SIMLA PAST AND PRESENT

SIMLA PAST AND PRESENT

BY

EDWARD J. BUCK

GYAN

Published by

Gyan Publishing House
5, Ansari Road
Daryaganj, New Delhi-110002
Phone: 011-47034999, 9811692060
E-mail: books@gyanbooks.com

Distribution Network
gyanbooks.com
India, USA, Canada, UK, Australia

ISBN: 978-93-6433-419-8 (PB)
First Published, 1904

2nd Impression 2024

Printed at: Gyan Press, Delhi.

SIMLA PAST AND PRESENT
Author: EDWARD J. BUCK

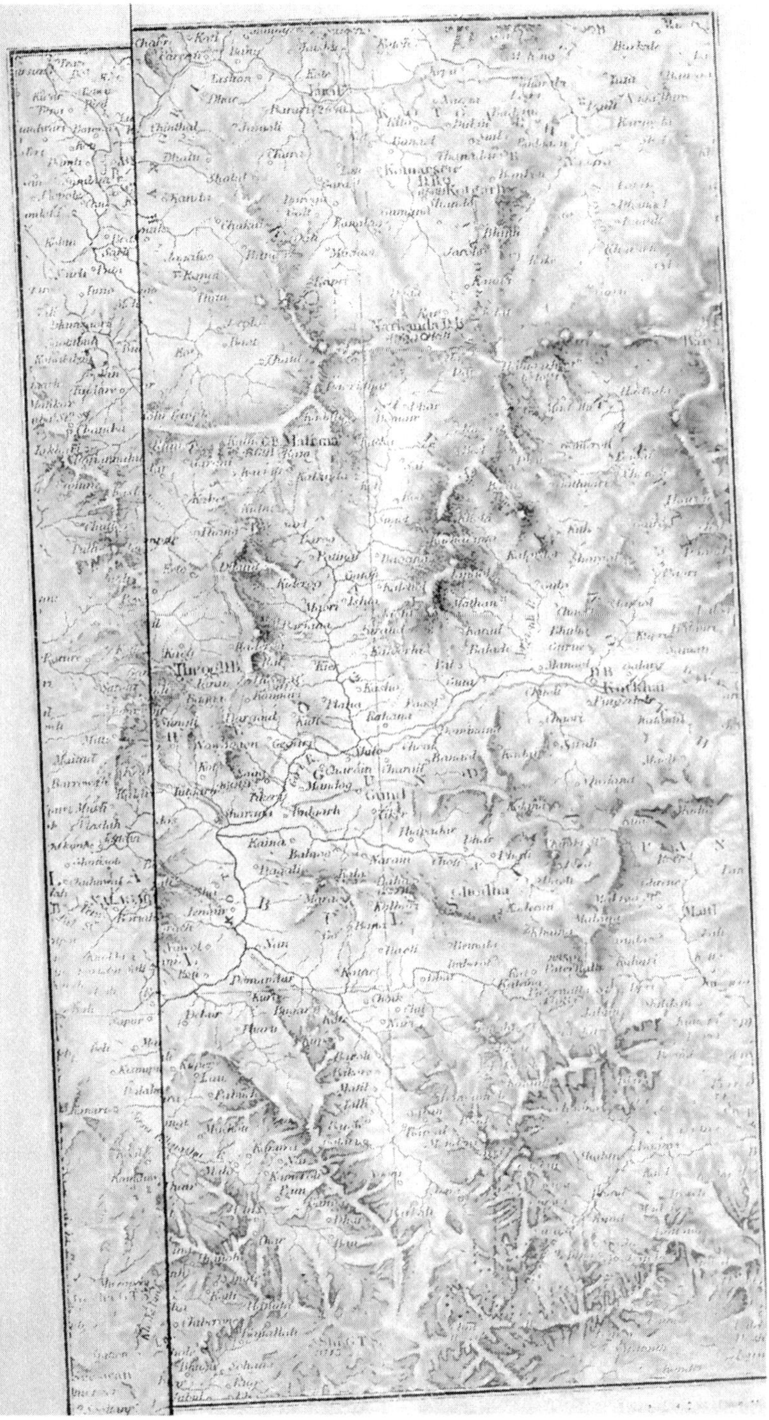

Narkanda
Matiana
Kotkhai

MAP OF THE SIMLA DISTRICT.

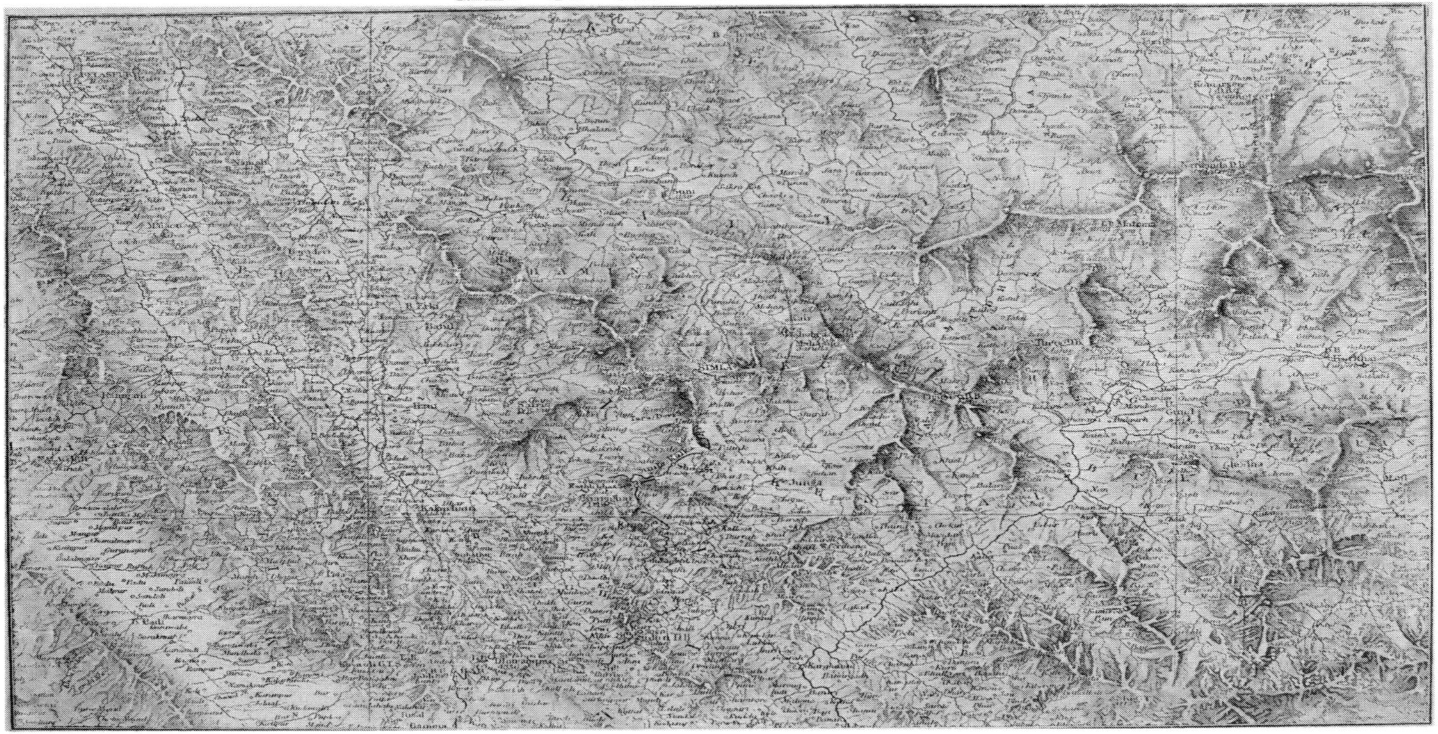

SIMLA

PAST AND PRESENT

SIMLA

PAST AND PRESENT

BY

EDWARD J. BUCK

WITH ILLUSTRATIONS

Calcutta: Printed by special permission at the Government of India Central Press, for Messrs. Thacker, Spink and Co., Publishers, Calcutta, 1904 . . . .

This Record of

SIMLA PAST AND PRESENT

is by permission dedicated to

HIS EXCELLENCY LORD CURZON, G.M.S.I., G.M.I.E.,

Viceroy and Governor General of India,

by his obliged and humble servant

The Author.

PREFACE.

THIS book on Simla is to some extent based on letters which recently appeared under the title of 'Old Simla' in the columns of the 'Englishman' and the 'Civil and Military Gazette.' The idea of amplifying and reproducing these in book form was first suggested to me by the Viceroy to whom with His Excellency's permission I have the honour of dedicating this volume. It includes a number of extracts from the writings of those who have known Simla in bygone time, which will I venture to think be found of interest to those who may visit the Simla of to-day. Its compilation, however, would have been a heavy, if not impossible, task had I not received much friendly assistance from many quarters. Thus to Mr. A. M. Ker I am indebted for the free use of his large and rare library at 'Chapslee,' to Sir Edward Buck, K.C.S.I., for permission to reproduce his paper on the 'Trees of Simla' and for his account of the Mashobra 'Retreat;' and for much valuable assistance to Mr. R. Nathan, C.I.E., Mr. D. E. McCracken, Mr. F. W. Latimer, C.I.E., Colonel F. Leigh, Mr. J. Elston, Mr. G. W. deRhé-Philipe, Mr. F. Bliss, Mr. W. G. A. Hanrahan, Mr. E. Hall, and Mrs. Alice Dracott.

My thanks are also due to Mr. R. D. Mackenzie, the clever artist now engaged by the Government of India in painting the official pictures of the Delhi Durbar, for having designed the sketch depicted on the cover of this book; to Major E. deV. Atkinson, R.E., Principal, and Mr. J. O'Neill, Instructor, of the Thomason College, Rurki; Messrs. C. J. Arbery and R. Graham, Army head-quarters, Simla; Mr. R. Hotz, and Messrs. Thacker, Spink & Co., for assistance in preparing sketches and pictures. Mr. R. Hotz, Messrs. Bourne and Shepherd, and Jadu Kissen of Simla have taken the greater number of the photographs which have been utilised for illustrations.

Imperfect as I feel it to be in many respects, I hope that the book will prove acceptable to those subscribers who have encouraged its production.

E. J. B.

CONTENTS.

CHAPTER VI.—Some Simla Institutions.

CHAPTER VII.—Annandale.

CHAPTER VIII.—Some Old Houses and their Owners.

CHAPTER IX.—The Amateur Dramatic Club.

CHAPTER X.—The Shops and Roads.

CHAPTER XI.—Simla Society.

ILLUSTRATIONS.

(*a*) From photographs taken by Messrs. Bourne and Shepherd.
(*b*) From photographs taken by Mr. R. Hotz.
(*c*) From photographs taken by Messrs. Jadu Kissen & Co.
(*d*) From sketches kindly lent by General S. B. Beatson, C.B.
(*e*) From sketches and photographs kindly lent by Mr. A. M. Ker.

JAKKO, FROM THE PUBLIC WORKS OFFICE.

SIMLA
PAST AND PRESENT.

CHAPTER I.

Origin, Early History, and Description of Simla.

SIMLA, the summer capital of the Supreme Government, of the Punjab Government and of the army head-quarters, is situated on several small spurs of the lower Himalayas, at a mean elevation of about 7,100 feet above sea level. Its latitude is 31° 6′ N., longitude 77° 13′ E. Its distance by the cart road from Kalka railway station at the foot of the hills is 58 miles. It is surrounded by the territories of about twenty minor independent chiefs under the control of the Deputy Commissioner of Simla, who is *ex-officio* superintendent of the hill states. In shape it has been described as an irregular crescent, a description which is still not inapplicable, although it has been in recent years much extended, and is now from one end to the other fully six miles in length. The various suburbs are called by distinguishing names, such as Burra (great) Simla, Chota (little) Simla, Prospect Hill, Elysium, Boileauganj, Summer Hill, Kaithu and Jakko. The official gazetteer describes the scenery of Simla as "exquisite." To the north and east a network of mountain chains, range rising over range, is crossed in the distance by a magnificent crescent of snowy peaks—the mountains of Kulu and Spiti on the north, and the central range of the eastern Himalayas stretching east and south-east as far as the eye can reach. The nearest of these peaks—that of Cheru on the confines of Kulu and Mandi, over 16,000 feet in height—is, as the crow flies, 27 miles from Simla, while the nearest of the central Himalayan peaks is double that distance; yet so sharply defined do they stand out against the horizon through the clear mountain air, that space seems annihilated, and the beholder might well believe that a short day's journey would carry him to their base. The records of the geological branch of the Government of India contain an interesting sketch of the geology of Simla and Jutogh by Mr. R. D. Oldham, an officer of the survey department, who made a special study of the neighbourhood in 1887. I do not propose to inflict on my readers any lengthy extracts from Mr. Oldham's scientific deductions, but many will doubtless like to know that his geological researches led him to write: "Taking everything into consideration we may, therefore, decide that when the Blaini group was being deposited, the spot now occupied by Simla was a sea on whose surface icebergs floated, melted, and dropped the stones which they carried on their surface, or imbedded in their substance." The economic geology of Simla is described as "very limited." Prospect hill is apparently a geological puzzle, and the surface geology of Simla is said to be "of considerable difficulty." Such is a brief and bare description of the famous summer capital of India.

Just a hundred years ago the Gurkhas, who had in 1804 suffered a severe defeat at the hands of the Sikhs at the battle of Kangra, a hill district about sixty miles beyond Simla, where according to some accounts they lost thousands of men in the fight and many others from disease, commenced to ravage the states and hills surrounding Simla. They committed many excesses, and according to Udhab Singh, Kumar, who recently published a short pamphlet entitled the 'Gurkha conquest of Arki,' ate so many goats that the price of these useful animals rose to R30 a head. The same writer tells us that the Gurkhas built numerous forts in the Baghal state, and that one of these strongholds, the Jagatgarh fortress, was the origin of the modern Jutogh, the well-known military cantonment adjoining Simla. The fortress at Sabathu still existent was also built by the Gurkhas. There is a second fort on the hill known from the similarity of its profile to that of Lord Bentinck, as "Billy Bentinck's nose," north-west of Simla, another at Dhami in the same direction, while the remains of a fourth can still be seen on the hill above the Sanjouli bazaar just beyond the station limits. By 1808 the invaders had conquered all the fortified posts between the Jumna and Sutlej, and from their capital of Arki began their ruthless rule over the neighbouring hill states, until at length the people in their wretchedness appealed to the British for help.

'The Journal of a Tour through part of the Himalaya Mountains' by James Baillie Fraser, published in 1820, gives a concise account of the war in which the British and Gurkhas engaged in 1815. Alluding to Nepal he wrote, "This power emboldened by a long course of success and conquest had commenced a deliberate system of encroachment on British boundaries, and a course of insult towards its lower ministers which at length it became absolutely necessary to repel." The British proclamation against Nepal showed that questions of usurpation had actually arisen in Purnea, Tirhoot, Sarun, Goruckpore and Bareilly, as well as in the protected territory between the Sutlej and Jumna. Accordingly four divisions were respectively formed at Dinapore, Benares, Meerut, and Ludhiana; the last named under the command of Brigadier-General David Ochterlony, who was instructed to proceed against the extensive cluster of posts held by Ummr Sing Thappah in the vicinity of Arki. Bravely as the Gurkhas fought, Ochterlony's force of less than 3,000 men, aided by the majority of the hill chiefs, took one fort after another, until the fall of Ramgarh left but one stronghold of importance unconquered, namely, Maloun. The 1st Gurkhas are now called the Maloun regiment in commemoration of this place. After desperate fighting in which the Gurkhas charged to the muzzles of the British guns, Bucktee Thappa, a famous Gurkha leader, was killed, many of his followers refused to continue the contest; finally Ummr Sing was on the 15th May induced to surrender, and Gurkha opposition in the vicinity of Simla ended.

Several uncommon incidents occurred during our struggle with the Gurkhas. Captain C. L. Showers, 19th Bengal Native Infantry, on one occasion engaged a Gurkha officer in single combat and slew him in an open space between the contending armies. Scarcely had he done so when he was shot dead. Among other officers who behaved with special gallantry was Lieutenant Lawtie, commanding an irregular corps, who also fell in the campaign. After Bucktee Thappa's corpse had been found on the battle field it was wrapped in rich shawls and sent to Ummr Sing by Ochterlony as a mark of respect. The following day after much preparation had been made the two widows of the fallen general committed "suttee" with his body, in view of both forces. Very shortly after the cessation of fighting followed a government proclamation by Sir David Ochterlony to the effect that all hill chiefs who had joined our forces in expelling the Gurkhas should have their lands restored, and should enjoy the benefits of our protection, as well as their previous rights and privileges.

Among other places which were retained as military posts by Ochterlony were Sabathu and Kotegarh, the former having been a stronghold of the Gurkhas. Here, later on, a political agent who was given control of all the hill states was appointed, and the post was apparently first held by the officer commanding the Nusseeree battalion. This corps was raised from the remnant of the Gurkha army which, at the close of the struggle with the British, laid down their arms, expressed a desire to enter our service, and formed a battalion which was posted to Sabathu, and which has since become the 1st Gurkha Rifles. A second battalion was stationed at Kotegarh, but was disbanded in 1829. It was during the campaign of 1815 that the Maharaja of Patiala rendered us valuable assistance by providing supplies, and was in return given land he now possesses in the neighbourhood of Simla. Other tracts he was allowed to purchase, and so became to all intents and purposes one of the hill chiefs. The village of Kalka at the foot of the hills, and the military posts of Kasauli, were later on transferred to the British Government by the Maharaja of Patiala at the requisition of Lord Hardinge, His Highness refusing to receive any compensation for the land thus given up.

Even to the present day the hill people talk of the Gurkha rule and its cruelty. Says a native writer on the subject: "The Gurkha army had no law to guide them, nor did they care for peace and prosperity. They valued their luxuries far above the rights of others, and hence their rule in the hills is regarded as nothing but a plague infection, ruinous to the hill subjects under them, and eventually to themselves . . . They took mercy upon nobody, nor did the idea of universal brotherhood ever occur to them. They had such a desire for revenge that if even a stone hurt their bare feet, they would not go further so long as it was not ground into powder."

On the other hand authorities are not wanting who declare that the Gurkhas' excesses and cruelty have been much exaggerated by native tradition, and that the only reason why the British took up arms and expelled them from the hills, was on account of their raids and a deliberate system of encroachment on British territory. To form any reliable opinion from the contradicting records which exist is not easy.

According to a Rev. Mr. Long, whom Mr. W. H. Carey mentions in his Simla Guide of 1870, Simla derives its name from 'Shyeamalay,' the house built of blue slate erected by a fakir on Jakko, the first nucleus of the settlement. But this derivation, be it noted, is regarded by many people as fanciful and far fetched, and probably 'Shimlah,' or 'Shumlah' as pronounced by the hill people, is the actual word from which the station takes its present name.

The original village of Simla was situated on the ground lying to the east of the present secretariat buildings above the road leading to the Ripon hospital, and immediately below the Roman Catholic chapel, S. Michael's school, and the court-house. A detailed portion inhabited entirely by charcoal burners lay just over the spur still further east, immediately below the spot where the Muhammadan mosque now stands. At the beginning of the last century, Simla was described as an obscure village taken from the Jhind Rana in 1815, and given to the Patiala Raja for assistance rendered to the British in the Nepal war, subsequently resigned by the Raja for a sanitarium. It is said that the first person who brought Simla to notice was a British officer who when moving Gurkha troops from Sabathu to Kotegarh about 1816, in passing through Simla, then a dense jungle infested with wild beasts, was struck by the cool temperature of the place. But it is claimed by Mr. A. Wilson in his 'Abode of Snow' that the hill on which Simla is situated was first made known by the visit to it of the brothers Gerard,

From a Sketch from nature. By Captain J. [illegible]

KENNEDY HOUSE, ABOUT 1824.

(THE FIRST HOUSE BUILT IN SIMLA).

two Scotch officers who were engaged in the survey of the Sutlej valley. Their diary, dated August 30th, 1817, ran: "Simla, a middling sized village where a fakir is situated to give water to travellers . . . We encamped on the side of Jakko, and had a very extensive and beautiful prospect." There were three brothers Gerard in India at this time, namely, Lieutenant (afterwards Captain) Alexander Gerard, 27th Native Infantry, who retired from the service on 15th February 1836, Lieutenant (afterwards Captain) Patrick Gerard, 9th Native Infantry, who was invalided on the 6th August 1832, and Assistant Surgeon James Gilbert Gerard, Bengal Medical Service, who died at Sabathu on 31st March 1835. Both Patrick and James Gerard served with the 1st Nusseeree battalion at Sabathu. The spot where the Gerards camped was probably somewhere above 'Walsingham,' to which a path ran direct from the western Simla village (near the secretariat buildings) through the present bazar which was then a dense forest. In his narrative of a 'Journey from Cawnpore to the Borrendo Pass,' Major Sir William Lloyd tells how he and Major Close, the representative of the government at Sindhia's court, reached Simla *viâ* Sabathu on 6th May 1821. The ascent from Syree, he says, was very great, but "the mountain air seemed to have instilled ether into my veins, and I felt as if I could have bounded headlong down into the deepest glens, or sprung nimbly up their abrupt sides with daring ease." The then splendid forests which clothed the sides of the Simla hills made a considerable impression upon the travellers, who after seeing a sunrise from Jakko and taking various observations journeyed on to Mahasu and thence into the interior. "It is impossible that Simla and its sublimity can ever be effaced from our minds," wrote Sir William Lloyd after he had reached Fagu. This author has in his book several interesting letters from Captain Alexander Gerard.

The picture here given of 'Kennedy House' as it appeared about 1825 is I believe the first picture made of Simla. It was drawn on the spot by Captain J. Luard, and published in London in 1833 in his 'Views of India from Calcutta to the Himalayas,' dedicated to the Earl of Amherst. As the author explains in the preface, "the enormous expense of line engraving induced him to draw the pictures himself on stone." The writer also says "all who have visited this charming spot have experienced Major Kennedy's kindness and hospitality."

The official history of the Simla 'ilaqa' or district up to 1850 has been given in the Settlement Report on the Simla district by Colonel E. G. Wace (1881-3), from which the following extract is taken :—

"The lands forming the 'pergannah' and the present station of Simla originally belonged conjointly to the Maharaja of Patiala and the Rana of Keonthal. As early as 1824 European gentlemen, chiefly invalids from the plains, had, with the permission of these chiefs, established themselves in this locality, building houses on sites granted them rent free, and with no other stipulation than that they should refrain from the slaughter of kine and the felling of trees, unless with the previous permission of the proprietors of the land. The station became favourably known as a sanitarium, and in 1830 the government directed that negotiations should be entered into with the chiefs of Patiala and Keonthal for as much land as was deemed sufficient to form a station. Accordingly Major Kennedy, the then political agent, negotiated an exchange with the Rana of Keonthal for his portion of the Simla hill, comprising thirteen villages, and yielding an estimated revenue of Rs. 987, making over to the Rana the 'pergannah' of Rajeen, yielding an annual revenue of Rs. 1,289, which had been retained by us on the first conquest of these hills, as its position was considered to afford a good military position. A portion of the retained pergannah of Bharaulie, consisting of seven small villages, was at the same time made over to the Maharaja of Patiala in exchange for his portion of Simla which was included in his territory yielding an estimated revenue of Rs. 245 per annum."

In 1831 M. Victor Jacquemont, the talented French traveller, in describing Simla said it was "the resort of the rich, the idle, and the invalid. The officer charged with the political service of this extremity of the empire which was acquired only fifteen years ago, bethought himself, nine years since, of leaving his palace in the plains during the heat of a terrible summer, and encamping under the shade of the cedars. A few friends came to visit him there. The situation and climate appeared admirable. Some hundreds of mountaineers were summoned who felled the trees around, squared them rudely and assisted by workmen from the plains in a month constructed a spacious house. Each of the guests wished to have one also, and now there are upwards of sixty scattered over the peaks of the mountains or their declivities: thus a considerable village has risen as if by enchantment."

The officer to whom Mr. Jacquemont here alludes was Captain Kennedy who was commanding at Sabathu, and was the first political agent or superintendent of the hill states. A residence which is described as "a mere cottage of wood and thatch" had been built in 1819 by Lieutenant Ross, the assistant political officer in the hills, but 'Kennedy House,' named after its owner, was undoubtedly the first permanent house in Simla. Some traditions have claimed this honour for 'Constantia,' now the 'Manse,' lying alongside the Union Church, and have also named 'Stirling Castle' as the second oldest house, and only given 'Kennedy House' the third place; but this historical residence appears to have much the strongest claims as the first substantial dwelling in the station.

In 1832 Captain Mundy, who was aide-de-camp to Lord Combermere in 1828, published a journal of a tour in India. Writing on 25th October 1828 he says, "the two parties of tourists dined with Captain Kennedy, the hospitable political agent. A merrier man I never spent an hour's talk withal." He explains in the preface that he scribbled for his own amusement and as a sort of promised sop held out to allay epistolary expectations at home, and that it was not until a year after his return to England that, prompted by the encouragement of perhaps partial friends, and finally rendered desperate by what may almost be said to have amounted to a paternal mandate, he found himself correcting the proofs.

Writing of Simla he says: "The political agent established a summer residence at Simla, a name given to two or three miserable shepherds' huts situated 24 miles north-east of Subbatoo beyond the British dominions, and in the territory of a native Ranee or feudal baroness, for the ruler of a small uncultivated cluster of mountains can scarcely be dignified with the title of queen. The climate of Simla soon became famous: invalids from the plains resorted there, and built houses, instead of breaking up establishments and sailing for the Cape of Good Hope with little hope of reaching it; and finally Simla was rendered fashionable by the governor-general, Lord Amherst, who resided there with his family for several months and brought back to Calcutta rosy complexions and some beautiful drawings by Lady Sarah Amherst to attest the healthful and picturesque properties of the spot."

Captain Mundy, who first reached Simla on May Day 1828, thus describes his arrival: "On reaching Simla we pitched our tents for the night and hurried to change our entire suit of white linen for a costume more suited to the temperature of 61°, which to us appeared almost inclement: indeed it was a dreadful night. I was completely drenched in my bed by the rain which fell in torrents; and the wind was so violent and the situation of our tents so exposed that I lay awake in momentary expectation of being blown away bodily into the valley 500 feet below. We found Lord Combermere with his surgeon and aide-de-camp established in Captain Kennedy's summer residence (Kennedy House), and the rest of the staff were either accommodated in the already existing houses, or busily employed in building—residing in the meanwhile in tents. The frequent clash of axe and hammer give evidence of the diligence with which they are labouring to provide roofs for themselves before the rains set in—nor have they much time to spare—. . . . Communication between the several residences and the bazaar is secured by well formed roads, which, though narrow, are tolerably safe for *sober* passengers. However, during our sojourn there, more than one neck was put in jeopardy by dark nights and hospitable neighbours. . . . .

"Many of the Simla householders have already cultivated small spots of ground for cabbages and potatoes and other vegetable esculents—the last named valuable root thriving remarkably well in these climates. Captain Kennedy is liberally disseminating it through the district, and the poor natives, who live almost entirely on the precarious fruits of a not very productive soil, are not a little grateful for this useful addition to their provisions."

The history of how the potato came to be cultivated in the Simla hills is of special interest, as later on the hill men, in their eagerness to grow this profitable root, cut down much of the splendid forest lying between Mahasu and Fagu, with the eventual result that the soil having lost the natural protection of the trees, was quickly washed away by the annual monsoon rains into the steep valley below. The potato, however, has continued to be a favourite crop in the Simla district, and a thriving trade is carried on to-day in this useful article of food between the Himalayas generally, and the plains of Northern India.

Captain Mundy's description of his residence will doubtless be read with interest by the more fortunate Simla aides-de-camp of the present day. He writes:

"I find the thermometer in May was never higher than 73 or lower than 53° in my *garret.* This apartment occupied by me during our stay in the hills, was pervious both to heat and cold, being, in fact, of that elevated character which in England is usually devoted to cheeses, apples, and onions, and forming the interval between the ceiling of the dining room and the wooden pent-roof of the house, which descending in a slope quite to the floor only admitted of my standing upright in the centre. Though this canopy of planks was lined with whitewashed canvas it by no means excluded the rains (the burra bursat!) so peremptorily as I, not being an amphibious animal, could have wished; and during some of the grand storms the hailstones rattled with such stunning effect upon the drum-like roof, that the echo sung in my ears for a week after. This my exalted dormitory was rendered accessible by a wooden ladder: but in spite of its sundry désagrémens I thanked my stars—in whose near neighbourhood I was—for my luck in getting any shelter without the trouble of building in the present crowded state of Simla. I enjoyed, as stated above, a splendid view from my windows (I beg pardon, window), and the luxury of privacy, except at night, when the rats sustained an eternal carnival, keeping me in much the same state as Whittington during his first week in London. I soon grew tired of bumping my head against the roof in pursuit of these four-footed Pindarees, and at length became callous to their nocturnal orgies and kept a cat. . .

"The temperature of Simla seems peculiarly adapted to the European constitution.

'The scorching ray
Here pierceth not, impregnate with disease.'

"We have reason to be thankful that we are here far elevated above the atmospheric strata that have hitherto been subjected to the cholera, a disease now raging at Calcutta. This destructive pestilence, two years ago ascended as high as Subbatoo, strewing Lord Amherst's line of march with dead bodies. The salubrity of this little abode of Hygeia is well attested by the presence of no less than sixteen ladies who gladly embrace the inconveniences attendant upon narrow accommodations and want of equipages for the advantages accruing from the climate to themselves and their children. Our native servants at first took fright at the cold, and some of them even refused to enter the hills, but others were persuaded by the promised advantages of additional warm raiment to accompany us."

Captain Mundy thus describes Lord Combermere's activity in 1828:

"Lord Combermere amused himself, and benefited the public, by superintending the formation of a fine, broad, level road round the Mount Jako, about three miles in length. It was worked entirely by hillmen and exceedingly skilfully done, and will, when finished, be a great acquisition to the loungers of Simla. Across a deep ravine, a quarter of a mile from the town, his Lordship erected a neat 'sangah,' or mountain bridge, of pines; and under it a capacious stone tank was constructed to obviate the great scarcity of water." This bridge which still bears Lord Combermere's name was the 'first step' towards the improvement of Simla (where there were then but two or three houses and no roads), and it 'counted' accordingly. It connected Simla with Chota Simla or Simla minor; and writing in 1846 Captain Thomas described the ravine as "a deep one down whose sides in the rainy season flows an impassable torrent. During the progress of this miniature Simplon which occupied the hours before breakfast and those after sunset, the attendant aide-de-camp amused himself by watching the formation of the mines for blasting the rocks, cutting down the prescribed pines, making grotesque rustic arbours at intervals on the road, or whistling after the huge blocks of stone, which moved by levers off the road, toppled, bounded and crashed through the wooden declivity into the valley below, reminding one of Homer's expressive line describing the retrograde descent of the stone of Sisyphus. When the longest half of the road was completed, the workmen were presented with two sheep on which they were to feast, after having offered them as propitiatory sacrifices to their deity."

As these animals did not, however, exhibit the proper signs of external agitation on being confronted with the little misshapen idol to whom they were offered, Captain Mundy proceeds to describe how—"The officiating pontiff advanced with all the solemnity due to the occasion, took a mouthful of spring water and squirted it into the ear of a sheep. The victim shook its head, the movement was held in triumph by the congregation, the priest's 'kukri' immediately severed its head from its neck, and its body was quickly roasting before a huge pine fire."

Before leaving Simla on October 20th, 1828, Captain Mundy correctly prophesied—"I cannot doubt but that Simla will rise in importance every year as it becomes better known. Its delightful climate is sure to recommend it for invalids; and its beautiful scenery, healthful temperature, and above all the *a procul negotiis* relaxation which they will there enjoy will induce the governors-general and commanders-in-chief to resort there, during the hot months, in their official tours through the upper provinces."

M. Victor Jacquemont who was travelling naturalist to the museum of natural history in Paris, published in 1834 the letters describing his journeys in India (really undertaken by order of the French government) between 1828 and 1831. They were written to his father, and in one of them dated June 21, 1830 and headed 'Semla, Semlah, Simla, Simlah *ad libitum*,' he gives the following entertaining account of life in the hills in that year:—

"Porphyre has a right to be jealous of my host (Major Kennedy). He is an artillery captain of his own age, and, like him, of long standing in his rank. He has a hundred thousand francs a year, and commands a regiment of highland chasseurs, the best corps in the army. He performs the duties of receiver-general, and judges with the same independence as the Grand Turk, his own subjects, and moreover those of the neighbouring Rajahs, Hindoos, Tartars, Tibetans; these he imprisons, fines, and even hangs when he thinks proper.

"This first of all artillery captains in the world is an amiable bachelor, whom the duties of his viceroyalty occupy for one hour after breakfast, and who passes the rest of his time in loading me with kindness. He had expected me for a month past; some mutual friends having informed him of my design of visiting Semla. He passes for the stiffest of dandies, the most formal and vainest of the princes of the earth. I find nothing of all this; it is impossible to be a better fellow. We gallop an hour or two in the morning on the magnificent roads which he has constructed, often joining some elegant cavalcade, among which I meet some of my Calcutta acquaintance. On our return we have an elegant and recherché breakfast; then I have the entire and free disposal of my day, and that of my host, whenever I think proper to put it in a requisition, to view men and things.

At sunset fresh horses are to the door, and we take another ride, to beat up the most friendly and lively of the rich idlers and imaginary invalids, whom we may chance to meet. They are people of the same kind as my host, bachelors and soldiers, but soldiers employed in all kinds of departments: the most interesting people in India to me. We sit down to a magnificent dinner at half-past seven, and rise at eleven. I drink hock, claret, and champagne only, and at dessert malmsey; the others, alleging the coldness of the climate, stick to port, sherry, and madeira. I do not recollect having tasted water for the last seven days; nevertheless there is no excess, but great cheerfulness every evening. I cannot tell you how delightful this appears to me, after the dryness, insipidity, hardness, and brevity of my solitary dinner, during two months in the mountains. And I have not one arrear to pay off. Having the approaching prospect of four months of misery on the other side of the Himalaya, I revenge myself by anticipation. I arrived here so much exhausted by fatigue and the consequences of an obstinate indisposition, that I thought I would avail myself of the period of my stay to recruit my health; but my host's cook cured me in four and twenty hours.

"Do you not see Semla on your map? A little to the north of the 31° of latitude, a little to the east of the 77° of longitude, some leagues from the Sutledge. Is it not curious to dine in silk stockings at such a place, and to drink a bottle of hock and another of champagne every evening—delicious Mocha coffee—and to receive the Calcutta journals every morning?

"The king of Bissahir's vizier, whose master is the greatest of my host's allies, is here at present; Captain Kennedy (that is my artilleryman's name) has introduced us to each other; and I am assured of receiving all sorts of attention at the other side of the Himalaya.

"One of his officers will follow me everywhere, and I shall take with me from hence a couple of Gorkha carabiniers belonging to my host's regiment, the most active and clever of them, and one of his tchourassis (a sort of usher or janissary) who has already visited that country, having gone thither with his master some years ago.

"The people on this side the mountains are horribly afraid of their neighbours on the other. It is rather difficult to procure porters for the luggage, and constitutionally it would be impossible to make a single domestic follow one thither; but Captain Kennedy has obligingly offered to imprison any of mine who refuse to accompany me; and although they declare that they prefer being hanged on this side the mountains to being free in Kanawer, I think that by availing myself, in one or two instances, of my host's kindness, I shall make the rest decide upon following me. What the simpletons fear I know not:—but it is no longer India on the other side; there are no more castes; instead of Brahmins there are Lamas. Besides, in my suite there will be perfect safety. The Rajah of Bissahir knows very well, that if any harm happened to me he would suffer for it, and he will take great care of the 'Francis saheb, captanne Kindi saheb ke doste,' which means 'the French lord, friend of the great General Kennedy'."

Mr. William de Rhé-Philipe, who contributed an article on Simla to the E. India United Service Journal in 1834, tells us that the road running below the club towards Chota Simla was then called 'the Combermere road,' and that to the Elysium hill, 'Bentinck road.' He alludes to the excellence of the vegetable gardens, remarks that cowardly, but ravenous, hyenas carried off all dogs, sheep and goats left outside at night, and in referring to high rents then prevailing, says that one-third of the cost of a house was usually charged as rent for six months.' Mr. Philipe became assistant-judge-advocate-general of the Bengal army in 1858, and was the father of Mr. G. W. de Rhé-Philipe, who has just retired after a service of more than thirty-six years in the adjutant-general's department at army head-quarters, and in the military secretariat of the Government of India.

In 'Five Years in India' published in 1842, Lieutenant Henry Edward Fane of the 90th Foot, aide-de-camp to Sir Henry Fane, the commander-in-chief, arrived in Simla on 21st April 1837, a place which his diary describes as "about the only thing in India we had not been disappointed in .....My Chief's house Bentinck Castle (now Peliti's Grand Hotel)," he wrote, "is perhaps the best in Simla; it is beautifully situated on this ridge, and was built for the late governor Lord William Bentinck. Houses generally let here very high, and to a person resident on the spot who can see them properly attended to are excellent property." Mr. Fane evidently found life in Simla rather dull, as he continued, "the sameness of our lives here, unless I make an expedition into the interior, will make it not worth while to continue my journal till we again descend into the plains." In September the commander-in-chief's staff made a trip out to Kotegarh, left Simla on the 25th October, and returned there on January 5th in the following year, when "many of the staff who had not seen snow for forty years were half crazy with delight charging out of their houses to make snow balls." In June came a trip to the Chor and neighbouring hills, and in November the remark," much as I have disliked Simla, I now leave it with regret, having got accustomed to its monotony and more particularly to this house and establishment here."

In 1838-9 Mr. Charles J. French, who accompanied Lord Auckland to Simla as a member of his staff, made copious notes about the station, and in 1853 published them in his 'Journal of a Tour in Upper Hindustan.'

His remarks on old Simla are so interesting that I make no apology for giving them at some length.

"Some of the hills and most of the houses have their peculiar names. Of the former there are Mount Pleasant, Mount Prospect, Mount Jako, Elysium Hill, and some others. Of the latter bearing the most fanciful names are Stirling Castle, Wharncliffe, Annandale Lodge, Oakfield, Eagle Mount, Longwood, Allan Bank, Union Cottage, Primrose Hill, Annandale View, Prospect House, the Crags, Bellevue, Rookwood, Swiss Cottage, Fountain Hall, Daisy Bank, the Hermitage, Blessington, the Briars, Victoria Lodge, Edward's Cot, Morna's Grove, Richmond Villa, Woodbine Cottage, Kenilworth, Abbeyville, Sunnybank, Holly Bank, etc. These form less than a third of a list with which I was kindly furnished by the principal house agent.

"This list with the names of 120 houses in it, exhibits upwards of Rs. 72,000 as the aggregate of their annual rent, which on the average is equal to Rs. 600 the year for each house. The minimum rent is Rs. 150, the maximum Rs. 1,500. The former is the rent of the Hermitage, the latter that of Abbeyville. However, the rent for the majority of the houses varies from Rs. 400 to Rs. 800, the one called Abbeyville being at present the only dwelling at Rs. 1,500 the season. When a house is let by the season, which is almost always the case, it gives the lessee the right of occupancy for only nine months out of the twelve, *i.e.*, from March to November, but if he wishes to live in it during the whole year he has, I think, to pay some additional trifle."

Describing the Simla house of the period Mr. French continued: "Attached to the house is a neat garden, consisting of flowering shrub and fruit trees of a tolerable great variety. At Simla almost every room in a house has a chimney, a most essential appendage in a cold winter's night, when the fireside has its peculiar charms. The walls of the houses are erected after a singular fashion unlike anything in the plains. Cement is seldom or never used except in the outer coatings. Instead of this a brittle kind of stone resembling slate, and which is procured in great abundance in the hills, is in the first instance shaped into squares or parallelograms by chipping off the ends and sides. These stones are then adjusted or laid down in layers of about two or two and a half feet in thickness, and this they do so regularly and neatly without the aid of lime or mortar, that the outer and the inner surface appear sometimes like one piece of slate with slight crevices running over them. For ordinary work, however, such regularity and preciseness are not by any means observed, and when this is the case, the wall wears the appearance of a rude pile of stones carelessly raised. At every two, three, or four feet of the height of the wall, the adjusted pile of stones is bound down with long pieces of timber laid horizontally over the edge on each side, and connected by cross bars of wood. It cannot well be conceived how this plan can lend much strength to the walls or promote their stability, but practically it has been found to succeed. Perhaps the equal pressure on all sides prevents the stones being dislodged. In some places, this mode of raising a wall has been carried to a very good state of perfection; of others the stones were so ill-adapted that it seemed wonderful they did not tumble down. The roofs of most of the houses are either slated or shingled in an angular form. Not a few are flat-roofed with a thick coating of earth, which is beaten down to render it impervious to the heavy showers which pour down in the rains. There are one or two thatched houses also, but none have I seen tiled. Slating is not brought to any perfection. Shingling is much neater and much lighter. Slate, however, is most effective against leaking, and when any part is observed to admit the rain, the remedy is easy and at hand, whereas flat roofs can only be beaten down when it ceases raining and then much to the annoyance of those below them. I have seen some gentlemen adopt the strange but effectual precaution of lining the outer surface of some of the flat roofs of their domiciles with tarpaulin, but this method is not universally adopted from the expense attending it. Although canvas for such a purpose is not easily obtainable, yet tar may be had for a song in the neighbouring pine forests, especially at Mahasu within twelve miles of Simla. It must not be inferred that tar is very extensively manufactured, or manufactured at all for trade. Very little indeed is made by a primitive process and that only for local wants. The Mahasu forest of pine and of fir supplies Simla with timber for building. Extensive groves of these gigantic trees adorn the spot."

Scarcely a visitor came to Simla in the early days who did not express admiration for the wild flowers with which the slopes of the station were then covered. In 'Views in India chiefly among the Himalaya Mountains,' by Lieutenant G. F. White, 31st regiment, which was edited by Emma Roberts in 1838, I find the following passage: "The gardens are numerous and thriving, potatoes, cabbages and other esculents grow freely, and beautiful parterres of flowers may be obtained by the mere trouble of transplanting the numerous wild varieties which wreathe the side of every hill." Now, alas! hardly a wild flower can be found in the vicinity of the station woods, chiefly owing to the fact that for many years past jampanis have constantly stripped the hill sides to decorate Simla dining tables. The Lieutenant White above mentioned was born in 1808, and died at the age of 91 after being chief constable of Durham for forty years.

In 1846 'Views of Simla' by Captain G. P. Thomas of the 64th regiment, Bengal Infantry, was published by Dickinson & Co., of 114, Bond Street. The book is now seldom met with, but occasionally a volume comes into the market. It contains some very interesting sketches of Simla as it then appeared, as well as a few of places in its neighbourhood. The author dedicated the book to the directors of the East India Company,

COMBERMERE BRIDGE, ABOUT 1840.

"impelled by a grateful sense of benefits received by his father General Lewis Thomas, C.B., and his children," and the following quotation on the title page expresses in unmistakable terms what he thought of Simla some sixty years ago:—

"A good land, a land of brooks of water, of fountains and depths that spring out of valleys and hills, a land of wheat and barley, vines, and fig trees, and pomegranates, a land of oil olive, and honey. . . . . A land whose stones are iron, out of whose hills thou mayest dig brass.—Deuteronomy, chap. viii."

The building of Combermere bridge has already been alluded to, and the sketch of it by Captain Thomas is reproduced on the opposite page. The armed mountaineers, or Pindarees, in the foreground are distinctly peculiar, and in describing the drawing Captain Thomas says:—

"Abbeville is the house in the centre of the drawing. For the carpet knight, 'the hero of a hundred balls,' this same Abbeville must be consecrated by a host of pleasant memories; for it is here that the best subscription balls and masquerades are given. Barrett's Boarding House is the building on the right, which is (like Wordsworth's violet) 'half hidden from the eye.' Its partial concealment, however, matters less, inasmuch as it has been knocked down and rebuilt within the last few months, and since this sketch was taken."

Captain Thomas attained the rank of major in the company's 3rd Bengal European regiment (now the 2nd Royal Sussex) and was mortally wounded in the battle of Shahganj, near Agra, on the 5th July 1857.

An observant visitor to Simla in 1858 was Dr. William Howard Russell, the famous war correspondent of the *Times*, whose trenchant remarks on the social life of Simla will be found in a later chapter.

Mr. J. F. Wyman, of Messrs. Wyman & Co., Calcutta, who was the author of 'Calcutta to the Snowy Range, by An Old Indian,' visited Simla in the winter about 1865, and on arrival at his hotel he says: "Mine host looked at us strangely, though not unwelcomely, wondering doubtless what on earth had induced us to visit Simla at such a time. He suggested perhaps that we should like a fire and said if he could find any wood that was not covered by snow we should have one. . . . Any place more undesirable for a residence in winter so far as comfort is concerned I cannot imagine. And yet to see Simla in the winter time, its fanciful summer house dwellings covered with cleaving roofs of snow; the tall pines fretted over with icicles and frosted with snow drift on leaf and branch, the lofty mountains around all white with their fleecy canopies, the valleys clothed with winter's thick smooth carpet, and above all the everlasting snowy range shining out in its grandest aspect, impressing the beholder with awe at its majesty and immensity, is indeed worth while to essay a winter journey to the Himalayas."

After strongly advocating a residence in Simla in the winter for the benefit of health, Mr. Wyman writes: "Truly one must have good lungs and stout legs to tramp up and down the declivities; but I suppose people get used to it, and the exercise at any rate seemed healthy, for everybody had the rosiest of complexions, and the cheeks of the young ladies absolutely invited kisses. . . . Since Government has been transferred to Simla in the summer months, rents have risen fearfully, and with the run of the fashionable world and its train to these breezy hills, all things else have proportionately increased in price."

I have been unable to find in any old or indeed in any new record of Simla a single complimentary remark on the native servants of the station. Mr. Wyman makes the following allusion to them in 1865: "Servants even in the Presidency towns far exceed in power and practice of annoyance Mayhew's 'Greatest Plague,' but in the hills whither he has with difficulty been seduced by offers of high wages and warm clothing, your servant becomes truly your master, and is ever ready, and it may be said ever able, to fleece you to his heart's content." Nearly every writer of early years indeed advises those who come to Simla to bring with them servants from the plains, and what held good in former times undoubtedly obtains to-day. One of the main causes of recent hotel development is alleged to have been the present servant difficulty in the station.

Mr. Andrew Wilson in his 'Abode of Snow,' writing about 1873 says plainly: "Simla is famous for its bad servants." On the other hand, there are residents in Simla to-day who stoutly deny these accusations and declare that Simla servants have only been spoilt by contact with undesirables brought up from the plains.

The Mr. Andrew Wilson just mentioned, was a well-known journalist who visited Simla in 1873; and the book above quoted contains two or three chapters dealing at some length with life in Simla at that period. Warm acknowledgment was made in it of the hospitality of two Bombay officers, Colonels Ker and Farquharson, who did a great deal to make his stay agreeable.

Lord Northbrook, who took a special interest in Mr. Wilson, subscribed for fifty copies of his book, a goodly portion of which was written at the Fagu Dâk Bungalow some 12 miles from Simla on the Tibet-Hindustan high road. Further quotations from this work will be found in subsequent pages.

And now for a few words about the journey up the hill.

It is less than a score of years ago since the railway was extended from Amballa to Kalka. Before that time the traveller to Simla had a choice

COMBERMERE BRIDGE, 1901.

(MR. G. T. FILLINGHAM'S TAILORING ESTABLISHMENT IN BACKGROUND.)

between the government van, and the 'dawk gari' to carry him over the 38 miles between the railway terminus at Amballa and Kalka at the foot of the hills. Either conveyance from the point of comfort left much to be desired, the springs of many of the 'garis' being actually packed with bamboo wrapped in rope to lessen the roughness of the jolting. Sometimes indeed these 'garis' broke down entirely, and the travellers spent their nights on the roadside.

In the rains, too, the Ghagar river, a few miles from Kalka, often became so swollen that bullocks were unable to drag conveyances through the water, and vehicles were constantly delayed for hours on the banks. Elephants also had to be constantly employed in the rainy season to carry over the post as well as travellers. The rapidity with which the floods rose was astonishing. On one occasion Sir Edward Buck wrote to me that his 'gari' arrived just as the 'postal' elephant was crossing the stream. By the time he had packed his own luggage on the travellers' elephant the water was too deep to be forded even by this huge animal, and he was kept for fourteen hours hungry and exceedingly cross until the water subsided. "Crusticus expectans dum defluit amnis" was his improvement on Horace as he sat watching the swollen stream. In August 1871 Sir Donald Stewart wrote from Simla—"Even if I had been well enough to start, I could not have left Simla during the past week, as both the roads are now impassable, the suspension bridge near Hurreepore having been carried away. There is the greatest difficulty in getting the mails up from Amballa."

Twice during the last thirty years Simla was entirely cut off for two or three days from communication with the plains below owing to excessive rainfall, and in the press agitation against Simla being constituted the summer head-quarters of the supreme government, this was one of the main reasons urged against the government isolating itself during the summer months. From Kalka, until the new cart road, originally called the grand Hindostan and Tibet road, was designed by Major Kennedy and executed by Lieutenant Briggs in Lord Dalhousie's viceroyalty in 1856, the mode of transit to the hills was by 'jampans' or by ponies, and all luggage was carried up by coolies or mules. The 'jampan' was really a sedan chair fitted with curtains, slung on poles borne by bearers who carried the passenger at an even sling trot. This was largely used by ladies, while men usually rode the 43 miles *viâ* Kasauli, Kakkarhati, Hurreepore, and Syree to Simla. Children and invalids were frequently carried in 'doolies' or light litters of wooden frames covered with canvas and waxcloth. After the new road passing through Dharampur, Solon, and Kairee Ghat to Simla, 58 miles in length, had been constructed, the 'ekka' or country cart at first held possession, then followed a bullock cart service for goods, while a 'tonga' service for mails and passengers soon afterwards came into general use.

The tonga, a two-wheeled cart drawn by a couple of ponies, harnessed curricle fashion, is familiar to all travellers who have been to Simla in past years. Under the able superintendence of Rai Bahadur Dowlat Ram, C.I.E., it attained the reputation of being probably the finest wheel posting service in the world. The tonga service originated with Mr. George Law, a retired military assistant engineer who brought the idea from the Central Provinces, and who was assisted with funds by Mrs. Burn, widow of Colonel Burn of the 53rd regiment. This service was afterwards bought by Mrs. Lumley, the owner of hotels in Amballa and Kalka. No less than three rivals, however, commenced to compete with her; a native contractor, a Mr. Wilkinson, and Mr. Lawrie, hotel proprietor of Simla and Kalka. The two latter formed a syndicate, the native retired from the contest, and in 1878 the 'Mountain Car Company,' as the combined venture was termed, was purchased by government. In 1881 Mrs. Lumley's interest was also acquired, a monopoly of the road was established, and the present tonga service came into being.

If the road is a triumph of engineering skill, the phrase can be applied with even greater truth to the wonderful mountain railway which has just been constructed under the supervision of Mr. H. S. Harington, chief engineer and agent of the Kalka-Simla railway.

On leaving Kalka, 2,100 feet, the line enters at once among the foot hills, commencing its picturesque climb immediately on its departure from the Kalka station. The first great difficulty met with was the huge landslip on the seventh mile of the cart road, which extends from the hill summit away down to the Khushallia river, 1,500 feet below. As it was impossible to find a good alignment passing either below or above the slip, and was out of the question to attempt to construct a line along the face of the landslide, the only alternative was to burrow under the hill by a tunnel, nearly ½ mile long, which has been constructed in the solid wall behind the disturbed surface strata.

Dharmpore is 4,900 feet above the mean sea level, so there is an ascent of 2,800 feet from Kalka to Dharmpore. The cart road with its steep grades surmounts this in a length of 16 miles; but in order to achieve the flatter gradients required for the railway, the new alignment has been purposely developed to make the line longer, three picturesque series of loops being adopted near Taksal, Gamma, and Dharmpore, respectively. The railway is thus 20 miles in length between Kalka and Dharmpore.

After leaving Dharmpore, the railway gains on the road by taking short cuts through tunnels, so that at the Taradevi plague post, the distance by

THE SIMLA KALKA RAILWAY.
(A HILL SLIP AND BREAST WALL).

rail from Kalka is actually something like ¼ mile less than the distance by road; in spite of the way in which the railway is handicapped by the longer alignment below Dharmpore. After leaving Taradevi it goes round Prospect Hill to Jutogh, and eventually curves round by Summer Hill, and burrows under Inverarm Hill to emerge at its 59th mile below the cart road on the south side of Inverarm, and so on to the terminus near the old Dovedell Chambers. At Dugshai, mile 24, the railway is 5,200 feet above sea, whence it falls to 4,900 feet at Solon, and to 4,667 feet at Kandaghat (mile 36½), where the final ascent towards Simla begins. Between Dugshai and Solon, the railway pierces the Barogh Hill by a tunnel, 3,760 feet long, situated 900 feet below the cart road. Throughout its length of 60 miles it runs in a continuous succession of reverse curves of 120 feet radius in and out along the valleys and spurs flanking mountains rising to 6,000 and 7,000 feet above sea level, the steepest gradients being three feet in a hundred. The works of construction involved are of first magnitude, comprising 107 tunnels, aggregating 5 miles in length, numerous lofty arched viaducts, aggregating 1¾ miles, and innumerable cuttings and stone walls; and the cost on completion will somewhat exceed one million sterling.

The first passenger trains began to run on 9th November 1903, and an illustration shews one passing round Taradevi mountain, 8 miles from Simla. There is a Hindoo shrine on the summit of this mountain, at which an annual fair is held. It was found necessary to construct a tunnel over ¼ mile long under this hill, and the hill people from the day it was first commenced declared that the goddess of the shrine would never permit of the tunnel being finished. Two years ago, when the tunnel was half bored through, great excitement among the natives was aroused owing to a report being spread that a huge snake, several hundred feet long, had been uncovered in the tunnel, and had effectually stopped all work. This wonderful reptile, however, turned out to be merely a large iron pipe running along the tunnel for the purpose of conveying fresh air to the inner workings. In a cutting close to the tunnel, seams of rock studded with small garnets were found, but these had no intrinsic value. Another view shews a construction train passing along a precipitous part of the line on the flanks of Prospect Hill, some 6 miles out of Simla, with the gang of Tibetan and Pathan labourers who are still at work in completing the cutting and walling. The hill side here appeared to be solid rock, and yet during the monsoon of 1903, an enormous slip (which can be seen in the illustration) occurred, extending to a height of 150 feet above the line. It has been necessary to build a wall here 60 feet high, at a cost of over half a lakh of rupees, to maintain the stability of the railway.

The third view of the line is taken from near Summer Hill, shewing

Government House on Observatory Hill, with a cutting 60 feet deep in the middle distance.

During the night of 26th December last an abnormal snowfall occurred, covering the ground, almost down to Kalka, to a depth of 2 feet, and causing drifts 6 and 7 feet deep in many cuttings. Passenger trains were for two days unable to get through, and were snowed up at small stations midway between Kalka and Simla. Two days later, however, the line had been cleared throughout, and all trains got through to their destination without further mishap.

Simla as a health resort has prominent merits and demerits. Its chief merit is negative—in that it affords an escape from the greater heat of the plains—but it can hardly be classed as a perfect sanitarium. As a distinguished medical officer said of it forty years ago, "Man, and notably the Englishman, was not created to live at an elevation of 7,000 to 8,000 feet, where he only inhales half the amount of oxygen that is required for working his machinery and digesting his food. Look at the natives. They live in the valleys, not on the hill tops. I cure 50 per cent. of my patients by instructing them to eat little and often, and by assisting their digestion with pepsine." And in the words of another, "A healthy man can enjoy life better at Simla than in the plains, but a sick man ought to go home."

The climate of Simla may be divided into four seasons of about three months each. The first quarter beginning with January—rough, snowy, stormy and raw. The second dry and sunny, with gradually increasing dust and heat. The third rainy, damp and relaxing. The fourth bright, clear and bracing. In no country perhaps are the seasons such seasons of rapidly changing extremes. Few exotic plants can stand them without careful protection, and the human exotic is no exception to the rule. The most trying periods for man are undoubtedly the latter half of the second or dry season and breaks in the rains. From the 15th of May till the rains fall at the end of June or beginning of July the sun gains in power, and so heats air and earth which are unprotected by any shield of moisture that a midday walk or ride alongside the glaring cliffs of the parched Mall makes one think of sunstroke. On one occasion the meteorological reporter noted that the "wet bulb showed absolute zero—a phenomenon unknown in any other inhabited part of the globe." At this time westerly winds blow from the deserts of the plains, filling the air with fine particles of dust and raising clouds of triturated filth from the bazaars underlying the Mall. A haze obscures the landscape. Suddenly is all this changed by the first burst of the monsoon, which is ushered in as a rule by thunder-storms of some violence, and which for uninterrupted hours pour torrents of refreshing

SIMLA KALKA RAILWAY

A CUTTING, VICEREGAL LODGE IN DISTANCE.

water on to thirsty hill and dale. The relief is great. But after a few days comes a 'break in the rains'—of perhaps short endurance; then another burst of rain—followed by another but longer break; and so on till the end perhaps of September, the rainless intervals becoming longer until the end of the wet season.

Sickness prevails chiefly in the weeks immediately preceding the advent of the monsoon, when the air is full of foul dust and the heat most trying, and again in the steamy days between successive rainfalls, favourable no doubt for the generation of the all-pervading 'germ.' At these times prevails the illness known as the "Simla ep—" a troublesome epidemic of mild choleraic character, but sometimes fatal to the weakly. With this exception, however, and that of the indigestion with which delicate constitutions are troubled, Simla is fairly healthy, although from May to September the climate is not of what is termed a 'recuperative character.' There is never enough cold, as at Ootacamund, for fires in the rainy season, and there is no bite in the air. The rains, however, are not so long in duration or so persistent in downfall as at other Himalayan stations further south, Naini Tal and Darjeeling, at which last place the sun is hardly seen from May to September.

About the third week in August the morning equestrian will come back from his ride round Jakko with the news "I have scented the cold weather," and thenceforth morning and evening there come whiffs of bracing air which increase in duration and intensity until towards the end of September they meet in one long day of the most delightful climate in the universe. But that an exceptional storm may interrupt the succession of such heavenly days, either at the close of that month or in early October, it is but the last gasp of the dying monsoon which ends as it began in thunder and lightning, due, say the meteorologists, to the battle between the electricities of dry and wet atmosphere. But thenceforward the season grows towards perfection. Just as, in England, a cloudless day of delight follows a week of mist and rain, so in the Himalayas of Northern India weeks of paradise follow months of purgatory. October and November are delectable months indeed—clear, bracing, exhilarating air then invigorates the body and makes the soul rejoice. Then too it is that the sportsman carries his gun over mountain ranges that would have appalled him a few weeks ago; and then it is that cavalcades of men, women and children stream along the road on foot, on ponies, or in rickshaws and dandies to the glorious woods of Mattiana and Huttoo. Life is no longer existence,—it is Life.

But one word ought to have been said in passing of a relieving feature in the monotony of the rains. It is doubtful whether in the whole world

*

there is more magnificent landscape than the cloud scenery which spreads ever the deep valleys and the mountain ranges that beyond Simla ascend in huge waves to the summits of Tibet. During breaks in the rains cloud masses form over them in giant steps and tiers which are lit up, as the day proceeds, by tints and colourings that are at once the delight and despair of the artist, and which mount in a Titan ladder to the everlasting snows. Well can one believe in the Olympian mansions of the gods when gazing on the glorious cloud-cities which surround the dazzling pinnacles of those snow-clad ranges that seem to end the world. And then in the mornings what a sight is there!—seas and lakes of white cloud sunk to sleep in the deep valleys, and awakening to life when the sun's warmth rouses them to fresh movement and to gradual climbing of the mountain sides. How Shelley could have enriched his wonderful poem on 'The Cloud' if he had written from the summit of Jakko! And yet there is a couplet in it which is sufficiently applicable to one of the varied landscapes of Simla cloudland:—

From cape to cape, with a bridge-like shape,
Over a torrent sea,
Sunbeam proof, I hang like a roof,
The mountains its columns be.

Such are the bridges which hang from Jakko or Mashobra to the Shali over the torrents of the Sutlej.

When the descent from Simla is over, all too soon, commences the real winter which is enjoyed or otherwise by the grass widows and children whose husbands and fathers have to tour round India or to continue writing interminable notes on official 'files' at Calcutta. However of late years a considerable number of officials are for economical reasons required to remain at Simla, and there is a goodly society still left at the summer capital who beguile the time with rink skating, children's parties and other domestic entertainments. The end of December brings storms, snow, and hail which are apt to continue at intervals till the beginning of March, and more than once dwellers on the summit of Jakko have been snowed up for three or four days, living on what tinned provisions might happen to be in the house. But the winter, though rough and often unpleasant, is undeniably healthy, and some of those ladies who return with pale cheeks after their Calcutta season envy the roses and ruddiness of the 'girls they left behind them;' while children thrive wonderfully, and look like Scottish bairns. Winter at an end, there comes an interval of bright, clear, pleasant weather when the rhododendron trees till the end of April, or even later, light up the landscape with splashes of brilliant scarlet. And then come again the scorching weeks of twelve months ago, and so the year goes round.

THE SIMLA KALKA RAILWAY.
(TARADEVI HILL, SIMLA IN DISTANCE).

The following table which has been supplied to me by Mr. W. L. Dallas, the assistant meteorological reporter to the Government of India, indicates the mean temperature of each month in the year.

Simla normals.

Month.	Mean maximum temperature.	Mean minimum temperature.	Mean temperature.	Average number of rainy days.	Mean rainfall.
January	44·5	34·5	39·5	3·60	2·71
February	45·9	35·6	40·8	4·00	3·00
March	56·4	46·0	51·2	4·30	2·07
April	65·2	52·2	58·7	3·10	1·70
May	73·1	58·6	65·9	5·20	3·06
June	74·4	61·0	67·7	9·80	7·85
July	69·2	60·1	64·7	18·90	16·84
August	67·1	59·5	63·3	18·90	17·67
September	66·1	56·4	61·3	8·70	5·87
October	62·4	51·0	56·7	1·30	0·98
November	56·1	45·0	50·6	0·70	0·61
December	49·4	39·1	44·3	1·60	1·23
Year	60·8	49·9	55·4	80·10	63·59
				TOTAL.	

There is a great difference between the north and south aspects of the mountain ranges in the Simla districts. In the summer houses facing the snows are preferable to those which look down on the plains; while in the winter, on the contrary, the northern slopes are bleak and almost sunless, and those who remain at Simla for the cold weather are fain to occupy houses in which they can be warmed by the same sun which would bake them in summer. For similar reasons houses on the two main spurs, Elysium Hill and Summer Hill, which jut out at right angles to the main ridge in a northern direction, are in request. These are neither scorched in summer nor frozen in winter. On the whole an east-north-east aspect for the dwelling-rooms of a Simla residence, provided it is open to the sun, is most enjoyable and most conducive to health. Such rooms are warmed in the morning, but not baked in the afternoon. The aspect certainly suits

English plants better than any other, and seems to be equally good for English men and women and specially for children. I venture to make these remarks (based on high medical opinion) because it seems desirable that builders of future houses should bear these facts in mind—facts which were not remembered when Viceregal Lodge, and many otherwise good houses were erected.

THE SIMLA RAILWAY STATION
(CHRISTMAS 1903.)

CHAPTER II.

Residences of the Governors-General and Viceroys.

Governors-General and Viceroys of India.	Period of Appointment.	Place of residence in Simla.
Earl of Amherst . .	1st August 1823 to 10th March 1828.	Kennedy House (then the residence of Captain Kennedy, Superintendent of the Hill States).
Lord William Bentinck .	4th July 1828 to 20th March 1835.	Bentinck Castle (now the site of Peliti's Grand Hotel).
Earl of Auckland . .	4th March 1836 to 28th February 1842.	Auckland House (the present Girls' School of that name).
Earl of Ellenborough .	28th February 1842 to 15th June 1844.	Auckland House.
Viscount Hardinge .	23rd July 1844 to 12th January 1848.	Auckland House.
Marquis of Dalhousie .	12th January 1848 to 29th February 1856.	One season at Strawberry Hill and two at Kennedy House.
Earl Canning . .	1st November 1858 to 12th March 1862.	Visited Simla in 1860 and resided at Barnes Court.
Earl of Elgin . .	12th March 1862 to 20th November 1863.	Peterhoff.
Sir J. Lawrence . .	12th January 1864 to 12th January 1869.	Peterhoff.
Earl of Mayo . .	12th January 1869 to 8th February 1872.	Peterhoff.
Lord Northbrook . .	3rd May 1872 to 12th April 1876.	Peterhoff.
Lord Lytton . .	12th April 1876 to 8th June 1880.	Peterhoff.
Marquis of Ripon . .	8th June 1880 to 13th December 1884.	Peterhoff.
Earl of Dufferin . .	13th December 1884 to 10th December 1888.	Peterhoff till June 1888, then Viceregal Lodge.
Marquis of Lansdowne .	10th December 1888 to 27th January 1894.	Viceregal Lodge.
Earl of Elgin . .	27th January 1894 to 6th January 1899.	Viceregal Lodge, and The Retreat, Mashobra.
Lord Curzon . .	6th January 1899 to . .	Viceregal Lodge, and The Retreat, Mashobra.

The first Governor-General who visited Simla was Lord Amherst, who in 1827 stayed with Major Kennedy, the Political Officer of the district, at 'Kennedy House.' It was Lord Amherst who said "The Emperor of China and I govern half the human race, and yet we find time to breakfast." While in Simla at Kennedy House he received visits from the Rajas of Garhwal and of Bussahir, and from the Rana of Jubal, as well as a complimentary mission from Ranjit Singh, the Sikh ruler of the Punjab. His impressions of the place were not, however, altogether pleasant. He quitted it in June under the belief that the vegetation which springs up rapidly in the monsoon made Simla unhealthy, and his medical officer and two civilians attached to his staff died from cholera at Pinjore, near Kalka, on the return journey to the plains.

The following paragraphs from the 'Rulers of India' series are of interest: "This lady (Lady Amherst) who seems to have been a person of great character, courage, and remarkable intelligence, has left a journal, perhaps almost unique of its kind, containing the history vividly and simply told of her husband's rule in India. The past is conjured up, still remembered names are familiarly quoted: we feel the temper of the times." And again: "It is not accurate to say that Lord Amherst invented Simla. Its claims were well understood by officers who served in the North-West, and they carried its fame to Government House. But he was the first Governor-General who made it a place of retreat from the discomforts of the plains. He set the fashion." (Lady Amherst's journal, although printed, has not been published.)

It was during Lord William Bentinck's time that Simla was really acquired by the Government of India, and it may not be generally known that one of his last acts was the purchase, from the Raja of Sikkim, of the site on which Darjeeling now stands. When he found the accommodation of Simla was insufficient for the requirements of his staff, Lord Bentinck proceeded for a season to Ootacamund. The old 'dâk' bungalow of Simla was demolished in order to provide a site for 'Bentinck Castle' (now Peliti's Grand Hotel), an account of which old house will be found in the next chapter. Lord Bentinck's hospitality has been recorded as 'magnificent,' and he is said to have worked hard to establish social relations between natives and Europeans. His wife who assisted him greatly in his endeavours has been described by Sir Charles Metcalfe as 'a most engaging woman,' whose charities were famous during her stay in India, and much missed after her departure. The year 1832 it may be noted was the first in which both the Governor-General and Commander-in-Chief were in Simla together.

One of Lord Bentinck's guests at Simla was Dr. Joseph Wolff, D.D., who, so it is stated in a volume dealing with his 'Travels and Adventures,' preached several times in the drawing-rooms of the Governor-General and of the Commander-in-Chief (Sir Edward Barnes), among the congregations being Sir William and Lady MacNaughton, and Colonel (afterwards Sir Robert) and Lady Sale. He also preached in Persian to the Muhammadan Nawabs.

During Dr. Wolff's stay in Simla Captain Hay (a relative of Lord Kinnoul) and Captain Bell (afterwards Resident in Nepal) fought a duel about some dispute at cards; while a dinner is mentioned as having been given by a Colonel and Mrs. Churchill, at which a whole party of dancing girls appeared. Dr. Wolff who afterwards "left Simla for Kurnaul with letters from the Governor-General for Lucknow, Calcutta, and Madras," received *en route* permission from the Maharaja of Kashmir to visit his State, the orders being that "he might remain there one month, that he should make slow stages and receive from every Raja he met on the road £25 a day and 20 pots of sweetmeats." On his arrival at Kashmir the Prince, Governor Sheer Singh, was to give him six shawls, and 1,000 'sicca' rupees equivalent to £100.

Lord and Lady William Bentinck, we are told, did much for the benefit of the station, "building a hospital and 'serai' (lodging-house) for natives out of their private purse, while their open-handedness and charity made them greatly beloved by all, high and low." It has already been noted that a prominent peak (on the north-west horizon) was called 'Lord Bentinck's nose' from the similarity of its outline to the profile of His Excellency.

Lord Bentinck's successor did not live at 'Bentinck Castle.' Lord Auckland chose a residence on the north-eastern spur of the Simla range, which during the summers of 1838-9 was known as 'Auckland House,' and for several subsequent years as Government House.

I have found two pictures of Simla, one drawn in 1838 by Captain G. P. Thomas, of the 64th regiment, Bengal Infantry—showing 'Auckland House,' 'Stirling Castle,' and 'Secretary's Lodge' (now 'Chapslee'),—and another drawing of the same subject taken about the year 1845 by Mrs. W. L. L. Scott. The particulars concerning these and other old houses which have been closely connected with the Governors-General and Viceroys of India have been extracted from old books and newspapers, and will indicate how simple were the conditions of Viceregal life in Simla sixty years ago.

The hill on which 'Auckland House' stood received its present name of 'Elysium' in 1838 as a delicate compliment to the Hon'ble Misses Eden, Lord Auckland's sisters. 'Auckland House' was destined to be "the scene of many a brilliant ball and amusing theatricals," and, as one of the oldest houses in the station, its history is of special interest.

In 1828, a Dr. Blake, Surgeon in the Honourable East India Company's service, obtained a grant of land from the Political Agent at Subathu. This was divided into two plots, registered as 13 and 54; on the former he built a large house which he let, and on the latter a smaller one in which he resided.

In 1836 this Dr. Blake sold plot 13 to Lord Auckland, and plot 54 to Captain the Hon'ble W. Osborne (Lord Auckland's nephew and Military Secretary), the Governor-General acquiring the smaller house from his kinsman in 1839. A year later Lord Auckland sold both properties to Dr. J. Ransford, Assistant Surgeon in the Company's service, for Rs. 16,000, the houses being respectively termed Government House and Secretary's Lodge in the conveyance deed. In 1858 Dr. Ransford obtained Rs. 24,000 for the two houses from Colonel Peter Innes of the Bengal Army. After ten years' proprietorship General Innes sold the 'Auckland House' estate (*minus* the ground on which the 'Elysium Hotel,' 'Kendal Lodge,' and 'Waverley' now stand) for Rs. 8,000 to the Bishop and Archdeacon of Calcutta, as Trustees for the Punjab Girls' School, and 'Secretary's Lodge' (now 'Chapslee,' *minus* the ground which 'Belvedere' now occupies) for Rs. 5,100 to Mr. W. Newman.

After serving as a residence for Lord Ellenborough and Lord Hardinge, 'Auckland House' dwindled from its proud position as the home of Governors-General, to the lower levels first of a boarding house, kept by a Frenchman and his wife, and next of a hotel kept by a native. In 1868, as already stated, it was purchased for the purposes of a girls' school which had been established in 1866 (with Mrs. Mackinnon as Head Mistress) at 'Holly Lodge.' The house was accordingly enlarged by the school authorities, and an upper storey erected. The school during its earlier existence met a long felt want in Northern India and Bengal. Later on, however, as facilities for proceeding to England increased it experienced a somewhat chequered career, and at one time nearly had to close its doors. It is now, however, a flourishing institution under the direction of Miss Pratt.

With reference to the early history of 'Auckland House,' it is described as a one-storied building, with a flat roof composed of a thick coating of earth well beaten down to render it impervious to rain. Notwithstanding this, on the occasion of a heavy downpour, the water settled on the ceiling of one of the principal rooms, which fell in and caused considerable damage. It is recorded of Lord Auckland's Staff that Captain M., after moving into every corner of his house, used to write under an umbrella, and Captain B. and his companion Dr. S. dined every day in their house with

Reproduced from "Simla," by Captain G. P. Thomas.

AUCKLAND HOUSE AND SECRETARY'S LODGE, ABOUT 1840.

umbrellas held over their heads and their dinners. It is also on record that fleas were then a terrible pest in the rains; for several nights the inmates of 'Auckland House' were unable to sleep, and the more the rooms were cleaned and overhauled the livelier these pests became. The Hon'ble Emily Eden, sister of Lord Auckland, thus wrote of the house in the years 1838-39:—

"On our arrival (in April) we found Simla white with snow—Giles (the servant) had preceded us by two days and had got all the curtains up, and the carpets down, and our house looked very comfortable. It is a jewel of a little house and my room is quite overcoming—so light and cheerful and all the little curiosities I have accumulated on my travels have a sweet effect now they are spread out . . . The views are only too lovely. Deep valleys on the drawing-room side to the west, and the snowy range on the dining-room side, where my room also is. Our sitting rooms are small, but that is all the better in this climate, and the two principal rooms are very fine. We have fires in every room and the windows open. Red rhododendron trees in bloom in every direction, and beautiful walks like English shrubberies on all sides of the hill. *April 22.*—The climate, the place, and the whole thing is quite delightful, and our poor despised house that every one abused has turned out the wonder of Simla. We brought carpets and chandeliers and wall shades (the great staple commodity of Indian furniture) from Calcutta, and I have got a native painter into the house, and cut out patterns in paper, which he then paints in borders all round the doors and windows, and it makes up for the want of cornices and breaks the eternal white walls of these houses . . . . We pass our lives in gardening. We ride down into the valleys and make the syces dig up wild tulips and lilies, and they are grown so eager about it that they dash up the hill the instant they see a promising looking plant and dig it up with the best possible effect except that they invariably cut off the bulb. We have not had a great many visitors. There are 46 ladies and 12 gentlemen in Simla independent of our party, and 40 more ladies and 6 gentlemen are expected up shortly. How any dancing is to be managed at our parties we cannot make out. The Aides-de-Camp are in despair about it. . . . . . There are several very pretty people here, but we can hardly make out any dinners. Most of the ladies send their regular excuse, that they do not dine out while Captain so-and-so is with the army. Very devoted wives, but if the war lasts they will be very dull women. It is wonderful how they do contrive to get on together as well as they do. There are five ladies belonging to the regiment all with families who have been living six months in one small house with only one common room and yet they declare they have not quarrelled. I can hardly credit it; can you?"

It was a free and easy kind of life in those days, compared with the somewhat official etiquette of the present day, for further on one reads that, "On fine evenings, in the rains, Lord Auckland and his sisters used to drop in familiarly after dinner to have tea and a rubber of whist with the Commander-in-Chief (General Sir Henry Fane) at 'Bentinck Castle.' Again Sir L. Ryan, the Chief Justice of Bengal, came to Simla on a visit to Lord Auckland, but there was no spare room in the house, so he stayed with a friend, and had his meals at 'Auckland House.'"

On the 8th May 1838, Lord Auckland held a Durbar at 'Auckland House,' where all the hill chiefs were received for the first time. They were introduced to him by Colonel Tapp, the Political Agent and Superintendent, Cis-Sutlej States. On the 7th May 1838 an embassy from the Lion of the Punjab (Ranjit Singh) was received in great state at 'Auckland House.' A company of Gurkha sepoys was drawn up on one side of the entrance, while on the other, in regular and gorgeous array, were the mace bearers and others of His Lordship's servants in their scarlet livery. It was described as a novel and imposing sight, and one well worth seeing. The visit of the Sikhs lasted about a week, and the ladies of Simla at first declined to dance in the presence of the envoys who were invited to Government House. Later on however they changed their minds.

On the 24th May 1838, the anniversary of H. M. the Queen of England's birthday was celebrated by a ball and supper at 'Auckland House,' and French's narrative of Simla gives the following description of the entertainment:—

"The preparations were suited to the occasion. A stream of light proceeded from two rows of lamps on both sides of the road leading to the house. The illuminations followed the curvatures of the path and its effect was thus rendered the more striking as it shone through the foliage. The lights at a distance appeared like clusters of stars glimmering through a sky of green. The music produced a fine effect. Its reverberation amid the neighbouring hills gave it a richness which is known only where echo after echo repeats in delightful mockery, the grand harmony produced by the effects of an Orphean band."

During the summer of 1839 at 'Auckland House,' Simla residents were favoured with a glimpse of a beautiful Mrs. James, "who looked like a star among all the others." She was so lovely that she drove every other woman with any pretensions to beauty quite distracted. This lady was the daughter and only child of Mrs. C., the wife of the Deputy Adjutant-General at Simla, and was afterwards celebrated as 'Lola Montez.'

Her history and doings could be made to fill a volume of romance, but they must be here briefly told. She was born in Limerick in 1822, and brought out to India as a child. Her mother took her back to England in 1837, and placed her in a boarding school in Bath. She did not, however, remain there long. We are told that she early developed great beauty, which, coupled with her vivacity of spirit, attracted an Indian officer, Lieutenant James, who had gone home on furlough "round the Cape" in the same ship with her. She made a run-away marriage from Bath with this gentleman. She was then only fifteen, while he was thirty. He brought her out again to the Punjab, and she came to Simla during the summer of 1839, on a visit to her parents. Simla society, it is reported, was much moved by her presence, and Miss Eden described her as "undoubtedly very pretty, and such a merry, unaffected girl." She had a very grand 'Jonpaun' with bearers in fine orange and brown liveries, and was a strangely fascinating woman. Her husband was then stationed at Kurnaul, where he was drawing a salary of Rs. 160 per mensem, as, at the age of thirty, he was only a subaltern in the army. On his visit to Simla he was described as "a sort of smart-looking man with bright waistcoats and bright teeth, riding a showy horse, in an attitude of respectful attention to *ma belle mère*." On her return after a Simla season to the quiet station of Kurnaul, Mrs. James naturally found life rather dull. When Lord Auckland visited Kurnaul in the course of a tour in November 1839, Miss Eden in her diary gives the following account of her, "Little Mrs. J. was so unhappy at our going that we asked her to come and spend the day here and brought her with us. She went from tent to tent and chatted all day, and visited her friend Mrs. — who is camped with us. I gave her a pink silk gown and it was altogether a very happy day for her evidently . . . . she is very pretty and a good little thing, apparently, but they are very poor, and she is very young and lively, and if she falls into bad hands, she would soon laugh herself into foolish scrapes. At present the wife and husband are very fond of each other, but a girl who marries at fifteen hardly knows what she likes." Shortly after this viceregal visit Mrs. James made a second elopement and re-embarked for Europe in 1842. She afterwards had a wild and very romantic career, and in course of time became the most notorious adventuress in Europe. As 'Lola Montez' she exercised a wonderful fascination over sovereigns and ministers alike and developed into an active and dangerous political intriguer. She gained unbounded influence over the King of Bavaria, who gave her an estate worth £5,000 a year with feudal rights over a population of 2,000 persons, and created her Countess of Landsfeld, and she is said for a time to have ruled her little kingdom quite wisely. Her acts and extravagances later on, however, became wildly scandalous, and she was ultimately compelled to fly in disguise. Eventually her intrigues, her marriages, duels, and horsewhippings made her notorious in London, Paris, and America, and after a most remarkable career, she died in New York, in January 1861, at the early age of 38.

The last four months of her life were devoted to ministering in a Magdalen asylum near New York. She wrote her autobiography (1858), and some years after her death her history was told under the title 'The Story of a Penitent' (1867).

To return however to my subject. Miss Eden was evidently very fond of Simla in spite of its undoubted drawbacks. "Poor dear house," she wrote on leaving 'Auckland House,' "I am sorry to see it despoiled, we have had seven as good months here as it is possible to pass in India: no trouble, no heat, and if the Himalayas were only a continuation of Primrose Hill, or Penge Common, I should have no objection to pass the rest of my life on them."

Miss Eden's charming letters to her sister were published in 1866, the writer having died in 1860 at the age of 72.

I have already alluded to the house known during Lord Auckland's first year in Simla, 1838, as 'Secretary's Lodge.' The accommodation in Auckland House being limited, the adjoining house was converted into offices for his Private and Military Secretaries, and set apart for the Secretaries and officials to meet in and conduct their business.

The year 1838 was memorable in Indian history, as one in which many weighty questions were considered, and several important measures adopted. During the summer of that year Lord Auckland and his advisers hatched the policy which led to the first Afghan war and to all its disastrous sequelæ. We read that he had a "Cabinet of Secretaries" with him, who turned a deaf ear to all peaceful representations. The famous "Simlah Manifesto" declaring war with Afghanistan was really issued from Secretary's Lodge on the 1st October 1838.

In the following year (shortly after Lord Auckland's arrival in Simla) Secretary's Lodge was turned into an abode for the Aides-de-Camp, who were many, and the two houses lying just below now known as 'Waverley' and 'Oakleigh' were at the same time respectively occupied by the Military Department and Foreign Offices.

Miss Eden writing from 'Auckland House' in March 1839 makes the following remarks about 'Secretary's Lodge':—

"Our Band twice a week is to be a great resource, Lord Auckland has bought the house adjoining ours and has made it over to the Aides-de-Camp, which saves them some money, and in the grounds belonging

CHAPSLEE IN SUMMER, 1903.

CHAPSLEE IN WINTER, 1903.

to it we have found a beautiful terrace for the Band, and the others have persuaded P., who is laying out the grounds, to arrange a few pretty paths for two, and also to make the gates so narrow that Jonpauns cannot come through them, so that the ladies must be handed out and walk up to the music. . . The Band played on Wednesday in the new place we have made for it in the adjoining grounds of 'Secretary's Lodge,' such a view of the Snowy Range and such a pretty spot altogether, and all the 'retired' ladies come to console themselves with a little music and to take a little tea and coffee and talk a little."

Here I must explain that 'retired' refers to several ladies in Simla who declined to accept invitations while their husbands were fighting in Afghanistan.

'Secretary's Lodge' again became the Secretariat during Lord Ellenborough's stay in Simla, and it is recorded that the failure of Lord Auckland's policy in Afghanistan was acknowledged, and the altered intentions of Government proclaimed, by Lord Ellenborough from the same building, in the same room, and on the very same day four years after the issue of the manifesto, namely, on 1st October 1842. In 1845, during Lord Hardinge's régime, 'Secretary's Lodge' was still used as the Government Secretariat. General Peter Innes, into whose hands the house afterwards came, was a large house-owner in Simla; he gave fanciful names to many houses, and changed the name of this one from 'Secretary's Lodge' to 'Chapslee.' Eventually, as already noted, he sold it to Mr. Newman, who in 1870 parted with it to General W. Gordon for R5,200. This owner spent a considerable sum on the property and then sold it for R27,000 to Mr. J. M. Macpherson, Secretary to the Government of India, who resided there for some years. The house was up to this time styled 'Chapslee, late Secretary's Lodge.' It afterwards became the residence successively of Sir Courtenay C. Ilbert, General Pemberton, General Sir C. E. Nairne, Mr. (now Sir) John Eliot (who purchased it in 1888 from Mr. Macpherson), Surgeon-General A. F. Bradshaw, Surgeon-General J. Cleghorn, General N. Arnott, and General Sir A. Gaselee. It is now the property of Mr. A. M. Ker, the well-known manager of the Alliance Bank of Simla, who bought it from Mr. Eliot in 1896, and who has within the last couple of years improved it beyond all recognition. In the opinion of many good judges 'Chapslee' is now surpassed by no other Simla residence in arrangement and general advantages.

Lord Ellenborough, who succeeded Lord Auckland as Governor-General, also resided at 'Auckland House.' Several of His Lordship's letters relating to his Indian Administration (edited by Lord Colchester and published in a volume in 1874) were written from Simla. Some of them were addressed to Her Majesty the Queen and others to the Duke of Wellington.

Lord Hardinge, the friend of Wellington, who landed in India in July 1844, was occupied with the Sikh war for several months after his arrival and did not visit Simla till 1846. In the 'Rulers of India' series in which his history is given by his son Charles, Viscount Hardinge, the only reference to his residence at Simla is the following: "The small bungalow (Auckland House) overlooking the snows was modest enough compared with the Government House which has since been erected. I can see him now pacing up and down the verandah, as he discussed with energy the contents of the latest dâk from Lahore with some of the Secretariat. After the labours and excitement of the campaign the repose now permitted, and the pleasant reflection that his rule was nearly at an end were meat and drink to him." On his return to England, Charles, Viscount Hardinge, published in 1847 a beautiful book of drawings which he styled 'Recollections of India.' The book was dedicated to the Queen, and the pictures represented many scenes and events that took place during Lord Hardinge's administration, and have the merit of coming from one who was himself an actor in some of the events which took place in 1845-46.

'Auckland House' apparently did not commend itself to Lord Dalhousie as a dwelling house, as he made his head-quarters for one season at 'Strawberry Hill' (of which a brief notice is given in a chapter dealing with old houses) and for two others at 'Kennedy House.'

It is reported on good authority that Lord Dalhousie was glad to have his head-quarters at Simla in the summer, because it enabled him to spend much of his time during the rainy season at Chini, 145 miles further inland, where the drier climate suited his health. Here he built a lodge, now utilised as a bungalow for travellers, which was broken into and plundered in 1858.

At a moment when the British mission to Tibet is attracting so much attention it is interesting to recall the fact that one of Lord Dalhousie's ambitions was to open up trade with Tibet, and a broad cart road at great cost was accordingly constructed under his orders from Simla to Chini. Much of this road is still utilized, although in many sections of it the tedious detours which the cart gradient demands have been abandoned for short cuts over the hills. Lord Dalhousie thus resided for some time at the termination of the grand road to Tibet. But it proved to be only a road towards and not 'to' Tibet, for the snowy ranges afford almost insuperable difficulties to its completion.

Sir W. W. Hunter, in his 'Rulers of India' series. says that Simla, formerly an occasional health resort, gradually grew at this period into the seat of the Government of India during the chief part of the year. Lord Dalhousie used it "as his eyrie from which to watch the newly annexed plains that stretch below."

Sir Richard Temple in his life of John Thomason, Lieutenant-Governor of the North-West Provinces, tells us that "He (Mr. Thomason) had the advantage of avoiding the hottest months by spending the time at Simla where all his correspondence followed him . . . He rightly resorted thither in order to be with the Governor General. Certainly it was thus he acquired a just influence over the mind of Lord Dalhousie."

Lord Canning, the first Viceroy under the Crown, arrived in Simla in April 1860. Lady Canning, writing from Barnes Court, said: "I think the beauty of this place very questionable, it is such a sea of hill tops, and the snowy mountains are so far off, and the dryness makes all look wintry . . . Here if one sees ten yards level one screams out, 'what a site for a house'" In May she wrote: "This place is very like a watering place, but we keep to our quiet end of it and private walks. I do not very much like this place, for I get so tired at the sameness of the roads, always with what we call here a 'khud' (a sort of earthy rocky precipice of hillside hundreds of feet down), and a wall of the same above." Owing to the illness of Sir James Outram, Lord Canning went down to Calcutta towards the end of May, and Lady Canning shortly afterwards left Simla on a trip along the Hindustan-Tibet road *viá* Chini to Landour and Mussoorie, which she reached after a thirty-one days' journey, the distance being about 300 miles. Her Excellency wrote of this journey that Lord Canning liked the notion of her trip, and that she was glad to go as she was not fond of Simla, and should of course avoid all society after he had gone to Calcutta. Neither Lord nor Lady Canning indeed cared for Simla, as the Viceroy was never free from neuralgia while in the hills, and Lady Canning objected to the place as 'very public,' and disliked the crowd which met daily on the Mall. Moreover she termed the Himalayas as 'giants detestable to live amongst,' though she was glad to have seen them. The forests, however, she wrote of as a real delight; "I have never before seen anything so beautiful, or such specimens of trees." Lady Canning died in Calcutta on 18th November 1861, and was buried in Barrackpore Park, near Calcutta. Lord Canning, who never recovered the shock of his wife's death, did not revisit Simla, and dying in London in June 1862, was buried in Westminster Abbey.

The first Viceroy who moved into 'Peterhoff' was the Earl of Elgin, who arrived in Simla on the 4th April 1863. Old records indicate that the first native cemetery in Simla was on the spot now occupied by this well-known house, and there seems to be no doubt that the Viceroy's summer residence was originally either on, or in close proximity to, a graveyard. Several cases of typhoid which occurred among the staffs and households of Lords Lytton and Ripon were openly attributed to this cause. A description of 'Peterhoff' itself (by Lady Dufferin) will be found further on in this chapter.

His Excellency described the journey to Simla as 'uninteresting,' but in alluding to the luxuriance in foliage and vegetation of Simla itself said, "this probably accounts for what otherwise seems strange, namely, that Europeans wishing to escape from the heat of the lowlands, should have fixed on a spot among the hills so distant from the plains." It was on 26th September that Lord Elgin left Simla for a journey through Kulu to Lahoul, dying amidst universal regrets at Dharmsala in the Kangra Valley on the 20th November.

Sir John Lawrence first visited Simla as Viceroy in May 1864, though he had made a previous acquaintance with the station as early as 1846 when holding the Commissionership of the Trans-Sutlej States. A residence in the hills in the hot weather was indeed insisted upon by the doctors as a condition of his accepting the Viceroyalty, and in spite of the expense, and the then unpopularity of the move, he brought his Council with him. Sir John Lawrence, however, always maintained that the arrangement was economical, if not of money, at least of men and work, and in one of his letters wrote: "I believe that we will do more work in one day here (Simla) than in five down in Calcutta."

A short residence in Simla confirmed the Viceroy in his opinion that the Government of the country would be benefited by an habitual residence in the hills during the summer, and he came to the conclusion that out of Calcutta there was no place better suited for the capital than Simla. He pressed the matter with much warmth on Sir Charles Wood, the Secretary of State for India, and the latter, in agreeing that the Governor-General and his Council should leave Calcutta in the summer, wrote: "With regard to yourself I have no sort of difficulty in saying that with, or without, your Council, you are quite welcome to be away from Calcutta for six months, and therefore you may set your mind quite at ease on that point. If you like next summer to go and see Madras and the Neilgherries, and put some life into their proceedings, or visit Darjeeling, and our new enemies in Bhutan, or go to Simla again, I have no objection." Sir John Lawrence, in replying, expressed his gratitude for Sir Charles Wood's very kind letter and said, "No doubt such a change as I propose is a serious one and requires much consideration. I do not, however, think that a better arrangement is to be made. The work now is, probably, treble, possibly quadruple, what it was twenty years ago, and it is for the most part of a very difficult nature. Neither could your Governor-General and his Council really do it in the hot weather in Calcutta. At the best, as you say, they would work at half speed. . . . This place of all hill stations seems to me the best for the Supreme Government. *Here* you are with one Government, I may say in the Punjab, and another in the North-West Provinces."

Neither Sir John nor Lady Lawrence cared much for social diversions. Lady Lawrence, writing in 1865, said: "There is not much to say about our domestic life at Simla. To me it seemed one long round of large dinner parties, balls, and festivities of all kinds. My husband did not at Simla go out for the long early rides of which he had once been so fond, and which he still kept up when he was in Calcutta. But he rose early and got through a fair amount of work before breakfast, and in the evening he either rode or walked by my side, while I was carried in a 'jampan.'" Later on in Calcutta she wrote: "The perpetual round of gaieties, both here and in Simla, though we tried to vary them by Shakespear readings, and tableaux, was trying to us both."

For the permanent location, therefore, of Simla as the summer head-quarters of the Supreme Government Sir John Lawrence undoubtedly deserves the credit, and though for many years the exodus to the Himalayas continued to be violently attacked by both the Anglo-Indian and vernacular press, and by none more vehemently than certain Calcutta papers, Simla has since remained, and surely will remain, the summer capital of India.

It is a curious circumstance that 'Peterhoff,' in which Sir John Lawrence lived during his Simla residence, is situated on a watershed, the drainage from which on the one side flows into the Sutlej and so into the Arabian sea, and on the other into the Jumna on its way to the Bay of Bengal. A suitable site for the residence of the Lord of the Indian Empire! The present Viceregal Lodge claims the same privilege.

Sir W. W. Hunter has left it on record in his Life of the Earl of Mayo that the fourth Viceroy was an indefatigable worker. Rising at daybreak he often laboured at his office 'boxes' till a late hour at night and left behind him a reputation for energy which few of his successors have equalled.

Of Lord Mayo's life in Simla but little is known to-day, and he apparently spent comparatively but few months there during his short term of Viceroy. To an officer who fancied that to come to Simla and hang around 'Peterhoff' would bring him into notice, Lord Mayo, through a third person, conveyed advice to return to his own sphere of duty and work quietly within it. Lord Mayo's practice at Simla was to work from early in the morning till the afternoon when he rode out for an hour or two, and returned to work again till the dinner bell rang. He generally gave one day in the week in fine weather to shooting in the interior near Narkanda, and bagged some fine black bears in his first two seasons. He thought little of a thirty-mile ride in the forenoon or afternoon. Lord Mayo was hospitable to the last degree and spent his money generously in entertainments of all kinds.

Lord Northbrook was the next Viceroy and he too lived at 'Peterhoff.' Mr. Andrew Wilson is my authority for the statement that while His Excellency's feats on horseback were not so extraordinary as some of those of his predecessors, still they were decidedly remarkable. The road from Simla to Kotgarh, 52 miles in length, he rode in a day, and it is on record that he also rode from Chini to Narkanda, about 100 miles, in a dangerously short period. Lord Northbrook, who made several trips to the forests and the interior, was a clever amateur painter, and his sketches of trees were especially admired. He frequently suffered from asthma during the rainy season, and so was obliged to spend a good deal of his time within the walls of 'Peterhoff.'

Lord Lytton, who followed Lord Northbrook in 'Peterhoff,' described the place as 'a sort of pigstye' and always said it was a most unsuitable residence for a Viceroy. In spite of its drawbacks there was a good deal of entertaining at the house in Lord Lytton's Viceroyalty, and numerous amusing stories, some of which should certainly be taken with the proverbial grain of salt, have since been told of social functions of that day. The mall leading from 'Peterhoff' through the bazaar and round Jakko was converted into a carriage road, and His Excellency took considerable interest in the improvement of the station. I believe however that it was Lord William Beresford, then the senior Aide-de-Camp on Lord Lytton's staff, who suggested to His Excellency the widening of the road round Jakko, and was the first to drive over it with a phæton and pair. The labour for constructing the road was supplied by a Pioneer regiment brought up to Simla for the purpose.

That Lord Lytton was fully aware of the drawbacks of 'Peterhoff' may be gathered from a speech which he made at the opening of the Fine Arts show held in the Theatre of the old Assembly Rooms in 1878. Captain Cole exhibited a picture of a Viceregal Lodge, the construction of which was then very much in the air, and Lord Lytton in the course of his remarks spoke as follows:—"Ladies and gentlemen, many of our other contributors this year have devoted, with marked success, a careful and experienced study of ærial effect to those extensive views and distant prospects in which this country abounds. But never was there so audacious, yet successful, an attempt to place before our eyes, without even recourse to colour, the contours of a distant prospect, as that which has been made—and most successfully made—by my friend Captain Cole, in his excellent etching of a prospect so distant that it is only possible to the eye of faith. (Cheers and laughter.) For the 'airy nothing' to which his constructive genius has given 'a local habitation and a name' is that visionary Viceregal residence which 'never is, but always *to be* built' at Simla." (Cheers and laughter.)

At a time when the possible future move of the Punjab Government summer head quarters from Simla to Dalhousie is under consideration, the fact that Lord Lytton in 1876-77 ordered the provincial Government, then located at Murree, to move up to Simla, may be fittingly recorded. The Lieutenant-Governor (Sir R. H. Davies) spent his first two seasons at 'Oakover,' now the property of the Maharaja of Patiala.

Referring to the Viceroy's departure for the scene of the Madras famine in 1877, Val Prinsep wrote: "I must say that Lord Lytton does not consult his personal convenience. I wonder how Viceroys and people managed in the old time when all went about in tall hats and voluminous neckties and neither ice nor soda water were to be had. Are we really gone off? Have we got soft and luxurious? Lord Lytton has certainly not an iron constitution, but he stands more work than most people, for he does not require exercise to keep him in good health. Now, he is sometimes days without going out. He writes day and night, and even when sitting to me he does business with Secretaries and others."

Lord Lytton, who suffered much from insomnia, rarely retired before 3 A.M. when he went to bed and slept from sheer exhaustion. He was generally in his office and at work about 10-30 A.M. Probably no Viceroy, with the exception of Lord Curzon, has worked harder or more continuously, or has covered more manuscript with his own right hand. Like Lord Curzon, he took intense interest in his work, and like him also he never allowed anything to interfere with the thorough performance of it. Those who knew him and were associated with him officially and privately at Simla remember him best for the artistic skill with which he treated the driest subjects and made them interesting reading; for his exceptional gifts as a public speaker; for the charm of his conversation; and, last but not least, for the lovable and whole-hearted nature of the man.

In the Hon'ble Mrs. Maxwell Scott's Biography of Henry Schomberg Kerr, who came out to India in 1880 as Lord Ripon's Domestic Chaplain, will be found an interesting account of how Father Kerr with Lord Lytton's successor reached Simla, with his impressions of the station at that time. The following are extracts from the Chaplain's diary:—

"By nine o'clock we had reached Solon, *i.e.*, a dozen tongas of men and baggage. Here—the half-way house—the Deputy Commissioner of Simla received and entertained us to an excellent breakfast, which I afterwards learned had come all the way from Government House. We now learned details of the full-dress reception that awaited His Excellency at Simla

Government House. Every arrangement had been made, and printed instructions issued. Five o'clock precisely was the moment at which Lord Lytton was to receive Lord Ripon under a shamiana on the lawn in front of Peterhoff—all the world looking on, salutes firing, band and banners playing in the breeze. This being so, Foote (who had not a full-dress coat) determined to come on with me and make a private entrance at an earlier hour. Accordingly we started in tonga soon after 11 A.M., and within three hours passed, two miles out of Simla, the tents where the Viceregal party were to stop and adorn themselves. By three and-a-half hours we had reached the precincts of Government House, where, accidentally meeting Captain Muir, A.-D.-C., we honoured him with our company at luncheon. Afterwards wishing to keep out of the way and so casting only a glimpse at my window at Government House, I went with Foote and rested in his bungalow on the crest of the knoll, named Mount Pleasant. In due time guns and music rent the air, but I was not moved. Presently I learned that all had been satisfactorily accomplished. The Supreme Council had listened to the mandate of the Queen-Empress appointing Lord Ripon, who now sat on the Viceregal throne. Towards the shades of evening I had determined, having nought to do with state dinners, to take possession of my room and there refresh the inward man, but Lord and Lady Lytton sent an express to beg me to make my appearance—a command which I obeyed.

"Then came the trying moment, when at last the host and hostess had to bid farewell to their guests and to the house. The custom is peculiar. The ex-Viceroy gives a state dinner to the new one, at the end of which he goes, leaving guests and house behind him; so that Lady Lytton dressed for dinner in her room, but never afterwards saw it. Quickly after the 'jampans' filed up one by one, and shipping their cargoes (Father Kerr it may be remarked had spent his earlier life as a sailor) passed noiselessly out of sight. Soon all had gone, leaving Lord Ripon and staff in quiet possession of Government House. By midnight silence reigned throughout, and we laid ourselves down with thanks—and with reason, for coffins are in readiness at every station along the line; and the driver and the guard of the train that left Bombay on the night previous to us were both taken out dead—heat apoplexy—at Kandura, where we breakfasted the morning after—all well. *Laus Deo semper.*"

The allusion to the coffins and the railway line may be explained by the fact that in former years most of the Indian trains carried these gruesome accompaniments in readiness for cases of heat apoplexy, cholera, and other sicknesses. By a printer's error this portion of Father Kerr's account of the journey from Bombay got mixed up with the account of the reception at Simla and appears in Mrs. Maxwell's book as quoted above. Father Kerr's further impressions of Simla are described in his diary as follows:—

"The main and only artery running through the station is called the 'Mall,' along which none but the Viceroy and the Lieutenant-Governor of the Punjab can drive, the rest being condemned to their feet, ponies, or jampans. Except the bazaars, there is not a street. Houses and shelters for human beings are dotted about on every available spot wherever a nook can be got sufficiently safe to stand the wash of a tropical shower. House and road building is expensive enough, for during the rains repairs are incessant. Every day slips of land carry away roads, dry walls, and even foundations. The whole place is a make-shift. Government House a shooting box. Government offices there are none. You would be surprised to see how the work is carried on. Houses peer out under every bank, lie so close to the hill, and are fronted by so much shade that they seem to breathe forth nothing but pains and fever. Happily Peterhoff is watered and crowned by the heavens alone. The Catholic church is fairly central, but down the hill and in a bad position. Being off the Mall not even the Viceroy can drive to the door."

Lord Ripon converted the small upper storied room in the south-east corner of 'Peterhoff' into a chapel where service was regularly held. I have been informed by an official who knew him well that Lord Ripon was never keen on pushing on the scheme for a new Government House, and that when the engineers tried to persuade him that the 'Peterhoff' hill was unsafe he merely remarked, 'I think it will last during my time.'

If 'Peterhoff' was a miserable residence for a Viceroy when Lord Lytton took office, it does not seem to have been much improved by the time that Lord Dufferin entered its doors, for we find Lady Dufferin writing in 'Our Viceregal Life in India' on 21st April 1885:—

"The house itself is a cottage, and would be very suitable for any family desiring to lead a domestic and not an official life,— so, personally, we are comfortable; but when I look round my small drawing-room, and consider all the other diminutive apartments, I do feel that it is very unfit for a Viceregal establishment. Altogether it is the funniest place! At the back of the house you have about a yard to spare before you tumble down a precipice, and in front there is just room for one tennis court before you go over another. The A.-D.-C.'s are all slipping off the hill in various little bungalows, and go through most perilous adventures to come to dinner. Walking, riding, driving, all seem to me to be indulged in at the risk of one's life, and even of unsafe roads there is a limited variety. I have three leading ideas on the subject of Simla at present. First, I feel that I never have been in such an out-of-the-way place before; secondly, that I never have lived in such a small house; and thirdly, that I never saw a place so cramped in every way out of doors. I fear this last sensation will grow upon me."

A year or two later in 'Helen Trevelyan' by John Roy (Sir H. M. Durand), 'Peterhoff' is described as a "small uncomfortable Government House."

Although all preceding Viceroys had complained of the house, yet partly on account of the continued 'financial difficulty' of the year, and partly, perhaps, of the natural disinclination to spend money on objects which only successors can enjoy, no Viceroy seriously took up the task of creating a fitting residence until Lord Dufferin came. Lord Dufferin determined, however, that it should be done, though he had little hope of ever sleeping under the roof of what Lady Dufferin calls 'our own house,' and when Lord Dufferin made up his mind that a thing should be done, whether it was the annexation of a new province, or the building of a new house, it generally was done. To continue Lady Dufferin's diary:—

"D. and I visited 'Observatory Hill,' which is a site Lord Lytton chose for the new Government House. At Calcutta it was proposed that we should alter this cottage into a fitting Viceregal residence, but the moment we saw the proximity of our precipice and the smallness of the house, we began to think that it would be a mistake to build here, and now that we have seen the new site we are convinced of it. There is a splendid view from it, and a large space of vacant ground to build on, and I should say it has every possible advantage over this."

Lord Dufferin himself suggested the general plan of Viceregal Lodge, and until the designs were completed, continually examined and modified the drawings in detail. While the construction of the building was proceeding he visited it almost every morning and evening somewhat to the perturbation of the then Public Works Member and his Department, for changes had sometimes to be made, estimates kept closely within limits, and work at the same time vigorously pushed on. In fact it was his one chief distraction from the heavy and serious business with which his Viceroyalty was occupied. Meanwhile Lady Dufferin made the best of 'Peterhoff,' and on Thursday, 28th May 1885, wrote:—

"I did very little all the day except to take an active interest in the arrangements for the ball, and particularly to superintend the decoration of the conservatory, which I did up like a sitting-room. It is at one end of the drawing-room, opening into it; so, when furnished, it added greatly to the available space and was really very pretty. Unfortunately at night it was very cold, and the frequenters of 'kala jagh' (or dark places) were

THE TOWN FROM JAKKO.

unable to enjoy it as much as I had hoped they would. There were many more odd corners curtained in, and whole verandahs utilised in the same way, and for supper we had a big shamiana, which held places for 100, and which was very well lighted, and looked very nice. Dancing was intended to be in two rooms, but there was a misfortune with the floor of one of them, so that practically the dancers were confined to one.

"However, the sun shone for us, and our cottage looked warm and comfortable. The very few improvements which we have ventured to make in this condemned house have been most successful; and a big verandah, which I have taken into the drawing-room, gives light and variety to what was a very dull and dark room. My own little boudoir is decked out in the freshest and most English of chintzes, and is a delightful sanctum. D. has had a great deal more light let into his study, and he looks very comfortable too, sitting over his fire.

"A little fire, and a wide-open window, and a balcony to wander out on and distant views of gleaming snows, help to make up a very endurable indoor existence. In the afternoon we ride, or walk or go to look at the new house as it rises from the ground; speculate as to whether the rooms are big enough; think what a splendid view there will be from almost all our windows; and watch the crowd of men at work.

"Our Queen's Ball was a very great success. The weather favoured us; and by dint of putting up one great shamiana for supper and another for sitting in; by dint of shutting in verandahs and taking off doors, we created a great deal of room, and there never was any inconvenient crush. We had two good floors and plenty of light. The high chimney-pieces, which reach to the ceiling, were filled with roses, all the men were in uniform, all the ladies in their smartest gowns, and everybody in the best of spirits—and what could you want more? Except perhaps supper, and that was good too, and looked very nice. The children are delighted with the small house, which they say is much bigger than they expected, and at the same time not too big to be home-like. They are glad the new 'Palace' is not finished. Watching its completion will be one of our amusements this year, and we have already made several expeditions to see it. D. is much pleased with it, and if only it is ready for us to go into next year we shall be quite contented. It ought to be roofed in before the rains, if there is to be a chance of its being dry."

On July 15th, 1887, Lady Dufferin, who with the Viceroy took a keen interest in the new house, wrote in her diary:

"D. took Hermie and me all over the house in the afternoon. We climbed up the most terrible places, and stood on single planks over yawning chasms. The work-people are very amusing to look at, especially the young ladies in necklaces, bracelets, earrings, tight cotton trousers, turbans with long veils hanging down their backs, and a large earthen-ware basin of mortar on their heads. They walk about with the carriage of empresses, and seem as much at ease on the top of the roof as on the ground-floor; most picturesque masons they are. The house will really be beautiful, and the views all round are magnificent. I saw the plains distinctly from my boudoir window, and I am glad to have that open view, as I shall not then feel so buried in the hills. Every day the news about our house gets worse and worse, and its state of unpreparedness is hopeless. The little cottage into which we have to squeeze is a tighter fit than ever, and the girls' maids greatly object to sleeping in the same room, and cannot believe that I am not concealing from them vast empty apartments which they might inhabit. We could not resist walking up to see how the new building looked. Stones and stone-cutters, and sheds, and scaffolding, occupy the whole front; the road is like a mountain torrent, and the boilers for the electric machine are only now being dragged up the hills. Inside also there is much to be done, and if we get into it in two months we shall be lucky. I do want to live there very much, for the house is beautiful and the views from it are quite splendid. Simla scenery is seen to greater advantage from it than from any other place I know. Half the servants are on leave, and the furniture in my rooms is partly in old covers matching the curtains here, and partly in new ones matching those in the other house. I no sooner arrange the drawing-room than a large sofa disappears and leaves a vacant space, and I am told it is gone to be re-covered—so I feel that I shall get more and more uncomfortable and untidy-looking until I take up my abode in that palace on Observatory Hill."

On 18th August 1887 at 'Peterhoff' Lord Dufferin entertained, at luncheon, three French travellers, Messieurs Bonvalet, Pepin, and Capris, who had crossed Central Asia into India by the Baroghil pass and Chitral, and paid a high tribute to their tenacity, courage, and endurance in surmounting numerous severe privations and hardships on their journey.

In September of the same year the Persian Consul-General came up from Bombay to present Lady Dufferin with the Order of the Sun. The Order was accompanied by a letter from the Shah of Persia, in which a benedictory hope was expressed "that Her Ladyship may adorn her virtuous heart therewith, and remain under the protection of gracious God." A special durbar was held at Viceregal Lodge, Lord Dufferin read a long Persian speech, and Lady Dufferin handed the Consul-General an autograph letter for the Persian Monarch.

On Sunday, 15th July 1888, Lady Dufferin continued: "I went up to the new house this afternoon, and it did look lovely. It was one of Simla's most beautiful moments, between showers, when clouds and hills, and light and shade, all combine to produce the most glorious effects. One could have spent hours at the window of my unfurnished boudoir, looking out on the plains in the distance, with a great river flowing through them: at the variously shaped hills in the foreground, brilliantly coloured in parts, and softened down in others by the fleecy clouds floating over them or nestling in the valleys between them. The approaching sunset, too, made the horizon gorgeous with red and golden and pale-blue tints. The result of the whole was to make me feel that it is a great pity that we shall have so short a time to live in a house surrounded by such magnificent views. The newest feature of the house, as an Indian house, is the basement. 'Offices' are almost unknown here, the linen, china plate, and stores are accustomed to take their chance in verandahs or godowns of the roughest description. Now each has its own place, and there is, moreover, a laundry in the house. How the dhobies will like it at first I don't know. What they are accustomed to is to squat on the brink of a cold stream, and there to flog and batter your wretched garments against the hard stones until they think them clean. Now they will be condemned to warm water and soap, to mangles and ironing, and drying rooms, and they will probably think it all very unnecessary, and will perhaps faint with the heat. We are sending things up to the house and hope to sleep in it on Monday.

"We really inhabit the new Viceregal Lodge to-day (23rd July 1888), so I left the old directly after breakfast, just returning there for an hour at lunch-time, and busied myself the whole day arranging my room and my things, and the furniture in the drawing-room. Happily the weather was very tolerable, and our beds got up here dry. D. and the girls did not come near the place till dinner time, when everything was brilliantly lighted up by the electric light. It certainly is very good, and the lighting up and putting out of the lamps is so simple that it is quite a pleasure to go round one's room touching a button here and there, and to experiment with various amounts of light. After dinner we went down to look at the kitchen, which is a splendid apartment, with white tiles six feet high all round the walls, looking so clean and bright. We sit in the smaller drawing-room, which is still a little stiff and company-like, but it will soon get into our ways and be more comfortable."

On August 8th, 1888, the journal contains the following remark:—

"We had our first entertainment in our new house to-night. It looked perfectly lovely, and one could see that everyone was quite astonished at it and at the softness of the light. First we had a large dinner for sixty-six people at one long table. The electric light is enough, but as candelabras ornament the table we had some on it. At one end of the room there was a side-board covered with gold plate, etc., and at the other end double doors were open, and across the ball-room one saw the band which played during dinner. We had all the Council and 'personages' of Simla, and the Minister, Asman Jah, from Hyderabad, who brought his suite. After dinner people began to arrive for the dance. When not dancing, everyone was amused roaming about the new rooms, and going up to the first floor, whence they could look down upon the party."

Although Viceregal Lodge was occupied in July 1888, various completion works went on till September of that year.

Mr. Henry Irwin was the architect and chief superintendent of works, but associated with him were Mr. F. B. Hebbert and the Hon'ble L. M. St. Clair as executive engineers, and Messrs. A. Scott, T. Macpherson, and T. English, assistant engineers. The names of the first three are inscribed in metal letters on the stone façade above the main porch. Only a few months ago the merits of Viceregal Lodge were discussed in my presence by several men, but when questioned as to the architect no one was able to recollect one of the engineers I have mentioned, and I have therefore used the opportunity to place their names on record.

Viceregal Lodge possesses, as it rightly should, one of the most commanding positions in Simla. It lies to the extreme west of the station, and is one of the first objects to strike the eye as the traveller approaches from Kalka. Described briefly it consists of a main block of three storeys, and another called the kitchen wing, of five storeys, but the latter is built on the side of a precipice, and commences three storeys below the ground level of the main block and east wing; so that viewed from the north-east the house has a very lofty, somewhat forbidding appearance, and might at a distance be mistaken for a mediæval castle.

The style of architecture throughout is English Renaissance (Elizabethan), the masonry of the walling is light blue limestone, and the wrought stone work is all of sandstone of a very fine grain and beautiful light grey tint. This stone is uniform in texture, and is capable of being worked to very sharp arrises; the mouldings are all true, and where carving has been carried out it is bold and sharp. Very little stone carving has been used, but what there is of it relieves the plain parts, and is very effective. The walling stone was quarried about five miles away and was transported to Simla on mules; the cut stone was brought in for 50 miles from the foot of the hills near Kalka. Carrying on the labour in the winter was a matter of much difficulty as the masons refused to work except for extremely high wages, while carpenters were not obtainable at any price. A small tower surmounts the house from which flies the flag which denotes the presence of the Viceroy in Simla. In this tower are the water tanks into which is pumped the supply from the municipal mains, and the view from its summit on a clear day is magnificent. To the north, and north-east particularly, the ranges of perpetual snows are seen to great advantage over the peaks of the nearer ranges, while on the west, especially in the rains, there is a grand view of the plains, with the Sutlej winding away in the distance. The house, grounds, and approaches are now lighted by electricity. There are about 1,000 lamps, the majority of 16 candle-power, and the engine is situated near the main entrance gate and close to the stable range. Inside, the house is beautifully built and finished, the fine entrance hall, with its gallery leading to the ball-room, being perhaps the main feature. This gallery is fifty feet in height, ninety feet long, but only eighteen feet broad, which is really much too narrow.

The woodwork, however, is beautiful. For instance, the treads, newels, and handrails of the main staircase are of teak, the balusters are solid walnut, the carriages and concealed portions of the framing of the stairs are of deodar, some of the carving being very bold and effective. Heavy velvet curtains divide the gallery from the ball-room, an apartment seventy feet by thirty feet with a side annexe seventy feet by ten feet on the west, and a vestibule seventeen feet by thirty feet on the east. These really are a portion of the room as they communicate with it by large openings twenty feet wide. Another velvet curtain hangs over the opening to the state drawing-room, sixty feet by thirty feet, a charming room, with the wall panels hung in silk tapestry and the woodwork painted white. The upper part of the gallery is hung with Japanese paper in white and gold heavily embossed. Perhaps the state dining-room appeals most to the ordinary visitor. This is panelled all round ten feet high with teak, the upper two feet being in pierced strap work, and supporting the shields charged with the armorial bearings of the several Governors-General and Viceroys of India, all illuminated in the proper heraldic colours. These now make a splendid decoration. The walls are divided by means of pilasters supporting the ceiling beams, and their upper portion is hung with crimson silk and woollen tapestry, while there is a good deal of bold carving in the room. On the occasion of a state dinner the scene is a particularly brilliant one. The furnishing of the house was originally done partly by Messrs. Maple & Co., who sent out their assistants for the purpose; many of the simpler articles, however, were made by Punjab carpenters whose work was excellent.

The advantage to the Simla public no less than to their Viceregal hosts was soon shown. Society in Simla has so much grown that whereas in Lord Lytton's day at 'Peterhoff' the official parties did not exceed 400 persons, over 800 are now invited to the state ball in Viceregal Lodge, and the annual levée held by the Viceroy in June is attended by an average of nearly 350 officers and officials. Lady Dufferin in her record of Viceregal entertainments at 'Peterhoff' in 1885, tells us that there were twelve big dinners in the season of 25 to 50 guests, and twenty-nine small ones, a state ball, fancy ball, a children's fancy ball, and six dances of 250 people each, besides a couple of garden parties, and two evening parties. Altogether there were 54 entertainments, while 644 guests dined at 'Peterhoff.'

Lord Lansdowne was the first Viceroy who really benefited by the construction of Viceregal Lodge. During his term of office the grounds surrounding the house were planted out with trees and shrubs, and many improvements which were designed mainly for the purpose of garden parties were carried out under the supervision of Mr. Parsons, the English gardener of Simla. The Viceregal entertainments could now be conducted on a far larger scale than had hitherto been the case, and no one was more capable of presiding over them than Lady Lansdowne, whose charm of manner as hostess endeared her to all who were fortunate enough to be her guests. Lord 'Bill' Beresford was a tower of strength as Military Secretary; the personal staff was notably smart and popular; and Simla seasons became renowned for their brightness and general success.

Lord Elgin who succeeded Lord Lansdowne secured the 'Retreat' at Mashobra as a suburban residence for future Viceroys, and made a constant habit of spending the week end out there with his family. Lord Elgin, as his personal staff occasionally discovered to their discomfiture, was a pedestrian of rare endurance, and was never known to ride a horse in Simla. Unlike Lord Dufferin who said he 'preferred men and women to trees,' Lord Elgin seldom missed a chance of spending a few days in the neighbouring woods of Mashobra.

Time has shown that it is rather a pity that the construction of Viceregal Lodge had to be hurried on with the rapidity necessary to permit Lord Dufferin to occupy it in his last summer, for a good deal of the work has been found to be lacking in strength, and it is doubtful whether the building possesses the stability that ought to attach to so costly and handsome a structure. Large sums have to be spent every year upon construction and repairs.

Considerable changes have been made in the interior in Lord Curzon's time. All the state rooms have been hung with damask, sky-blue and pale green in the two drawing-rooms, yellow in the ball-room and crimson in the dining-room. These have replaced the lincrusta and paper ornamentations that had been bequeathed by Messrs. Maple. The carving has been completed in the dining-room, and the ancestral shields of the Governors-General, which were found to be incorrect, have been verified, and now

VICEREGAL LODGE FROM PROSPECT HILL.

represent with accuracy the long list of Governors-General, from Warren Hastings to the present day. The beautiful carved screen of teak-wood in the dining room was made under Lord Curzon's instructions on the model of the screen that stands behind the Emperor of China's throne in the Imperial Palace, at Peking. The Council chamber which is a handsome room with teak panelling has been hung with silk, and is now adorned with a complete collection of engraved portraits of every Governor-General and Viceroy, which has been made by Lord Curzon, by personal reference to the families, or descendants of his predecessors. The upper walls of the main gallery (which was unfortunately unduly contracted in width in order to save expense in the original building, and which was intended and ought to have been 12 feet wider) are now decorated with a collection of Indian arms; and over the mantelpieces are hung mirrors in frames of Burmese glass mosaics, which were brought by Lord Dufferin from King Thebaw's Palace at Mandalay. Both in the Council chamber and in the Viceroy's study upstairs are ceilings of Kashmir wood in geometric patterns, which were erected respectively by Lord Elgin and Lord Curzon. The exterior tower, which was out of proportion to the rest of the building and was found to be in need of repairs, has also been raised in height by the latter.

There are lawns and gardens both on the south (or main) and north fronts of Viceregal Lodge, but owing to the limited space on the summit of the hill, even after the latter had been cut down in order to admit of the building and its surroundings, these are of restricted extent. It was originally intended to complete the terraces on the northern side with stone balustrades and flights of steps. But this has never been done, and they were converted into lawns and flower beds, with a rose 'pergula,' by Lord Curzon. The lower lawn on the north which was laid out as tennis courts was the scene of the state garden parties until recent years, when they have been held on the southern lawn in front of the house. The avenue of fast growing limes and the shrubbery that screens the eastern face of the house was also planted under the instructions of the present Viceroy.

From first to last Viceregal Lodge has cost about sixteen and-a-half lakhs, of which actual building operations have absorbed over eleven lakhs.

The fact is truly significant of the development and growth of Simla and of the Indian Empire, when it is remembered that the two houses (Auckland House and Secretary's Lodge) which Lord Auckland owned in 1840, were sold by him on his departure from the hills for Rs. 16,000.

Immediately to the east of Viceregal Lodge stands the 'Observatory House' which has of recent years been reserved as the residence of the

Private Secretary to the Viceroy. Sir Donald Mackenzie Wallace and Sir John Ardagh, respectively, occupied it in Lord Dufferin's and Lord Lansdowne's Viceroyalties, Mr. Babington-Smith while Lord Elgin was in India, and finally Sir Walter Lawrence, late Private Secretary to Lord Curzon, and Mr. J. O. Miller, the present Private Secretary, have made it their home. The original house was built in 1844 by Colonel J. T. Boileau for the purpose of an observatory, from which it derived its name. It was well fitted with magnetic instruments, and valuable papers issued from it for several years. In 1850-51 Colonel Boileau was ordered away on some other duty, and the Government of the day apparently did not think it worth while to appoint a successor to him. The instruments were removed to Agra, where they were destroyed during the Mutiny, and 'Observatory House' began to fall into ruin. There were two brothers called Boileau in Simla at this period, the western end of the station now called 'Boileaugunge' being named after them. Reliable authority states that the brothers were decidedly eccentric in their habits, and that they once received the then Commander-in-Chief at a dinner party in their house, each brother standing on his head by one of the main pillars of the central porch! Eventually the house was repaired, and among its residents afterwards claimed Sir Henry Norman, Sir Henry Durand, and Sir John Strachey, Mr. C. U. Aitchison (afterwards Sir Charles, and Lieutenant-Governor of the Punjab), the Hon'ble Mr. Gibbs, Member of the Viceroy's Council, and Sir Henry Cunningham, Secretary to the Government in the Legislative Department, and afterwards a Judge of the Calcutta High Court. A later occupant about 1887 was Mr. Quinton, who afterwards became Chief Commissioner of Assam, and was murdered at Manipur in 1891.

It is a fact not generally known in Simla even at the present day that the northern slopes and summit of 'Prospect Hill,' the fine spur to the south of Viceregal Lodge, are actually within the Government House boundary. The public have free access to this hill, but its grounds are kept in order by the gardeners of the Viceregal Lodge.

Behind Observatory House is the electrical engine house for Viceregal Lodge, and behind this again the little chapel of ease for All Saints. Between the chapel and the Viceroy's stables near the entrance gates stood till lately a gun-shed containing a gun that was fired daily at noon, and on other occasions. Its unexpected salutes were found to be so disconcerting to equestrian visitors that it was recently removed.

It may be of interest to mention that the entire viceregal estate at Simla, which covers the whole of Observatory Hill, Bentinck's Hill, Prospect Hill, and a portion of the hill on which stands 'Peterhoff,' embraces an area of 331 acres. Upon it there stand 26 houses, and in them reside some 840 persons, of whom 40 are Europeans and 800 Natives. The annual up-keep of the entire estate amounts to little short of £10,000. The responsibilities connected with this are so great that Lord Curzon found it desirable to appoint an English clerk of the works, who is now invested with the exclusive charge of the Viceregal estate.

Among the houses in the grounds of Viceregal Lodge which are occupied by members of the Viceregal staff are 'Squire's Hall' (famous in recent years for Colonel Baring's hospitality), at the northern extremity of Bentinck's Hill; 'Curzon House,' rebuilt by Lord Curzon on a site once occupied by a house that was similarly called after Lord Lansdowne, and 'Courteen Hall,' now the office of the Military Secretary to the Viceroy. Quarters for the clerk of the works, the electrician, the band, the body-guard and police guard are planted in other parts of the estate. Immediately below Peterhoff is a covered tennis court, built by Lord Dufferin upon the model of one that he had erected at 'Rideau Hall,' Ottawa, in Canada, and which has itself supplied a model for other courts that have been built in different parts of India.

Before this volume has been published another Viceroy—Lord Ampthill—will in all probability be moving into temporary possession of Viceregal Lodge, and another name will be added to the list of the Rulers of India who have resided in Simla.

CHAPTER III.

Residences of Commanders-in-Chief in India.

Names.	Assumed charge of office.	Place of residence in Simla.
General Stapleton, Viscount Combermere, G.C.B., G.C.H.	7th October 1825 .	Kennedy House.
General George, Earl of Dalhousie, G.C.B.	1st January 1830 .	" "
General Sir Edward Barnes, G.C.B. .	10th January 1832 .	Barnes Court.
General Lord Wm. C. Bentinck, G.C.B.	15th October 1833 .	Bentinck Castle.
General Sir Henry Fane, G.C.B. . .	5th September 1835	" "
General Sir Jasper Nicolls, K.C.B. .	7th December 1839	" "
General Sir Hugh Gough, G.C.B. .	8th August 1843 .	" "
General Sir Charles James Napier, G.C.B.	7th May 1849 .	Barnes Court.
General Sir Wm. Maynard Gomm, K.C.B.	6th December 1850	" "
General The Hon'ble Geo. Anson .	23rd January 1856 .	" "
General Sir Colin Campbell, G.C.B. .	13th August 1857 .	" "
General Sir Hugh Henry Rose, G.C.B. .	4th June 1860 .	" "
General Sir Wm. Rose Mansfield, K.C.B.	23rd March 1865 .	Woodville.
General Robert Cornelis, Lord Napier of Magdala, G.C.B., G.C.S.I.	9th April 1870 .	"
General Sir Fred. Paul Haines, K.C.B. .	10th April 1876 .	"
General Sir Donald Martin Stewart, G.C.B., C.I.E.	7th April 1881 .	" and Snowdon.
General Sir Fred. Sleigh Roberts, V.C., G.C.B., C.I.E.	28th November 1885	Snowdon.
General Sir Geo. Stewart White, V.C., G.C.I.E., K.C.B.	8th April 1893 .	"
Lieutenant-General Sir Charles Edward Nairne, K.C.B. *(provisional).*	20th March 1898 .	"
General Sir William S. A. Lockhart, G.C.B., K.C.S.I.	4th November 1898	"
General Sir Arthur P. Palmer, K.C.B. .	19th March 1900 .	"
General The Right Hon'ble Horatio Herbert, Viscount Kitchener of Khartoum, G.C.B., O.M., G.C.M.G., R.E.	28th November 1902	"

Lord Combermere, the first Commander-in-Chief to arrive in Simla, made his head-quarters at 'Kennedy House,' and has left a perpetual memento of his visit in the Combermere bridge, of which an account has been given in an earlier chapter. 'Kennedy House' possesses the honour therefore of having been the house at which both the first Governor-General and the first Commander-in-Chief who visited Simla, made their temporary head-quarters, and by a curious coincidence of having been the birth place of General Sir Arthur Power Palmer, the late Commander-in-Chief in India. In 1870, the estate consisting of Kennedy House, Lodge and Cottage was the property of Major S. B. Goad, but for many years past has been in the possession of the Maharaja of Kuch Behar, a frequent visitor to Simla. Within the last few months this historic estate has been purchased from the Maharaja by the Government of India for Rs. 1,20,000, and will in future, it is believed, be set aside as a residence for a member of the Viceroy's Council.

One of the tenants of Kennedy House in recent years was Mr. S. S. Thorburn, a well known Punjab civilian and author. Mr. Thorburn's audacious attack on the Government of India's frontier policy, delivered in Lord Elgin's presence at the Town Hall in June 1898, at the close of Colonel Hutchinson's lecture on the 'Lessons of the Tirah Campaign' will long be remembered as the official sensation of the Simla season of that year.

An interesting account of the journey to Simla in August 1830 is given in the memoirs of Colonel Armine S. H. Mountain, C.B., afterwards Adjutant-General of Her Majesty's forces in India, who (then a major) visited the Earl of Dalhousie, the Commander-in-Chief, who like his predecessor also lived at 'Kennedy House.' The passage by raft over the Ghagar river near Kalka, then heavily swollen by the rains, was only accomplished with much difficulty. On reaching Simla Major Mountain wrote, "I met with a very kind and warm reception both from Lord and Lady Dalhousie. He expected me to wait and go down with him to the plains, but I think I shall be off sooner, though I should like to see his camp which will assemble at the foot of the hills. The camp of the Commander-in-Chief, who is attended by the heads of the staff, contains 5,000 souls, elephants, camels, horses, oxen, cows, goats, dogs innumerable, and two of his own tents are each of them fifty feet long, thirty high, and twenty wide. What was the progress of a European sovereign in old times to this?"

Sir Edward Barnes, the next Commander-in-Chief, who had been the Duke of Wellington's Adjutant-General at Waterloo, has left a lasting record of his short term in India in 'Barnes Court,' the present residence of the Lieutenant-Governors of the Punjab in 'Chota Simla.'

Connected as it is with both the military and Punjab history of past and present years, 'Barnes Court' has distinct claims to be considered one of the most famous old houses in Simla. The following, briefly told, is its history:—The earliest portion of the estate, amounting to 200 square yards, was granted by Captain C. J. Kennedy, Principal Assistant to the Political Agent at Delhi, to a Dr. J. Ludlow on the 1st of January 1830, subject to a ground tax of Rs. 40 per annum. Lieutenant J. K. McCausland, of the Nusseeree Battalion, whose head-quarters were at Subathu, also had an interest in this grant of land on which a house was built, and which seems to have been the nucleus of the present greatly enlarged residence. Sir Edward Barnes acquired the right and title of this estate for a sum of Rs. 14,000. On the 1st of May 1832, an adjoining piece of land, amounting to 50 square yards, was granted by the Principal Assistant to a Mr. McDermott of the Adjutant-General's office, subject to a ground tax of Rs. 10 per annum, and to the sanction of the Principal Assistant for felling trees. The right and title of this plot of land seems to have been also secured by Sir Edward Barnes, who in the same year was permitted to take up at an annual rental of Rs. 40, an additional piece of ground which was described as being, from "its precipitous and rocky nature, wholly useless for any building purpose." The whole estate, which by this time aggregated some 42 acres, subsequently fell into the hands of the late Major S. B. Goad, who, on the 15th of May 1875, sold it to Major General Sir Peter Lumsden, late Quartermaster General in India, for Rs. 23,000. On the 21st of May 1879, General Lumsden resold the estate to the Punjab Government for Rs. 50,360. Sir Lepel Griffin, at that time Secretary to the Punjab Government, was one of the witnesses to the deed of sale. The official description of the property when this purchase was effected by the Punjab Government was as follows:—

"Barnes Court is a partly single and partly double-storeyed building facing west and south, the principal entrance being on the latter side. The building is so arranged as to have a good view on three sides, *viz.*, on the west, south, and east. It is built on a spur running out due south from Jakko, the front of the house being raised on a masonry terrace flanked at either end with a masonry sentry box. There is a level lawn to the west of the house between it and the hill. The ground is of very considerable extent running out in a kind of arm for about half a mile on the south-east of Jakko, and a good distance up the hill side."

This description practically holds good to the present day. Extensive improvements have, however, been made from time to time to the property which is now valued at about Rs. 2,50,000. The principal addition is a double-storeyed building erected during the Lieutenant-Governorship of Sir C. U. Aitchison, the lower storey being a ball-room, and the upper

PELITI'S GRAND HOTEL.

rooms the offices of the Lieutenant-Governor and his Private Secretary. The ball room is charmingly decorated and painted in eastern Moorish style, this work having been supervised by Mr. Lockwood Kipling, for many years the Principal of the Mayo School of Art, Lahore. Much of the stone used for the Punjab Government offices at 'Ellerslie' was quarried in 1900-01 from the precipitous hillside described in 1832 "as being wholly useless for any building purpose," a fact which considerably reduced the actual cost of the offices. The Lieutenant-Governors who have resided in 'Barnes Court' are: Sir Robert Eyles Egerton, Sir Charles Umpherston Aitchison, Sir James Broadwood Lyall, Sir Dennis Fitzpatrick, Sir William Mackworth Young, and at present Sir Charles Montgomery Rivaz.

General Lord William Bentinck, in addition to ruling India as Governor-General, also held command of the army from May 1833 till he was succeeded by Sir Henry Fane in September 1835 and he lived, as has already been shown, in 'Bentinck Castle' (now Peliti's Grand Hotel). Sir Henry Fane, Sir Jasper Nicolls, and Sir Hugh Gough followed him, and resided in the same house. An account of the house may therefore be appropriately given here.

In 1829 when Lord William Bentinck gave orders for a residence to be prepared for him in Simla, the site selected for the purpose was that now occupied by the Grand Hotel. In that year, however, the dâk bungalow of the period was perched on the summit of the hill. The house which replaced it was called 'Bentinck Castle,' and was built by Captain McCausland, Assistant to General Tapp. After it had been occupied by the distinguished officers already mentioned it became the property of Sir Henry Lawrence but subsequently passed into the hands of the Simla Bank, in whose possession it remained from about 1850 to 1887, when the Bank went into liquidation. The premises were then purchased for Rs. 35,000 by the New Club, who commenced to rebuild and alter the whole place. Hardly had this been done, however, when a fire broke out and the entire property was burned to the ground. Luckily for the Club an insurance had been effected, and a new and really fine set of buildings were speedily constructed. For a year or two the New Club threatened to prove a serious rival to the older Club—the United Service. Its rooms were spacious and well built; it possessed a fine dining-room with an excellent dancing floor, and its members gave smoking concerts at which Sir Frederick Roberts (then Commander-in-Chief), the Lieutenant-Governor of the Punjab and the Members of the Viceregal Council often attended and joined heartily in the choruses. The late Lord William Beresford took a warm interest in the Club's welfare, Colonel A. R. D. Mackenzie, who led the mutiny veterans at the Delhi Durbar, was its President, Dr. (now Sir George) Watt, Mr. B. Ribbentrop, late Inspector-General of Forests, and many well-known residents were prominent members. For some months it looked as if the Club would easily hold its own. But the United Service Club suddenly woke up to the danger of competition and recognised the fact that a dangerous rival had come into existence. Major (now Surgeon-General Sir William) Taylor induced the committee of the older Club to sanction extensive improvements and alterations in their property, and a good deal of private pressure was brought to bear on members of the Government Services to induce them to support the United Service Club. Eventually the New Club had to go into liquidation, and the buildings passed into the hands first of M. Bonsard, who had been brought out as viceregal cook by Lord Lytton, and afterwards by Signor, now Chevalier, Peliti who had been brought out as viceregal confectioner at the same time. M. Bonsard, who had then become the proprietor of the well-known Bonsard Hotel in Dhurrumtollah in Calcutta, only held possession for a season, and though there were rumours that he was about to join hands with Chevalier Peliti, and run a combined hotel, the estate became the property of the latter in 1892, for, I think, two lakhs of rupees, and has since remained the largest and best known hotel in Simla. Its position could certainly not be improved upon, and its management is excellent. More than one new building has been erected on the hill since it came into Chevalier Peliti's possession, and among other improvements may be mentioned the erection of the necessary machinery for the manufacture of ice. The hotel is now managed by Chevalier Peliti's sons, the father having retired to his beautiful estate at Carignano near Turin, where he has erected extensive factories for conserving and tinning vegetables and fruits grown on his farms, whence his Simla hotel and Calcutta restaurant are kept supplied.

Simla has to thank Sir Henry Fane for the road round Prospect Hill, and it is understood that he defrayed its cost from his private purse. At Auckland House in the following year Sir Henry Fane presented to Runjeet Singh two brass nine-pounder howitzers, which were afterwards used against and captured by the British in the first Sikh Campaign.

Sir Charles Napier was the first of five Commanders-in-Chief who successively elected to live in 'Barnes Court.' It is no secret that Sir Charles Napier, who resigned after holding command of the Indian Army for some twenty months, did so on account of his perpetual quarrels with Lord Dalhousie. His orders restricting leave to the hills were much resented by the British officers of the day, and the Delhi Sketch Book not only caricatured the Commander-in-Chief, but also published several skits on the subject.

"THERE IS AN OLD MAN WHO SITS ON A HILL,
AND IF HE'S NOT GONE, HE SITS THERE STILL."

OLD NURSEY RHYME.

Reproduced from
"The Delhi Sketch Book."

One was headed 'The Hills.' "Sir Charles Napier says he does not like the hills. Do you believe him?" *Private letter* :—

Sad Fate compels me—I must go,
  Though me the climate kills,
To Simla I must wend my way—
  I do not like the Hills!

The offices are all up there,
  Governor and Councils,
And I must go, though not from choice—
  I do not like the Hills!

The enduring British soldier
  Stays in the plains and grills,
The subaltern should suffer too—
  I do not like the Hills!

In the plains you are well off,
  And seldom vex'd with drills,
You should not scamper from the heat—
  I do not like the Hills!

Urgent affairs form your excuse,
  We beg in gentle trills,
I'll let you go for a month or so—
  I do not like the Hills!

For more than that you shan't have leave,
  From that arise no ills,
For all affairs that is enough—
  I do not like the Hills!

I go, alas! you know I must,
  Though I do hate the chills,
My Lord resolves on staying there—
  I do not like the Hills!

Another 'Song' "dedicated in all humility to the Commander-in-Chief of the Indian Army by a British subaltern," contained a verse which though capable of improvement in rhythm was certainly to the point:—

And all leave to the hills
Has been stopped, and one grills;
In the plains, like a Shadrach in his furnace flame;
While all the time he swears
That public affairs
Prevent him from doing, *as he'd like to do*, the same!

In June 1850 the grand Hindustan and Tibet road already alluded to was planned and commenced by Major Kennedy, Secretary to Sir Charles Napier.

Sir William Gomm apparently purchased 'Barnes Court' for his residence during the four years he resided in Simla. On the 17th September 1851, Lady Gomm laid the foundation stone of the chapel of the well-known Lawrence Asylum for the orphan children of soldiers. This institution stands on the Sanawar hill close to Kasauli, and the boys wear the artillery uniform as a compliment to its founder, Sir Henry Lawrence. General the Hon'ble George Anson, Sir Colin Campbell, and Sir Hugh Rose followed in turn as tenants of 'Barnes Court.'

It was on the 12th May 1857 that Sir Henry Barnard's son, who was acting as A.-D.-C. to his father, galloped into Simla from Amballa bringing the news of the Mutiny to General Anson, the Commander-in-Chief. Towelle's Hand-book to Simla thus describes the panic which is said to have taken place in the station on this occasion :—

"The memorable year of the Mutiny, 1857, commenced in Simla, as all over India, with a feeling of some coming, yet undefined, evil, though outwardly all was apparently safe. On the 11th May the storm broke, and a panic seized the unprepared inhabitants. Hastily orders were issued, by some who took the command of affairs in hand, for all the ladies and children to assemble first at the church and subsequently at the Simla Bank, in case a necessity arose to seek a place of refuge. Great was the confusion which ensued; on the signal agreed upon (the firing of two guns) being given, a few rolled up bundles of bedding and clothes, and hurried to the place of rendezvous. Some did not even wait to collect the necessary garments, but started as they were, with alarm depicted on their countenances. Unfortunately there was no one to take the lead and restore any kind of order. Thus ladies were in hysterics, children crying, and the gentlemen hastily endeavouring to erect barricades on the top of the hill on which the Simla Bank, now the Grand Hotel, once stood. After a time the rumour came that the Goorkha regiment stationed at Jutogh had mutinied, and that some of the Goorkhas were coming to 'loot' Simla. This made matters worse, and immediately not only was the bank deserted, as it was supposed that would be the first place the mutineers would try to seize—but some went off by bye-paths, avoiding the main road, to Kussowlie and Dagshai to seek protection in the European barracks; some sought shelter in the territories of the Hill Chiefs of the neighbourhood; others rushed into the interior of the hills, filling the dâk bungalows on the road—all appeared to be bereft for the time of their senses. The scenes that followed were so ludicrous, seeing the utter want of adequate cause of alarm, and shed so little glory on the courage of those in authority and of the inhabitants, European as well as Native, that the less written on the subject the better. Suffice it to say that in a few weeks order was restored, people returned to their houses, surprised to find them and their property intact, for, notwithstanding the dire confusion, it was astonishing that no robberies took place, scarcely even a petty theft, though the opportunities for being unmindful of the laws of *meum et tuum* were so numerous, houses having been left open and unprotected, even keys and cash having been heedlessly forgotten on tables and drawers. The cash in the Simla Bank was perhaps saved from being made away with by the simple fact of the Secretary having the key of the strong room in his pocket when he, with others, left the bank to take care of itself."

I cannot, however, allow my readers to accept this thrilling account as altogether correct. That a panic did occur on the outbreak of the Mutiny is undeniable, but the facts, and I give them on the authority of Mr. G. W. deRhé Philipe who was resident in Simla at the time, were as follows:—The Deputy Commissioner, Lord William Hay, being aware that the Gurkhas at Jutogh were disaffected, and hearing that they had become mutinous and had hustled their officers on the parade ground, proceeded there to reason with them. Meanwhile in consequence of positive intelligence reaching the station that the Gurkhas had broken out into mutiny and were coming in to loot the place, a considerable number of citizens, in accordance with arrangements made the day before, assembled at the Bank under the command of Major General Nicholas Penny, C.B., for the purpose of making a stand, and here they remained until Lord William Hay came back from Jutogh late at night, and reported that the troops had returned to duty and advised those at the Bank to proceed to their houses. Even after this announcement, however, many remained at the Bank during the night. At the same time a report quickly gained credence that Lord William Hay had hinted it would be as well if everyone left Simla for a while, and accordingly on Saturday, the 16th May, there was a considerable, but, considering the circumstances, a quiet and orderly exodus to Mashobra and the Junga state. A certain number of bolder spirits however steadily declined to leave until danger had really declared itself. There is no doubt that people living in Chota Simla were at the outset informed that the Gurkhas had arrived in the main station and that they were in possession of the bazaar. Hearing this, and finding their only road to the Bank was closed, almost all these residents dispersed down the 'khud' sides without further ado, and many of them suffered considerable hardships before returning. It was amongst these people that the so called 'Simla panic' of May 1857 occurred, not amongst those who assembled at the Bank as is generally but quite erroneously supposed.

In 'Delhi, 1857,' in which an account is given of its siege, assault, and capture, from the diary and letters of Colonel Keith Young, C.B. (at one time Judge Advocate-General of the Bengal army), the following passages occur:—"14th May.—A meeting at Mr. Peterson's to arrange for the defence of Simla. 15th May.—Hear a rumour of the Gurkha corps (Nusseree Battalion) in open mutiny and refusing to march. Ride towards Boileaugunge. Great alarm; many cutting off. 16th May.—Home at sunrise. All quiet. Two sepoys came to the house soon after I got there:—very civil, and declared they never intended to alarm any of the 'sahib logue.' The scoundrels! Determine after due consideration to go and sleep at the Rana's again (the Rana of Keonthal), and to start at moonrise in the early morning for Joonug, his country seat, some twelve miles off; arrange accordingly, send everything off, and go and dine about 4 at General Gowan's, May Day Hill. 17th May.—Off with difficulty about 4 A.M., dreadful scrimmage, reach Joonug about 8 o'clock. Such a scene of confusion."

In a letter dated 17th May Colonel Keith Young wrote to Colonel H. B. Henderson, London:—"I write a line to tell you that there is not a word of truth in the reported 'Simla massacre.' F. and I and the dear 'babies' are as well as you could wish, enjoying ourselves at this place, some sixteen miles from Simla. We came out here this morning—'fled,' you may say—for fear of the mutineering Nusseree Battalion at Jutogh rising against us and resorting to deeds of violence. We are here under the protection of a friendly Raja and shall probably remain two or three days longer and then return to Simla or go on to one of the European hill cantonments as circumstances may render desirable. . . . . Our party consists of Colonel and Mrs. Greathed, and the wife of the Umballa Brigadier, Mrs. Hallifax; and in the adjacent houses and tents there must be some forty ladies and gentlemen, and nearly double the number of children."

The return to Simla took place on the 20th May when Colonel Keith Young remarked, "Ellerslie was found just in the same state as we left it."

Mr. Towelle's account was evidently compiled from hearsay and after numerous hysterical reports had been spread abroad. He was not in Simla at the time. Mr. Philipe on the contrary was one of those who assembled at the Bank, and his memory may be confidently relied on. The whole of the cash of the Bank (about R80,000) was on the 16th May undoubtedly placed in charge of a Gurkha guard by Mr. Fleming, the manager.

General Anson, who hurried down to the plains immediately the news of the mutiny reached Simla, was seized with illness on the road and died before he could reach Delhi.

Sir Hugh Rose, who was the last of the Commanders-in-Chief to reside at 'Barnes Court,' was given a farewell entertainment at Simla on the 27th September 1864, when Sir Robert (afterwards Lord) Napier paid a high tribute to the retiring Commander-in-Chief.

On Sir William Mansfield's arrival at Simla, in 1865, 'Woodville' was honoured by becoming the residence of the Commander-in-Chief, and later on both Lord Napier of Magdala and Sir Frederick Haines respectively occupied it during their term of office. Sir Donald Stewart, after living there for a short time, deserted it for 'Snowdon,' which has since become the official residence of the head of the army in India. The lawn at 'Woodville' was evidently the scene of many a hard fought game of croquet in the sixties, for Mr. G. R. Elsmie in his book on Field Marshal Sir Donald Stewart wrote: "The game of croquet had then become highly popular and was eagerly played by young and old. The Viceroy, Commander-in-Chief, Members of Council, and many others were thankful for this newly discovered means of taking air and exercise at the end of a long day's work. No votary of the game was keener than Donald Stewart."

After the Commanders-in-Chief ceased to reside in 'Woodville' it became the property of Sir James L. Walker, and its latest tenant has been the Hon'ble Sir T. Raleigh, Legal Member of Council.

Lord Roberts' connection with Simla throughout his military career was so close that it is difficult to allude to his association with the place without entering into historical details of his life.

His first visit to Simla was in August 1855 when as a subaltern he marched across the hills from Kashmir *viâ* Chamba, Dharmsala, and Bilaspur. He reached Simla when Sir William Gomm, then Commander-in-Chief, was about to give up his command, and when, as he wrote, "the Simla of those days was not the busy and important place it has since become, the Governor-General seldom visited it, and the Commander-in-Chief only spent summer there occasionally." Lord Roberts tells us in his 'Forty-one years in India' that a lunch he then had with Colonel Arthur Becher was the turning point in his career, for his host said he should like some day to have him in his department. At that time there was no limit to the tenure of staff appointments, and the ambition of every young officer was to join the political, civil, or army staff, and Lord Roberts' remarks on the subject will be found particularly interesting to the youthful military officer of to-day. His book runs "My father had always impressed upon me that the Political Department was the one to aspire to, and failing that the Quartermaster-General's, as in the latter there was the best chance of seeing service. I cherished a sort of vague hope that I might some day be lucky enough to become a Deputy Assistant Quartermaster-General, for though I fully recognised the advantages of a political career, I preferred being more closely associated with the army, and I had seen enough of staff work to satisfy myself that it would suit me. So the few words spoken to me by Colonel Becher made me supremely happy." How the future

Commander-in-Chief joined the department a year later, how he was forced to vacate his appointment on account of his ignorance of Hindustani, how within a few months he passed the necessary examination and rejoined the office, only to leave it as Quartermaster-General in 1878, is all duly set forth in the military records of India.

Lord Roberts went home and married in May 1859, and returned to India in July with his wife. Lady Roberts made her first journey to Simla in a 'jampan' carried by four coolies, while Lord Roberts walked or rode by her side. Their first house 'Mount Pleasant' was on the crest of the 'Inverarm' hill, above the Choura maidan, and commanded a glorious view. "Life at Simla," Lord Roberts writes, "was somewhat monotonous. Society was not very large in those days; but there were a certain number of people on leave from the plains, who then, as at present, had nothing to do but amuse themselves. Consequently, there was a good deal of gaiety in a small way; but we entered into it very little."

In 1862 Lord Roberts wrote, "At the best one gets very tired of the hills by the close of the summer," and judging from various passages in his book neither he nor his wife cared much for the social gaieties of the station. In 1864 the Roberts' changed their house for one "near the Stewarts" and in 1868 appear to have occupied 'Winscottie.' In 1869, being left in charge of the Quartermaster-General's office, Lord Roberts resided in 'Ellerslie'—a house which has recently been demolished to provide room for the new Punjab Secretariat offices.

In 1873-4 His Excellency purchased 'Snowdon,' which had originally been used as a dispensary, from General Peter Innes, and at once commenced to materially improve his property. Simla was more than usually gay in 1887 in consequence of the numerous entertainments held in celebration of the Queen's Jubilee, and a fancy dress ball was given at 'Snowdon' to inaugurate the opening of the new ball-room.

In 1892 Lord Roberts, who in the course of his residence in Simla made several trips into the interior, returned to Simla for the last time, and towards the end of this season at a special gathering at 'Snowdon' a substantial sum of money for her 'Homes in the Hills' with a diamond bracelet were presented to Lady Roberts by her Simla friends, Lord Lansdowne acting as spokesman for the donors of the souvenir.

Shortly after Lord Roberts' departure the Government of India purchased 'Snowdon' for Rs. 79,187 as the official residence for the Commander-in-Chief in India, and as there was a slight flaw in the title the property was, with the owner's consent, taken up under the Land Acquisition Act. Later on, a new double-storeyed building was constructed to provide accommodation for a portion of His Excellency's personal staff, and quite recently an

SNOWDON.

imposing gate-way, with large pillars on either side supporting mortars, have been added to the public entrance to the house. The probable value of 'Snowdon' to-day is over three lakhs of rupees. Sir George White, who succeeded Lord Roberts, lived in 'Snowdon' for five years, and during that period Lady White established a reputation as a hostess which will long be remembered in Simla, her dances and theatricals being as numerous as they were successful. Sir Charles Nairne having acted as provisional Commander-in-Chief for a few months, was followed by that popular frontier soldier Sir William Lockhart, who after several months of ill-health in Simla, died in Calcutta on the 18th March 1900, and Sir Power Palmer, whose recent sudden death is deplored by many old friends in India, next resided in 'Snowdon' in the summers of 1900 and 1901.

One of Lord Kitchener's first visits when he had a few days to spare from the Delhi Manœuvres, which claimed his attention almost as soon as he landed in India, was paid to Simla, where he inspected the house which was to be his home for so large a proportion of his service in the country, and those who remember the original and lower bungalow previous to his occupation will not wonder that its structural and internal shortcomings at once attracted his attention. The result was that the Government of India admitted Lord Kitchener's strictures, and placed a sum of money at his disposal for the improvement of the entrance and staircase of the house with the present very satisfactory result. By the sacrifice of a large but dark and useless bed-room on the ground floor, a fine hall shaped like the letter "L" was added; while instead of the straight staircase, suggestive of a lodging house, which used to rise abruptly from the front door, a broad staircase with three turns was introduced from the hall. This staircase, which lands on a corridor outside the upper rooms, is entirely constructed of walnut wood, as is also the panelling of the hall and the columns on which the corridor is supported. A curious coat-of-arms in carved oak confronts the visitor at the first turn of the stairs, and this originally formed the back of the canopy under which President Kruger used to sit in the Raad Saal at Pretoria, and beneath which the famous ultimatum which heralded his ruin, and that of his country, was signed. Close below the ceiling of the hall hang a long row of banners, those at each end being respectively the flags of the Free State and the Transvaal, the latter being a specimen of silk manufacture and worked with the golden Dutch motto, "May God preserve us," by the ladies of Wakerstroom for the local Commando. After the first stage of the war it was however buried for safety from the Rooincks and lay hidden in the neighbourhood till near the end of the struggle, when it was unearthed and presented to Lord Kitchener by Lieutenant-Colonel Stewart's column.

The flags in the centre, over a dozen in number, are Dervish banners captured in the Omdurman campaign. Besides making these alterations Lord Kitchener pulled down a former dairy and china cupboard (which with truly Indian inappropriateness had been located at the end of the drawing-room), and with the space thus acquired constructed a handsome billiard-room, the chief ornament in which is a fine mantelpiece of carved walnut wood, designed by himself from an old English model, the motto on which "Strike and feare not" gives characteristic advice to players at the game which Lord Kitchener is never disinclined to follow. The illustration here given depicts the three blocks which constitute the 'Snowdon' of to-day. Since Lord Kitchener has occupied the place it has become a residence worthy of the soldier who, out of England, holds the most important army office under the crown. All these improvements have been carried out in the first year of the present Commander-in-Chief's residence, and plans have also been prepared under His Excellency's direction for the immediate completion of a suitable dining-room to take the place of the somewhat low and dingy apartment which has hitherto existed.

In June last Lord Kitchener gave the largest and most successful ball which has yet been held at 'Snowdon.' Two supper-rooms were organised for this dance—the ordinary large apartment in the ball-room building, and the smaller dining-room in the lower house. In the latter were displayed Lord Kitchener's splendid gold and silver presentation plate, the first including large cups presented by the City of London and Ipswich, with smaller ones from the Fishmongers' and Grocers' Companies, a magnificent rose water ewer and dish, presented by Liverpool (which once formed part of the famous "Peel heirlooms"), and two pairs of large and small gilt candelabra, with a plentiful supply of salt cellars, mustard pots, pepper castors, etc. The chief feature of the silver service was the soup and dinner plates, the gift of Sheffield, on which the supper was served; large silver trays presented by Chatham and Liverpool completing the unique and valuable collection.

MR. H. B. HARINGTON, *Additional Member of Council.* — SIR CHAS. TREVELYAN, *Finance Member.* — SIR HUGH ROSE (LORD STRATHNAIRN), C.-in-C. — SIR JOHN LAWRENCE (afterwards LORD LAWRENCE), *Viceroy and Governor-General.* — SIR ROBERT NAPIER, *Military Member* (afterwards LORD NAPIER OF MAGDALA.) — SIR H. S. MAINE (SIR HENRY MAINE), *Law Member.* — SIR WM. GREY, *Home Member.*

SIR JOHN LAWRENCE'S COUNCIL, 1864.

CHAPTER IV.

The Government of India.

THERE is only one correct answer to the question 'What is Simla famous for?' and that is 'It is the summer head-quarters of the Government of India.' It is true that the Lieutenant-Governor of the Punjab with his Secretariat and satellites reside here in the hot weather, and also that the Commander-in-Chief of the Army with the Army head-quarters form no small portion of the population from year to year, but both of them sink into insignificance by the side of the Imperial Government, for the Provincial Government is in dire danger at the moment of transportation to Dalhousie, and even the General Officers of the Army head-quarters fail to compare in importance with those who may be said to compose the great 'Sarkar,' or Supreme Government of Hindustan. Had it not been for official patronage, it is practically certain that Simla would never have come into existence. She really owes, as has been already shown, her being to officialdom, and her character, as an official centre, is her main trait to-day. Thus it comes that Simla has been constantly described as the 'home of the heaven-born' (the covenanted civilians), 'the abode of the little tin gods,' the 'Capua of India,' 'Olympus,' and at times by other titles scarcely as complimentary. To be caught up to the Supreme Secretariat has long been, and still doubtless is, the ambition of many a budding civilian, and countless in Simla have been the reputations made and blasted, numberless the hopes and fears, and the joys and disappointments, that have centred around these famous Himalayan hills.

"How mysterious and delicious," wrote George Aberigh-Mackay in his inimitable 'Twenty-one days in India,' "are the cool penetralia of the Viceregal Office. It is the sensorium of the Empire; it is the seat of thought; it is the abode of moral responsibility! What famines, what battles, what excursions of pleasure, what banquets and pageants, what concepts of change have sprung into life here! Every pigeon-hole contains a potential revolution; every office box cradles the embryo of a war or dearth. What shocks and vibrations, what deadly thrills does this little thunder cloud office transmit to far away provinces lying beyond rising and setting suns."

To those who would read a full and what is probably the best account yet written of the Supreme Government, let me recommend General Sir George Chesney's 'Indian Polity.' I beg however to be allowed to make a few remarks on the origin of this august body which, as already shown, permanently located itself here during Sir John Lawrence's rule. In the early days of 'John Company Bahadur' the settlements at Madras and Bombay and in Bengal were governed by Councils of the principal merchants, the senior being the President of the Council (hence the term Presidency). Each settlement was independent of the others and transacted trade and administrative business directly with the Court of Directors in London. When worthy Job Charnock founded the City of Calcutta, the Bengal settlement was a very small concern, and it was not until Clive's *Jagir* endowed it with the fertile provinces of Bengal, Behar, and Orissa that it became the most important of the Company's possessions. In 1773 the "Regulating Act" of that year appointed a Governor General and four Counsellors for the Government of Bengal and declared the supremacy of the Bengal Presidency over those of Madras and Bombay. As the possessions of the Company became gradually welded into a dominion, the control exercised by the Governor General of Bengal in Council increased, and at last he was declared by an Act of the year 1833 to be the Governor General of India. He still continued to rule Bengal until a Lieutenant-Governor was appointed to that province in the year 1853. The Governor General in Council now became the general controlling authority over the various provinces of India, and the circumstances which led him to establish his summer capital at Simla have been set forth in earlier chapters. As Sir George Chesney has explained, "The decision was arrived at rather as a gradual outcome of circumstances than of deliberate purpose from the first, and it is probably far from being the best possible arrangement."

At first the Council of the Governor General was a purely consultative body, every case was circulated to each Member of the Council, and after they had recorded their opinions the decision was given by the Governor General. Business, however, soon increased to a point at which this arrangement threw an impossible amount of work on the Governor General, and after Lord Dalhousie had recorded a strong opinion on the subject, Lord Canning introduced the present system under which each Member of the Supreme Council holds charge of one or other of the principal departments of business. These Departments are: the Foreign Department, the Home Department, the Revenue and Agricultural Department, the Finance Department, the Legislative Department, the Public Works Department, and the Military Department. The Viceroy himself takes direct charge of the Foreign Department, and the present heads of the other Departments are as follows:—Finance, Sir Edward FG. Law; Military, General Sir E. R. Elles; Public Works, Sir A. T. Arundel; Home, Revenue and Agriculture, Sir Denzil Ibbetson; and Legislative, Mr. H. E. Richards.

A GOVERNMENT MESSENGER.
(THE HOME SECRETARY'S HEAD ORDERLY).

There are thus five ordinary Members of Council; in addition the Commander-in-Chief of the Forces in India is an extraordinary Member of Council and takes rank next below the Viceroy. The Foreign Department deals with the external politics of India and conducts the business connected with the numerous Feudatory Chiefs; the Home Department conducts the ordinary internal administration, including such matters as education, police and the medical branches of the service; the Revenue Department is concerned in the first place with the administration of the land revenue and the well-being of the agricultural population; it also controls the forest, survey, geological and other departments connected with economic purposes and administration, and supervises the measures for protection against famine; the Finance Department deals with both finance and commerce and administers the sources of revenue (other than those controlled by the Revenue Department); the Legislative Department conducts the legislative business of the Supreme Government and advises other Departments in legal questions; the three main branches of the business of the Public Works Department are railways, irrigation, and roads and buildings; the Military Member of Council holds a position somewhat analogous to that held by the Secretary of State for War before the recent changes of system effected in England. For purposes of legislation several members (both nominated and elected) are added to the Council; and while most of the important legislative business is conducted at Calcutta, the Legislative Council also holds occasional meetings at Simla. Both the Executive and Legislative Councils sit at Viceregal Lodge.

Under the Member of Council each Department is controlled by a Secretary, under whom again there is a small staff of Deputy, Under, and Assistant Secretaries: their number and designation vary from Department to Department, and they are generally officers of the Indian Civil Service, military officers, or officers of the Public Works Department. Next in the official hierarchy come the office establishment, most of whom are natives of India.

Last, but by no means least, we come to the outward and visible sign of the Government of India, the red chuprasies, the official messengers who carry the office boxes which hold the mysterious 'files,' who wear the Imperial livery, and who are attached to the civil offices. As Aberigh-Mackay has somewhat severely written "The chuprasie is to the entire population of India the exponent of British rule; he is the mother-in-law of liars, the high priest of extortioners, and the receiver-general of bribes."

Such is a bare description of the power known to the natives of the country as the 'burra sarkar.'

In a later chapter which deals with Simla society, quotations will be found which allude in unmistakable terms to the fact that the Government's main object in coming to Simla was to find amusement and relaxation, and there is no doubt that until comparatively recent times this belief has been largely held by those whose only knowledge of Simla is gathered from descriptions of social gatherings.

Never was there a greater fallacy, a more erroneous idea, for Simla, as Lord Curzon has truly remarked, "is no longer a holiday resort of an Epicurean Viceroy and pampered Government." Still, whether the belief has arisen from ignorance or from malice, the old proverb of 'give a dog a bad name,' might appropriately be applied to Simla in this regard, for there are people to-day who refuse, or pretend to refuse, to be enlightened on this point. As an instance of how easily misconceptions occur, it may be explained that in 1849–52, the break-down from which many Punjab officers suffered, and which sent numbers of them to recruit in the Murree, Dalhousie, and Simla hills, resulted in the term 'Punjab head' coming into vogue. In later years the origin of the term became forgotten, and the supreme authorities have more than once been accused of collectively suffering from this complaint while in Simla. As a matter of fact there is probably no other centre of civilisation where officials, both civil and military, work harder than those connected with the machinery of the Imperial Government. And no one is more ready to admit this than the critic who is willing to study the subject for himself. Mr. Andrew Wilson, previously mentioned, has left the following remarks on record after witnessing the work of officials in Lord Northbrook's time :—

"Some sneers have been indulged in of late, even in Parliament, at the alleged industry of Members of the Supreme Council and other officials to be found at Simla, as if a certain amount of hospitality and of mingling in society were incompatible with leading a laborious life. But if we except the soldiers and regimental officers, it will be found that most of the English in India, be they civilians, staff officers, educationalists, surgeons, merchants, missionaries, or editors, are compelled to live very laborious days, whether they may scorn delights or not. A late Indian Governor, accustomed to Parliamentary and ministerial life in England, used to declare that he had never been required to work so hard in London as he was in his comparatively unimportant Presidency town. 'Everyone is overworked in India,' was remarked to me by an Oudh Director of Public Instruction, who was himself a notable instance of the assertion; and I have often had occasion to notice how much overtasked Indian officials of the higher grades are, and that in a country where the mind works a good deal more reluctantly and slowly than in Europe, and where there is very little pleasure in activity of any kind for its own sake."

Sir H. M. Durand. General Sir E. Collen. General R. C. B. Pemberton.

Sir Charles Aitchison. Sir Andrew Scoble. The Earl of Dufferin. General Sir George Chesney. Sir James Westland.
General Sir Frederick Roberts. Sir Charles Elliott.

LORD DUFFERIN'S COUNCIL AND SECRETARIES.—1888.

Judged from an English standpoint and having due regard to the complexity of the business connected with the growing civilisation of the Indian Empire, the staff which may be said to compose the Government of India is an absurdly small one. It appears all the smaller too because it is so seldom seen, the harder worked officials certainly find far more pleasure in escaping from, than in attending, social functions, and to the casual visitor large and somewhat ugly buildings, for which Lord Ripon's Government were mainly responsible, and which deface the landscape, are the principal evidence that for eight months in the year Simla rules India. The days have long since gone by when a Dalhousie could spend the rainy season at Chini, or Viceroys come to Simla to banish dull care and repose in peace under the deodar. As one who has been somewhat intimately connected with the official life of Simla for over seventeen years, I should say its prominent feature is the incessant toil attached thereto. Also be it said that the following remarks, made by Lord Dufferin at the Mansion House when presented with the freedom of the city on the 29th May 1889, applied no less to the officers at head-quarters than to those whose work is performed in the districts. Lord Dufferin then said, "Indeed I may say, once for all, without disparagement to the accepted standard of public industry in England, that I did not know what hard work really meant until I witnessed the unremitting and almost inconceivable severity of the grind to which our Indian civil servants, and I will add our military employés, so zealously devote themselves." And perhaps this chapter cannot close more appropriately than with a quotation from a Viceroy whose own industry and wonderful power of work has been a constant theme of admiration in official circles during the last five years.

Lord Curzon when announcing his extension of office on the 4th August last at Simla, alluded to the immense strain upon the labours and energies of the official world throughout India who are the direct instruments for formulating and carrying through the administrative programme which he had initiated. "The loyalty with which they have responded to every appeal, and the zeal and devotion with which they have played their part I can," he said, "never sufficiently acknowledge and praise."

CHAPTER V.

Imperial Properties.

PREVIOUS to the year 1888 the Government of India owned several houses in Simla besides Viceregal Lodge, and was tenant of others. The most important public buildings in its possession were the offices of the Government of India Secretariats, the Army Head Quarters offices, the Public Works Secretariat, the Government Central Press, the Foreign Office, the Post and Telegraph offices. In the year 1888 the question of providing suitable accommodation for the viceregal establishments came under consideration when it was decided to place certain outlying dwelling-houses on the market, and to retain only those in the vicinity of Viceregal Lodge. This has resulted in the convenient arrangement of the Viceroy's clerical staff being housed either on the slopes of the hill on which the Lodge stands or in proximity to it. The houses put on the market were 'Beatsonia' (now called Wind Cliff), 'Primrose Hill' (now called 'Khud Cottage'), 'Mount Pleasant,' 'Annandale View,' 'Tara Hall,' 'Sherfield,' 'Milsington,' and 'Winterfield.' The last named, situated just above the cart road and immediately below the Secretariats and Army Head Quarters offices, now belongs to the Punjab Government, the building, which has been much improved, being now the office of the Executive Engineer, Public Works Department, Simla Provincial Division. The other houses have passed into the hands of private individuals. 'Tara Hall' for instance was purchased by Colonel J. Robertson, C.I.E., for some time president of the Simla Municipality, and is now the property of the Loretto Convent, having been converted into a school for girls and young boys under the supervision and tuition of a staff of nuns.

I will now proceed to give some details of the houses which were retained by the Government of India. The Government of India Secretariat and Army Head Quarters buildings are centrally situated just below the Mall near the 'Kutcherry' (Court House), and the Telegraph and Post offices, and were built in close proximity to one another for the convenience of public business. In former years the different offices had been most inconveniently situated in private dwelling-houses, ill suited for office purposes, and scattered over both Burra and Chota Simla. For instance, the work of the Military Department had, previous to 1884, been carried on successively in 'Bantony,' 'Portmore,' 'Lowville,' 'Dalzell Cottage,' and finally in 'Race View.' In order to find land for the new buildings, it was necessary to take up sites which old residents of Simla will remember as 'Little Hope,' 'Littlewood,' 'Greves Cottage,' 'Dahlia Lodge,' and the shop of the late Mr. Crayden, bootmaker and saddler. The block containing the Government of India Secretariat offices is erected on the site of 'Dahlia Lodge,' originally the property of Mr. F. Dalton, Postmaster of Simla, killed at Delhi in 1857. It was commenced in August 1881 and cost 7½ lakhs, while that containing the offices of the Army Head Quarters was commenced in September 1882, and completed in March 1885 for a similar sum. On the site of this latter block once stood 'Littlewood' which was acquired by Government from Mrs. Byrne. The two blocks are substantial in appearance, are fire-proof, and though not possessed of remarkable architectural beauty, are a noticeable feature of the station to travellers by the tonga road. The first impression indeed to visitors is generally one of surprise that an apparently precipitous hill-side can bear such cumbrous structures. The surroundings of the buildings have been improved almost out of recognition by the construction of approaches and by tree planting, the only reminder of the past being the two fine horse chestnut trees at the porch of the Military Department, which once stood at the entrance of the old Kutcherry. It is expected that about July next the big Civil Secretariat now being erected on the Gorton Castle hill will be completed, when both the blocks I have mentioned will be handed over for occupation by the various Military Department and Army Head Quarters offices.

The Public Works Department Secretariat offices, situated on the main mall close to the new Imperial offices now under construction, on the Gorton Castle hill, occupy the site of old residences known as 'Herbert House' and 'Lowville.' These houses after having been rented by the Government for some years were purchased and demolished, and a handsome structure in brick and timber erected in their place; but this latter was burnt to its foundations on the night of the 12th February 1896. The present building is substantial and serviceable in appearance, and is also fire-proof. It was commenced in April 1896, and completed in August 1897, at a cost of just over four lakhs.

The buildings constituting the Government Press are conveniently situated close to, and immediately below, the Government of India Secretariats and Army Head Quarters offices. They occupy sites of houses formerly known as 'Tally Ho Hall,' and the old Masonic Lodge. The press is one of the few buildings in the station which possesses an electric installation, and it turns out excellent work under the superintendence of Mr. W. Jones.

The Foreign Office was in Lord Auckland's Viceroyalty situated in

Waverley,' just below 'Chapslee' (then 'Secretary's Lodge'), and later on, apparently after several changes, it was removed, and for many years occupied 'The Tendrils' (now the Hotel Cecil), on the Chaura Maidan. About the year 1875 extra accommodation being needed to provide for an increase of establishment, the office again moved into 'Rock House' and 'Valentines' (once known as 'Valentine House'), a small double-storied building being added for the special use of the Secretaries of the department. In 1887 the office made a final exodus and took up its quarters in the picturesque Swiss chalet building it now occupies in the vicinity of Viceregal Lodge. The chalet, which stands on the site once occupied by a house called 'Prospect,' is certainly the most picturesque of all the Government buildings, and has been considerably improved and enlarged within the last two years.

For the present convenience and speedy despatch of public business the Imperial departments of state are now located in four great buildings all within a few hundred yards of each other, but thirty years ago the wheels of the Government machinery certainly moved with much less speed than they do to-day. A map of Simla issued by the Surveyor General's Department in 1875, indicates that in that year the offices were located as follows—the Home office was in 'S. Mark's,' the Finance in 'The Yarrows,' the Public Works in 'Herbert House,' the Foreign in 'Valentines,' the Military in 'Dalzell Cottage,' and the Revenue and Agricultural in 'Argyll House.' The Adjutant General carried on his work in 'Strawberry Hill' and the Quarter Master General in 'Portmore.'

Among other public edifices which deserve mention is the Post Office situated in the centre of Simla, on the site of a house originally known as 'Conny Lodge' purchased from Mr. Peterson, formerly the proprietor of Enjalbert & Co. and afterwards Manager of the Simla Bank. Messrs. Enjalbert & Co. were the pioneer European tailors in Simla, and were followed by Messrs. Coutts & Co. and Ranken & Co., before the ground was acquired for the post office of the station. The Telegraph Office, a handsome structure which stands close by below, is on the site of the old station library house 'Conny Cot' which was removed to the Town Hall in 1886.

Below the Telegraph Office is the Court House or 'Kutcherry,' once known as 'Gaston Hall,' and afterwards as 'Rosna Hall,' in which are the offices of the Deputy Commissioner, the Court of the District Judge, the Treasury, and other offices. 'Clermont' on the Mall near the 'Chaura Maidan' was formerly the office of the Financial Department, but has since been allotted to the Imperial Forest, Survey, and Veterinary Departments.

Situated on Kaithu hill near the Jail on the main road to Annandale

THE MAIN MALL AND MILITARY OFFICES.

are a number of houses known as 'Clerks' Cottages.' The heavy rents which began to be demanded by Simla house owners, for inferior and inadequate accommodation, led the Government about the year 1880 to build a number of cottages for the use of clerical subordinates. These cottages are rented on reasonable terms to clerks in public offices, and are a great boon to a deserving class of men on whom the increasing cost of living in Simla bears heavily. Were there indeed treble the number of these houses there would be none too many. On the cart road, below the Government Press, are the native clerks' barracks which are let out on equally favourable conditions. Two other houses which are Government property are 'Armsdell,' once the residence of the late Mr. D. Panioty, for so many years Assistant Private Secretary to the Viceroy, and since occupied by his successor, Mr. F. W. Latimer, C.I.E., and 'The Burj' which is generally tenanted by a member of the Viceroy's Staff, or used for the reception of native Chiefs who may visit Simla. 'West End Hotel,' 'Boswell Villa,' and 'Boville' are all occupied by the members of the Viceroy's band. 'Hawthorn Cottage' and 'Willie Park' are respectively utilised as the Viceroy's dispensary, and as the printing office of the Private Secretary. Both these latter houses were purchased by the Government for about Rs. 12,000 each, and in order to ensure compliance with certain legal formalities were taken up under the Land Acquisition Act.

'Inverarm' which in the sixties belonged to General Innes, who was also the owner of 'Peterhoff,' passed subsequently into the hands of the Sirmur Raja and finally into the possession of the Government. Some forty years ago 'Inverarm' was a small mud-roofed house which rented for Rs. 700 per annum, and it was apparently taken over by the Imperial Government at the same time as 'Peterhoff.' It was then enlarged, and became for many years the private residence of Lord William Beresford, Military Secretary to the Viceroy. After Lord William Beresford left India it was occupied for some years by General Sir Edwin Collen, who was succeeded by the present tenant, Sir Edward Law, the Financial Member of Council.

Owing to the steady growth of the station the difficulty experienced by high officials in obtaining suitable houses at reasonable rents for the summer season reached an acute stage in 1901. Accordingly the Government of India in that year appointed a small committee consisting of Mr. H. M. Baines, Executive Engineer, Mr. A. Craddock, Architect, and Mr. G. H. leMaistre, Under-Secretary in the Public Works Department, to make proposals for the acquisition by purchase, or on long lease, of suitable residences for Members of the Viceroy's Council. This measure resulted in the acquisition of the two properties known as 'The Mythe' and 'Craig Dhu.' The former house was once the property of Mr. Whitley Stokes, the famous legal official, during whose occupation it was known as 'Laurel Hall,' and though somewhat low lying it is one of the most picturesque properties in Simla. It was acquired by the Government of India on a long and repairable lease from the executors of the late Lieutenant-General George Leslie, R.A, and has been much altered and improved since it became a Government possession. It is now occupied by General Sir Edmund Elles, K.C.B.

'Craig Dhu,' situated on a commanding position on the Elysium Hill, is a house which was built by Mr. Macpherson, then Deputy Secretary in the Legislative Department, in 1882. It was erected on the site of an older house known as 'Stirling Hall,' once the property of Mr. D. O'B. Clarke, which had been pulled down many years before, and after this the ridge on which the house had stood was used as an archery ground. The present house was designed by General C. W. Hutchinson, then Inspector-General of Military Works, under the supervision of Mr. H. B. Goad, the Secretary to the Simla Municipality. Great care was taken in the construction, with the result that the house is one of the best built and most perfectly finished private residences in the station. Mr. Macpherson after living in it for twelve years sold it to Colonel Joubert, I.M.S., by whom it was transferred three or four years later to General Sir E. Locke Elliot. It was sold by the latter to Government under whose direction it has been much improved, and is now tenanted by Sir A. T. Arundel, the Public Works Minister.

As the visitor to Simla proceeds down the mall towards Viceregal Lodge, he is confronted by the great masonry pile, mainly constructed from stone quarried from the hills near the Sanjouli bazaar, which constitutes the new Civil Secretariat buildings. Here until quite recently stood 'Gorton Castle,' one of the most conspicuous buildings of the station. In 1863 'Gorton Castle' which stood on its own hill in close proximity to 'Kennedy House' belonged to Colonel T. D. Colyear, who had previously purchased it from Government for the sum of Rs. 5,000. At his death it was left by will to his native wife, and on her decease it passed into the hands of Miss Colyear, the daughter of his adopted son, Mr. David Colyear. Later on various complications arose with regard to the estate, and it was eventually sold by the Administrator-General in satisfaction of estate debts for Rs. 26,000 to Mr. Tuther in 1879. It was this owner who parted with the property to the Roman Catholic community who at one time had some idea of erecting a chapel there. By private arrangement, however, Mr. (afterwards Sir) Theodore Hope, Member of the Viceroy's Council, took the place over, giving the Roman Catholics in exchange a property called 'The Groves' which is now the site of the present Roman Catholic Chapel. In more recent years Sir Philip Hutchins occupied the house, and it was during his tenure of possession that the dancing floor for which the place

SIMLA IN THE WINTER.

became so famous, was laid down. The story of how this happened is not without interest. Mr. B. Ribbentrop was then head of the Forest Department, and was anxious to push the padouk timber of the Andaman Islands on to the open market, being personally firmly convinced as to its real merits and value. Sir Philip Hutchins, however, was not persuaded that the new wood deserved special support. But the Inspector-General of Forests discovered that the Member of Council's wife required a dancing floor, and he guaranteed to provide her with the best in Simla. The necessary padouk was imported to the Himalayas, a perfect floor resulted, the Honourable Member had practical proof of the quality of the timber, and to-day the demand for the wood in the timber market exceeds the supply. 'Gorton Castle' then changed owners as Sir Theodore Hope sold the place to Colonel (now Sir William) Bisset for Rs. 40,000. About five years ago a mild sensation was caused by the news that Mr. (now Sir James) Walker, of Alliance Bank and Simla Volunteer fame, had purchased the house for Rs. 80,000, and as he had retired from India there was considerable speculation as to his purpose. Some declared the place would be given to the station as a Library, and others that it was intended as a gift to the Volunteer Corps. At length came the announcement that the owner wished to present the place to the station as a hospital for Europeans. It was a splendid gift, and the Simla residents were not slow to record their appreciation of the donor's liberality. But gradually the feeling grew that so central a site was scarcely a suitable one for hospital purposes, and after careful consideration it was decided with the donor's sanction to hand the site over to Government for its proposed Civil Secretariat block and to spend the money thus obtained in building a hospital elsewhere. This proposal was carried through and the Government of India agreed to give Rs. 1,20,000 for the house and grounds. Now a huge pile of new offices costing about eleven lakhs has arisen under the supervision of Major H. F. Chesney, R.E., on the old site where once stood 'Gorton Castle,' perhaps in some ways the finest house in Simla. The original design was made by Sir Swinton Jacob, but it has been considerably modified during the course of construction, as when the site was cut down it was found that there was not as much building space as had been anticipated. Moreover the necessity of providing more accommodation for all the Government departments has steadily increased during the last few years.

Many reflections may occur to the mind of the Simla public as they admire this great and imposing structure in the future, but none, I take it, will be more striking than the fact that property which Government parted with for some Rs. 5,000 about 1860, they thought fit to repurchase for Rs. 1,20,000 in 1900.

CHAPTER VI.

Some Simla Institutions.

IT is perhaps only fitting that a chapter which deals with local institutions should commence with some account of the Municipality which is so largely answerable for the health and welfare of the townsfolk of Simla.

Municipal Government was first introduced into Simla in December 1851 under the provisions of Act XXVI of 1850, and the Simla Municipality is the oldest in the Punjab. The Corporation was at first purely elective, but subsequently became also partly nominative, and several changes have, from time to time, been since made in its constitution. The President has frequently been a non-official, but the present head of the Committee is the Deputy Commissioner of Simla, and amongst other members are the Civil Surgeon, the Executive Engineer of the Simla Division, and half a dozen public spirited residents.

The most important Municipalities in India have been frequently abused, and that of Simla has been no exception to the rule. It has been subjected of recent years to severer criticism and attack than perhaps any other, and because it legislates for the summer head-quarters of the Imperial and Provincial Governments, it is exposed to the fierce light which beats upon two thrones. And naturally as the number of houses has increased from 100 in 1844 to some 1,400 in 1904, so have the responsibilities of the Municipal Councillors steadily grown heavier. The water-supply, sanitation, taxation, road-making have all in turn proved burning questions, and in June 1898 a Committee, consisting of Mr. J. P. Hewett (now the Chief Commissioner, Central Provinces), President, the Hon'ble Mr. J. S. Beresford, Colonel H. P. Leach, R.E., Mr. L. W. Dane, C.S., Mr. J. E. Hilton, Colonel L. Grey, Members, and Mr. E. Ducane Smythe, Secretary, was appointed by Government to consider various questions connected with the extension of the station.

The recommendation of this Committee resulted in about fifteen lakhs of rupees being expended in works connected with the water-supply and sewage system, and the attention of the Municipal authorities is now being directed to the improvement of the road communications.

A few months ago it was officially announced that the possible transfer of the Punjab Government summer head-quarters from Simla to Dalhousie was being seriously considered, and since that time the question has been argued with considerable warmth in the press. While those in favour of the move point to the congested state of the station, the certainty of a steady increase in the population, and for political reasons the desirability of the ruler of the Punjab possessing his own summer capital, the general public seem to be strongly opposed to the scheme. There are indeed cogent arguments regarding the heavy cost of the exodus, the increase in taxation which would fall on future residents in Simla (at least one-third of Municipal revenue is now paid by the Punjab), together with the comparatively small relief in other directions which would be experienced by the move of some 2,000 souls, which cannot be lightly dismissed.

It is generally believed that Lord Curzon and his Government are in favour of the move, and it is also whispered that if the Provincial Government disappears, the present Municipal system will be abolished and Simla will be converted into an Imperial Cantonment. In which case house-holders may find they have only exchanged the rule of King Log for the tyranny of King Stork.

The fact that Simla was practically created by the Government has not unnaturally been constantly urged as a strong reason why the station should receive special assistance from the Imperial funds, and the announcement that twenty lakhs of rupees have been specially allotted in the late Financial Budget for its improvement shows that the Supreme Government has now admitted its obligations in this respect. A considerable portion of this sum is likely to be spent in acquiring outlying pieces of ground and so extending the station limits.

While it can hardly be contended that the Municipal rule in Simla has always proved satisfactory to residents, it is only fair to say that the Committee has struggled hard against many difficulties, that it has received but scant praise or encouragement from tax-payers, and has often been too harshly attacked. And it is an indisputable fact that, owing to the exertions of Colonel H. Davies, President, and Mr. B. G. Wallis, Engineer and Secretary (the latter a retired officer of the Punjab Public Works Service), a marked advance in Municipal control has been noticeable during the last two years. Cleverly written as were a series of letters on ' Degenerate Simla,' in the *Pioneer* in 1903, their influence was somewhat marred by a too bitter criticism of some of Simla's defects. But I have no desire to inflict a controversy upon my readers on the delicate questions here alluded to. To-day Simla possesses a summer population of about 38,000 souls, of whom about 7,000 are Europeans and Eurasians. This population however falls to some 19,000 during the winter months. The Municipal revenue is about six lakhs of rupees which, after the necessary expenditure has been provided for, leaves a balance of about R60,000 for the annual improvement of the station, and the incidence of taxation a head per annum is slightly under R12-8-0.

The Municipality possesses an imposing Town Hall which, though by no means free from structural defects, is fairly suitable for the needs of the station. The Hall contains the Municipal offices, ball and supper-room, the Freemason's hall, Library and reading-rooms, and the Gaiety Theatre. Among other properties owned by the Municipality are the Ripon Hospital and its adjuncts, the police station, the Municipal markets, a fire brigade, extensive fruit orchards on the Mahasu range, and a number of grain shops and sheds in the bazaar ward. The difficulty of furnishing Simla with an adequate supply of pure water has always proved a serious one. To-day the supply is obtained from the slopes of the Mahasu range known as the catchment area, the water being conveyed into reservoirs in the station by two gravitation lines some seventeen miles in combined length.

About ten years ago however more water was urgently required in the hot weather, the catchment area was largely extended, and a powerful pumping installation which lifts up 200,000 gallons water, 1,300 feet per diem, was erected in the Charot Nullah. Many improvement schemes in connection with the water-supply have from time to time been propounded, and the latest is that of General Beresford Lovett, C.B., R.E., now being considered by Government which is estimated to cost about sixteen lakhs. Briefly the idea is to utilise the power of the water in the Nauti Khud stream which runs into the Sutlej about sixteen miles from Simla, not only for the provision of an efficient water-supply, but also for the electrical lighting of the station.

Amongst the many able men who have sat in the Presidential chair perhaps Colonel Parry Nisbet, was the most prominent. Of Secretaries no one will be so long remembered as Mr. Horace B. Goad who was the prince of managers and the terror of all evil doers. His appointment was really due to the recommendation of a Committee which sat under Sir Lepel Griffin in 1877.

The following are the Presidents and Secretaries of the Municipality since its formation :—

List of Presidents and Secretaries, Simla Municipality.

Chairman or President.	Term of Office.	Secretary.	Term of Office.
Mr. F. Peterson	August 1855 to October 1855.	Mr. F. D. Vivian .	1858.
Mr. C. H. Barrett . .	1855—1856.	There appears to have been no regular Secretary until Mr. H. B. Goad was appointed. The work was certainly done for a few years by the Assistant Commissioner of the district.	
Major S. B. Goad .	1856—1857.		
Colonel C. D. Blair, C.B.	1857—1858.		
Major-General P. Innes.	1858—1859.		

CHRIST CHURCH, ABOUT 1870

List of Presidents and Secretaries, Simla Municipality—*contd.*

Chairman or President.	Term of Office.	Secretary.	Term of Office.
Major S. B. Goad .	1859—1860.		
Mr. G. E. Pool .	1860—1861.		
Mr. F. Peterson .	1861—1862.		
Major S. B. Goad .	1862—1863.		
Mr. F. Peterson .	1863—1870.		
Mr. J. Craddock .	1870—1871.		
Major S. B. Goad .	1871—1872.		
Mr. F. Peterson .	1872—1873.		
Mr. J. L. Walker .	1873—1874.		
Major S. B. Goad .	1874—1875.		
Colonel C. A. McMahon.	1875—1876.		
Colonel C. H. Hall .	July 1876 to October 1876.		
Colonel C. A. McMahon.	Oct. 1876 to March 1877.		
Captain R. Parry Nisbet.	March 1877 to Oct. 1881.	Mr. H. B. Goad .	Jan. 1878 to Nov. 1895.
Captain J. B. Hutchinson.	Nov. and Dec. 1881		
Captain R. Parry Nisbet.	Jan. 1882 to April 1882.		
Mr. W. Coldstream, I.C.S.	May 1882 to Sept. 1883.		
Surgn-Genl. J. Cunningham.	Sept. 1883 to Aug. 1884.		
Mr. James L. Walker	Sept. 1884 to Mar. 1887.		
Mr. E. V. S. Cullin .	May 1887 to July 1891.		
Colonel John Robertson, C.I.E.	Oct. 1891 to Oct. 1897.	Major W. P. Carson	Dec. 1895 to Dec. 1903.
Colonel L. J. H. Grey, C.S.I.	Nov. 1897 to April 1899.		
Mr. P. Donaldson .	April 1899 to April 1902.		
Major (now Colonel) H. S. P. Davies, I.A.	April 1902 to date.	Mr. B. G. Wallis, M.I.C.E. (late P. W. Dept.)	24th Feb. 1903 to date.

This list is compiled from information supplied by the offices of the Deputy Commissioner and Municipal Secretary.

I am indebted to Mr. J. E. Wilkinson, Clerk of Christ Church, for permission to extract a short history of this Church from his neat little volume, 'The Parochial History of Simla,' which has only just been published.

Prior to 1836 Simla residents attended divine service in a building which stood on the site now occupied by Northbrook Terrace, which possessed a thatched roof and accommodated a hundred people, but there was no regular Chaplain until the Rev. J. Vaughan was appointed in 1842. Even then services were only held intermittently until April 1845.

The corner stone of the present Church was laid in September 1844, but though the building was apparently ready for the consecration some years earlier, this did not take place till the 10th January 1857, when the ceremony was performed by the Right Reverend Thomas Dealtry, Bishop of Madras. In 1849 Lord Hardinge presented a mortar, taken or found at Hoshiarpur, which was erroneously believed to have been cast into a bell and placed in the tower. As a fact it was broken up and sold, the proceeds being credited to the Church Building Fund. In the same year the Lieutenant-Governor of the North-West Provinces presented a font and a pulpit, the latter since replaced by a stone one in memory of Bishop Milman. Colonel Boileau, too, gave a reading desk which was afterwards moved to All Saints' Chapel at Boileaugunge. The first organ was erected in the Church in 1855, the major portion of its cost, £250, being subscribed by Lady Gomm, the wife of the Commander-in-Chief. The Church was taken over by Government as a public building in 1856, and in the fifties and sixties various improvements were carried out, including the erection of the clock tower, extension of the aisles and chancel, provision of a new roof, and the construction of a porch, the latter in 1873. The clock was put up in 1860 by Colonel Dumbleton.

The Simla Church is none too large, and tradition relates that recognising this fact a certain Chaplain some forty years ago preached a sermon against the enormity of the crinoline, the extravagance of its wearers, and the room it took up in the sacred edifice to the exclusion of would-be worshippers. And it has also been left on record that the ladies of the congregation took the discourse so much to heart that on the following Sabbath they all appeared in riding habits!

In 1875 Lady Gomm's organ was replaced by a new instrument, which again in 1899 was sold to the Rawalpindi Church to make room for the present organ built by Messrs. Morgan and Smith of Brighton, and erected on the 29th September 1899. This organ has cost R23,000; the two most expensive stops were presented by Sir Mackworth Young and Sir James Walker, while the cost of decorating the pipes was defrayed by the Countess

LORD AND LADY CURZON DRIVING TO CHURCH FOR THE CORONATION SERVICE, JUNE 1902.

of Elgin to commemorate the marriage of her daughter Lady Elizabeth Bruce with Mr. H. Babington Smith in the Church on the 22nd September 1898. During the winter of 1900 the six bells which cost over R2,000, were hung in the tower. The actual cost of the Church has been about R89,000.

In 1901 the European and Eurasian Church of England population numbered 1,950, in addition to 120 Native Christians, out of a native population of nearly 40,000. The largest congregation for which the Church has been asked to provide accommodation was on Coronation Day, 26th June 1902, when 825 seats were required. The first Chaplain gazetted by the Government was the Rev. T. Vaughan in 1843. Among those of more recent years have been the Rev. H. J. Matthew, 1877—1885, the Reverend Archdeacon W. H. Tribe, 1886—1892, whose daughter is now the Duchess of Bedford, the Rev. G. W. Tomkins, the Reverend Archdeacon A. N. W. Spens, 1894-1898, and the Rev. M. C. Sanders, 1898—1902. The present Chaplain is the Rev. G. E. Nicolls, who was previously Chaplain in 1892—1894.

The chancel window of Christ Church was erected by subscription to the memory of Bishop Matthew's wife who died in England while he was Chaplain of Simla, and is an allegorical representation of the 'Te Deum.' The fresco surrounding it was designed by Mr. Lockwood Kipling, and carried out under his supervision by his pupils of the Mayo School of Art, Lahore. A fine stained glass window representing Faith, Hope, Charity, Fortitude, Patience, and Humility is to the memory of the wife of Mr. (since Sir) James Lewis Walker, and there is another in memory of General Sir Henry Godwin, who commanded the expedition to the Rangoon River in 1852, which resulted in the annexation of Lower Burma. There are also mural monuments to the memory of Sir T. D. Baker, K.C.B., Lieutenant-General Sir William K. Elles, K.C.B., Colonel A. C. Cruickshank (killed in the Black Mountain Campaign of 1888), Lieutenant-General Julius George Medley, Lieutenant-Colonel Roger John Madock, R.A., Surgeon-General Oliver Barnett, Major-General Thomas Elliott Hughes, Major-General Samuel Compton Turner, R.E., Fred. Corbyn, Esq., Robert Harris Greathed, Esq., B.C.S., General Frederick Charles Maisey, Rev. Thomas Edwards, Pastor of the Native Church, Lieutenant-Colonel E. E. Money, 9th Bengal Lancers, Constance Stanley, wife of Colonel S. J. Home, R.E., and Arthur Bridge Wilson, Esq., killed by the accidental discharge of a gun, near Sambhur, Rajputana, on 7th December 1897.

The little Chapel of All Saints, Boileaugunge, is built on ground just within the Viceregal Lodge Estate, and was consecrated by Bishop French on the 6th April 1885, and assigned as a perpetual chapel of ease to Christ Church. Here Lady Dufferin used to play the organ and train the choir during her residence in Simla. Colonel Conway-Gordon spent three years in building an organ, which was replaced by an American instrument in 1892. In 1897 Lord Elgin presented a white marble font in commemoration of the baptism of his son Victor Alexander Bruce in that year. The chapel possesses a stained glass window erected by Miss Matthew in 1900 to the memory of the son of Bishop Matthew of the Punjab diocese. This Bishop was for many years intimately connected with Simla and much loved by the residents of the station. He died at Lahore on 2nd December from a stroke of paralysis which seized him in the Cathedral immediately after preaching a sermon on the evening of Advent Sunday, 27th November 1898.

The erection of the Simla Union Church, which stands on a portion of the 'Constantia' estate (purchased by the trustees for R19,000), was commenced in 1869, but this site was not chosen until after a piece of ground had been obtained near the Combermere bridge and levelling operations had been commenced there. Dr. Murray Mitchell and the Rev. John Fordyce were two of the earliest ministers connected with this Church. Dr. Mitchell afterwards became a Moderator of the Free Church of Scotland, and the Rev. John Fordyce, who for many years was Secretary of the Indian Evangelisation Society, died at home at a ripe old age two years ago. The Rev. Mr. Smith, who, after some fifty years' valuable service in the Baptist Mission at Delhi, gave some of the closing years of his life to the pastorate of the Union Chapel, is commemorated by a brass tablet. The Rev. J. H. Bateson, now well known as the Secretary of the Royal Army Temperance Association, also ministered to the congregation from 1892 till 1899. The Rev. William Wilson, Minister of the Trossachs Parish, was pastor in 1903, and the Rev. A. M. Maclean of Cramond, Edinburgh, is the present minister.

St. Thomas' (Native) Church, which is situated in the centre of the Native Bazaar, has accommodation for about 150 persons, and its construction was mainly due to the efforts of the Rev. Thomas Edwards, a Bengali by birth, and formerly clerk at Christ Church. It was consecrated by Bishop French on the 9th August 1885, in the presence of a congregation which included Lord and Lady Dufferin. The services are now held both in English and Urdu.

The first place of Roman Catholic worship erected in Simla was the little Chapel still existing at the west end of the Lower Bazaar. The ground on which it stands was granted on the 1st of March 1850 by Mr. William Edwards, Superintendent of Hill States, to Messrs. J. Rebello, J. Walsh, R. Cantopher, L. E. James, and J. Nash. Prior to this grant the land had been occupied by a public hospital, and for this reason had also been free of ground rent. The deed of grant to the Roman Catholic community recites that the

WOUNDED OFFICERS AT SIMLA, 1857-58.

"land being now appropriated for the erection of a place of worship, the same indulgence will be continued so long as it is used for that purpose." From the year 1885, when the new Roman Catholic Chapel under the Cutchery came into use, up to the year 1902, the little Chapel was used as a school; at present it is in disuse, and the right of ownership to a portion of the site is the subject of litigation. In the year 1850 the ground near the site of the Chapel, now occupied by a densely crowded part of the Bazaar, must have been covered with trees, for the deed of grant contains the usual stipulation that no trees were to be cut without the permission of the grantor. The new Chapel was constructed at a cost of about R80,000, this sum having been raised entirely by voluntary contributions, the largest subscriber being the Marquis of Ripon, who had entered the Roman Catholic Church not long before his appointment as Viceroy. And the Misses Fitzpatrick, daughters of Sir Dennis Fitzpatrick, formerly Lieutenant-Governor of the Punjab, were also consistent supporters of the Chapel. The ceremony of consecration was performed in 1885 by the Archbishop of Agra, and the building was completed in the year 1900 by the addition of a steeple and peal of bells. The present senior Chaplain is the Rev. Father Calistus, O.C., and a popular visiting preacher for some years past has been the Right Reverend Monsignor W. Tylee, M.A., Domestic Prelate of the Pope.

One of the most valuable properties in Simla to-day is that owned by the United Service Club. This popular institution was originally a private dwelling house built by Sir Jeremiah Bryant, and remodelled by Mr. Thoby Prinsep, a member of Lord Auckland's Council, the father of Sir Henry Thoby Prinsep, who until recently, as Judge of the Calcutta High Court, held the position of 'the father of the Civil Service.' It was apparently re-named by Mr. Thoby Prinsep as 'the Priory,' and its rent in 1844 was Rs. 1,400. Mr. Prinsep was a popular and hospitable entertainer; indeed the sound of revelry emanating from his house was often heard far down the Mall at night, and the residence received in his honour the title of 'Thoby Priory.' After he vacated it, it fell, as so many houses in the olden days appear to have done, into ruin, and was rebuilt by Captain Pengree some years later. The house in the fifties was called 'Belvedere.'

In 1858-59 Dr. W. H. (afterwards Sir William) Russell, the famous correspondent of *The Times*, paid his visit to India, and on June 14th arrived at Simla in a jampan "at a large ostentatious building called the Simla Club—in truth an hotel." "It was"—he writes in his 'Diary in India'—"nearly 5 o'clock ere my jampan was laid alongside the club steps, and I limped into a decent apartment which was ready for me. The landlord, however, told me that the club was nearly full. Many sick and wounded officers were up here." (The illustration here given of wounded officers in Simla is reproduced from Captain G. F. Atkinson's 'Campaign in India,' 1857-58.) Dr. Russell had not long occupied his room before Captain Alison brought him an invitation to Lord William Hay's residence, and he says: "I was carried off jampan and all, and I must say the air of the club did not make me quit it with regret, though some subsequent acquaintance with the place induced me to modify a little my first unfavourable impression."

The following description of life at the Club nearly fifty years ago, written by Dr. Russell when he had been about six weeks in Simla, will doubtless be read with mixed feelings by past and present members:—

"Let us go over to the Simla Club. It is nightfall, for the last moments of the day are absorbed in the canter round Jacko, the closing gallop down the Mall, billiards, the racket-court, the library, or lounging from one shop into another. Lights are gleaming from the long row of windows in the bungalow. Syces holding horses, and jampanees sitting in groups by their masters' chairs, are clustering round the verandah. Servants are hurrying in to wait on the sahibs, who have come to dinner from distant bungalows. The clatter of plates and dishes proclaim that dinner is nearly ready. The British officers and civilians, in every style of Anglo-Indian costume, are propping up the walls of the sitting-room, waiting for the signal to fall on. The little party in the corner have come down from the card-room, and it is whispered that old Major Stager has won 700 rupees from young Cornet Griffin, since tiff; but Griffin can never pay unless he gets his Delhi prize-money soon; and that little Shuffle, the Major's partner, who does not look twenty yet, but who is well known as a cool hand, has extracted nearly twice as much from that elderly civilian, who has come up with a liver and full purse from the plains. The others are the soldierless officers of ex-sepoy regiments, Queen's officers, civilians, doctors, invalids, unemployed brigadiers, convalescents from wounds or illness in the plains; and their talk is of sporting, balls, promotions, exchanges, Europe, and a little politics, re-chaufféd from the last *Overland Mail;* but, as a general rule, all serious questions are tabooed, and it is almost amusing to observe the excessive *esprit de corps* which is one of the excellences as one of the defects of the English character, and which now breaks up the officers of the Queen's, of the Company's service, and of the civil departments into separate knots. Dinner is announced, and the members and guests file into a large room with a table well laid out with flowers and plated epergnes, round which there is a double file of the club servants and of the domestics which each man has taken with him. The dinner is at all events plentiful enough, the pastry and sweets being, perhaps, the best department. Conversation is loud and animated. Among Indians the practice of drinking wine with each other has not yet

THE CLUB.
Simla Season 1854.

SUCH A JOLLY BALL.
Simla Season 1854.

Reproduced from
"The Delhi sketch Book."

died out, and the servants are constantly running to and fro with their masters' compliments, bottles, and requests to take wine with you, which are generally given to the wrong persons, and produce much confusion and amusement.

"Cheroots follow closely on the removal of the last jelly-brandy-panee, and more wines not very infrequently succeed, while parties are formed and set to work in the inner room, and the more jovial of the gentlemen proceed to the execution of vocal pieces such as were wont to be sung in Europe twenty years ago, generally enriched by fine choral effects from the combined strength of all the company. The usual abandon of such reunions in Europe is far exceeded by our Indians, who, when up at the hills, do not pretend to pay the least attention to the presence of old officers, no matter what their rank or age. The 'fun' grows louder and faster as the night advances. The brigadiers look uneasily or angrily over their cards at the disturbers, but do not interfere. There is a crash of glass, and a grand row at the end of the room, and the Bacchanalians, rising with much exultation, seize 'Ginger Tubbs' in his chair, and carry him round the room as a fitting ovation for his eminent performance of the last comic ballad, and settle down to 'hip-hip-hurrah, and one cheer more,' till they are eligible for their beds or for 'a broiled bone' at old Brown's. *Hinc illæ lachrymæ.* Hence the reports of the bazaar people of the rows and scrapes that reach us in the mornings. But by midnight nearly all the guests and members have retired to their rooms or bungalows."

For a short period the so-called club was in the possession of Captain Levinge, formerly in the 93rd Highlanders, but about 1863 it passed into the hands of a joint stock company under the name of the Simla Club and North-West Wine Company, and was managed by Mr. C. Wilson, until in 1865-66 it came into the possession of proprietary shareholders and was turned into a more or less private hotel for members of the service visiting Simla for short periods. Colonel W. Gordon appears to have been the first Honorary Secretary of the Club.

The real turning point in the history of the present club came in the years 1888 to 1901 when a rival 'New Club,' as it was called, sprang into existence on the site now occupied by Peliti's Hotel. For a time this seriously threatened the prosperity of the senior institution. Luckily for the latter, however, it possessed in its Honorary Secretary, Surgeon-Major 'Billy' Taylor (now Surgeon-General Sir W. Taylor, K.C.B.), an excellent man of business, as energetic and far seeing as he was shrewd and popular. He induced the committee to at once add a huge new block of quarters and to thoroughly refurnish, and more or less rebuild the existing public rooms. So attractive indeed was the service club rendered that the 'New Club,' of which Mr. H. Birch (now Secretary of the Bengal Club in Calcutta) was Secretary, was compelled, in spite of many advantages, to close its doors after an existence of about a couple of years.

The club now consists of four really splendid blocks of buildings with accommodation for 70 members. It possesses too a fine covered tennis court, a game which was introduced into Simla by Lord Dufferin, while its private electric plant, and its general fittings and arrangements are perfect. In the spacious dining room are capital portraits of the late Sir George Chesney, formerly President of the Club, and of Lord Roberts. Saturday night is the guest night, when a band supplies the music, and over 100 diners sit down together. Not the least popular adjunct is the 'Chalet' (irreverently termed the 'Hen house'), a pretty cottage overhanging the old band stand, in which the members of the Club entertain the ladies of Simla, and in which, after dinner, even members of the Viceroy's Council have been known to unbend so far as to play 'musical chairs.'

As it will probably interest some members past and present, I give the list of Presidents and Secretaries from 1879 to 1903:—

Year.	President.	Honorary Secretary.
1879	Sir A. Arbuthnot	Dr. Hamilton.
1880	Major A. J. Filgate, R.E.	A paid Secretary.
1881	Ditto	Ditto.
1882	Colonel A. J. Filgate, R.E.	Captain Gloscock.
1883	Ditto	A paid Secretary.
1884	Ditto	Ditto.
1885	Ditto	Lt.-Colonel Henderson.
1886	Ditto	Ditto.
1887	Ditto	W. Ross, Esq. (paid Secretary).
1888	General G. T. Chesney	Surgeon-Major W. Taylor.
1889	Colonel Bushman	Ditto.
1890	General Sir G. T. Chesney, K.C.B.	Ditto.
1891	General A. R. Badcock, C.B.	Ditto.
1892	Ditto	Ditto.
1893	A. U. Fanshawe, Esq., C.S.	Captain W. E. Bunbury.
1894	General A. R. Badcock, C.B.	Major H. Finnis, R.E.
1895	Ditto	Ditto.
1896	A. U. Fanshawe, Esq., C.S.	Ditto.
1897	Ditto	Ditto.
1898	Ditto	Captain T. A. Robertson.
1899	Ditto	Lieut.-Colonel H. Finnis.
1900	Ditto	Ditto.
1901	Surgeon-General W. Taylor	Captain J. B. Robertson.
1902	A. U. Fanshawe, Esq., C.S.I.	Captain G. B. Hingston, R.E.
1903	Surgeon-General Sir B. Franklin, K.C.I.E.	Ditto.

The principal school in Simla is that known as Bishop Cotton School.

This school, originally known as the 'Simla Public School.' was founded by public subscription with the assistance of Government at the instance of the late Right Reverend G. E. L. Cotton, Bishop of Calcutta, as a thank-offering to Almighty God for His deliverance of the British people in India during the Mutiny of 1857. The school, which was designated Bishop's School, came into existence at Jutogh in the year 1863 in several detached bungalows, but as the cantonment proved an unsuitable locality, was removed to its present site on the 'Knollswood' spur on ground given by the Raja of Keonthal in exchange for a village near Sabathu. The foundation stone of the building was laid by Sir John Lawrence, Governor-General of India, on the 26th of September 1866. Within a fortnight of this function Bishop Cotton was drowned, and the name of the institution was then changed to 'Bishop Cotton School:' and building operations were completed in 1869. The education given in the school is planned with reference to the wants and circumstances of the class for whose benefit the school is especially designed, *viz.*, the sons of Government officers in receipt of small salaries, and others who cannot afford to send their children to Europe, it having been the desire of Bishop Cotton to establish for the middle classes of Anglo-Indians three public schools—one of which should be at Simla—" not less secure and by God's blessing not less useful than Winchester, Rugby, and Marlborough." The school, which is capable of accommodating 150 boarders, is affiliated to the Calcutta University and prepares boys for the examinations of this University. Special effort is directed to the preparation of boys for entrance to the Roorkee Engineering College and for special examinations preceding admission to various Government departments. The students attend divine service in the School Chapel which was erected by public subscriptions. The school has always received warm support from the Punjab Government, successive Lieutenant-Governors having taken a personal interest in its affairs, and making, from time to time, in addition to the grant-in-aid admissible under the provisions of the Punjab Educational Code, substantial grants of money for the improvement of the buildings. Boys who come up to the military requirements of age and physique receive a military training in the cadet company of the Simla Volunteer Rifles.

The trustees of the school property are the Bishop and Archdeacon of Calcutta; there are four elected governors who must be residents of Simla, and four *ex-officio* governors, namely, the Lieutenant-Governor of the Punjab, the Bishop of Lahore, the Commissioner of Delhi, and the Deputy Commissioner of Simla. H. E. the Viceroy, as 'Visitor,' interprets the school statutes in case of any dispute and takes measures for their observance, his decision on any point of interpretation being final. The headmasters have been the Rev. S. Slater, 1863—1885; the Rev. H. M. Robinson, 1885-1886; the Rev. E. A. Irons, 1886-1901; and since that date the Rev. H. M. Lewis. On the 17th September 1903, Founders' Day, Lord Curzon presided at the annual distribution of prizes. After delivering a highly interesting speech on European schools in India he said that "not a single lad who is worthy of his salt need despair of getting creditable and remunerative employment." Lord Curzon concluded his impressive and eloquent speech with words that should remain engraved on the heart of every Bishop Cotton School boy,—"When you go out into the world do nothing without an object. Have an object in your work, have an object in your play, let there be an object in your heart where your emotions are supposed to be—in your mind with which you think and in your soul where is the touch-stone of right and wrong. Life without an object is as cold as a furnace without fire—is as empty as a religion without a God. When you are successful it will be because you have pursued an object. When you fail sit down and create for yourself the object you have hitherto ignored."

The Masonic Lodge Himalayan Brotherhood, the oldest and largest Lodge in the Punjab, and the first established in the Himalayas, was founded in 1838 by Messrs. G. L. Hoff, H. G. Goulard, R. B. Macdonald (a leading tradesman), and Mr. Henry Torrens, Secretary to the Government. On St. John's Day, the 24th June 1839, the members of the Lodge assembled at the Royal (now Lowrie's) Hotel, and marched in a procession to church, where a sermon was preached by the Chaplain and a collection was made for charitable purposes. The Governor-General allowed the use of his band for the occasion, and French's journal of 1838-39 has left it on record that "the music afforded great èclat to this novel scene in the hills. The natives and others thronged in numbers to witness it, some called us 'Jagoodurs' or magicians, and others with equal wisdom and sagacity said we must have dealings with the devil!" The 'Royal' was utilised for the meetings of the Lodge until a Masonic building was erected on the cart road, and here dances and other convivial meetings were also held. The old Masonic Lodge is now a part of the Government Press, and the meetings of the Craft have for some years been held in their subterranean rooms at the Town Hall, which is a much more convenient centre. In addition to the Himalayan Brotherhood Lodge, a Mark Lodge, and a Royal Ark Mariner, and a Royal Arch Chapter 'Dalhousie' hold their meetings in the Masonic Hall, as do also the Knights Templar and Knights of Malta belonging to the Himalayan Preceptory. The Sovereign Princes of the Order of Rose Croix of Heredom or the 18 also hold meetings in the same hall.

Many prominent citizens and officials have been members of the local Lodge, and its list of past Masters includes the names of H. G. Goulard, J. T. Giels, J. G. W. Curtis, G. Cox, J. B. Dodd, J. J. Marshall, J. S.

MAIN BLOCK, BISHOP COTTON SCHOOL.

Chisholm, H. A. Ebden, S. W. Ferguson, J. Mackenzie, G. Jeffery, Lord W. M. Hay, H. Tapp, W. A. Hoghton, T. Fleming, M. Clarke, T. Wood, W. B. Grant, T. E. Cooke, T. M. Bleckley, Colonel Gardiner, W. Ball, H. R. Cooke, A. Litster, F. Von Goldstein, J. Robertson, W. C. Willson, J. K. Rawlins, G. H. M. Batten, J. Phelps, B. L. Freeman, Colonel Sanford, Dr. R. Worsley, W. P. Carson, H. P. Burt, J. Burt, R. A. English, E. van S. Cullin, J. McDermott, General Sir E. H. H. Collen, H. Elkington, R. Burton, Sir A. Miller, R. Watson, A. B. Patterson, W. Alves, Colonel A. E. Sandbach, G. H. C. Anderson, Colonel C. P. Lukis, and J. B. D'Silva.

The present Master is Mr. E. O. Wilsey, Adjutant-General's Department.

For many years past the Freemasons have given an annual installation banquet in June and a ball at the Town Hall in September, the latter being invariably attended by the Viceroy, the Lieutenant-Governor, Members of Council, and other distinguished guests. The archives of the Lodge are not conclusive as to the date of the first banquet, but there is little doubt it has been a recognized function since 1838. The ball has been regularly given since 1873, and may also have been held in previous years. It is one of the most brilliant functions of the Simla season, as the Viceroy and his wife are given full Masonic honours both on arrival and departure, and there is always a big gathering of Masons from other Indian Lodges for the event. Since Lord Kitchener's arrival in Simla a new Lodge, entitled the 'Kitchener,' has been organized, which with Colonel J. Shearer, I.M.S., as its first master, already enrolls a goodly number of members.

One of the principal events of a Simla season is the Fine Arts Exhibition. The Fine Arts Society, which sprang into existence in 1865, held their first show in September of that year in the present Bishop Cotton School, when nearly five hundred exhibits were displayed. In the following year the Exhibition was held in Auckland House, with Lord Mayo as President, on 24th September, when the exhibits reached 600 in number. In the 'Story of my Life' Sir Richard Temple wrote of the year 1868: "In art work I found indeed congenial spirits. There was a galaxy of amateur talent in water-colour painting then at Simla. Who that beheld them can forget the productions of Colonel Walter Fane, of Colonel (now Sir Michael) Biddulph, of Major (now Sir Peter) Lumsden, of Colonel Strutt or Major Baigree, of Captain Strahan, of Colonel (now Sir Richard) Sankey." In 1876 the Exhibition was held in 'Oakover,' and Lord Lytton who opened it made the following remarks at the conclusion of his speech:

"But I must apologise, ladies and gentlemen, for the length at which I have detained your attention. A poet has said that art is long, but life is short, and really life is much too short for long discourses upon art. There is a pretty aphorism by an old Latin philosopher that poetry is vocal painting, painting mute poetry. I think that aphorism exceedingly pretty, but don't think it quite true. All good has a tense and articulate language of its own, and the most and the utmost we can any of us say about it, or of it, is much less to the point than what it can say for itself.

"You may perhaps, remember, ladies and gentlemen, that when the Greek orator Hyperides was defending the cause of the beautiful Phryne it occurred to him that the best way of winning that cause would be to cease speaking and unveil his client. He did so, and at once the judges became her admirers. Allow me to imitate that wise example. Allow me to cease speaking, and unveil my client—in other words, to declare this Exhibition open."

Lord Lytton contributed to the show a copy painted by himself of Titian's 'Peraro Madonna' in the Frari Chapel at Venice. In the following year the Exhibition was held in 'Inverarm,' and in 1878 the ball-room of the Assembly Rooms was lent for the occasion, Lord Lytton making another felicitous speech.

Since 1887 the Exhibition has been held in the Town Hall, and has almost invariably been opened by the Viceroy, or in his absence by the Lieutenant-Governor of the Punjab. In speaking at the opening on 18th September 1885, Lord Dufferin said he could not help expressing his surprise that there should not exist in India a more favourable field for the exertions of the professional artist, and remarked that if a real and genuine love of art were widely diffused among our wealthier Indian fellow subjects, a highly honourable, lucrative, and useful career would be opened to hundreds and hundreds of aspiring young men, whether as painters, engravers, sculptors, architects, designers, illuminators, enamellers or otherwise. In 1893 the Exhibition was opened by Lady Lansdowne, Lieutenant-General H. Brackenbury making a speech on her behalf. Lord Elgin and Lord Curzon have since discontinued the practice of making speeches at the opening.

About eighteen years ago a clever skit on the Simla Picture Show, supposed to have been contributed by Rudyard Kipling, appeared in the *Pioneer*. Many officials were humorously chaffed, and the following are not the least amusing: "Mr. C. P. I....t's (now Sir C. P. Ilbert) 'There's no place like home,' though a palpable plagiarism from Sir E. Landseer, will, it is to be feared, be caviare to the general. A soft eyed wombat has apparently strayed from its home in the Zoological Gardens, and on a grey cold morning presents itself at the door of its cage, a comfortable nest enough from which it is not likely to run away again.

"A grand subject by the same is 'Better fifty years of Europe than a cycle of Cathay.' All that is seen in this ultra Whistlerian canvas is the stern of a P. and O. steamer looming through the fog.

"Just before his departure to England Mr. D. M. B.. ..r (now Sir D. M. Barbour) completed a perspective drawing of the greatest interest described as the vanishing point. In the far distance is a rupee dim and minute, and by an ingenious arrangement of lines, which has all the relation of a picture, and all the force of a geometrical diagram, the gradual steps of the most distressing disappearance of modern times are fully explained. Too many modern painters neglect perspective. This scientific though painful study should convince them of their error."

In 1890 a clever little book of skits was published on the Fine Arts show of that year, and copies were freely sold at a bazaar which Lady Roberts organised for her 'Homes in the Hills.' These skits were the production of Lieutenant F. C. Colomb, 44th Gurkhas, and Lieutenant Cardew, 10th Bengal Lancers, and the edition was very quickly sold out, bringing in a handsome sum. For four years following, books of skits were produced and sold at the Fine Arts show, many of the best being the work of Captain (now Colonel) G. S. Ommaney, whose talent as an artist is well known in Northern India. The preface in the volume for 1894 ran as follows: "Charity is said to cover a multitude of sins, and the fact that the proceeds of this little book are from year to year devoted to charitable purposes, is the only apology the authors have to offer for its production." In order to allay suspicion, those who were responsible for the skits were often extremely severe on each other's pictures.

The value of the money prizes offered annually for competition amounts to something over R2,000, about one-fourth of this sum being found by the Society, while the remainder is contributed by various individuals in Simla. Pictures are sent in for competition from all parts of India, and sometimes from home, to the number generally of about 700. Of late years, the committee have attempted, with much success, to raise the standard of exhibits by judicious rejections. Among recent winners of the Viceroy's gold medal have been Mrs. Barber, Captain Molyneux (twice), Mr. R. D. Mackenzie, Mr. F. Swynnerton, the two latter gentlemen being professional artists. The Lieutenant-Governor's prize has been won by Mrs. Barber, Captain Molyneux, Colonel E. R. Penrose and Colonel Ommaney, and the Commander-in-Chief's prize by Colonel Hobday, Colonel Ommaney (twice), and Captain Molyneux. Prizes for the best water colour in the Exhibition have fallen to Colonel Strahan, Mrs. Cunliffe, Miss H. Supple, Mr. G. A. Anderson, and Mrs. Arthur Waterfield.

Few pictures perhaps of recent years have attracted more attention than those of Mr. R. D. Mackenzie, the distinguished artist who has been commissioned by the Government of India to paint the official picture of the State entry at the Delhi Durbar of 1903. 'Our Restless Neighbours' and 'the Baluchis,' exhibited in Simla in 1899 and 1900, were both splendid paintings, and were a marked feature of the Paris Salon in 1901. Among other noticeable productions may be included Mrs. Gauntlett's 'Festival at Hyderabad,' Portrait of the Maharaj-Kumar of Sikkim by Mrs. E. A. Newton, 'The Lower Bazaar, Murree' by Mrs. Williamson, 'A Cornish Cliff' by L. de Renault, 'Atlantic Breakers' by Captain Molyneux, and 'A Portrait (pastel)' by Mrs. Moylan.

Besides those already mentioned, there are many others who have won prizes and honourable mention for excellent work at the Simla show, among whom may be named Colonels Tanner, Donne, Hart, and Supple, Major Colomb, Messrs. W. Poole, R. Graham, Mesdames Latimer, Cowper, W. Beadon, Cunliffe, and Aker. Prominent among professional artists have been Misses McCracken, A Smedley, and N. Haddow; Mr. Dudley Severn (President of the Irish Water Colour Society), Messrs. Alex. Caddy, Percy Brown, F. A. Grace, and Pithawala.

The onerous post of Honorary Secretary was held by Major J. Day, R.E., in 1896—99; by Mr. E. Harvey in 1899—1901; and by Major M. Cowper from 1901—04.

For the existence of the Ripon Hospital, the native community of Simla are in the main indebted to Mr. A. O. Hume and Sir Benjamin Franklin, Director-General of the Indian Medical Service. Prior to the year 1882, at which time Dr. Franklin was Civil Surgeon of Simla, the existing hospital accommodation was wholly inadequate and a standing reproach to the summer capital of the Government. For European patients there was no hospital accommodation at all; while the buildings available for the native population were in the midst of most unhealthy surroundings. The Simla Municipal Committee, however, on the 21st of September 1882, appointed a sub-committee consisting of Mr. A. O. Hume, Surgeon-General Townsend, Inspector-General of Civil Hospitals, Punjab, Mr. J. Elston, a leading resident of Simla, Mr. (now Sir James) Walker, Lala Ram Narain, and Surgeon-Major (now Sir Benjamin) Franklin, Civil Surgeon, to deal with the question, and on the 20th of the following month the foundation stone of the hospital, known as the 'Ripon,' was laid by the Marquis of Ripon in the presence of a large crowd of Europeans and Natives. A guard-of-honour of the Simla Volunteers under Captain F. Leigh, together with detachments of Gurkhas and Pioneers, was on the ground. Mr. Hume and Dr. Franklin, who had been appointed respectively President and Secretary of the Committee, were indefatigable in prosecuting the scheme. Subscriptions came in freely, and on the 14th May 1885 the hospital was declared open by Lord Dufferin. The results thus achieved were described by the correspondent of the *Bombay Gazette* who wrote: "Lady Ripon proposed the hospital, Mr. A. O. Hume gathered the subscriptions, Mr. H. Irwin designed the buildings which Mr. Campion and Mr. Learmouth have built, and Dr. B. Franklin, our Civil Surgeon, has been the presiding genius of the whole. From the 1st May 1885 neither European nor Native need remain sick or sorry for want of proper attendance and accommodation, and the ancient stye which has hitherto done duty for an hospital may be devoted to its original pigs." The Ripon Hospital is on a spur on the southern slope of the hills about the centre of the station, is conveniently situated for the inhabitants of the bazaar and commands glimpses of the beautiful valley to the south of Simla, and also of Kasauli, Sabathu, and the plains in clear weather. The ground on which the hospital is constructed was given by the Municipality, and comprises former estates known as 'the Briars' and 'Glen Cottage,' valued in the seventies at Rs. 30,000. Both these houses were burnt down in 1881. The other principal subscribers were Lord Ripon, the Maharajas of Vizianagram, Patiala, Dholpore, Kotah, Travancore, Durbhanga, Jodhpur, and Kashmir, the Nawab of Bahawalpore, and the Maharani Surnomoyee of Murshidabad. Numerous other Native Chiefs and European and Native gentlemen also subscribed liberally to the building fund, and the actual amount collected was Rs. 1,47,184.

For the much appreciated Walker Hospital, the European population of Simla in particular, and of the Punjab in general, are indebted to the initiative of Surgeon-General Sir Benjamin Franklin and to the generosity of Sir James Lewis Walker.

In May 1899 General Franklin, when Inspector-General of Civil Hospitals in the Punjab, visited the Ripon Hospital and found that the native patients had been ousted from four of their wards, in order to provide room for the increasing number of Europeans who came to the hospital for admission. The accommodation remaining for natives was not sufficient for the pressing requirements of Simla, and as the Ripon Hospital was primarily intended for natives, General Franklin suggested to the Punjab Government the appointment of an *ex-officio* committee to consider the question, and proposed 'Gorton Castle' as the most suitable house for a sanitarium. 'Gorton Castle' was then the property of Mr. J. L. Walker. Immediately on hearing of the condition of affairs in the Ripon Hospital, and of the recommendations submitted to the Punjab Government, Mr. Walker replied to overtures made for the purchase or lease of 'Gorton Castle' with a telegram which ran: "I make a free gift to Simla of 'Gorton Castle' for a hospital for European and Eurasian patients."

The gift was a noble one, and was accepted with gratitude by the residents of Simla. But 'Gorton Castle' was after all not destined to become a refuge for European invalids. In view of the objections raised to the location of a hospital on the main mall, the Managing Committee re-sold the property for Rs. 1,20,000 to the Government of India as a site for new civil offices, and obtained another plot of ground, where the Walker Hospital now stands, as a free gift from the Punjab Government, who also subscribed Rs. 40,000 to the building fund. The hospital was opened on the 1st May 1902, and has accommodation for 20 patients. As the hospital is self-supporting, having no income other than the fees paid by the patients, in order that Europeans who could not afford to pay Rs. 5 a day should not be debarred from its advantages, Lady Franklin founded the 'Lady Franklin's Free Bed Fund,' which pays the whole, or a portion of the fees, according to the circumstances of the patient. It had been a special condition of Mr. Walker's generous gift that accommodation should be provided for poor Europeans.

There is no more popular or interesting event of the Simla season, than that of the Durand Football Tournament, which is usually held towards the end of September. It was instituted by Sir H. Mortimer Durand, who, when Foreign Secretary to the Government of India, in 1888, presented a challenge trophy to be played for annually in Simla. In 1889 the tournament was placed under the direction of a committee of management, of which Sir H. M. Durand became the first President, being represented during his absence from Simla by his brother, Colonel A. G. A. Durand.

In 1888 six teams competed, the Royal Scots Fusiliers (21st) being winners, and the Highland Light Infantry (74th) the runners up. The Royal Scots Fusiliers again won the cup in 1891 and 1892.

In 1895 the cup passed permanently into the hands of the Highland Light Infantry, who by brilliant play had won three years in succession.

The trophy was at once replaced by Sir M. Durand and again won outright by the Black Watch (42nd) in 1899. In 1900 Sir Edwin Collen, Military Member of Council, accepted the post of President of the Committee, and he was succeeded by his official successor, Sir Edmund Elles, in 1901. It was during this year that Sir M. Durand suggested to the Committee that as he had now permanently left India the present trophy would be the last he would present, and that the cup should be made an annual challenge cup, which could never be permanently won, while a smaller one should be given for retention by the winning team. This suggestion was accepted, and the smaller cup has since been generously presented by Sir E. Elles, who has intimated his intention of presenting it as long as he is associated with the tournament. Besides these trophies the Committee give a small silver goblet to the captain, silver medals to each member of the winning team, and bronze medals to the runners up.

The tournament is deservedly supported by public subscriptions, for it is quite the most sporting event of a Simla season. For a considerable time Captain E. Weston, Simla Volunteers, took an active part in its management, while of recent years the post of Honorary Secretary has been filled by Captain C. C. Onslow. For the last five seasons the duties of referee have been admirably performed by Captain C. Wigram, A.-D.-C.

CHAPTER VII.

Annandale.

THERE is possibly no name connected with Simla which to thousands of Anglo-Indians, past and present, can revive more memories of a pleasant nature than that of Annandale. This must be my excuse for dealing at length with the history of this well-known play-ground.

In an article published in the East Indian United Service Journal in July 1834 Mr. William de Rhé Philipe, afterwards the first Assistant Judge Advocate-General of the Bengal Army, in alluding to Annandale, wrote, "Beyond the glen is a small patch of table-land about a quarter of a mile in circumference, and a village called Khytoo containing 30 houses. Annandale will ever remain celebrated as the spot where a fancy fair and *fête champêtre* were held in September 1833, for the purpose of instituting a school at Subathoo for the instruction of native females. On that occasion the place was thronged with the inhabitants temporary and constant of Simla, the sale produced near Rs. 900, and after its conclusion a collation was served up, and the visitors returned to their homes."

The Annandale of Great Britain is I believe a little valley in Dumfries-shire, whence came the Hope Johnstones and several other families well known in the Indian service. The Marquis of Annandale of olden times was a Johnstone. As Mr. Philipe in 1834 calls the Simla valley Annandale who shall say that this name was not bestowed by some Scotchman to whom the place recalled some real or fancied resemblance to the dale of his own loved land.

Or was it a lady with the Christian name of Anna after whom the now famous recreation ground of Simla was called ? I ask the question, because in 'Views of India chiefly among the Himalaya Mountains' published in 1838 by Lieutenant G. E. White, 31st Foot, afterwards Colonel White, and for forty years Chief Constable of Durham, we find the following remarks :—

" Simla is often, when visited by the rich and the fashionable portion of the Company's civil and military servants, the scene of great gaiety. During the sojourn of Lady Barnes and Lady Bryant, a fancy-fair was held in a romantic glen, named Annandale from the lady who first graced its solitude. The talents of both ladies and gentlemen were put into requisition to furnish drawings and fancy articles of every kind, while there were many goods for sale, for use as well as ornament ; the proceeds being collected in aid of a native school, to be established at Subathoo, for the purpose of

Reproduced from "Simla," by Captain G. P. Thomas.

FANCY FAIR AT ANNANDALE, 1839.

affording mental instruction, needle-work, and other useful arts, to the female Goorka children; a boys' school at the same place having been found to answer. A fête of this nature seemed particularly adapted both to the features of the scene, and the talents of the subordinates employed: native genius always appearing to great advantage in the open air, tents were pitched amid the pine-groves of this romantic spot, and the interiors spread with productions of great taste and elegance, drawings and sketches of the magnificent scenery around, forming a very appropriate contribution. The most interesting, however, of the numerous objects of interest was a profusion of garlands, wreathed of the flowers of the Himalaya, and brought to the fair by the first class of the boys of the Subathoo school, attended by the old 'gooroo,' their superintendent. These were offerings of gratitude to the ladies who had so benevolently sought to extend the advantages of instruction to the whole of the native community, whether male or female, who were so fortunate as to be within the circle of their influence. Between seventy and eighty pounds were collected, very high prices having been cheerfully given for the articles put up for sale, the drawings especially being in great demand."

In support too of the fact that the public play-ground of Simla derived its name from some fair lady it may be noted that Captain George Powell Thomas of the 64th Bengal Infantry, writing in 1846, has several allusions to *Anna* dale, both in his letter-press and in connection with his sketches. I have also found in the 'Complete Guide to Simla and its neighbourhood' (a small book published after 1881) the following paragraph:—"Colonel Faddy, who was so long a resident at Simla, tells us the origin of the gardens. He says—You have omitted a little story about *Annadale* which touches in romance. It is misnamed Annandale. The story as told me some ten years ago (in 1861) by Major Wight of the late 4th Bengal Cavalry (Lancers) is as follows:—Major Kennedy I believe the first political agent, and one of the first explorers of these hills, was so struck with the beauty of the valley that he named it after a young lady to whom in his boyish days he was attached at home, whose first name was Anna, hence the name of Dale. Major Wight has known Simla since its formation."

Another early mention of Annandale occurs in the journal of Mr. C. S. French (1838-39) whose description of an Annandale fair of sixty-five years ago is worth quoting:—

"There was a fancy fair at Annandale," he wrote, "after the style of all fancy fairs with which Christians have anything to do. The one in the hills had the advantage of a peculiar locality which added a charm to it which I have not elsewhere witnessed. If one can pourtray to his imagination a tolerably large dell shaded by the pine and fir, with a semi-circular amphitheatre of hills and a somewhat comparatively level spot of a few acres in extent lying below, one may form an idea of the Annandale valley as it is popularly termed. The dell itself is composed, as I have said, partly of a level spot of ground generally under cultivation in the month of September, and partly overshadowed by a grove of tall pines. On this picturesque site were erected about eight or ten neatly decorated pavilions. These were arranged so as to surround three sides of a quadrangle, the fourth being left open for egress and ingress. The open space on the opposite side of a pathway was faced by a line of tents thrown together, forming one canopy under which luncheon, in its hundred varieties, was enjoyed for a trifle. A vast collection of fancy articles were here exhibited for the ends of charity, and reflected infinite credit on the benevolence and industry of the ladies and gentlemen who so humanely and readily contributed towards so good a purpose. It would be impracticable to detail the pretty commodities which took their places here. All that silk, satin, lace and embroidery, with their manifold concomitants, could produce, were laid out in elegant style, and the rapidity with which the whole or the greatest part of them were sold by the evening showed the merits attending these manufactures.

"Each stall had an appropriate designation after fancy, and a reverend gentleman established a picture gallery in miniature. Noted as an amateur painter, he took the opportunity of making a goodly display of all his best productions and of such others as were in his possession. It was a fine collection and well worth seeing, and not among the least was an encased panorama of Simla itself.

"While these characterised the internal attractions of the tents, the external bustle of the scene was varied and enlivened by the presence of mock gipsies who went about singing and begging in tattered raiments. Postmen were seen distributing letters and newspapers, and other characters were equally well sustained on the occasion, to say nothing of the recruiting officer who, followed by a fifer and drummer, went beating about for volunteers. Skittle playing, quoits, sword-fights and wrestling added much to the amusements of the day. Sections of Gurkha sepoys were likewise drawn up in another part to shoot at a given mark, which was a brass vessel of twelve or thirteen inches in circumference, stuck up on a small pole. Those who succeeded in hitting the object carried away sundry prizes. Kookries or Nepaulese daggers formed two of them, one richly set in silver with a velvet sheath; the other, though ill-sheathed, being a valuable blade once belonging to the late Bheem Sein Thappa of Nepaul. In 1838 the gifts were a silver lota or drinking vessel, a powder flask made of the same metal and two or three good swords, besides sums of money. The Gurkhas were proud of these trophies (for they were presented by the Governor-General and the

Reproduced from "Simla, | by Captain G. P. Thomas.

RACE COURSE AT ANNANDALE, ABOUT 1840.

Commander-in-Chief in person) and bore them away as flattering tokens of their steady aim. The last, though not least of this scene of ephemeral attractions, were the races. Amateur jockeys, bedecked in all the colours of the rainbow, acquitted themselves in style. The race course was about a mile and a half in circumference round a field on the table-land of the Annandale dell.

"Annandale is frequently resorted to by pic-nic parties. Its retired situation renders such parties extremely pleasant, blended as it is with other advantages of a local nature. There is a small but neat Hindu shrine of worship at the place constructed principally of wood with a profusion of carved work peculiar to the taste of the hillmen. It is now considered a spot of little or no sanctity if I may judge from the paucity of its visitors. It is possible that the former supplicants at this temple of idolatry are kept back from a silly prejudice that the presence of the Christian pollutes and desecrates their places of prayer."

Thus also wrote Miss Eden in her diary of April 19, 1839:—

"Our Aide-de-Camp gave a small *fête champêtre* yesterday in a valley called Annandale. The party, consisting of six ladies and six gentlemen, began at ten in the morning and actually lasted till half-past nine at night. Annandale is a thick grove of fir trees, which no sun can pierce. They had bows and arrows, a swing, battledore and shuttlecock, and a fiddle, the only one in Simla; and they danced and ate all day and seem to have enjoyed it all throughout wonderfully." Apparently the picnic was much appreciated, for a second, including yet another fancy sale, took place a few days later beginning at seven in the morning and lasting till eleven at night.

On May 24, 1839, the Viceregal dance in honour of the Queen's birthday was actually held at Annandale, for the Hon'ble Emily Eden wrote on 25th May:—"The Queen's ball came off yesterday with great success. I went down by myself to Annandale on Thursday evening to see how things were going on there. It was a very pretty fête; we built one temporary sort of room which held fifty people. I and ten others dined in two large tents on the opposite side of the road, but we were all close together and drank the Queen's health at the same moment with much cheering. Between the two tents, there was a boarded platform for dancing, roped and arched in with flowers and then in different parts of the valley, wherever the trees would allow of it there was 'Victoria,' 'God save the Queen,' and 'Candahar' in immense letters twelve feet high. . . . We dined at six, then had fireworks and coffee, and then they all danced till twelve. It was a most beautiful evening, such a moon, and the mountains looked so soft and grave after all the fireworks and glare.

"Twenty years ago no European had ever been here, and there we were, with the band playing the 'Puritani' and 'Masaniello' and eating salmon from Scotland, and sardines from the Mediterranean, and observing that St. Cloud's potage à la Julienne was perhaps better than his other soups . . . and all this in the face of those high hills some of which have remained untrodden since the creation, and we one hundred and five Europeans being surrounded by at least three thousand mountaineers, who wrapped in their hill blankets looked on at what we call our polite amusements, and bowed to the ground if a European came near them."

The proceeds of the sale were Rs. 3,400, twenty drawings by the Hon'ble Emily Eden fetching Rs. 800, while her stall produced nearly Rs. 1,400. As the best fancy sales in Calcutta in that day never raised more than Rs. 2,000, and as there were only one hundred and fifty Europeans then in Simla, the result was considered highly satisfactory.

The Hon'ble Emily Eden has left it on record that at the second fancy fair on 25th September 1839, X. and L. and a Captain C. were disguised as gipsies, the most villainous looking set possible, who sang songs and told fortunes; while two of her pictures raffled at three rupees a ticket fetched £75. . . . . L. E. was old Weller; and so disguised she could not recognise him; X. was Sam Weller; R., Tingle; and Captain C., Mrs. Weller; Z., merely a waiter, but all acted up to their character and the luncheon was very good. Altogether the fair produced Rs. 6,500, or enough to keep the hospital going for four years, by which time, Miss Eden reckoned that another Governor-General would be in Simla.

An allusion to the Annandale fancy fair is embodied in some amusing remarks on Simla society in Captain G. P. Thomas' book of about the same date. "Simla," writes Captain Thomas in 1839, is "indifferent stupid for the first few weeks, for, despite the maxim that everybody knows everybody, nobody knows anybody for about that time, and society is accordingly as stiff and hollow, if not quite as deceptive as a horsehair petticoat. But towards the end of the season, just when it is time perhaps to bid an eternal farewell people get up an eternal friendship, all becomes holiday costume; and what with balls, races, pic-nics and exploring parties, we prove our belief, that it is the business of true wisdom to enjoy the present moment, and let care go hang herself in her garters. Then come on (or come off, which is it?) at the same time, the races at Annandale, the race ball and the fancy fair. The fancy fair takes place between the first and second days of the races, and affords very good sport in its way. The season and the scene are alike delightful. The rains are just over, the air is once more dry and bracing, the sky is clear, the sun not warm, and nature is looking more charming than ever in her new green dress; moreover, half the pretty women in Simla are established in their stalls selling their wares for *less than nothing*. And (to be guilty of an anti-climax) still further in 'the merry green wood' stands a most spacious tent, to which a *posse* of butlers and khidmatgars are perpetually running with goodly freights of champagne, and no end to hams and patties, so that they bid fair to have 'that within which passeth show,' when one is tired of being actor or sufferer, seller or buyer.

"The accompanying drawing (here Captain Thomas alludes to his sketch) is an attempt to commemorate one of the very best of these charitable and social meetings. It was that of 1839, when Lord Auckland and his fair sisters added materially, by their kindness and hospitality, to the gaiety and sociability of Simla. But it is high time to say a few words about our *dramatis personæ*, as well as about the scene itself. Of the 'scenery' it may be proper to explain that the house, or toll-bar of charity, is made of canvas, and both *that* and the magpie and cage on the wall beside the window were *painted* for the occasion. Sam Weller is one of Lord Auckland's Aide-de-Camps; Mr. Pickwick is a portly doctor! the Dragoon and Hussar are officers in the Sikh service of that day (one French, the other English); and it may be seen, in spite of her petticoats, that even our gipsy girl wears the breeches."

I can discover no record of any fancy fair having been held at Annandale in any recent year, and perhaps a revival of the old custom in aid of our station charities, is an idea that Simla philanthropists of the future may like to consider.

The picnics and fairs of the earlier period were held on the small level space under the deodars at the back of the present club-house. Later on it became customary to hold picnics under some beautiful walnuts and willows that stood on the north-eastern end of what is now the cricket and polo ground inside the race-course.

In October 1845, Prince Waldemar of Prussia, accompanied by the Counts Grubbe and Orisk, and Dr. W. Hoffmeister, visited Simla, travelling in from the inner hills Numberless balls, dinners and fêtes were given in his honour, attentions which the Prince returned by a brilliant *fête champêtre* at Annandale. "On a large floor, laid with cloth which was arranged in the centre of the lawn, before three spacious tents hanging with elegant drapery, dancing was carried on, and the collation—the so-called 'tiffin'—was served in the middle tent." As the evening closed in, hundreds of lamps are said to have been suspended to every branch and twig forming a brilliant magic illumination. The splendour of this fête, we are told, won a great and far-spread fame.

It was apparently in 1847 that a scheme for public or municipal gardens was initiated under the superintendence of Dr. Jameson of the Saharanpur Botanical Gardens. Mr. W. H. Carey, in his guide to Simla (1870), however, states that Colonel McMurdo laid out the gardens in 1852, and the same authority says that it was once intended to affiliate them with the Agricultural Society of the Punjab in order to form a collection of indigenous alpine trees and to distribute the better sort of grafted fruit and timber trees to the neighbouring ranges of hills. This latter function, it may here be said, is performed by the municipal orchards on the Mahasu ridge in the catchment area which really owe their origin to the efforts of Sir Edward Buck, who from 1881 to 1896 held the post of secretary to the Government of India in the revenue and agricultural department, and who was one of the first officials to advocate general fruit-growing in the Himalayas.

Through his influence Mr. A. Parsons, one of the Kew gardeners attached to Lord Mayo's cotton commission, was brought to Simla in the early eighties and placed in charge of the orchards and of the Annandale gardens by the municipality. Mr. Parsons, whose employment continued for some fifteen years, lived in the present club-house and did much to improve flower cultivation and road-side arboriculture in the station, until in 1896 the municipal committee under Colonel John Robertson's guidance perhaps unwisely dispensed with Mr. Parsons' services. He then, with Sir Edward Buck's assistance, established himself at Hazelmere on Summer Hill where his orchards and conservatories, managed as they are by professional skill, have supplanted the Annandale gardens which have now been definitely closed by the municipality.

In connection with fruit-growing it is interesting to learn, on the authority of Lieutenant G. E. White, already mentioned, that the first English apple tree imported into India was taken to Mussoorie. "This plant came from Liverpool and proved the only one which survived the long journey to the upper provinces of India, whence being transferred to the hills, it was preserved from the heat and rain of the plains, which are found so destructive to European plants. This single apple tree cost upwards of £70, before it was planted in the botanic garden at Mussoorie where it flourishes luxuriantly, and will, in all probability, be the means of bringing its congeners of the hill to perfection."

To return, however, to Annandale. In 1847 a cricket ground was also laid out and the race-course improved. The descending road was then terribly steep, but in 1877-78 the 23rd Pioneers constructed the broad road through the forest which is now used by nearly all who are in the habit of making frequent journeys down the hill.

In May 1851 there was a flower fête at Annandale, which is thus described in the 'Delhi Sketch Book' by one Stiggins, who wrote from the Hovel, Simla, on 21st May:—

The Annandale Fête.

Air—The Mistletoe Bough.

The morning was warm, and the sun shining bright,
And the company teeming with joy and delight;
The gardens were deck'd in gorgeous array,
The ladies, like flowers, were blooming and gay;
The Malees and Dalees were waiting to be
Beprais'd and bepriz'd by the great committee.
But alas! that sage council, so careless and free,
Had forgotten refreshment for their companie,
Oh! the Annandale Fête! Oh! the Annandale Fête!

The bandboys were blowing their hardest they say,
And at "I Puritani" too-tooing away,
The Jampanees listening very intent,
Wondering what all the tamasha meant,
When a rather stout gentleman rush'd from the crowd
And shouted in voice both discordant and loud,
"Why here's a nice go! Here's the devil to pay,
I shan't get a morsel of tiffin to-day."
Oh! the Annandale Fête! Oh! the Annandale Fête!

The president winced, the committee looked blue,
As did all the hungry spectators there too.
The wearied and hunger'd look'd wretched and wan,
And testily snappish as hungry folks can—
For, barring a sluppy unwholesome affair
Call'd ice, in a degchee, no refreshment was there,
And one or two picnic feasts scattered about,
Seem'd mocking unfortunates, "going without."
Oh! the Annandale Fête! Oh! the Annandale Fête!

The flowers were fading, the band waxing warm,
And the sky became cloudy, portending a storm,
The Redowa's last notes, mingled with the warm air,
And by five, very few of the guests linger'd there.
The natives, poor wretches, who "tom-tom'd" had been,
So far from their homes, scarce could hide their chagrin
For they came to see much, and to benefit more,
But they vow'd they had never been sold so before.
Oh! the Annandale Fête! Oh! the Annandale Fête

Moral.

Now all sage committee men, take my advice,
When you get up a flower fête, provide something nice;
Be sure that, however the flowers may tell,
To the eye, that the body must be fed as well;
Be careful, that whenever Englishmen meet,
They never depart, without something to eat.
For success in such things on this adage depends,
"Good viands and wine to good fellowship tends."
Oh! the Annandale Fête! Oh! the Annandale Fête!

Mr. W. H. Carey also informs us that in 1869 were held a flower show and a dog show, which were well attended, and another poet who was moved to express his feelings in verse then wrote :—

"The tent is filled with flowers from roof to floor,
Creepers its very pillars are enwreathing,
And through the shrubs about the open door,
A soft low breeze is blowing.
It toys with tendril, blossom and green leaf,
It lifts long curls and flutters floating dresses
Of dainty damsels: Zephyr, the winged thief,
Woos with his sly caresses
And oh so rare, so beautiful are they,
The blossoms and the beauties in the bower;
Vainly of either would the heart essay
To choose the fairest flower."

In 1869 there is also a record of an archery society which used to hold regular annual meetings at Annandale, and in the year mentioned the competition among the fair sex was very keen. The names of the winners cannot be traced, but two prizes were presented by the Maharaja of Jeypore, two by the Simla cricket club, and three season prizes by the society.

In the sixties croquet made its appearance in the hills and became quite a fashionable game at Annandale. Mr. William Taylor, the author of 'Thirty-eight years in India' has left it on record that "it was delightful to see Sir John Lawrence with other high and mighty statesmen, at the close of a laborious day, entering with the zest of boys into the intricacies of the laborious game."

On the 8th May 1886 Lady Dufferin in 'Our Viceregal Life in India' notes that—"The gymkhana to-day was a very amusing one. The commander-in-chief (Sir Frederick Roberts) led off with tent pegging, and himself won the prize amid the cheers of the bystanders. There was a little steeple-

ANNANDALE FROM THE MALL, 1893.

chase in which all the horses went the wrong side of the jumps, and ran up banks which were off the course and behaved generally in a frolicsome manner. Then three buckets were laid down, and, gentlemen on horseback tried to drop potatoes into them as they rode by at a gallop, and never succeeded. The prettiest race of all was a tandem race, riding one and driving another pony in front. The three couples kept very evenly together and the finish was most exciting."

Again on October 15th, 1887, Lady Dufferin continues :—

"Our last dissipation in Simla was a very amusing gymkhana for which we stayed at home one day longer than we had intended. There was to be a ladies' hack race, and the exciting part of it was that a gentleman had presented Rs. 250 for a prize. Lord William appeared on Victoria's pony and easily took first place in the race and won it for her . . . . Another very amusing race was that ridden by the 'heavy' gentlemen on our staff, persons who had never ridden or won races before, Sir Donald Mackenzie Wallace on the 'Masher' fiying round the course had the best wishes of all the spectators, but he did not win. Mr. Grant carried off the cup which the staff presented to itself. Then there was a rickshaw race, and Blanche came in triumphant directing her men when to spare themselves and when to strive. The family went home happy and triumphant, and Blanche was quite as pleased at having won a pair of gloves for being last in the ladies' hack race as Victoria was with being first in it."

And on 5th June 1888 :—

"The Simla races began to-day and the weather caused everyone the greatest anxiety. Captain Burn, who had been starving for weeks and who has just reached the proper weight, is most anxious to get the races over that he may eat and drink again, and other officers who had only come to Simla on short leave bringing their race horses with them are equally fearful of their being postponed. When there has been rain here the ground gets so slippery that sharp turns on the tiny course are positively dangerous, and all the riders are nervous on that score. However, they decided to risk it, and they did manage to have two races, but during the second one a tremendous storm came on, and Captain Burn won it in a downpour. The spectators all crowded into the stand, and watched with amusement the jockeys, grooms, and natives who had no shelter. One man turned up the tails of his long coat, squatted down on his heels, and sat motionless under a thin white cotton umbrella, through which the rain came freely, for a good quarter of an hour, and until the advancing puddles invaded his toes, others got under the shamiana where the cloths on the refreshment tables had turned blue with the rain and a large party of men walked about under a long rug they had taken up from the ground. It can rain here, and you would scarcely believe how soon dry ground becomes a lake, and how the water pours off the roofs in sheets and comes out of the pipes in torrents. It was hopeless to wait till it was over, and we had to pass through some very respectable little rivers across our path as we went home."

The Simla volunteer corps, formed in 1861, has always used Annandale for its principal parades and annual sports, and in 1872 it held a camp of exercise under Colonel F. Peterson, its first commandant, on the spot then used as a croquet ground, which was also the base point of the archery competitions already referred to. The croquet ground, together with two magnificent walnut trees on it, noticeable features of the landscape, were swept away during the initial improvements by Lord William Beresford. Before these improvements were commenced the lower part of Annandale was only a huge basin in which the collection of water to a considerable depth made, after heavy rain, any use of the ground an impossibility. Up to about the year 1876 the volunteer targets had been placed on the far edge of the basin, the ranges from 100 to 600 yards running through the middle of the lower ground and gardens up to a point just under 'Arthur Villa' on the main road down to Annandale past the jail. The substitution of the 'Martini-Henri' for the old 'Enfield' necessitated the use of longer ranges and the consequent removal of the targets to their present position. The old race-course was nothing more than a hard road that ran round the outside of the gardens and pleasure ground. It had a steep and dangerous descent through the village, with an extremely sharp turn immediately behind the old volunteer rifle butts. At one race meeting a rider, with his horse, went over the wall at this angle, both being killed, and this put a temporary stop to races of importance. As early, indeed, as 1848 Dr. C. F. Francis, M.B., of the Bengal medical establishment, wrote:—"It is extraordinary that races should ever be attempted at Simla, yet they are held from year to year; and rarely does a meeting pass without some serious accident, such as a rider rolling down a precipice either with, or without, his horse into the valley below."

There are many still in India who remember the keen interest the late Lord William Beresford evinced in the racing at Annandale, and how under his management the grounds and course were steadily improved.

When military secretary to Lord Dufferin he conceived the ambitious idea of extending the ground by cutting into the hillside, so as to provide not only a larger course for racing but also a polo ground. These changes were effected at a cost of about Rs. 80,000, most of which was privately subscribed, several native chiefs who desired themselves to play polo when resident in Simla for the summer contributing handsome sums. The improvement scheme was a great success, and among other advantages brought about the playing of football in the summer capital, Sir Mortimer (then Mr.)

AN ANNANDALE GYMKHANA, 1903.

Durand inaugurating the annual tournament which still bears his name. Lord William gave the cricketers a new pavilion, and a tablet on its walls records the appreciation of the Simla public of his services in the interests of sports. He acted as honorary secretary of the general committee controlling the ground, and it was chiefly owing to his personal efforts that the transformation of Annandale was brought about. Simla will always be grateful for the great improvements that he effected. In 1896 Captain R. E. Grimston was honorary secretary of the club, and it was mainly due to his energy that some Rs. 25,000 was spent under the able direction of the late Mr. A. Younghusband, executive engineer in the Punjab, not only in cutting away a big piece of the hill and so enlarging the race-course, but also in considerably improving more than one dangerous corner.

The interest, indeed, which the members of the Viceroy's staff have ever taken in this public play-ground has been proverbial, and to Colonel the Hon'ble E. Baring, Military Secretary, and Captain C. Wigram, A.-D.-C., is due much of the marked success which has just attended the opening of the new Annandale club. The former worked out the main idea and details, and the latter undertook the post of honorary secretary. From the fact that there are already some five hundred members, of whom nearly two hundred are ladies, the popularity of the club will be understood.

A few remarks indicating the advantages of the reforms which have been recently made in the constitution of the club, will bring the history of Annandale up to date. Under the old régime there existed a general committee with an honorary secretary who derived their funds from the rents separately paid by gymkhana, polo and cricket clubs, race committee, volunteer club and new club for the use of the ground, as well as from any surplus balance that the gymkhana club or race stewards might hand over at the end of the year. The system was not altogether satisfactory. The apportioning and payment of the rent in the case of some of the clubs was always difficult, and there was no proper controlling authority to give orders to the men employed on the ground, and to check the various accounts for coolies and materials supplied. Each club ran on independent lines, and at times considerable friction resulted. Under the new scheme all this has been altered. The 'Annandale gymkhana club' has been formed, and comprehends under its management the races, gymkhanas, polo, cricket, horse and dog show, while the volunteer and new clubs pay a fixed rent for the use of the ground on certain days in the week. The Viceroy is patron of the club, which possesses a strong committee with an honorary secretary and an assistant honorary secretary. Each of the sports named above as well as the show is under the control of a separate sub-secretary who submits his accounts monthly to the honorary secretary whose sanction is required for all arrangements and expenditure. The club house, which hitherto had been occupied by the municipal gardener, was, with the grounds, secured by Colonel Baring when the gardens were closed, and is now used to great advantage for breakfasts, picnic lunches, and teas for which formerly private arrangements had to be made. Colonel Baring too effected many improvements in the house and grounds, including the erection of a kiosk.

Among other improvements may be noticed the sloping on the railroad principle at the dangerous corners of the race course with the result that accidents have so far ceased; the construction of tennis courts adjoining the club; the amalgamation of all subscriptions under one head; and the admission of visitors to the polo and race weeks as temporary visitors.

Quite recently Colonel Baring has successfully launched a new and ambitious scheme involving the removal of the greater portion of the steep hill facing the stand on which has hitherto stood a village and the Annandale garden. This scheme which is now being actively carried out will enable the ground to be converted into a first class and full-sized polo ground, will greatly improve the racing track which will be six furlongs in length, instead of four as at present, and will enable several sports to be carried on at one and the same time. The cost will probably run into a lakh of rupees, but satisfactory financial arrangements have been made to cover it, and to quote from the *Pioneer*—"The late Lord William Beresford was not more conspicuously associated with the brightening of existence in the summer capital of India than will be Colonel Baring in virtue of this remarkable project."

CHAPTER VIII.

Some old Houses, and their Owners.

IN the opening pages of this book I have already quoted some of Mr. C. T. French's remarks on the houses in the station fifty years ago, but the rapid development of Simla must serve as my excuse for here placing on record some detailed accounts of, and incidents relating to, a few well-known dwelling places.

The nomenclature of Simla houses often strikes the newcomer as peculiar, and a reference to old lists of residences shows how many of the earlier names have been either altered or forgotten. 'Alan Bank' for instance in the forties, and for many years afterwards, was called 'the Nunnery,' because it was for some time occupied by three unmarried sisters. The Roman Catholic Orphanage, an admirably conducted institution, is located on a spur long ago christened 'Chota Chelsea,' where once stood 'Eagles Mount.' 'Wheatfield,' now the property of the Maharaja of Durbhunga, may once upon a time have been surrounded by cornfields; there are certainly few in its vicinity to-day. 'Violet Hill,' on Jakko, for several years the property of the late Mr. W. S. Halsey, is appropriately named from the modest flower which adorns the surrounding wood. 'Melville Lodge' for years was known as 'Leopard's Lodge' as it used to be surrounded by thick jungle, and was the constant lair of leopards which prowled through its verandahs at nightfall. 'Rooks-nest,' 'Strawberry Hill,' 'Race View,' 'The Cedars,' 'Pine House' and others are titles which may be said to speak for themselves. To-day, scattered over the station, there are dozens of 'Lodges,' 'Cottages,' 'Villas' and 'Banks,' some still bearing the name of early owners, and others with modern fanciful prefixes, all of which may at any moment be altered at a new purchaser's whim. Owing moreover to building operations, numerous old landmarks, such as 'Gorton Castle,' 'The Tendrils,' 'Cross Buildings,' 'Northwood,' 'Bentinck Castle,' 'Bantony' and others have of necessity disappeared for all time. Did not Mrs. Charlie Baker in 'Jadoo' on first arrival tell her jampanies to take her to the 'Repository,' "the long wooden shop with a range of glass windows, where behind the counter a charming old lady (Mrs. Corstorphan) sold every variety of article from furniture to children's toys, and had all the gossip of the place at her fingers' ends." But the 'Repository' has shared the fate of other buildings, and it is, alas! no longer a landmark of Simla. Because there appears to be no reliable record of old houses in Simla, I have endeavoured to trace the history of some of the more prominent, and I will begin with two closely connected with the Punjab. The first of these is 'Ellerslie,' already mentioned as the residence of Colonel Keith Young in 1857, which lies on the road round Jakko close to the Chota Simla Bazaar, and is on a continuation of the spur on which the 'Barnes Court' estate is situated. The property, a large one of 22,579 square yards, belonged to Captain John Pengree of the old Invalid Establishment, and on his death was absorbed in the 'Pengree estates' in Chota Simla. In 1881 these estates were sold by the executor, Lieutenant H. H. Pengree, to the Punjab Government for Rs. 30,000, and the deed giving effect to this transaction bears the signatures of two names well remembered in Simla—Mr. Mackworth Young, afterwards Lieutenant-Governor of the Punjab, and Mr. F. Peterson, for many years Secretary of the late Simla Bank. At the time of the purchase 'Ellerslie' was rented by Brigadier-General Arbuthnot, Adjutant-General of Royal Artillery in India. On his vacating the house in 1881 it was altered and adapted for use by offices, notably by the old Military Department of the Punjab Government, which was abolished in the year 1886. In 1899 the house was dismantled, and the handsome buildings, designed by Lieutenant-Colonel H. E. S. Abbott, R.E., and now known as the Punjab Government offices, 'Ellerslie,' were erected. The structure accommodates the offices of the several departments which accompany the Lieutenant-Governor to the hills for the summer months, and is conveniently near to His Honour's residence. It is constructed of iron and stone, the stone having been obtained partly from a quarry on the neighbouring 'Barnes Court' estate, and partly from the quarries at Sanjaoli. Building was commenced in April 1899, under the supervision of Colonel Abbott and Major H. E. Chesney, both Royal Engineer officers of the Provincial Public Works Department, and was finished in May 1902, when the offices for whom it was intended moved into it. The total cost of the structure was about Rs. 3,00,000. The crest of the Punjab Government:—The sun rising over the five rivers of the Punjab, with the motto 'Crescate fluviis' is engraved on a stone slab over the entrance porch.

The second house 'Benmore,' which was built nearly half a century ago, is on land near 'Barnes Court,' granted to a Captain Simpson by Lord William Hay, then Superintendent of the Hill States, and is one of the landmarks of Simla, from both a social and official point of view. In 1863 the property passed into the possession of Major Percy Innes, and in December 1869 was sold by him to Herr Felix von Goldstein for Rs. 20,000. Mr. Goldstein, who was a professional musician, and Bandmaster to the Viceroy at the time of his death ten years ago, added a ball-room with subsidiary accommodation—used also by the Freemasons of Simla—to the house in 1872 which cost Rs. 10,000. In 1875 a rink which cost a similar sum was constructed by a body of gentlemen who registered themselves under the title of 'The Rink Company, Limited' with shares at Rs. 250 each. The scheme was originated and the rink designed by Mr. A. B. Sampson, Under Secretary to the Government of India in the Public Works Department. Among the shareholders were Mr. Sampson, Mr. Frank Barnes, Examiner of Accounts, Public Works Department, Mr. G. W. Allen (afterwards the late Sir George Allen of the *Pioneer*), and Mr. G. H. M. Batten, Secretary to the Government of India in the Revenue and Agricultural Department, the latter an accomplished performer on the violoncello, and a thorough musician in the best sense of the term. The shares were gradually bought up by Mr. Goldstein as their holders left Simla. Eventually, the Imperial Rink Company, Limited, died a natural death on the 1st of November 1882 by the mutual consent of the few remaining shareholders assembled on that date for the purpose of winding up the concern. From 1872 to 1885 old records show that 'Benmore' was the 'Kursaal' of Simla. All concerts, Monday 'Pops,' dances, meetings of Lodge 'Himalayan Brotherhood' and public gatherings generally were held there, the conveniences provided by Herr Goldstein having caused the disuse of the old Assembly Rooms and Theatre, which, about 1875 were partially destroyed by fire and were afterwards converted into what is now the Municipal market. In 1885 the present Town Hall being in process of construction, Herr Felix von Goldstein, seeing one of his means of living slipping, sold 'Benmore' to the Punjab Government (Sir Charles Aitchison being then Lieutenant-Governor and Colonel D. Limmond, C.B., Chief Engineer) for Rs. 50,000. The Provincial Government took possession in 1886, and until 1892, when new offices were opened near the Chota Simla Bazaar, 'Benmore' was occupied by the Civil Secretariat of the Punjab Government, by the offices of Inspector-Generals of Police, Prisons and Civil Hospitals, and by those of the Director of Public Instruction, and Sanitary Commissioner. The Punjab Government had to make considerable alterations and improvements to adapt the building to office requirements. The old-fashioned shingle roof was replaced by corrugated iron, and light was let into all the rooms. The building is now occupied by the offices of the Judge Advocate General, Army Head-Quarters, the Director-General of Education, the Consulting Architect to the Government of India, the Chief Inspector of Explosives, and the Director-General of Archæology. When the new Government of India offices now under construction at 'Gorton Castle' are ready for occupation, 'Benmore' will probably be vacated and be on the market. The present value of the property is roughly estimated at a lakh of rupees. Other houses that have been occupied by the Punjab Government are 'the Parsonage' in 1871, a very old house near the church, razed to the ground some four years ago, and replaced by the large premises now occupied by Messrs. Rivett and Sons; Craigs Court, 1872—76; Belvedere, 1876; River View, 1877; Rockcliffe, 1878; Craigsville, 1879 to 1884; Strawberry Hill, 1895; and Benmore as above noted.

In Chota Simla, below the bazaar, stands one of the finest houses in Simla—'Strawberry Hill'—which was apparently originally occupied by Colonel Tapp, who succeeded Captain Kennedy, the first Political Agent of the Hill States, and who subsequently moved into 'Barnes Court.' Later on the place seems to have been much improved by a Colonel Churchill, Military Secretary to Sir Edward Barnes. 'Strawberry Hill,' it is interesting to learn, was the name of a residence of the Duke of Marlborough at home, and according to one story which has been handed down, it was in honour of His Grace that Colonel Churchill, a scion of the family, called the place and house 'Strawberry Hill.' It was then, however, only a single storeyed building, subsequently it was altered to its present dimensions by Captain Pengree as a residence for Lord Dalhousie in 1849, and I am told that the knocker on the main door which was placed there in his day still remains in the present year of grace. The size of the house may be imagined when it was rented for Rs. 2,000 in the early forties, 'Strawberry Hill' has for many years been the property of Mr. T. S. Bean, Deputy Manager of the Alliance Bank, and a large portion of it is now occupied by the Survey of India offices. The grounds have been much improved, and are extensively planted with fruit trees.

In close proximity to 'Strawberry Hill' is 'Torrentium' House and estate, so called after its builder Major-General R. Torrens, C.B., formerly Adjutant-General of the Army. In 1870 the house was described as follows:—

"The house itself is built after a taste which combines the English with Indian, and is substantial and commodious, attached to it is a neat garden consisting of flowering shrubs and fruit trees of a tolerable great variety. One of its best features is a small artificial pool having a little wooden bridge thrown across it, which leads to the main entrance to the house. The pool is surrounded with weeping willows which extend their graceful branches over the cistern. Perhaps one of the greatest attractions to this spot is its fine park which is one of the largest in Simla. This estate was once called 'Roseville' from the numerous rose bushes which then covered the grounds. The old name, however, has since been resumed." The lake and its willows do not exist to-day, the former was filled up and a tennis court has taken its place. The park, too, such as it now is, consists of deodars and pines. The garden, however, is one of the best in Simla, and in the hands of its present tenant Colonel J. W. A. Morgan, Inspector-General of the Civil Veterinary Department, is not likely to deteriorate.

After leaving Chota Simla and approaching the centre of the station we come to a large house in a commanding position on the lower slope of Jakko known as 'Kelvin Grove.' This house, in which the Alliance Bank of Simla, the principal Bank, is situated, was built by Mr. Campbell about 1850, and was first used as a general shop. In 1865, the United Bank of India was started by some of the house proprietors in Simla, in opposition to the old Simla Bank. Its capital was five lakhs, Captain C. H. Levinge was appointed Secretary, and business was carried on in 'Kelvin Grove' until 1873, when the institution was wound up, and its goodwill was taken over by the Alliance Bank of Simla. The Bank commenced its operations in 1874 under the management of Mr. (now Sir) James Walker, and owing to his influence and ability soon became a flourishing institution. For ten years or so, it paid 8 per cent., and since 1883 has regularly paid 10 to 12 per cent. Commencing with a capital of half a lakh, it now possesses a paid up capital of 15 lakhs, has a reserve of 19 lakhs, and a working capital of considerably over three crores of rupees. Mr. A. M. Ker has managed the Bank for many years past, and to his good judgment and energy this continued success has been mainly due. Among directors now deceased have been the late Colonel T. D. Colyear, Mr. G. M. Bryan, Mr. H. G. Meakin, Mr. P. Mitchell, Mr. K. Murray, Mr. H. B. Goad, Mr. A. E. Dyer, and Mr. L. J. Arathoon. Colonel John Robertson, C.I.E., and Mr. R. Dixon now in England have also sat on the board of management. The present directorate consists of Sir James. L. Walker, Mr. J. Elston, Mr. A. M. Ker, and Mr. E. J. Buck, and the Bank has branches at Agra, Ajmere, Bombay, Calcutta, Cawnpore, Darjiling, Lahore, Murree, Mussoorie, Rawalpindi, and Umballa.

On a prominent spur, below the Alliance Bank, is 'Ravenswood,' also one of the ancient houses of Simla. For many years afterwards it was the property of the late Mr. A. O'Meara, the well known, and for 20 years the only, dental surgeon in the Punjab. Mr. O'Meara came to Simla in 1850, and his reputation spread far and wide. On one occasion, the Amir of Afghanistan sent for him, and the journey to Kabul and back occupied Mr. O'Meara for six months. On his return, Mr. O'Meara gave his friends many interesting particulars of his visit to the Amir's Court, which was not then so well known as it is to-day. He amused his hearers specially by describing how the Amir required him to extract teeth from his courtiers, before operating on himself.

It may be mentioned here, that during Napoleon's captivity at St. Helena, Dr. Barry O'Meara, Mr. O'Meara's uncle, was the Emperor's medical attendant. When Napoleon died, Dr. O'Meara planted a weeping-willow over the great man's grave. Cuttings from this tree were afterwards sent round the Cape (then the route to India) to Mr. O'Meara, and consequently several real St. Helena weeping-willow trees may now be seen growing in and about Simla, the best specimens being at 'Sherwood,' Mr. A. M. Ker's Mashobra residence.

In 1867 'Ravenswood' became the property of Mr. F. Lushington, Financial Secretary to the Government of India, who lived there during his term of office. The house was subsequently sold by Mr. O'Meara to the Raja of Faridkot, who, with the architectural aid of Mr. T. E. G. Cooper and a large expenditure of money, made it into the palatial residence it now is. The house was later on occupied by Colonel Cecil Beadon, Deputy Commissioner of Simla and Superintendent of the Hill States, and, after he left Simla, Colonel R. Home, head of the Irrigation Department, and later still General Sir Henry Brackenbury, Military Member of Council, lived there.

Close by on the main mall is 'Aln Cottage' or 'Regent House,' now occupied by Messrs. Peliti, Messrs. Richards & Co., Messrs. Thacker, Spink & Co., and Messrs. Watts & Co., which was formerly a 'Poor house' of Lady William Bentinck's, whence it is said she used to distribute blankets and food to needy hill people. The premises, which were then mere outhouses, were afterwards converted into an ice house, which was sold later on for a few hundred rupees to the officers of the 19th Hussars who, by the addition of some rooms above, turned it into a mess house. It later on fell into the hands of Messrs. Anderson & Co., who sold it for Rs. 7,000 to Messrs. A. and S. Wallace. The latter firm greatly improved the place, and on the death of Mr. Wallace it was purchased by Mr. Francis (Messrs. B. Francis & Co.) for Rs. 18,000.

As an instance of the remarkable changes which continue to take place in Simla may be mentioned 'Bridgeview' situated above the Combermere Bridge. The 'pottah,' or lease, granting the land on which this house is built is dated the 8th December 1842, and is signed by John C. Erskine, Sub-Commissioner, North-West Frontier, Simla being then on the actual frontier of the British possessions in India. Even in these early days, the necessity for protecting the Simla forests from denudation was recognised, as the 'pottah' stipulated that no trees of whatever description should be cut without the Sub-Commissioner's sanction. The fifty yards of building ground comprising the estate was subject to an annual quit rent of Company's rupees ten, payable in advance.

The first owner of the property was Mr. Barrett, a large house proprietor, and the house as erected by him was single storeyed with a mud roof. The property next passed into the possession of a local merchant, named Esanoolla, for Rs. 2,235. In 1870, Mr. Patterson purchased the estate for Rs. 2,750, and in 1874, it was bought by the late Mr. L. J. Arathoon, a well known local solicitor, for Rs. 5,000. The last owner added an upper storey with an iron roof, and generally improved the house. The property being centrally situated has naturally much increased in value.

Also on Jakko, but situated above the Lakkar Bazar, are two of the largest houses in Simla.

The first of these is the 'Crags' estate dating from 14th June 1841, when a grant of building ground was made to Dr. C. B. Handyside by the Political Agent. Since then the estate has passed through many hands, *e.g.*, J. P. Gubbins, C.S., 1843—47, Colonel H. I. Tucker, 1847—55; Captain R. M. Paton, 1855—61; Major J. Tickell, 1861—64; General Sir P. S. Lumsden, 1864—72; General E. L. Thuillier, 1872—79; Sir J. B. Lyall (afterwards Lieutenant-Governor of the Punjab), 1879—83; General Sir C. M. MacGregor, 1883 to 21st October 1885, when it was bought by the present owner, Colonel A. R. D. Mackenzie, C.B., the gallant soldier who led the Mutiny veterans in their never-to-be-forgotten march into the arena at the Delhi Durbar on the 1st January 1903. In the story of the distinguished career of Major G. Broadfoot, C.B., Governor-General's Agent, North-West Frontier, 1844-45, occurs the following passage: "In May (1845), Broadfoot went up to Simla. His health had suffered much from anxiety and overwork; and at Lahore, matters were quieter than they had been. The house he took was called 'The Crags.' It is well situated on Jakko, the highest of the Simla hills; and from it there is a most magnificent view of the Snowy Range. Here he remained during the summer and early autumn, with a houseful of guests. . . . Naturally Havelock was much at the house as were Edward Lake, and Herbert Edwardes, who lived in the smaller house just below, and who both owed to Broadfoot their selection for civil employment. Lake became one of his assistants. Edwardes was not appointed till after the first Sikh war, as there was no vacancy before. At one period for a short time the 'Crags' was known as 'Stoneham,' but it soon resumed its original name of the 'Crags,' which is quite an appropriate one for it, situate as it is on a huge rock jutting out from the side of Jakko." Colonel Mackenzie, who has settled down in Simla, has greatly improved the house, which can now be best described as a charming English villa. The house possesses one of the best ball-rooms in Simla, and its situation is unsurpassed.

The other house is 'Rothney Castle' which stands above the 'Crags' high up on Jakko. This was first known as 'Rothney House,' and was built by Colonel Rothney in 1838, who resided there for several years. He sold the place in 1843 to Dr. Carte, who started the Simla Bank Corporation in the house on the 19th November 1844. Dr. Carte, the first Secretary of the Bank, was succeeded a few years after by Mr. Arnold H. Mathews. It is now difficult to understand what business the Bank could carry on in a locality so isolated and difficult of access, but considerable transactions evidently took place. The following is the abstract of the balance sheet of the Bank in 1847:—Capital (paid up) Rs. 8,00,000; deposits, Rs. 1,32,710; undivided profits, Rs. 38,280; total Rs. 9,70,990, advances and investments, Rs. 8,75,040; cash and Government securities, Rs. 95,950; total Rs. 9,70,990.

In the following year the capital was increased to 16 lakhs, and there were 3,200 shares of Rs. 500 each subscribed for of which Rs. 14,62,000 was paid up, and it is recorded that "the business of the Bank chiefly consisted of Indian exchange, and loans to the Services." At any rate the following dividends were declared:—the first on 1st May 1845, 10%; the second on 25th November 1845, 8%; the third on 25th July 1846, 8%; the fourth on 30th January 1847, 9%; the fifth on 3rd August 1847, 9%; the sixth on 1st February 1848, 9%; and the seventh on 10th August 1848, 8%. In January 1851, the bank removed its premises to 'Bentinck Castle,' this being considered a more central position for business.

'Rothney House' next became the personal property of Mr. Arnold H. Mathews, who continued attached to the Bank till 1854, when he was appointed Manager of the Agra Bank, at Agra. In 1867, 'Rothney House,' then called 'Rothney Castle,' passed into the hands of the late Mr. P. Mitchell, C.I.E., a well-known personage in Simla during his day. He resided in 'Rothney Castle' for some years, and afterwards sold the place to Mr. A. O. Hume, then a Secretary to the Government of India. Mr. Hume proceeded to convert the house into a veritable palace, which tradition says he fully expected would be bought for a Viceregal residence in view of the fact that the Governor-General then occupied 'Peterhoff,' a building far too small for Viceregal entertainments. From first to last he spent over two lakhs on the grounds and buildings. He added enormous reception rooms suitable for large dinner parties and balls, as well as a magnificent conservatory and spacious hall on the walls of which he displayed his superb collection of Indian horns. He engaged the services of an European gardener, and with his aid he made the grounds and conservatory a perpetual horticultural exhibition, to which he courteously admitted all visitors.

But, possibly because 'Rothney Castle' can only be reached by a troublesome climb, any anticipations which Mr. Hume may have formed of the pur chase of the building by Government were not realized, and Mr. Hume himself made little use of the larger rooms otherwise except that he converted one of them into a museum for his wonderful collection of birds, and for occasional dances.

Mr. Hume, a grandson of the celebrated politician Joseph Hume, was himself a remarkable character. Of exceptional ability and brain power, and endowed with a wonderful talent for organisation, he was not free from the eccentricity which sometimes accompanies genius. Lord Mayo, attracted by his reputation and personality, placed him in charge of the Agricultural Department which, with the co-operation of Sir John Strachey, His Excellency had, in 1870, created for the development of agricultural improvements and reforms.*

Mr. Hume was essentially a man of hobbies, and whatever hobby he took up was ridden well and hard. At the time that he was brought to Simla the special subject to which he had been devoting his energies was that of ornithology. Possessed of ample private means, he had in his employ an army of collectors, some of them Europeans working on liberal salaries even beyond the limits of India proper, while many private collectors, falling under the influence of Mr. Hume's genius, gave him strenuous assistance in all parts of the Indian Empire. Many birds new to science were discovered by himself or by his agents. The specimens were all brought to 'Rothney Castle' and arranged there in classified order in cabinets which lined the walls of the room utilized as a museum. The collections were rapidly augmenting when suddenly Mr. Hume mounted another hobby. This time it was Theosophy! And one of the tenets of that creed being to take no life, telegrams were sent to the collectors to stop work and shoot no more birds, while at the same time an offer was made to the authorities of the British Museum to present the entire collection to that institution on condition that they would send out an expert to overhaul the specimens at 'Rothney Castle.' The offer was naturally accepted; Mr. Sharpe, one of the staff, was sent to Simla and the collection removed to the British, and then the Kensington Museum, where it forms one of the most valuable assets.

Mr. Hume was undoubtedly led to the worship of Theosophy by the High Priestess of that cult, Madame Blavatzky, at whose disposal the hospitality of 'Rothney Castle' was always placed. A Theosophical society was formed of which the leading spirits were Madame Blavatzky, Mr. Hume himself and Mr. Sinnett, then editor of the *Pioneer* and still, it is believed, a leader of Theosophical work in London. Strenuous efforts were made to

* Mr. Hume held charge of the Department for five years when, for financial reasons, it was abolished, though five years later, it was, at the instance of the Famine Commission, re-established and placed under the charge of Sir Edward Buck.

bring into the fold influential officials and other residents of Simla, and it was even whispered that Madame Blavatzky, who when first arriving in the country had been placed under the surveillance of the police as a suspected Russian agent, had a political object in gaining adherents to her creed! Certain it is that Madame Blavatzky and her American disciple, Colonel Olcott, preached the doctrine that the knowledge and learning of the East reached far higher planes than the science of the West, and that the oriental should not look upon the occidental as a superior being.

Madame Blavatzky was in the early eighties a constant summer guest at the Rothney palace, the situation of which on Jakko, whence is commanded an uninterrupted view of the snowy peaks of Tibet, was peculiarly favourable for the intercourse of the Theosophical priestess with her familiar 'Kút Humi,' who in astral form (or otherwise) had chosen for his home the isolation of the Trans-Himalayan steppes. More than once did Madame Blavatzky invoke his aid at 'Rothney Castle.' But on two notable occasions she gave, unaided, manifestations of her power with the object of gaining the faith of those doubting votaries of Theosophy who called for a sign. One of these miracles is of historical interest. There were gathered together at the 'Rothney Castle' dinner table all the believers and possible believers in the Theosophical creed then at Simla. Madame was solicited, probably by her own arrangement, to give an example of the power which the true Theosophist acquires by asceticism, faith and self-denial. She protested like a young lady asked for a song: "It is very trying to me; it exhausts much; no, no, I cannot, I cannot;" but further pressed, at last exclaimed, "Well then, I must, but it is hard, it is hard! Mrs. Hume! (turning to her hostess) what is there that you would like? You shall say. Have you lost anything that you would find?"

Mrs. Hume.—"Yes. A year or more ago I lost a brooch. Find that and it will be indeed wonderful."

Madame.—"It is hard but IT SHALL BE DONE!! Khitmatgar! Bring me one lantern!" The lantern brought, Madame rose, led the way through the opened doors leading to the garden; there halting, she pointed to a bush and commanded, "Dig there!!" A spade produced, earth was removed and lo! there was the brooch. The guests wonderstruck and, some of them at least, convinced, returned to the table where a succinct account of the miracle was drawn up and signed by all present, including two Honourable Members of Council. Is not this miracle with many more recorded in the chronicles published by Mr. Sinnett shortly after the event? On another occasion a picnic party was troubled by the circumstance that there was one tea cup short. "Never mind," said Madame, who was present and in a complaisant humour, "I shall find one!" and sure enough a cup (of the same pattern !) was dug up from under another bush, and again the miracle produced a profound impression.

Sir Edward Buck, who, as already noted, succeeded Mr. Hume in charge of the Agricultural Department, has told the writer of the attempt made to bring him, among others, into the Theosophical fold. The story may be given in, as far as they can be remembered, his own words :—

"I was one," he said, "of a small dinner party, men only present, at which Mr. A., a leading theosophist, was also a guest. After dinner a discussion took place on the miracles recorded in the then recently printed booklet issued by the Editor of the *Pioneer*. Mr. A., an exceedingly clever man, held his own surprisingly well against the scoffing antagonists who attacked the Theosophical faith. Although always interested in the questions with which Theosophy was concerned, I refrained from joining in the discussion, which circled round one of the leading tenets of Theosophy, *viz.*, that such power could be gained over matter by 'adepts' who by asceticism had reached the 'higher planes' that they could disintegrate a solid body, pass it through another, and reconstruct it on the other side, as well as transfer it any distance. This granted, of course all kinds of developments were possible. Walking home with Mr. A. to Jakko where I was living in a house above 'Rothney Castle,' I told him that I believed that I could explain the whole series of miracles in a more simple way. 'What way?' said Mr. A. 'It is too late now,' I replied, 'but I will call at "Rothney Castle" to-morrow evening at 9 o'clock and tell you over an after-dinner cigar.' I kept my appointment, but was a quarter of an hour late. I asked the servant who opened the door to let Mr. A. know I was there, but instead of being taken to his private room, was ushered into the small drawing-room where a congregation of Theosophists was assembled in full force. I apologized, explaining that I had only come for a chat with Mr. A. 'Oh! we know what you arranged to chat about,' said Mr. Hume, who presided, 'and all want to hear what you have to say.' I protested that what I might say would offend some of those present, but protests were useless. I referred, of course, to Madame Blavatzky, who was reclining in one of those long deck chairs familiar to the P. and O. traveller, and enjoying a cigarette. She however made no sign. 'It is a pity,' began Mr. Hume, 'that you were a quarter of an hour late. If you had been here at 9, you would have seen the arrival of a communication from Kút Humi (handing me a letter), which those present (turning to the congregation) will tell you descended from the roof a few minutes ago.' I read it. Addressed to Madame, the purport of it was that she need not trouble herself with attempts to make proselytes of the incredulous. Enough that those who believed and practised should gain the higher planes of knowledge and power. What mattered it to them that the rest of human kind wallowed in ignorance. The adepts could smile at them in contempt from their superior height! The text of the letter might indeed have been that to preach to the ignorant would be to 'cast pearls before swine.' Reading through the letter it struck me that Kút Humi must have had considerable intercourse with America, as more than one of the phrases appeared to savour of the Yankee dialect. And did not Colonel Olcott come from America? However, this episode concluded, began my cross-examination.

Mr. H.—You assert that you can explain the miracles recorded by Mr. Sinnett in a simple way. How?

Sir E. B.—Which one do you choose?

Mr. H.—The discovery of the brooch.

Sir E. B.—Is not Madame Blavatzky a powerful mesmerist?

Mr. H.—Yes.

Sir E. B.—Had she not been for some time at 'Rothney Castle' before the occurrence of the miracle?

Mr. H.—Yes.

Sir E. B.—Is Mrs. Hume a believer in her powers?

Mr. H.—Certainly.

Sir E. B.—Then let us assume that Madame Blavatzky had acquired such mesmeric power over Mrs. Hume as to make her give utterance to a certain wish. Is not the rest easy?

Mr. H.—You imply that the brooch was already buried!

Sir E. B.—You have drawn the inference.

Madame B. (rising from her chair and waving her cigarette in Sir Edward Buck's face).—You come here, sir, to *insolt* me. You call me cheat, etc., etc., etc.!!

"Madame Blavatzky, be it said, was a powerfully made woman of about 50 years of age—almost a virago—somewhat coarse in feature. She was still attractive in the intellectual force which was expressed in her countenance, and I had always felt a certain admiration and respect for the strength of her character. At this moment she appeared formidable, and I sought to assuage her assumed fury. The conversation continued:—

Sir E. B.—Madame Blavatzky, pray be calm! Of course *you* know that my explanation is absurd. But have you not erred in neglecting the principles so clearly expressed in this letter of Kút Humi's? Have you not cast pearls before swine? We ignorant people who live on lower planes have not attained to the spiritual level of the initiated, and are obliged to seek for foolish explanations of miracles which to them are no mystery. Why, then, publish your miracles to the world?

"Madame Blavatzky, who had not done with me yet, sank again into the deck chair and Mr. Hume continued his cross-examination. Other miracles, such as that of passing a ring into a cushion, were cited, a similar explanation being suggested by me in each case, to the accompaniment of angry growls from Madame Blavatzky. But she had been waiting all the time to play her trump card, as the ensuing dialogue will show.

M. B.—Now, sir, I will show you one thing that shall convince you! You have something to do with agriculture?

Sir E. B.—Yes, I have the honour to administer the Department of Agriculture.

M. B.—Well, sir, *you* shall plant a seed and it shall grow in six months! *I* shall plant that seed and it shall grow in six minutes!

Sir E. B.—Madame, I pray you spare yourself that trouble. No doubt you can do as you say, but I, in my ignorant scepticism, should only believe it to be the mango trick of the Madras conjurors.

M. B. (rising in fury).—What, sir! you class *me* with those vulgar impostors? You call yourself gentleman, etc., etc.

Sir Edward Buck.—Mr. Hume, I begged you not to open this conversation. I foresaw the result, and it is better that I should now retire (bowing adieu and moving to the door). But before leaving I should wish to make one suggestion to Madame Blavatzky. Will she permit me to go to the Viceroy to-morrow and ask His Excellency to transfer the Agricultural Department from my charge to hers? For that Department was recently created to deal with the protection of the country against famine, and if Madame Blavatzky can raise crops in six minutes, what more is wanted? Good night!"

"I did not venture to call at 'Rothney Castle' again, at any rate while Madame was there. But I always regretted that I had so far lost my temper as to decline seeing that six-minute trick, which would have at any rate been interesting. I never saw Madame Blavatzky again. And it was not long afterwards that her clever impostures were exposed at Madras. But I have always said of her, as the two clerical dignitaries said of Mrs. Proudie, 'She was a wonderful woman.'"

Thus far Sir Edward Buck. Mr. Hume, in a printed brochure on Madame Blavatzky, said that she was the most marvellous liar he had ever met, but excused her on the ground that she used deception with the honest object of converting to a higher faith. So far as that faith is expressed by 'Theosophy' its temples have since Madame Blavatzky's departure been transferred from 'Rothney Castle' to Paris and London.

In the later years of his residence at 'Rothney Castle' Mr. Hume devoted his time to the furtherance of what had been ostensibly one of Madame Blavatzky's objects, though no doubt from better motives, *viz.*, the elevation of the native community to a higher and more dignified status. In all honest sincerity he to this end became President of the Congress and aided that body with much good advice and with much good money. But he was more than once constrained to charge his followers with failure to themselves contribute that practical and financial support to the movement which he considered it demanded. However this may be, there is no doubt that in being deprived of the able leadership of Mr. Hume on his retirement to England the Congress sustained a severe loss. And of Mr. Hume too, may it be said "He was a wonderful man!"

'Rothney Castle' was afterwards the residence of Sir William Rattigan for a couple of years. Subsequently Baron Gaertner, and then Herr von Walthausen—both German Consul-Generals—occupied the palace, and the latter's princely entertainments were, for several seasons, the talk of Simla. Herr von Walthausen, indeed, thought seriously of purchasing the place as an official residence for German Consul-Generals, but negotiations fell through, and subsequently there arose a chance of 'Rothney Castle' changing hands for Rs. 80,000 for conversion into a Convent School. Mr. E. N. Baker, the Financial Secretary to the Government of India, now lives in 'Rothney Castle.' For the last few years, however, the house has been untenanted, as, with its extensive grounds, it is an expensive residence to keep in proper order. Moreover, the hill path which leads up to the house, just above the Church, is, as already indicated, one of the steepest and most trying in the station.

Another house which must not be omitted from my list is 'The Priory' originally constructed by Captain Sunderland, R.A., occupying a position on Jakko about fifty feet above the road leading to 'Snowdon.' This was in 1858 rented furnished for the season to Dr. W. H. Russell of the *Times* and Captain Alison for £60. Its roof was then of shingle, and the flower garden was narrow and neglected. The eve of Dr. Russell's departure from Simla on 6th October was celebrated by a banquet at the 'Priory,' which was chiefly remarkable for the exhaustion of the little cellar and the great conviviality which was elicited by very scanty fare, and a limited supply of liquids. The host then wrote: "Indeed not only the Priory, but all Simla is just now without any stock of wine, beer, or spirits on hand. It is impossible to get brandy or pale ale, claret has ceased to exist, and sherry is supposed to be half way up to the hills, and the only wine to be had is some curious sparkling Johannesberg at about £1 per bottle, which tastes like ginger beer adulterated with Warren's blacking, and some quaint old '20 port which I believe to have been made in the neighbourhood." Dr. Russell's diary in Simla contains numerous allusions to his fondness for natural history, and while in the 'Priory' he made quite a large collection of birds and beasts. Miss C. F. Gordon Cumming, who in 1884 brought out her book 'In the Himalayas,' and who lived in 'Raby Lodge,' a house adjacent to the 'Priory,' alludes to it as the place where Dr. Russell wiled away the weary hours of convalescence with all his pets—"his menagerie, I might say—his young hill bears, monkeys, mountain rams, costurah (or hill thrush), green parrot, chikore, ninety-six aberdavats, besides hill minahs or black-birds." Another resident at the 'Priory' during his short stay in Simla was Prince Alexis Soltikoff, who produced a book of Indian scenes and characters in 1858.

'Stirling Castle,' which is by no means inappropriately christened, is one of the oldest houses in Simla, and the first reference that can be found to it is in 1833, when it is alluded to as the house belonging to Mr. Stirling, perched on the summit of an isolated and thickly wooded hill. Captain G.'s wife died at 'Stirling Castle' in September 1838, and a long account of this sad event is recorded by the Hon'ble Miss Eden. The following paragraphs, written some time afterwards, are taken from her book:—"*March 1839.*—The Aides-de-Camp have engaged a house for the Misses S. and their aunt, quite close to ours, called 'Stirling Castle'—a bleak house that nobody will live in, and that in general is struck by lightning once a year—but then it is close by, and they are preparing for a ball. . . . The Aides-de-Camp are about as much trouble to me as grown-up sons. One remarked that, 'those two little windows in the gable end of Stirling Castle look well, and when two little female forms are leaning out of them, nothing could appear more interesting. . . . I met that sedate Captain P. the other day carrying a little nosegay to Stirling Castle, which looked suspicious. He followed me into my room after breakfast and thought it right to mention that he had proposed to Miss S. . . . P. is quite altered since he has been engaged, and will talk and joke and dance in the most debonair manner. He danced three times with the same lady, but got up early next morning to write an account of himself to his 'Clarissa' at Stirling Castle."

Since the above remarks were written 63 years ago, 'Stirling Castle' has been the residence of several well-known personages. From 1844 to 1850 it was the residence of Sir Frederick Currie, Foreign Secretary to Lord Hardinge—and afterwards a Member of Council during Lord Dalhousie's term of office. Some time after this the house was struck by lightning, became a ruin, and it was not occupied for many years. In the early sixties it was the residence of Mr. D. O. B. Clark—who kept a school there. Then in 1865 'Stirling Castle' became the property of Mr. Moore, a solicitor, and in 1870 was bought by Mr. Cotton (of Messrs. Cotton and Morris, well-known Simla merchants). He sold it to Mr. S. T. Berkeley in 1873, and seven years later Sir W. W. Hunter purchased the house and resided there for several years. While he occupied 'Stirling Castle,' he wrote his 'History of the Indian people.' Mr. F. H. Skrine in his 'Life of Sir W. W. Hunter' says that when Sir W. Hunter first moved into 'Stirling Castle' it was "a dilapidated house perched on the summit of a wooded hill which commands a glorious panorama of the snowy range and had a large but neglected garden. So delighted was the tenant with the isolation and pure air of the place that he afterwards purchased it and made it his head-quarters during the remainder of his stay in India. It was soon shared by a congenial spirit, Sir Courtenay Ilbert, who had become Legal Member of the Viceroy's Council." After this it became the residence of Colonel (now Lieutenant-General Sir) Ian Hamilton, then it passed into the hands of Colonel (now Lieutenant-General), R. M. Jennings, C.B., and when he vacated, Mrs. Meakin lived there from 1896—98. The 'Stirling Castle' of the present day belongs to General A. S. Hunter (retired list), who has greatly improved the house, and has made it his permanent residence. 'Stirling Castle' has an imposing appearance, and commands magnificent views on all sides. This beautiful and extensive estate actually changed owners in the sixties for the modest sum of Rs. 2,450. Those were certainly 'good old days,' for there are many who now pay considerably over that sum for a single season's tenancy of a comfortable house.

Quite one of the finest houses on the Elysium hill is 'Kelston,' now the property of Mr. H. S. Harington, the Agent and Chief Engineer of the Kalka-Simla Railway. In 1850 the house, which was then known as 'Elysium House,' belonged to the Roman Catholic Society, and was used as a school for boys and girls, but in 1856 the boys were moved to Mussoorie and the girls to Chakrata. The house was afterwards rented to various tenants, and the estate, then assumed as extending to the circular road below and to Petersfield, was sold to Colonel Gay, R.A., for Rs. 15,000. Among subsequent tenants were Sir George Greaves and Sir William Elles, who successively held the appointment of Adjutant-General in India. In 1893 Major Kemp purchased the property, for the purpose of running a dairy farm, and lived in it till 1900, when it passed into the hands of its present owner, who re-named it after an old family estate in Somersetshire, and has practically re-modelled the entire house.

Returning once more to central Simla we find that the 'Dalzell House' premises now occupied by the Bank of Upper India near the Public Works Offices, were for some years usually inhabited by the Civil Surgeon of Simla. The main mall which in the earlier months of the year is generally ankle deep in thick dust, runs past the house, and the remarks made by Captain G. D. Thomas in 1847 scarcely hold true in 1904. He then wrote:

"I have a leaning to this house (Captain the Hon'ble H. B. Dalzell's) and like it almost as much as the Mount, though the scenery is not nearly so

Reproduced from "Simla." by Captain G. P. Thomas.

CAPTAIN THE HONOURABLE H. B. DALZELL'S HOUSE, ABOUT 1846.
(NOW THE BANK OF UPPER INDIA).

beautiful as that from thence. But the fact is, that I once went up to Simla dangerously ill, and recovered in an incredibly short time in this house. By the way, it is impossible to describe the delicious feeling of awaking at Simla for the first time, and looking out upon the purple and shadowy dells below, and the dark dense woods around, and the spotless Himalayas in the distance, and the moss and ivy on the trunks of the oak and pines about your path, and the dewy English wild flower and fern under foot. The intensity (as the phrase runs) of such a moment can neither be described nor forgotten. A delicious home feeling wells up and refreshes the sick man's heart, and home itself arises 'to his mind's eye,' not as he last beheld it, but arrayed in all its brightest hues."

The sketch which appeared in Captain Thomas' book nearly sixty years ago, shows 'Dalzell House' in the foreground.

A few minutes' walk from 'Dalzell House' is 'Northbank' which from being a small cottage is now a comparatively large house, and has for some years contained the head office of the Countess of Dufferin's Fund. It was towards the end of the year 1886 that unusually heavy rains in Simla caused numerous landslips, and one of the most serious occurred at 'Northbank,' where Mr. C. S. Bayley (now the Agent to the Governor General for Central India) and his wife were then living. Lady Dufferin has left the following account of the occurrence on record:—"They (Mr. and Mrs. Carlo Bayley) had had guests dining with them who about one o'clock decided that they must go home, and they had just seen them off and were talking over their entertainment in the drawing-room, when the house shook and they heard a terrible noise, and rushing to see what had happened discovered that a landslip had come bang into their dining room and that it was full of mud and stones. The staircase was shut off, and two babies were sleeping upstairs. Mr. Bayley managed to get at a second narrow staircase, and taking his children out of bed he and his wife and her sister and the nurse with these two bundles of children wrapped in bed clothes, had to scramble over the débris in the dining-room and to go out as they were in their evening dress in the pouring rain. They walked some distance in this melancholy condition to their nearest neighbour's house, and were taken in for the night, and clothed and warmed. I believe a big tree came down upon their house, after they had left it, and all their things in the way of china and ornaments were smashed."

Later on the house passed from a native owner into the possession of Sir Edward Buck, and when he first occupied it, large troops of monkeys, he has told me, daily visited the lawn tennis ground to warm themselves in the rays of the morning sun; the monkey children gambolling the while in playful quarrel and rough games. One of the smallest became tame enough to climb to his window for a share of 'chota haziri' and became the envy of two of the large hill crows which frequented the grounds. At last the birds flew at the infant monkey from whom they tried to snatch his bread and butter. Seeing which the 'Raja' monkey followed by his attendants first drove away the crows who took refuge on the branch of a neighbouring deodar, and then swarming unseen up the trunk of the tree, with a sudden bound caught one of the crows, carefully plucked its feathers out one by one, and then tore it to pieces.

Rudyard Kipling was staying with Sir Edward Buck at 'Northbank' when this occurrence took place and in a recent letter to the author (who now owns the property) he wrote,—"The name at the head of your letter revives many old memories. Do the monkeys still come into the upper bedrooms at 'Northbank' and take the hair brushes off the table?"

'Knockdrin,' a well known house on the main mall below 'Kennedy House,' about 1862 was owned and occupied by General Butler of the old Indian Army. It was acquired, enlarged, and its name changed from 'Will Hall' to 'Knockdrin' about 1868 by Captain Levinge, and it was purchased from his estate for Rs. 23,000 by Colonel H. K. Burne, Military Secretary to the Government of India, who afterwards sold it for half a lakh to its present owner, the Maharaja of Faridkot. During the period he was Foreign Secretary to the Government of India Sir Mortimer Durand (now British Ambassador at Washington) resided in 'Knockdrin,' and it has for several years past been occupied by Sir A. U. Fanshawe, Postmaster-General in India.

The 'Tendrils,' on the 'Choura Maidan,' was in 1844 a small one-storeyed house known as 'Tendril Cottage.' About 1850 it passed into the possession of Mrs. Barlow Colyear, and was sold by auction on the 29th June 1850 by the Simla Civil Court, in the suit of Mr. David Colyear *v.* Mrs. Barlow Colyear, for Rs. 2,410, being bought by the former. It was later on sold in a slightly improved state by Mr. Colyear for Rs. 18,000 to Mr. H. R. Cooke, then Registrar, afterwards Assistant Secretary, in the Foreign Office, on the 17th November 1877. It was rebuilt about that time, but had to be almost immediately pulled down and again built up as its construction was unsatisfactory. For many years it has been let in three flats to various residents in Simla. Mr. Cooke disposed of it in 1902 for Rs. 45,000 to Mr. R. Hotz, a well-known Simla photographer, who has since added largely to it, and has re-christened it the 'Hotel Cecil.' It is centrally situated and is now one of the finest hotels of Simla.

Just opposite the 'Cecil' is 'Holcombe,' for many years the property of Mr. J. E. O'Conor, C.I.E., the late Director-General of Statistics to the Government of India, and then known as 'Jim's Lodge.'

HÔTEL CECIL

'Holcombe' is now the property of Mr. Everard C. Cotes, a well known Anglo-Indian journalist, and here Mrs. Everard Cotes (Sara Jeannette Duncan of literary fame) has written more than one of her delightful books.

It is not many years ago since a comparatively few house owners practically owned the whole of Simla, and not the least of these proprietors was Major S. B. Goad, who at one time was second-in-command of the Simla Volunteers. 'Mr. Carey's Guide of 1870' gives Major S. B. Goad as the owner of no less than thirty-three houses with a rent-roll of over Rs. 38,000 per annum. Among these houses were Barnes Court and Kennedy House, rent Rs. 3,000 each; Victoria Place and Holly Lodge, Rs. 1,800; Sam's Lodge, Rs. 1,600; Yates' Place and Office, Rs. 1,520; Tara Hall, Rs. 1,400; and the Park, Snow View, Victoria Cottage, Willie Park, Morley Villa, Cutcherry House, Grant Lodge, Holly Oak, Kennedy Lodge and Villa, all from Rs. 1,200 to Rs. 1,300 each.

Another of Major Goad's properties was 'Tally-Ho Hall,' which used to stand on the site now occupied by the Government of India press. The house was so called by its sporting owner, who, it may be mentioned, also possessed a large residence in Ferozepore known as 'Goad's Folly,' which he purchased from a Mr. Coates for a lakh of rupees. At Ferozepore he kept a pack of hounds, and used to entertain in a truly old English fashion. In the hot weather the hounds were brought up to Simla and were regularly exercised by their master at Annandale, their kennels being then situated on the site now occupied by the 'Glaciers,' below the Choura Maidan. Major Goad, who was a man of robust constitution, lived to the age of 70, and, to the regret of many friends, terminated his life by his own hand in Tally-Ho Hall.

Major Goad's son, Mr. Horace B. Goad, entered the police, in which department he gained the reputation of being the smartest police officer in the North-West Provinces. He joined the Simla Municipality in 1877, and was still on the active list of the police force, serving for pension with the Municipality, until a short time before his retirement from it in 1895. His extraordinary knowledge of the native language and customs, combined with a genius for disguising himself, rendered him a terror to all evil-doers within his jurisdiction. In many respects he was an excellent secretary, and no figure was better known or respected in the station. Even the ayahs regarded him as a man to hold in awe; indeed many of the little ones they tended were quieted by the threat of being handed over to 'Goad Sahib' unless they behaved as good children on the Mall. It is sad to relate that Mr. Goad, following his father's example, took his own life at Umballa on the 12th February 1896, and it was a strange coincidence that the Public Works Secretariat was burnt to the ground the same evening in Simla. By many hundreds of natives in the station this was solemnly regarded as 'Goad Sahib's' funeral pyre, especially as it was rumoured he had, probably in a jocular moment, foretold a disaster in Simla when he should die. At any rate many natives to this day declare that they saw his spirit in the flames. *De mortuis nil nisi bonum.* Mr. Goad kept the market 'bunnias' and dealers in better control than any man had done before, or I think has done since. He was a keen fruit grower, and made an attempt to improve the Simla hill cattle at the suggestion of Sir Edward Buck, by crossing them with imported Brittany and Kerry cattle, the latter being presented by Lord Lansdowne. His farm on the Tara Devi hill, a few miles out of Simla, was a favourite picnic ground fifteen years ago, and is now in the possession of his son, a distinguished young officer in the United Provinces Police.

Another big house owner in the seventies was Colonel T. D. Colyear, who was, I am informed, twice married to native ladies, and who died in August 1875. In support of this statement may be quoted the marriage register in Christ Church which runs—"T. D. Colyear, widower, son of the Right Honourable the Earl of Portmore, and Alice, spinster, daughter of Jewtoo, Hindu. By Licence—11th December 1865."

A list of Simla houses, compiled about 1870, shows that Colonel Colyear then owned no less than seventeen residences, including Gorton Castle, Newlands, Marsden Grange, Portmore, the Tendrils and others. By his will, made shortly before his death, he made certain bequests of house property and personalty to his wife Alice, and to David, his stepson by his first wife. Colonel Colyear also left certain other property which remained undisposed of by will, and thus some residences fell to the Government as an escheat. Certain claims were made to houses and jewellery by David Colyear and his daughters which were favourably considered, and the properties were given to the claimants, the rest of the estate lapsing to the Government.

The largest proprietor in Simla to-day is undoubtedly Mr. J. Elston, a popular landlord whose residences are much sought after. These comprise Armadale, Armadale Cottage, Grant Lodge, Southwood, Mansfield Lodge, Forest Hill and Lodge, Long View, The Monastery, Raby Lodge, The Priory, Abbotsford, Newstead, Annandale View, Alderton, Mount Pleasant, and Merlin Lodge.

High up on Jakko, above the United Service Club, is 'Bonnie Moon,' one of the oldest boarding houses in Simla, and here in years gone by was a curious and valuable museum belonging to the late Colonel Tytler of the Honourable East India Company's service. The museum, which was open to the public, consisted chiefly of a large collection of birds from all parts of the world, including animals and shells from the Andamans, oriental manuscripts, and geological, mineralogical and mythological specimens. Lord Mayo specially placed Colonel Tytler's services at the disposal of the Home Department in order to enable him to exhibit his museum, and it was only closed after his death in 1872. Mrs. Tytler has preserved the ornithological specimens, and has expressed her intention of giving them to Simla, in memory of her husband, should a museum be ever formed there.

Mrs. Tytler in 1869 established at 'North Stoneham' house, now known as the Mayo Industrial School, an 'Asiatic Christian Orphanage,' for boys and girls, and though later on the idea of a native orphanage in Simla was dropped, the present useful Mayo School undoubtedly owes its origin to Mrs. Tytler's energy and benevolent initiative. As its name denotes, it was named in honour of the Viceroy who opened it in June 1870. After Colonel Tytler's death in September 1872 the institution which Mrs. Tytler had built at her own risk was purchased by a committee of gentlemen, and it has since been supported by public contributions, a Government grant, and from the income on its invested funds, under the management of a small committee of which the Bishop of the diocese, and the Chaplain of Simla are '*ex-officio*' members. A free home is thus provided for a number of European and Eurasian orphan girls, and the daughters of poor parents who cannot afford more expensive schools are also allowed to reside in the home at a small charge till the age of seventeen. A scheme is now being considered for the entire re-construction of the present building as the old house is practically past repair. Soon after the Asiatic Christian Orphanage was established, the grand-father of the present Maharaja of Patiala endowed it in perpetuity with an annual gift of Rs. 1,000, but this was withdrawn shortly after the place became a school for European girls.

One more personal sketch, and I must close a chapter which is already of inordinate length. In 1871 there arrived in Simla a man who will ever be remembered as a character in the station. I refer to Mr. A. M. Jacob, the famous art dealer and jeweller. Who Mr. Jacob really is, and whence he came, is, I fancy, only known to himself, though, possibly, the mysterious Secret Department of the Government of India may also have a record on the subject. Suffice it to say that Mr. Jacob appeared in the year mentioned, that he had previously been serving in Dholpur as a member of the State Council, and that he has since supplied three novelists with a character for their books. It has long been an open secret, for instance, that Marion Crawford's 'Mr. Isaacs' was no other than Mr. Jacob. This novelist makes his hero say:—"I am a Persian, a pure Iranian, a degenerate descendant of Zoroaster, as you call him, though by religion I follow the prophet whose name be blessed. I call myself Isaacs for convenience in business. There is no concealment about it, as many know my story; but it has an attractive Semitic twang that suits my occupation, and is simpler and shorter for Englishmen to write than Abdul Hafiz-ben-Isak, which is my lawful name."

Mr. Jacob, in his capacity as a curiosity dealer, has had many famous customers on his books, and rare beyond measure were scores of the treasures he collected from all parts of the East in his house, 'Belvedere,' below the Lakkar bazaar, and his quaint little shop on the Mall. Marion Crawford in 1879 wrote of his room as follows:—"At first glance it appeared as if the walls and ceiling were lined with gold and precious stones; and in reality it was almost the truth. The apartment was small—for India at least—and every available space, nook and cranny, were filled with gold and jewelled ornaments, shining weapons, or uncouth but resplendent idols. There were sabres in scabbards set from end to end with diamonds and sapphires, with cross hilts of rubies in massive gold mounting, the spoil of some worsted Raja or Nawab of the Mutiny. There were narghyles, four feet high, crusted with gems and curiously wrought work from Baghdad or Herat; water flasks of gold and drinking cups of jade; yataghans and idols from the far East.

"Surgeons' lamps of the octagonal Oriental shape hung from the ceiling, and fed by aromatic oils, shed their soothing light on all around. The floor was covered with a soft, rich pile, and low divans were heaped with cushions of deep-tinted silk and gold. On the floor in a corner which seemed the favourite resting place of my host lay open two or three superbly illuminated Arabic manuscripts, and from a chafing dish of silver near by a thin thread of snow-white smoke sent up its faint perfume through the still air."

Kipling, too, in 'Kim' has also immortalised Mr. Jacob as 'Lurgan Sahib' of whom he wrote: "The back verandah of his shop was built out over the sheer hillside, and they looked down into their neighbours' chimney-pots, as is the custom of Simla. But even more than the purely Persian meal cooked by Lurgan Sahib with his own hands, the shop fascinated Kim. The Lahore Museum was larger, but here were more wonders—ghost-daggers and prayer wheels from Tibet; turquoise and raw amber necklaces; green jade bangles; curiously packed incense-sticks in jars crusted over with raw garnets; the devil-masks of overnight and a wall full of peacock-blue draperies; gilt figures of Buddha, and little portable lacquer altars; Russian samovars with turquoises on the lid; egg-shell china sets in quaint octagonal cane boxes; yellow ivory crucifixes—from Japan of all places in the world, so Lurgan Sahib said; carpets in dusty bales, smelling atrociously, pushed back behind torn and rotten screens of geometrical work; Persian water-jugs for the hands after meals; dull copper incense-burners, neither Chinese nor Persian, with friezes of fantastic devils running round them; tarnished silver belts that knotted like raw hide; hair-pins of jade, ivory, and plasma; arms of all sorts and kinds, and a thousand other oddments were cased, or piled, or merely thrown into the room, leaving a clear space only round the rickety deal table, where Lurgan Sahib worked."

And yet a third author, Colonel Newnham Davis, has recognised Mr. Jacob as a local celebrity, for in his novel 'Jadoo,' published in 1898, is found the following allusion to this strange character: "When they came to the spot where the path joins the broad road there was at the junction a pale-faced, fat, black-eyed little man sitting on a Burmese pony with a jewelled tiger's claw round its neck. He was waiting there apparently to see the people come up from Annandale . . . . . 'Who is the little man?' asked Dita. 'Oh! Emanuel. A man who knows more of the mystic secrets of India than any other man. He hears things that other men cannot hear, sees things that other men cannot see. The natives believe that he has the power of *jadoo* (magic), the white *jadoo*, the clean *jadoo* that gives the power to see and sometimes the power to save.'"

To further describe Mr. Jacob it may be said that he was undoubtedly a clever conjuror and mesmerist. He has been supposed to have been a Russian spy, a political agent, an astrologer and magician. He was certainly a wonderful linguist, for he could talk, amongst other languages, English, Urdu, Persian, Turkish, Arabic, and French with considerable fluency. The stories that have been woven around him, the rumours of the fortunes he has made and lost, are legion. Unhappily in recent years Mr. Jacob has been pursued by misfortune, and Simla now knows him no more. His auctions, his tea and dinner parties, are things of the past. And it was one of the world's famous diamonds that really began his ill fortune. It was in 1891 that the Imperial Diamond Case created such a sensation in India. Mr. Jacob, in a word, contracted to deliver a certain diamond, then in England, to the Nizam of Hyderabad for the sum of forty-six lakhs of rupees (about £300,000). He received a deposit of 23 lakhs but the Nizam declined to ratify the agreement. How a commission proceeded to Hyderabad to examine His Highness of Hyderabad and Sir Dennis Fitzpatrick, the Resident; how the trial in which a large number of the leading barristers of India were engaged, was concluded in Calcutta on the 22nd December 1891, after a sensational fourteen days' trial; and how a verdict of acquittal was given in Mr. Jacob's favour: was all duly reported at extraordinary length in the papers of the day. But though Mr. Jacob won his case, his expenses were great. His reputation suffered, his good luck deserted him, and many of his possessions were eventually sold at a considerable sacrifice in Simla about two years ago. I have heard that a life of this interesting man will presently see the light from the pen of an American lady who has secured the necessary details from Mr. Jacob himself. It will certainly be worth reading.

Mr. Jacob treated his regular customers at Simla with fairness and often with generosity. But he was 'down' as a rule on the English tourist, as may be gathered from the following anecdote:—One of his favoured customers, having to receive Rs. 8 change from a note given in payment for a small purchase, said to him "Oh! can't you give me something out of the shop instead of cash?" "I don't deal in such trifles," replied Jacob, "as a rule, but it so happens that there is a brass camel from Jaipur which is priced at Rs. 12. You may have that for your Rs. 8, especially as I sold the last one for Rs. 600." "How on earth was that?" asked his surprised customer. "Well," said Mr. Jacob, "one of those wandering Lords came round and looked over the shop. Seeing the camel, he asked how much for that gold animal. 'Rs. 600,' said I. You see I didn't say it was gold; he did, and he paid up." Saying which, Mr. Jacob went into the back room, pulled down a ledger from a shelf, turned over the leaves, and pointed to an entry "Lord —, one brass camel, Rs. 600." Under English law, by the way, this constituted no offence, as was proved in a trial concerning the sale of a picture under similar circumstances. [It so happens that this eight-rupee camel has passed into my own possession, having been presented to me by the customer (a well-known official), who told me the story.]

As a curiosity dealer Mr. Jacob has been succeeded by Mr. Imre Schwaiger, whose collection of curios will be well remembered by the Durbar visitors at Delhi, and whose establishment in Simla is one of the main attractions on the Mall.

ART IN SIMLA.

Show-room at Mr. Imre Schwaiger.

CHAPTER IX.

The Simla Amateur Dramatic Club.

THE Simla Amateur Dramatic Club, or the A. D. C. as it is popularly and familiarly termed, has always occupied so large a place in the affections of the Simla public, that I make no apology for giving its history at somewhat unusual length in this chapter. Anglo-Indian society, especially in northern India, is to a great extent dependent upon its own resources for any form of popular entertainment, and it has only been, comparatively speaking, of recent years that professional companies from abroad who have visited the cities of Calcutta and Bombay have met with any fair measure of success. Several theatrical ventures in this country have indeed, as is well known, ended in what can be truly termed financial disaster, and until quite lately theatrical managers have been chary of sending out first-rate companies on tour, even to the provincial capitals of India. The Brough Company stands out perhaps as one of the few instances of a superior company achieving any real success. No professional performers of any standing have yet visited Simla. Simla has ever been the home of amateur theatricals; the Gaiety Theatre has time after time produced the best London plays, and Poona, Ootacamund, and Mussoorie have not yet succeeded in vieing with the talent of its actors, or the all-round excellence of its plays.

If Colonel Newnham Davis, himself no mean actor, may be taken as an authority, Simla is the Mecca of amateur actors in the East, and the A. D. C.—probably the best equipped amateur club in the world—is an example of the pitch of efficiency to which an amateur organisation can be brought abroad.

It is highly probable too that Simla is the oldest home of amateur acting in India, as I find that Miss Eden wrote on 9th June 1838:—

"We went to the play last night. There is a sort of little theatre at Simla, small and hot, and somewhat dirty, but it does very well. Captain N. got up a prospectus of six plays for the benefit of starving people at Agra, and there was a long list of subscribers, but then the actors fell out. One man took a fit of low spirits, and another who acted women's parts well, would not cut off his moustachios, and another went off to shoot bears near the snowy range. So the scheme fell through, which was a pity, as the subscription alone would have ensured £30 every night of acting to these poor people. So when the gentlemen gave it up, the uncovenanted service (the clerks in the public offices) said they wished to try. We went and lent them the band, and the house was quite full, and they really acted remarkably well, one Irishman in particular."

On August 18th Miss Eden wrote in her Journal:—

"We had to go to another play last night. Luckily they only acted two farces, so we were home at ten, but anything much worse I never saw. There were three women's parts in the last farce, and the clerks had made their bonnets out of their broad straw hats tied on; they had gowns with no plaits in them, and no petticoats, nor *bustles.* One of them—a very fat black half-caste—stood presenting his enormous flat back to the audience, and the lover observed with great pathos, 'Upon my soul that is a most interesting little *gurl.*'"

The following epilogue was delivered on this occasion, the actual theatre being a portion of the Royal, now Lowrie's Hotel:—

"At length on old Himalaya's lofty brow
For the first time, the curtained stage we show!
Some small deficiencies may meet the view
For these our best apologies are due.
Next ought we, if we followed ancient use,
T' invoke the Tragic and the Comic Muse;
To place their portraits in our audience' eyes,
And trust to them our future destinies;—
But who alas! has heard the muse's name,
Since in sad hour to Eastern climes she came?
E'en in these scenes, where varied nature showers
Her fairest gifts, and puts forth all her powers,
In no best spot have classic forms appeared—
No lyre divine amid the wilds been heard—
No heavenly visions throng the flowery vale
Though temple yields to lovelier Annandale.
Though Jakko raises high his grassy crest
No light-heeled Oreads tread his spacious breast:
Though dark the forest on Mahassoo's side,
No buskin'd Dryads there are seen to glide;
Though clear the stream, and lost the waveworn hall
No Naiad haunts the Simla Waterfall!
Then who shall o'er our rising hopes preside?
Whom shall we call? What deities provide?
But stay! What needs it wand'ring far to seek
For fabled muses, and for sounding Greek,—
Where lo! before us, all that we require,—
The mind to judge, the beauty to inspire,
Fair ladies! your protection we engage,—
To you we dedicate our infant stage.
Then kindly listen, while, our cares and pains
Left far beneath us in the sultry plains,

We strive to wile the passing eve away
And cheer you with a laughter-moving play.
Then, if our enterprise, not wholly vain,
Shall add one pleasant hour to memory's train—
If we shall light one joyous sparkle more
In eyes whose triumph was too sure before,
Would you deny from gratitude displayed?
Grant but your praise, and all our toils are paid."

On September 13th Miss Eden's diary runs: "This is the first time I have had an evening quite alone in an English fashion since we came to India, not even a stray Aide-de-Camp about. They are all gone to the last of the Simla theatricals. I had seen four out of five plays, so excused myself."

Later on, however, matters seem to have improved, for Miss Eden wrote on October 20th:—"We had such an excellent play last night, or rather two farces, acted chiefly by Captain X. and M. and Mr. C. and by Captain Y., one of Sir G.'s Aides-de-Camp. Captain X. is really quite as good as Liston, and I think he ought to run over a scene or two every evening for our diversion. It is supposed that R. was never seen to laugh till he cried before, which he certainly did last night. It is astonishing how refreshing a real good laugh is.'

Some years after this a building in the shape of a quadrangle was erected in the lower bazaar which was used by the Simla community as Assembly Rooms, a portion being set aside as a theatre. In 1852, an accident which might have been attended with far more serious results occurred here on the occasion of a dance. It appears that some days previously a Frenchman had given a theatrical performance, and not finding the stage wide enough for his scenery, had removed two of the main supports of the roof. On the day of the dance the rain had been pouring down in torrents, and just before the hour appointed for the supper, which had been arranged in the centre room, the roof came in with a crash, burying all the tables and furniture. The musicians had luckily just left the room, but their instruments were destroyed in the ruins. A few minutes later and the dancers would have been seated at supper, and the loss of life would have been serious.

The theatre was next moved to 'Abbeville,' a house which had been built by a Frenchman, and which after being altered and improved by some officers who purchased it during Lord Ellenborough's time, became the Assembly Rooms of the station. The property is reported to have changed hands in 1863, when the proprietor added a handsome stage, and here a memorable ball was given by the Maharaja of Jeypore in 1869, to the Earl and Countess of Mayo. The Assembly Rooms, including the adjoining racquet court, constructed by Captain Tytler at a cost of about Rs. 24,000, were converted into a Limited Company with a capital of Rs. 70,000 in 280 shares at Rs. 250 each, and for some time is understood to have returned shareholders nine per cent. These buildings have long since disappeared, and the Simla meat market now stands on the site of the racquet court.

Mr. William Tayler of Patna fame has left it on record that in 1864 'Still Waters run deep,' 'Betsy Baker,' and 'She stoops to conquer' were performed in Simla, and among those who acted were Mrs. Innes, Mrs. C. Johnston, Mrs. Strachey, Mrs. Johnson and Miss Butler, Majors Allen Johnson, Innes, and Burne (the latter afterwards Sir Owen). The theatrical managers were Major Innes, Colonel Massey, and Mr. William Tayler.

In 1865, Mr. William Tayler conducted, at the residence of Sir John Lawrence, by the latter's request, the production of scenes from the 'Talisman' and 'Ivanhoe.' Sir John took much interest in the preliminary arrangements and rehearsals, and both he and Lady Lawrence expressed special satisfaction at the result. The gentlemen actors included Colonel Blane, Majors Vicars, O. Wilkinson, and Lumsden, Captain Lockwood, Messrs. Gossett, Onslow and Macnabb, and have been described as well suited to their characters. The ladies who formed a picturesque and captivating group included Mrs. F. Hogg, Misses Durand, Plowden, Lawrence, A. Norman, Bazley and Anson.

'The Rivals,' 'Box and Cox,' and 'The Day after the Wedding' were other plays at this period, and among the actors were Captain W. Harbord, General Brind, Captains Minto Elliot, A. Prinsep, Edwards, Butler, and others.

Lord Mayo, who was very fond of theatricals, on one occasion gave an entertainment at 'Peterhoff' at which he had engaged Dave Carson, formerly a well known and popular favourite of the Calcutta stage, to amuse his guests. The income tax was then a burning question of the day, and Carson had been warned that personalities regarding any of the high officials would be unwelcome. In a song, however, called 'The blue tailed fly' he introduced allusions about the odious tax which were so clever and comical that both the Viceroy and the Finance Minister (Sir Richard Temple) were quickly in uncontrolled fits of laughter.

Val Prinsep tells an amusing story of the theatre in August 1877. The Maharaja of Nabha went to see the burlesque of 'Robert Macaire' in which the following verse was sung:—

When my wife against my will
Goes out, I never stops her;
But when she's gone a little way,
I calls her back and 'whops' her.

The Foreign Secretary at the Maharaja's request translated the above words as best he could. "We do not do that," responded Nabha gravely, "we shouldn't let our wives go out at all." "He probably thinks," adds

Prinsep, "that the above song is a picture of an English gentleman's behaviour, and that Lord Lytton continually 'whops' his lady." Prinsep also wrote that theatricals were much in vogue, and he was asked to get up a piece. But he found this next to impossible, since Mrs. M. whom he wanted to act with Mrs. N. refused to do so, while Mrs. X. would act with neither!

From the interesting volume published in 1898 by W. G. Elliott on 'Amateur Clubs and Actors,' which contains a delightful chapter by Lieutenant-Colonel Newnham Davis on 'Amateurs in foreign parts,' I glean a number of interesting facts about the A. D. C. in the seventies.

Although there were several theatrical performances at the Commander-in-Chief's house—Lady Mansfield being particularly fond of them—as well as elsewhere, it is on record that Sir John Lawrence, the Viceroy, did not encourage acting, and it was not perhaps till Lord Lytton's viceroyalty that any real encouragement from high quarters was given to acting in Simla. Since then the Viceroy has always continued to support the stage. Dramatic plant exists at both the Commander-in-Chief's and Lieutenant-Governor's official residences; theatricals were constantly given at Snowdon in the days of Lord Roberts and Sir George White; and Lord Lansdowne caused a special stage to be built, scenery and a drop scene to be painted for Viceregal Lodge when he entertained Lord and Lady Harris on a visit from Bombay. The theatre, which in Lord Lytton's time stood alongside the main block of the present market, consisted of two large rooms, one of which, the auditorium of the theatre, had a splendid dancing floor. The building was, however, in a very inconvenient position with the native bazaar in close proximity. 'Plot and Passion' and 'The Ticket of Leave Man' were among the earlier plays put on, the latter play being acted for the benefit of Rosa Cooper, a professional actress who had played with Phelps. In 1877 a version of the 'Contrabandista' with "a very original dialogue" was produced, and Val Prinsep, who had come to India to paint a picture of the Imperial Assemblage of 1877, wrote the libretto. 'The Passing Cloud,' also by Val Prinsep, was staged in this year, and Colonel Newnham Davis tells us that the ranks of the A. D. C. were strengthened by the advent of the lady who afterwards played on the English stage under the 'nom-de-plume' of Madame San Carolo, that "Bwab" made an appearance in 'Society,' and Lord 'Bill' Beresford was the Irishman in the Owl's Roost scene.

To quote from the writer I have mentioned: "These were the days that dwellers in Simla with long theatrical memories always talk of as the 'Riddell and Liddell time.' They were both young officers on the Viceregal staff; now the former is the trusted business manager to the Kendals, the latter a light of the Stock Exchange, one of Her Majesty's Gentlemen-at-arms and a star of the yearly performances of the 'Windsor Strollers': and Lord Lytton, the Viceroy, encouraged theatricals unreservedly. The theatre was re-decorated, three boxes were built for the three great powers of Simla, the Viceroy, the Commander-in-Chief, and the Lieutenant-Governor of the Punjab; and the season of 1878 commenced with the production of the first Lord Lytton's drama 'Walpole,' the rehearsals of which were superintended by the Viceroy. It is an old-fashioned play, dealing with Jacobite plots, and written in rhymed Alexandrine verse. Report says that some of the actors found the lengths of verse anything but easy matter to commit to memory; but then a viceregal stage-manager does not appear every day. This was not the only play produced under the direction of the Viceroy, for at Calcutta, during one of the winter seasons, 'The School for Scandal' was rehearsed under the viceregal eye. It was no doubt an invention of the enemy; but those who were inclined to gird at the Viceroy for his love of gorgeousness, declared that he could never superintend a rehearsal until an especially resplendent sofa, all gilding and yellow satin, had been placed facing the stage, and His Excellency duly enthroned thereon.

"A period of wars followed; the news of the death of Cavagnari arrived at Simla during one of the A. D. C. performances; and the fortunes of the club ebbed, for nearly all the men who should have played or paid were away in Afghanistan. There came a dire day when the A. D. C. owed two years' rent of the theatre and had not the wherewithal to pay. Lord Bill Beresford came to the rescue. He was Military Secretary to the Viceroy, and was the guiding spirit of all race-meetings and gymkhanas in the summer capital, but he cheerfully took a new burden on his shoulders. He made an arrangement as to the rent; the resources of Peterhoff were brought to bear to aid the theatre; the wars ceased, and the men swarmed back to Simla; little suppers after the performances, to which each actor was entitled to ask a guest, became so popular, that the competition to be allowed to play, even as a super, was keen; and Hobday and his burlesques sprang into prominence. Major, then Captain, Hobday was one of Lord Roberts' Aides-de-Camp, and could not only write very witty doggerel, but was a clever burlesque actor and an excellent stage manager. A burlesque, put upon the stage regardless of expense, became one of the events of the A. D. C. season; the fairest of Capua's daughters sang in the chorus; and the art of stage-dancing was much cultivated. Elaborate scenic effects were attempted, and one at least of the burlesques played almost as long on its *première* as a Drury Lane pantomime does."

Continuing his remarks on the Simla stage, Colonel Newnham Davis wrote:

"The Deanes, Mrs. Wheler, Mrs. Fortescue-Porter, Mrs. Harry Stuart, Percy Holland, C. de C. Hamilton, Hunter Weston, Yeatman-Biggs were the stars of the dramatic side; while in musical pieces, the direction of which were in the safe hands of Major H. Clarke, Miss Ribbentrop, Miss Collen, and Miss Halliday made special successes."

Soon after Lord William Beresford came to the rescue of the theatre, Colonels P. D. Henderson and J. Deane joined him as lessees, and continued to manage and run the performances till 1888, when the present A. D. C. was formed at a breakfast held at 'Valentine,' then Colonel Henderson's residence, at which some eighteen persons, interested in Simla theatricals, were present. Mr. and Mrs. D. McCracken are now the only representatives in Simla of that historic gathering. The A. D. C. then formally took over the theatre from Lord William Beresford, Colonels Henderson and Deane, and commenced its present successful career. The first formal meeting of the Executive Committee of the A. D. C. was held on 21st May 1888, at which Colonels Deane and Morton, Major Rowan Hamilton, and Mr. D. McCracken were present. In the same year the club was registered as a joint stock company under Act XXI of 1860. The club at this time numbered only 20 members; to-day there are 350 on its rolls. The profits of the performances have been expended from time to time in improving the theatre, both before and behind the curtain. Much has been done, but the structural defects of the building have considerably hampered the arrangements for shifting and storing scenery, and stage management generally. Up to 1896 the theatre continued to be lighted by oil lamps, a source of great inconvenience and danger, which on one occasion nearly led to a catastrophe. Just after the curtain had fallen at the close of a burlesque, a whole row of kerosene oil headlights fell with a crash on to the stage, and set fire to the scenery. The fire was, however, promptly extinguished with the sand stored for the purpose at the wings. The actors and audience behaved with admirable restraint on the trying occasion and there was no panic. The installation of the electric light, while adding to the safety of the theatre, has brought the lighting of the auditorium and stage thoroughly up to date. It cost from first to last about Rs. 15,000, and the same plant is used for lighting the Masonic Lodge and the ballroom of the Town Hall.

The auditorium of the theatre has been repeatedly altered and improved. At one period there were six upper boxes, three on each side with a gallery in the centre. Next three large boxes took the place of the centre gallery; now a gallery runs right round the theatre with seats raised in tiers so as to give an uninterrupted view of the stage.

The A. D. C. pays the Municipality Rs. 3,000 per annum for the use of the theatre on condition that no other portion of the Town Hall is let for theatricals, or entertainments for which stage fittings are required. On the other hand, the theatre cannot be let for concerts pure and simple.

The old theatre continued, however, to be used after the new theatre was opened in June 1887, for performances given by non-members of the club, till it was burnt down in the great fire of May 1889. This fire consumed a large portion of the eastern end of the main bazaar with the Municipal Market, and at one time threatened to destroy the church. Just as the roof of the sacred edifice had commenced to burn, however, a contrary north wind fortunately sprang up, and beat the flames down on to the old theatre and market, thereby saving the church. The small grove of trees between the church and Lowrie's hotel was completely destroyed, and the whole side of Jakko, then dry as tinder, seems to have had a narrow escape from destruction. The A. D. C. in this fire lost a good deal of scenery which was on loan in the old theatre at the time.

On the 30th May 1887, at the opening of the new Gaiety Theatre, Mrs. 'Joey' Deane spoke the following prologue which was specially written by Colonel Deane:—

Ere yet we bid the dear old boards adieu,
And raise the curtain which conceals the new,
Let truant Fancy pause, and call to mind
The triumphs past, which oft we there designed,
To pass an hour midst follies of the age,
Remembering yet that 'all the world's a stage.'
How deftly Lytton helped us thro' the plot
Of *Walpole*, nor in *Scandal's School* forgot
The maxim Sheridan was wont to take,
That play and players follow Nature's wake.
The *Overland Route*, Lord Ripon's toils assuaged,
His glances following throughout *Engaged*,
Our Simpson sweetest, there seen at her best,
Plaintive, yet charming, easily impressed.
Like her, let others merit your applause,
By sparking mimicry in woman's cause,
As many have, with every graceful art,
Both charmed your fancy, and e'en reached your heart.
To name them all would trespass on your time,
And make you weary of the Poet's rhyme.
Yet still indulgence from your ears we sue,
The sentimental muse to bring in view,
The *Frozen Deep* was watched with glance severe,
And yet its scenes developed pity's tear,
Helped by triumphant art, midst captious smiles,
With Sarto's brush, and Kenny-Herbert's wiles,

Liddell, MacCall, in *Plot and Passion* try,
Nor vainly, they, with Sinkinson, to vie.
The *Roses* twain, by Foote, ne'er trampled were,
In *School's* flirtation Cunningham did stir
Our Boys to efforts which their *Caste* displayed,
In *Home's* bright scene. *The Parvenu* dismayed
Straight sought *The Magistrate* and vowed, forsooth,
Blank verse to try, in Gilbert's *Palace o' Truth.*
Pygmalion's Galatea then was made,
To win poor Chrysos o'er in Delphic shade.
Our wings of fancy soon took higher strokes,
And operetta critic's wit provokes.
In *Trial by Jury*, *Patience*' holy laws
Were broke, when *Pinafore* was made a cause
For *Pirates* wild a *Crimson Scarf* to wear.
Mikado followed with his music rare,
In quaint Japan, the eccentric plot was laid;
Combs decked the warrior, fans concealed the maid.
McCracken's scene no stage would e'er disgrace,
Where praise is due, to him the foremost place.
But yet, we've had our impecunious days,
For ancient comedies and modern plays,
Financial rules are posts that mark the course,
Which way our William shall direct his horse;
He took the fence which others shirked, yet still,
Forgets how much we owe our little Bill.
Shall we behold each face with pleasure glow,
Unthankful to the friend who made them so?
To-night, let busy man to pleasure spare,
The hour New Gaiety claims—abandon care,
No stolid Monarch of a puppet age
Is here to-night to view our new born stage,
The Earl who bears the Royal sceptre here,
To all our efforts, lends a gracious ear.
His consort, too, untwists the mingled fame,
That sinks the player in the poet's name,
She knows what gives each sentence strength and grace,
And shapes the pliant mien of Thalia's face.
Sir Frederick, too, must have a 'play' to-night,
And starve those warriors who so bravely fight.
Pardon the boldness that we here should dare,
These names so famous on our stage to bear,
Has not the fate of men and Empires been
The common business of the tragic scene?
Who writes should follow Nature without fail,
Mix shades with light, and paint the unvarnished tale,
Since plays are but the mirrors of our lives,

On this new stage, let maidens, widows, wives,
Essay the art to please, and nothing more,
And add to past success another score.
Some active minds, in Simla, oft must be
Weighed down by idleness to misery,
No fool should thus his time in suffering waste,
The stage here offers an amusement chaste,
Which in its proper use, may surely try
To help the lessons of the Church close by.
So let us strive each other to excel,
Shall we succeed or not? Why—' *Time will Tell.*'

Time will Tell' was the opening play of the new theatre, hence the allusion in the last line. Among the actors in the play were Colonel Stewart (known as Red Stewart), Colonel Henderson, Captain Rowan Hamilton, Captain (now Colonel) Rundall, Captain (now Colonel) Davies, Miss Carter, and Mrs. Fletcher.

This prologue called forth on the 9th June 1887 some amusing verses in the columns of the *Civil and Military Gazette,* which were at once declared to be the work of Rudyard Kipling.

In the matter of a Prologue.

"The best actors in the world, either for tragedy, comedy, history, pastoral, pastoral-comical, historical-pastoral, tragical-historical, tragical-comical-historical-pastoral, scene individual, or poem unlimited."

For past performances, methinks, 't were fit
To let the patient public give the chit,
Albeit, scarce their memory can score,
Your triumphs since the season " seventy-four "
When Lytton ruled the roast, and—so it is sung—
The Empire and the Amateurs were young.
You, then as now, were Irvings, Baretts, Keans,
For you the local Stansfield painted scenes.
The lenient eyes of Marquises and Earls
Watched, then as now, your not too girlish girls,
And deftly praised with diplomatic guile
The high-strung pathos that provoked a smile,
Survivors of a score of Simla years—
Hot for fresh praise and panting for fresh cheers—
Why tell us this? Full oft have we confessed,
But Smith to-day is gone, and gone is Jones,
He of the nut-brown curls and dulcet tones,
'Macready' Boffkins left in ' seventy-eight,'
And Burbles is a Minister of State.
Yea, these are gone, and Time, the grim destroyer,
Already blurs their photos in your foyer,

Though Boffkins' sneer throughout the hills was known,
And Burbles' Faust was mentioned in Ceylon.
Sweet must it be to you, remembering these,
To gild afresh half-faded memories,
Belaud the past, and, in the praise you paste,
Praise most yourselves—the Perfect and the chaste.
Why "chaste" amusement? Do our morals fail,
Amid the deodars of Annandale?
Into what vicious vortex do they plunge
Who dine on Jakko or in Boileaugunge?
Of course it's "chaste." Despite the artless paint,
And P—mm's best wig, who dares to say it ain't?
Great Grundy! Does a sober matron sink
To infamy through rouge and Indian ink?
Avaunt the thought. As tribute to your taste,
We certify the Simla stage is chaste.
Mellowed by age, and cooled by tempering Time,
We find it venerable and sublime.
But newer generations take their seats
Unversed in Boffkins' or in Burbles' feats,
And these perhaps exacting babes may say:—
"The audience, not the actors, judge the play,"
Nor think that lady-critic over bold,
Who said not "Time will tell" but "Time hath told."

It was in this year that the little stage at Snowdon was opened in the new ball-room, and a performance was given in aid of Lady Roberts' 'Homes in the Hills.' Captain Carter, 5th Northumberland Fusiliers, painted a pigsticking drop-scene for the occasion, the Deanes played 'Delicate Ground,' and Colonel Neville Chamberlain produced the burlesque 'Lucia di Lammermoor.' The prologue which was composed by Rudyard Kipling was spoken by Miss Kipling (now Mrs. Fleming), and the opening lines contained the following:—

The others, who portray poor Lucia's griefs,
Are all in their respective lines the chiefs.
The army list eluci(a)dates this fact.

Miss Kipling was dressed as a nurse, and it may be mentioned as an instance of Lord Roberts' wonderful memory that in 1902 he sent a charming message concerning the prologue, and her costume, to the lady who had delivered it with such delightful effect fifteen years before. In June 1888 there were some particularly amusing 'Wax works' at Snowdon in which Miss (now Lady) Aileen Roberts took part.

About this time 'A Scrap of Paper' was played at Lady Dufferin's request in aid of the building fund of the Roman Catholic church then being built: the cast included Rudyard Kipling as 'Brisemouche,' Major Burton,

Colonel Rundall, Major Medley, Mrs. Burton, Mrs. Freddy Atkinson, Mrs. Levett-Yeats, and Mrs. 'Theosophist' Gordon.

Colonel Newnham Davis has a highly appropriate allusion to the services of Mr. D. McCracken, now the head of the Thagi and Dakaiti Department, who has for so many years lent such unselfish and invaluable aid in the onerous work of scene painting. He also tells us how the foyer at the Town Hall led to the Freemason's Lodge as well as to the Gaiety; how dates clashed, and how the supporters of the theatre talked of the convenience of the Viceroy or Commander-in-Chief, while the Freemasons fell back upon Solomon and Hiram of Tyre. With references to the 'Midsummer Night's Dream,' played in aid of Lady Roberts' Homes in the Hills, which had to be suddenly transferred from the open grounds of Peterhoff to the ball-room of the Town Hall, and with allusions to successes scored by Fritz Ponsonby, Baden-Powell, Wilkinson and Mrs. Wheler, Colonel Newnham Davis' most readable article on Simla acting closes.

A play which was excellently acted at Viceregal Lodge in Lord Lansdowne's viceroyalty was 'A Sheep in Wolf's Clothing' in which Colonel Newnham Davis, Captain G. Williams, Mr. P. Holland, Mrs. Little, Mrs. Lambert, and Miss Way took the principal parts.

Two very prominent supporters of the Simla A. D. C. were Colonel and Mrs. Deane, whose connection with Simla theatricals extended over several years. At a dinner given in their honour on the occasion of the Colonel's leaving Simla in May 1898, some interesting speeches were made, of which I give a few extracts. Among the hosts were the late Sir James and Lady Westland, the Hon'ble Mr. (now Sir Charles) Rivaz, Sir William Cuningham, General Morton, and in fact all the leading lights of the theatrical world of Simla. Sir James Westland, who proposed the toast of the evening, said he was proud to be spokesman on the occasion because he thought he could claim a longer acquaintanceship with Colonel and Mrs. Deane than anyone else present. Having made some amusing remarks regarding the impropriety of alluding to a lady's age, Sir James referred in sympathetic terms to the long connection of the guests of the evening with the Simla stage, and to their numerous histrionic triumphs which had given so much pleasure to the public. His remarks were greeted with loud applause, which was renewed when he also alluded to General Morton's efforts to improve the local drama. He would, he said, leave General Morton to speak of the numerous characters the Deanes had filled during past years. They had been the best of actors, there had been no tinge of jealousy in their dispositions, and all had gone to them from time to time for advice. It was largely due to their efforts that the present high standard of acting had been reached in India, and that amateurs in Simla could almost compare at times

MAJOR 'JOEY' DEANE.
IN 'THE MIKADO,' 1885.

COLONEL R. S. S. BADEN POWELL.
IN 'THE GEISHA,' 1894.

with the best actors at home. They left the impression of good work behind them, and all who were with them on the present occasion looked forward to meeting them on the other side of the water later on. Colonel and Mrs. Deane's healths were then drunk with musical honours. Colonel Deane in the course of his reply said:—

We are indeed fortunate in having secured Sir James Westland as president of our club, and in knowing that he not only takes an interest in our financial success, but reviews and advises us on our monthly expenditure. We may therefore feel assured that we are reasonably safe, for does he not hold the purse strings of the Empire, and is he not one that displays the same kindly interest in almost every analogous institution in the amusement and recreation of Simla? With him is associated on our finance committee my old friend General Morton, who, out of pure love for the drama and its surroundings, gives some of his, alas! all too few leisure moments to doing everything to advance and elevate our club and its productions. To him is mainly due the lighting of this theatre with electricity and many other improvements in regard to decorations, etc., which have made it more appreciated than formerly. And this reminds me how steady has been our advance in the past few years, and of a name to which I would like to refer as one who has also done a great deal for our stage and for sport in Simla (I allude to our friend Bill Beresford). Before this theatre was built, our theatricals took place close by, in a building which is now the municipal market. Many were the good and successful plays there produced, and at one time, when financial difficulties threatened a closing of our doors, he came forward in the most public spirited manner with the necessary funds to keep our show alive. For several years thus was the venture conducted, he supplying the sinews of war, and I—well, something else. I remember that it used to be generally thought he made vast sums out of the transaction. These were the days of champagne suppers, generally provided at his expense, now we have to be content with the "wine of my country," so I am well aware that he was always on the wrong side of the book . . . . I may perhaps refer to one in front of the curtain, who has invariably been kind to us all, and that is my friend Mr. Hensman. It is needless for me to refer to the influence which the press exercises in all parts of the world over the stage and all connected with it. The space which is occupied in the papers at home in regard to matters theatrical is significant testimony of the very great interest taken by the public in such matters. The articles are usually written by gentlemen of known learning, ability, and discretion, but I doubt whether any of them has during a long period of theatrical review displayed comment so fair, and in such good taste and judgment, as he whose twinkle of the eye I now catch. He has never forgotten that we are, after all, but amateurs, that we do our best to please, that encouragement is needed, and so the theatre and its actors remain his debtors. It is not too much to say that had our press treatment been severe, the local drama would have languished, and, perhaps, have died. This would have been a pity, for it seems to me, looking back, that Simla is really a sufficiently dull place and cannot dispense with one of its intellectual amusements. Some such distractions are surely admirable, and having been enjoyed, perhaps the machinery of state will go round none the worse therefor. We are apt to forget in the press of officialdom how much we lose by turning out here music, pictures, sculpture, the drama, and the many things of beauty that are joys for ever. Well, I hope you will all live to enjoy them, and when the time comes to turn your back on India, I cannot wish you better, than to have as happy a retrospect, as I am glad to say I enjoy. In a few hours I shall be on my way to other climes, to the rattle of the tonga bar, which already seems to say to me, in the words of Lepel Griffin,—

Farewell to Peliti, whose menus delicious,
  Have helped our digestion the long season through,
Farewell to the scandals so false and malicious,
  And all the more piquant, for not being true.
Au revoir to the ladies, farewell to them never,
  Who are most of them pretty, and all of them good,
Whose saintly example and gentle endeavour
  Would surely reform me, if anything could.

No retrospect of our connection with Simla theatricals would be complete without some allusion to happy performances at Viceregal Lodge and Snowdon. I can, however, go back further still, for my first Viceregal performance was before Lord Mayo, in Calcutta, in 1871, and almost my first at Simla was in aid of the Mayo Memorial Hall, when Lepel Griffin gracefully wrote :—

Then fitly we give the last night of the season
  Ere the last curtain falls, and our comedy ends,
To recall our lost leader, whom red-handed treason
  Snatched too soon from his country—too soon from his friends.
Fame dwells not in halls of memorial beauty,
  In the wealth of the brush, or praise of the pen,
But for those who have seen nought in living but duty,
  She lives in the loving remembrance of men.

No more staunch supporter of the drama ever came to India than Lord Lytton. Under his own auspices the original play of 'Walpole' by his father was produced with great success in 1878, and in 1880 the 'School for Scandal' was played at Government House, Calcutta, with lavish expenditure in costumes, and great success. Lord Dufferin loved the stage, and took the keenest interest in all its productions, and every Viceroy has more or less patronised the drama and given performances in which we have shared. At Snowdon, too, we have had very delightful performances; they are too many to refer to now, but some of them have been mentioned in Sir James Westland's all too flattering speech. In connection with one of them given during Lord Roberts' time, I must, at the risk of being thought vain, quote a few lines by Rudyard Kipling :—

Then having met all possible detractors,
We will not ask you to excuse our actors,
  Some you know well—their art in bygone years
  Has moved the Gaiety to mirth and tears,
Brought as the act-drop closed upon the scene
  To English lips the Moslem cry of 'Din' (Deane).

Well, I have no doubt other Deanes may be forthcoming to uphold the reputation of the Simla stage. I am leaving some of that name behind me here, to await your call, and if they should fail you, I have no doubt there will be in the future, as in the past, others of a different name, far more worthy of your recognition and entertainment than I have proved. In saying farewell to the Simla A. D. C., I wish it every success, and hope it may be fortunate in securing in future such assistance as has been hitherto given it by Sir James Westland, General Morton, Mr. McCracken, Colonel Jerrard, Colonel Craigie, Captain Pressey, and in its actor management by Captains Holloway, Samson, Hobday, Fraser and many others.

General Morton then following, said:—

In obedience to the president's orders, the archives of the club have been searched to trace the history of the Deane family from a dramatic point of view. Thomas—otherwise Joseph—Deane exhibited remarkable precocity as an infant in arms, and later on his talents developed to such an extent, that an infant relative was with difficulty rescued from a watery grave in the family bath tub, due to a rehearsal of the celebrated scene out of 'The Colleen Bawn,' in which the aforesaid Thomas played the part of Danny Man. Coming to India to join the King's Dragoon Guards, Mr. Deane, then a 'nubilis juvenis,' was able, owing to his very beardlessness, to take parts now assigned to the fair sex. Fate transferred him to Calcutta, where he acted so well, in one part at least, that he persuaded Miss Jessie Murray, now Mrs. Deane, to share his fortunes. In 1872 he was seen with that accomplished lady as Citizen Sangfroid and his wife in 'Delicate Ground' at Calcutta. Transferred to the Military department at Simla, Colonel and Mrs. Deane played in a succession of sterling plays between 1877 and 1898. It would be impossible to recount all the parts they have played, but the following are the more important, and these plays fully exhibit the wonderful versatility of talent they possess: Colonel Deane—Sam Gerridge in 'Caste,' Perkin Middlewick in 'Our Boys,' Mr. Lovibond in 'Overland Route,' Jack Merridew in 'My Milliner's Bill,' in which Mrs. Deane played Mrs. Merridew and in which they repeated the thrilling scene of Danny Man and Eily O'Connor of 'The Colleen Bawn,' Desmarets in 'Plot and Passion,' Wilfred Shadbolt in 'Yeomen of the Guard,' Chrysos in 'Pygmalion and Galatea,' and to come to more recent performances, Our Mr. Jenkins in 'Two Roses,' the Dean in 'Dandy Dick,' and Sir Richard Kato in the 'Case of Rebellious Susan.' Mrs. Deane's best parts were those of Mrs. Bunter in 'New Men and Old Acres,' Polly Eccles in 'Caste,' Mrs. Sebright in 'Overland Route,' Mrs. Pinchbeck in 'Home,' Maggie MacFarlane in 'Bonnie Fishwife,' Georgina Tidman in 'Dandy Dick,' Lady Teazle in 'School for Scandal,' Our Mrs. Jenkins in 'Two Roses,' Peg Woffington in 'Masks and Faces,' and The Blind Mrs. Preston in 'Cape Mail.' The places of two such amateur actors on the Simla stage cannot be filled. To-night we part with Colonel Deane, but we may perhaps induce his wife to appear again on these, to her, familiar boards. They carry with them our regrets at their loss, but they leave behind them the memories of the past and the pleasure they have given to their numerous audiences.

The members of the Simla A. D. C. similarly entertained Major-General G. de C. Morton (with his wife and daughter) at a farewell dinner on his departure from India in October of the same year. Sir James Westland occupied the chair, and over 40 members of the A. D. C. were present. Sir

James, in proposing the health of the guests of the evening, referred to General Morton's long connection with the Simla stage, and the loss that would be sustained in theatrical circles by his departure. Actors and public were alike indebted to him for all he had done, not only in the general management, but in attention to all details connected with the production of plays, stage management, and instruction of actors. Sir James paid a tribute to the acting of Miss Morton, and concluded by asking all present to drink the health of their guests, with musical honours. General Morton, in replying, acknowledged the honour done to his wife and daughter and himself by the members of the Simla A. D. C., and his regret at leaving a place endeared to him by so many recollections and associations, and enriched by so many friends. He went on to say :—

Here in 1871 I began my amateur career, and though for several of the years between 1871 and 1898 I was absent from Simla, I have been here sufficiently long to see several generations (I may call them) of actors and actresses play their parts and move on elsewhere. It is now my turn to move on, and in this my farewell speech I should like to recall the names of the more prominent of those who in their day gladdened their audiences and assisted in raising the standard of our amateur performances to its present level. Some of these names will be unfamiliar to those sitting round me. It is the great drawback of the actor's art that his art departs with him : the poet, the sculptor, and the painter hand down their work to posterity ; but beyond tradition there is nothing to give the existing generation a tangible idea of the genius which animated the leading actors of the past century. I do not, of course, pretend that such dramatic genius as I have alluded to is to be found in our small band of amateurs and students of the art, but among the names I am about to give will be found some who, with professional training and more experience, would have risen to high rank on the professional stage.

The names I propose to recall are those of Mrs. Westmorland, Dr. Clifton, Colonel and Mrs. Deane, Norton, Henderson, McCall, Riddell, and his twin A.-D.-C. Liddell, Colonel Dick-Cunyngham, Baden-Powell, Mrs. Le Mesurier, and her talented daughter Mrs. Sinkinson, Percy Holland, Captain and Mrs. Williams, the late and much lamented Yeatman-Biggs and Dacres Cunningham, Mrs. Cunningham, Ponsonby and Crowe, Rowan Hamilton, Colonel and Mrs. Leach, and Miss Collen. To come to more recent times, we have, or hope to have again, Mrs. Owen, Hobday, Wilkieson, Fraser, De Courcy Hamilton, and Mrs. Yeats Hunter, in addition to those now sitting round this table whose recent performances have made their names as familiar in our little world as household words. I can confidently say that my best friends have been made in the cricket field and on the stage. There is in both, but especially in the latter, a spirit of true and a strong feeling of mutual sympathy which bind more closely than is usual in the ordinary avocations of life, and I know no better place or condition for enabling a judgment to be formed of the character and qualities of an individual than associations with him or her during rehearsals or performances. When the club was formed in 1888 I, for one, never contemplated to what it would grow in ten years' time. In my earlier days, the seventies, players were few and far between :

the dramatic instinct which many possessed found expression generally in charades and dumb crambo in private houses; and on these occasions high officials descended from their pedestals and threw themselves into these pastimes with as much zest as their younger friends. A few of the more ambitious spirits got up an occasional play either at the old theatre (the present market of Simla), or at 'Oakover,' or at 'Kennedy House,' the then home of the talented Strachey family, whose descendant is one of our present company. But this venture not only required ambition, but entailed an immense amount of personal labour and energy. In those days there were no Holloways, McCrackens, Brownes, and Simpsons. There was no organisation to meet demands, and scenery, properties, dresses, and the many requirements of the stage had to be created by the promoter at his own risk and by his own hands. We have now in this club an organisation which—with the various improvements, introduced from time to time—has stood the test of ten years' experience, and has enabled us to produce a class and variety of play in rapid succession which would have been impossible without an organised system. I may here allude to the following high class plays which have been produced during the last ten years, and produced, I think I may add, to the satisfaction of our audiences and in a manner which has raised the reputation of the club:—Plot and Passion, Dandy Dick, The Hobby Horse, Overland Route, Masks and Faces, The Red Lamp, Major Hobday's and Captain Fraser's Burlesques, Faust, Ali Baba, Bluebeard Retrimmed and Merry Merchant of Venice, Captain Swift, Jim the Penman, The Money Spinner, Diplomacy, Iolanthe, Liberty Hall, Yeoman of the Guard, The Masqueraders, The Geisha, An Ideal Husband, The Home Secretary, and The Mountebanks. Plays of such a variety are not, I think I am correct in saying, produced in any London theatre. Each theatre there has its own line, and adheres to it; but in our small world here, small though it be, there are varying tastes, and these tastes must be studied and provided for by the management of the one theatre to be found here. We have also produced plays by amateur dramatic authors, and among them I would name Mrs. Scott's 'Minor Poet,' Captain Fraser's plays, and Mr. Irvine's opera 'The Mahatma.' We have had our failures as well as our successes—and what manager has not? Sometimes the style of the play has failed to please, and sometimes our acting may not have been up to the increasingly high standard our admirers have been led to expect; but failure, like adversity, has its wholesome influence, and serves to show that success can only be attained by distinct and sustained effort, by mutual co-operation, and, in short, by strict attendance to business. To bring my remarks up to date, I may now allude to the dramatic season we have just brought to a close. I think we may consider it a success, both dramatically and financially. In the dramatic results we owe much to Mrs. and Miss Wheler, Mr. Jacob, Captain and Mrs. Strachey, Captain Baker-Carr and the Beresford-Lovetts, and, though I say it, who should not, my débutante daughter has played the parts of a cook and a wilful but fascinating young lady with some success . . . We shall start next year with a valuable asset in the shape of the electric light installation and good assets in dresses, scenery, and property. This club has been patronised and supported by every Viceroy who has reigned since its inception, and to His Excellency the present Viceroy we owe our cordial thanks, not only for the personal support and presence accorded by himself, Lady Elgin and the Ladies Bruce, but also for his readiness in placing at our disposal his band for musical plays and (indirectly) for placing on his staff officers so valuable to us as Captains Ponsonby, Pollen and Baker-Carr have been. We are losing from among us several valuable members—Captain Holloway, our stage manager, to whose untiring efforts so much of the success of seasons 1896 and 1898 is due; Mr. Lionel Jacob; Mrs. Deane, whose loss, with that of her husband, we recorded at the commencement of the year; our committee colleague and kindly press critic, Mr. Hensman, whose advice we have always found of such great value; Captain Pollen, our newly discovered 'Jeune Premier;' and last, but not the least, our president, Sir James Westland, with Lady Westland, and his daughters. In Sir James Westland the club loses a president who during his term of office has ever had its interest and welfare at heart. In Lady Westland it loses an actress of great capacity, who always enters into the business of her part, whether it be sweeping a room or disturbing the occupants of a sleeping car, with the full desire to do that part full justice. In the Misses Westland we lose two young actresses of great promise. I have to thank you, ladies and gentlemen, for the very kind reception you have given to the president's toast, and to assure you that, though absent from Simla, I shall always maintain my great interest in the Club, its welfare, and prosperity.

A piece which was extremely well played at Viceregal Lodge, at Lady Elgin's desire, was 'Still Waters Run Deep,' in which Mrs. Beresford-Lovett, Mrs. Barber, Colonel Gunter, Captains Baker-Carr and Ponsonby took part. Last August 'A Scrap of Paper' was most successfully performed at Viceregal Lodge at Lady Curzon's request, the cast including Mesdames Bingley and Wheler, Misses Macquoid, Tandy, Wilcocks and Wheler, Colonel C. de C. Hamilton, Majors Marker and Poynter, Captains Baker-Carr and Wigram. Colonel Hamilton and Miss Macquoid were especially excellent in the leading characters.

To mention the most successful plays that have been performed of recent years on the Gaiety stage is not an easy matter, but the following drew the largest houses and were enthusiastically received:—'The Mikado' (Colonel Deane, Major Barrington Foote, Mr. Du Cane, and Mrs. LeMesurier), and its revival in 1900 under Colonel Kuper's guidance (Colonel Thomson, Major Burt, Mr. Waymouth, Mrs. Iggulden, Misses Turner and Hoseason); Captain Hobday's burlesque 'Ali Baba' in 1893 ran for ten days and was excellently acted by Captains Hobday, Holloway, Baynes, Crowe and Annesley, Mrs. Iggulden and Miss Poyser; and 'Dr. Faust and Miss Marguerite' by the same clever author (Captains Hobday, Holland, Annesley, Fegen, and Crowe, and Mesdames Fegen, Skrine, and Hobday), was also a brilliant success. Few plays have been better staged and acted than 'The Red Lamp' in 1894, in which Generals Morton, Yeatman-Biggs, Captains Ponsonby and Holland, with Mrs. Beresford-Lovett and Mrs. Barber filled the principal characters; while 'The Money Spinner' (Major Simpson and Mrs. Wheler) and 'Diplomacy' (General Yeatman-Biggs, Captains Holland and Ponsonby, Mrs. Wheler, and Miss Collen) were both much

Mr. F. W. Sumner. Miss Frances Macquoid. Major W. L. Conran. Mrs. Mallaby. Lieut.-Col. H. G. Kennard.

"FLORADORA" AT THE GAIETY, 1902.

enjoyed and talked of in Simla. 'The Merry Merchant of Venice,' by Captain Fraser (Major A. Pressey, Captains Fraser and Annesley and Mrs. Iggulden) was the last really good burlesque we have seen in the station. 'The Geisha,' in which General Baden-Powell, of Mafeking fame, played with Miss Turner and Mrs. Elsmie, was an extremely popular production, as was also the 'Masqueraders' (Captain Wilkinson, a born stage manager, Mr L. Jacob and Mrs. Wheler). In 'The Adventures of Lady Ursula,' 1901, Mrs. Coffin, a charming actress, and Captain Finlay, acted perfectly, and in 'Under the Red Robe' Mrs. Tyler and Colonel C. de C. Hamilton scored a big success.

As a musical production it will probably be many years before the 'Cavalleria Rusticana' of 1901—in which Mrs. Carthew Yorstoun, Mrs. Hawkins, Miss A. Watson, and Major J. Turner took part,— is equalled on the local boards. Both music and singing were excellent.

If takings are any criterion of a popular success, 'Floradora,' with a run of eleven nights in 1902, promises to hold the record for some time to come. The principal parts were filled by Colonel H. G. Kennard, Major W. L. Conran, Mrs. Mallaby (a sister of the talented Misses Vanbrugh), and Miss Frances Macquoid with remarkable skill. Miss Macquoid is considered by many competent judges to be the best all-round actress Simla has yet seen.

In addition to plays which have been already alluded to, others which, I think, deserve special mention in more recent years are The Pickpocket, The Private Secretary, Patience, Pinafore, Sweet Lavender, The Gondoliers, In Chancery, Aunt Jack, The Silver Shield, The Critic, Nemesis, The Sorcerer, Niobe, Sunlight and Shadow, Les Cloches de Corneville, The Magistrate, Colonel Othello, V.C., School, The Profligate, The Three Hats, The Chieftain, The New Boy, The Case of Rebellious Susan, The Colonel, David Garrick, Charley's Aunt, The Passport, The Frozen Deep, Ours, His Excellency the Governor, The Liars, My Friend the Prince, Runaway Girl, Manœuvres of Jane, A Royal Family, Gaiety Girl, Lord and Lady Algy, Brother Officers, Miss Hobbs, Lady Huntworth's Experiment, The Late Mr. Costello, Mice and Men, Dorothy, The Second in Command, A Marriage of Convenience, The Marriage of Kitty, An American Citizen.

In addition, too, to names already alluded to, I would mention the following as having contributed in large degree to the high reputation of the Gaiety theatre. I apologise at the same time for the omission of many others who have rendered yeoman service :—Captain Swiney, Colonel Thornycroft, Captain Norton, Colonel Duncan, Colonel Woodthorpe, Mr. Jabez Lightfoot, Mr. A. Williams, Major Colomb, Colonels Hunter-Weston, O'Grady, Haly and Clarke, Mr. Burt, Surgeon-General Taylor, Major Medley, Majors

Simpson and Bythell, Mr. Beynon, Colonel Mathias, Mr. Waymouth, Mr. C. Hallé, Dr. Barrett, Colonel Mason, Colonel A. Barrow and his brother W. Barrow, Mr. Baynes, Captain Fane, Colonels Ommaney and Kuper, the Craigie family, Majors Fegan and Marker, Mr. Ross Alston, Mr. Sydney Jones, Mr. Bosanquet, Captains Simpson, J. Turner and Owen, Majors Fletcher, Barrington-Foote and Keith, Mr. G. Nicoll, Lord Bingham, Captain A. Gordon, Mr. Lawson Smith, Colonels Howard Melliss, Percy-Smith and Sanford, Captain Pakenham, Mr. Markham, Lord Suffolk, and Captain Dowding; Lady Westland, Mrs. Simpson, Mrs. Bonham Carter, Lady Colleton, Miss Roberts, Mrs. McCracken (who opened the first matinée at the new Gaiety theatre), Lady Collen, Mrs. Dallas, Mrs. Keith, Mrs. Stewart, Mrs. T. P. Smith, Mrs. Dunsterville, Mrs. Patterson, Mrs. Warburton, Mrs. Williams, Mrs. Leslie Porter, Mrs. Hilliard, Mrs. B. Duff, Mrs. Lightfoot, Mrs. Bell, Mrs. Obbard, Mrs. Ford, Mrs. Joubert, Mrs. Bingley, Mrs. Parsons, Mrs. Franklin, Mrs. Vans Agnew, Lady Symons, Mrs. Hawkins, Mrs. Rimington, Miss Waterfield, Mrs. Fane, and Miss Kennet.

The Presidents and Honorary Secretaries of the A. D. C. who have held those offices since the year 1888 are:—Presidents:—Hon'ble Sir A. Scoble (1888-90), Lord Roberts (1891-2), Sir D. Fitzpatrick (Lieutenant-Governor of the Punjab) (1893-5), Hon'ble Sir J. Westland (1897-98), Sir C. M. Rivaz (Lieutenant-Governor of the Punjab) (1899-1903). Honorary Secretaries:—Colonel G. de C. Morton (1888), Captain G. Williams (1889-90), Mr. P. Holland (1891-2), Colonel Percy Smith and Colonel Mathias (1893), Captain F. Ponsonby (1894), Mr. Fraser and Colonel Jerrard (1895), Colonel Jerrard (1896), Colonel Jerrard and Colonel Craigie (1897), Colonel Craigie and Captain Pressey (1898), Captains E. and A. J. H. Swiney (1899), Captain A. J. H. Swiney (1900), Captain Finlay (1901), Captain H. H. Dowding (1902), and Major Caruana (1903).

It only remains for me to add that Colonel C. de C. Hamilton, R.A., a first-rate actor, and popular president of the executive committee in 1903, has just been succeeded by Mr. D. McCracken, that Major A. J. Caruana continues to fill the onerous post of honorary secretary to the club with tact and success, and that Mr. H. de la Rue Browne, who has been connected with the theatre since 1889, is the committee's invaluable business manager.

TALBOT HOUSE.
(Messrs. Bourne and Shepherd's Studio, Christmas, 1863.)

CHAPTER X.

The Shops and Roads.

THERE is perhaps no surer sign of the increasing prosperity of Simla than the excellence of many of its shops, for nothing now-a-days strikes the casual visitor from the plains more than the number of well-appointed business houses which are contained in its straggling bazaar. Chief among these is undoubtedly the fine block called 'Bank Buildings' near the Post Office, a structure which would be a credit to any English town. These handsome premises, which occupy an unrivalled position for trade purposes, have lately replaced an old ramshackle house which once belonged to the old Upper India Commercial Association, Limited, and was called the "Central Exchange." On the Association going into liquidation in the year 1867, the premises were purchased from the liquidators, Messrs. F. Peterson and S. Pittis, by Messrs. Francis, Ramsay & Co., of Calcutta, for the Simla branch of their firm, and they changed the name of the premises to "Somerset House." In March 1892, Messrs. Francis, Ramsay & Co. sold the premises to the Punjab Banking Company, who in 1895-96 pulled down the house and erected in its place the present Bank buildings. In the course of the dismantlement of the old building a serious accident occurred by the falling in of a floor on coolies who, contrary to orders, were working in a room on the ground floor, and two men and a woman were killed. The Bank has retained the centre buildings for its offices, while the portions to the right and left are the property, respectively, of Messrs. Ranken & Co., civil and military tailors, and Mr. E. Clarke, draper. Beyond these premises lies the Central Post Office of Simla.

Said a writer over thirty years ago, "What cannot be purchased at Simla? Here is an abstract of the business portion of Simla, and as the wares are displayed in a most tempting manner to the eyes of passers-by on the Mall, what wonder that the number of 'jhampanis' are numerous at almost every shop at the time of 'eating the air' in the evening." The list given is as follows, and it will doubtless prove of interest to many Simla residents of to-day.

Photographers.—Messrs. Bourne & Shepherd, Craddock, and De Russett.

Dentist.—Mr. O'Meara.

Jewellers.—Messrs. Hamilton & Co., and Charles Nephew & Co.

Watchmakers.—Messrs. Hamilton & Co., Charles Nephew & Co., and M. Kleyser.

Professors and teachers of music and pianoforte tuners.—Messrs. Goldstein, Cockburn, Williams, and Mack.

Saddlers.—Messrs. Cotton & Morris, and C. Crayden.

Clothiers.—Messrs. B. Francis, and Francis, Ramsay & Co.

Druggists and Chemists.—Messrs. Symes & Co., E. Plomer & Co., and S. T. Wallace.

Civil and military tailors.—Messrs. A. Ramsay, Phelps & Co., W. Coutts, Davidge Brothers, and J. C. Lewsey.

Printers and publishers.—Messrs. Cotton & Morris, J. Elston, and S. T. Wallace.

Hair-cutters and perfumers.—Messrs. Watson & Summers.

Hosiers and milliners.—Messrs. Campbell, Francis, and Phelps.

Wines, spirits, beer, and miscellaneous stores.—Messrs. Goldstein, Cotton & Morris, H. T. Ball, M. Kleyser, Davidge Brothers, and C. J. Harding & Co.

It seems to be a generally admitted fact that Messrs. Barrett & Co. were the first European merchants in Simla, for Mr. C. J. French, whom I have already freely quoted, wrote in his journal of 1838:—"Messrs. Barrett & Co. have long established themselves as merchants and agents here. Their efforts to accommodate the community have been successful in every way, notwithstanding the many difficulties which had attended their early exertions Everything suited to the wants of a European is procurable at their place. But for their endeavours and the example set by them, the lovers of the 'roast beef of Old England' would have been deprived of this article of food. The slaughter of kine consequent on the resort hither of Europeans was once strictly prohibited on account of the prejudices of the natives, but now this rule is somewhat more honoured in its breach than in its observance. This law in theory has long since been abrogated in practice, and so long as a cow or bullock is not slaughtered in the face of open day, the natives care little about the number that are destined to pass under the butcher's knife. The same prohibitions not being extended to Mussalman prejudices, one may (to use a cant phrase) go the whole hog and kill as many pigs, and as publicly as one pleases. A good library and reading room, with periodicals and newspapers, supply no little variety for the gratification of different tastes and capacities. Added to these, and judging from the number that resort thither, Messrs. Barrett & Co.'s billiard rooms are not the least attractive of the appliances."

The same writer, in alluding to the journey up to Simla says:—"Besides the bungalow at Barh, there is a coarsely constructed suite of 'godowns'

BANK BUILDINGS—A BUSINESS BLOCK ON THE MALL

appertaining to the firm of Barrett & Co. at Simla. These are intended as receptacles for palanquins, carriages, elephant litters, tents and anything else which one may not wish to take up with him either from choice or necessity. A trifling charge is levied for the safe custody of these articles until the traveller returns. The 'godowns' are superintended by an active and intelligent man called Bustee Ram, a specimen of the genteel and decently equipped natives of the hills."

In 1845, according to Towelle's hand-book, the enterprising Mr. Barrett opened an hotel, which was called the Pavilion (afterwards the Royal, now Lowrie's Hotel). The Pavilion was erected on the site of a two-roomed cottage built by a Mr. Ewart in 1827. An establishment of the kind had been opened in 1843 at a house called 'Abbeville,' but shortly afterwards this house was purchased by several share-holders, for the purpose of converting it into public assembly rooms for theatrical performances, balls, and suppers. Subsequently (about 1850) a racquet court owned by Major Goad was added, and after changing hands several times the buildings were all destroyed by fire in 1889, and the market now stands on the sites of the assembly rooms and the racquet court. It was, too, Mr. R. B. MacDonald, a partner in the then leading firm of the place, Messrs. Barrett & Co., who was elected Master of Lodge Himalayan Brotherhood in 1839, while Mr. Barrett himself proposed and started the old Simla Bank after a dinner party in 1845. Captain Hay, the Governor-General's Agent for the Protected Hill States, was the first secretary to this Bank. A branch was opened in Umballa in 1846, and another in London, about the same time, under Dr. Stephens, who nearly swamped the Bank by granting irrecoverable loans. This led to the closing of the London office, and the Simla Bank Corporation was eventually wound up.

In Carey's Guide of 1870 is found the following remarkable account of the building now known as Lowrie's Hotel:—"The spot where the Royal Hotel now stands, the most centrical in Simla, was, at the period of Lord Combermere's visit to the station, a perfect wilderness, covered thickly with pines and cheels, and with dense undergrowth, wild roses and raspberries and other entangling shrubs, inhabited by bears and leopards. Messrs. Ewart and Zeigler attached to Army head-quarters were the first to build here a cottage, where they lived in constant dread of the ravages of a leopard that nightly roamed in search of prey, until it was destroyed by a party purposely collected to hunt it down. Old Mr. Munro, of Agra, improved the estate in after years, and then Barrett & Co. enlarged its building for the purpose of holding general assemblies and making it do duty similar to what the present Assembly Rooms now do on occasions of reunions, theatricals, concerts, balls, and other similarly social parties. Subsequently,

appertaining to the firm of Barrett & Co. at Simla. These are intended as receptacles for palanquins, carriages, elephant litters, tents and anything else which one may not wish to take up with him either from choice or necessity. A trifling charge is levied for the safe custody of these articles until the traveller returns. The 'godowns' are superintended by an active and intelligent man called Bustee Ram, a specimen of the genteel and decently equipped natives of the hills."

In 1845, according to Towelle's hand-book, the enterprising Mr. Barrett opened an hotel, which was called the Pavilion (afterwards the Royal, now Lowrie's Hotel). The Pavilion was erected on the site of a two-roomed cottage built by a Mr. Ewart in 1827. An establishment of the kind had been opened in 1843 at a house called 'Abbeville,' but shortly afterwards this house was purchased by several share-holders, for the purpose of converting it into public assembly rooms for theatrical performances, balls, and suppers. Subsequently (about 1850) a racquet court owned by Major Goad was added, and after changing hands several times the buildings were all destroyed by fire in 1889, and the market now stands on the sites of the assembly rooms and the racquet court. It was, too, Mr. R. B. MacDonald, a partner in the then leading firm of the place, Messrs. Barrett & Co., who was elected Master of Lodge Himalayan Brotherhood in 1839, while Mr. Barrett himself proposed and started the old Simla Bank after a dinner party in 1845. Captain Hay, the Governor-General's Agent for the Protected Hill States, was the first secretary to this Bank. A branch was opened in Umballa in 1846, and another in London, about the same time, under Dr. Stephens, who nearly swamped the Bank by granting irrecoverable loans. This led to the closing of the London office, and the Simla Bank Corporation was eventually wound up.

In Carey's Guide of 1870 is found the following remarkable account of the building now known as Lowrie's Hotel:—"The spot where the Royal Hotel now stands, the most centrical in Simla, was, at the period of Lord Combermere's visit to the station, a perfect wilderness, covered thickly with pines and cheels, and with dense undergrowth, wild roses and raspberries and other entangling shrubs, inhabited by bears and leopards. Messrs. Ewart and Zeigler attached to Army head-quarters were the first to build here a cottage, where they lived in constant dread of the ravages of a leopard that nightly roamed in search of prey, until it was destroyed by a party purposely collected to hunt it down. Old Mr. Munro, of Agra, improved the estate in after years, and then Barrett & Co. enlarged its building for the purpose of holding general assemblies and making it do duty similar to what the present Assembly Rooms now do on occasions of reunions, theatricals, concerts, balls, and other similarly social parties. Subsequently, after Mr. White had built the house now called the Assembly Rooms, Mr. Barrett converted his buildings into accommodation for travellers and visitors, and named it the 'Pavilion.' The premises afterwards passed into the possession of Mr. MacBarnet, who named the hotel the Royal Hotel."

In Carey's Guide a Mr. Munro is described as 'the greatest philanthropist Simla ever had,' being credited with the institution of the Royal Hotel, the Fountain Hall Hotel, while he was the builder of Harding's Hotel (then 'Bondgate'), was a prime mover in the scheme which gave the station its assembly rooms and racquet court, and was the promoter of the 'Old' Brewery, about 1860. Mr. Munro, who was the principal partner in Messrs. Munro & Co., was without doubt at one time a considerable house-owner.

Although Simla residents are apt, especially in the months of May and June, to vehemently abuse the state of the station roads, and to upbraid the municipal fathers for carelessness, indolence and general ineptitude whenever the inevitable hot weather dust becomes unpleasantly conspicuous, there is no doubt that our main thoroughfares are very much better than they used to be in the olden days. Even in 1869 the Mall was but an ordinary hill road, fit for use only by pedestrians, horses, jhampans and dandies. Some idea of the width of the Mall in the years gone by is given by the road on the south of the Gorton Castle estate which formed a part of the old Mall, and which, though still narrow, is wider now than it was in 1869. Then in many parts of the Mall only two horses could go abreast, and this not without some danger to the riders, as in early days ponies were generally unruly, squealing beasts, always ready to kick or bite, and very different from the well trained animals which are now ridden in Simla. Lord Mayo, the Viceroy, was, as all know, a splendid specimen of a man, and the pedestrian often had to bear well into the railings at narrow portions of the road to avoid inconveniencing the Viceroy as he rode by on a powerful hill pony. At that time, too, the present open ridge by the Town Hall was occupied by what was then known as the 'Upper Bazaar,' the town of Simla being then divided into an upper, a main, and a lower bazaar. The houses in the upper bazaar extended on both sides of the ridge from the turning down to Blessington to the take off to the Lakkar bazaar, with a narrow road of about ten feet running between them. This bazaar contained, besides a crowd of native shops of the ordinary kind, the Kotwali, the business premises of De Russet, a photographer, Messrs. Hamilton & West, drapers, Messrs. O'Connor & Peliti, confectioners, and the native firms of Hussain Bakhsh, Ahsanoollah and Alif Khan. A portion of De Russet's house was occupied by the office of the Revenue and Agricultural Department of the Government of India. In 1875 a fire broke out in the premises of Messrs. Hamilton & West, and several houses in the upper

GANESHI LALL & Co
GANESHI LALL & SON
JEWELLERS &
GANESHI LALL & Co GENERAL DRAPERS
ERS
MERCHANTS
FRANK BLISS & Co

THE BAZAR

bazaar were burnt to the ground. The municipality wisely prohibited rebuilding, compensated proprietors for their lost sites, levelled down the crest of the road, and planted the flourishing copse now existing between the Town Hall and the Church. Later, when the construction of the Town Hall was decided upon, the upper road was galleried out, the result being the fine open ridge now enjoyed by the inhabitants of the town. Fire has undoubtedly been answerable from time to time for marked improvements on the upper mall, and many people wonder that the crowded native bazaar of wooden houses has hitherto escaped destruction. The last big fire in Simla occurred a couple of years ago, when a big block of old wooden buildings opposite the Telegraph office was burnt out, the damage being estimated at about four lakhs of rupees. A well built range of business premises has since been erected, and I may here mention that to the efforts of two architects, Mr. T. E. G. Cooper and Mr. A. Craddock, the station owes much of its recent solid and artistic improvement.

As already stated in an earlier chapter it was in 1878, during the Viceroyalty of Lord Lytton, that the first impetus to really good roads in Simla was given, for in that year both the wide road under the Gorton Castle estate, and 'Ladies' Mile' at the back of Jakko were constructed, and by degrees the whole Mall stretching from Viceregal Lodge round Jakko, some ten miles in length, was widened and improved into a carriage drive. In 1879, consequent on the improved condition of the Mall which admitted of wheeled traffic, the jinrickshaw commenced to supersede the jhampan and dandy. Both these latter were atrocities; the jhampan with its curtains for protection against sun or rain, not altogether unlike a miniature four-post bedstead, was carried by four coolies and was a jolting, back-aching abomination. The dandy, a piece of loose durry or carpet fixed by iron rings on to a single pole, so as to form both seat and footrest, was, if anything, even worse. If the getting into the durry was not carefully negotiated, a half somersault backwards resulted, and even when the entrance was safely accomplished, the rider always appeared to be occupying an undignified position. Both jhampan and dandy are now, except for occasional travelling in the hills in the neighbourhood of Simla, things of the past. The general use of the jinrickshaw has compelled house proprietors to improve the private roads leading to houses, and these, which were in many instances mere bridle paths, are now in the majority of cases often quite as good as the main mall.

As for the jinrickshaws, they have also vastly improved of recent years, and the price of a first rate modern vehicle, fitted with luxurious cushions, and possessing wheels with rubber tyres, glass window and modern improvements, now costs something like Rs. 750, as compared with the Rs. 300 or Rs. 400 of ten years ago.

CHAPTER XI.

Simla Society.

IT is not without somewhat serious misgivings that I venture to write on the delicate subject of this chapter. For it must be admitted that, to a large majority of people both in England and in India, Simla, although the initiated well know that all its women are beautiful and all its men are clever, possesses a social reputation which cannot be described as altogether enviable. How this has arisen, and how far it is to-day capable of being refuted, I will endeavour to show. But before attempting the latter task let us examine the opinions of those who have written of Simla in bygone years.

That Simla has not altered in some respects from its customs of the past, may be gathered from the following paragraph by Mr. C. J. French, who was in Lord Auckland's camp in 1838-9, and who dedicated his journals to Sir Frederick Currie, Baronet:—

"Mount Jakko seems to be the pivot around which the Simla community revolve in their morning and evening perambulations. The circuit round this hill is about two or three miles, and consists of a broad pathway rendered as level as the nature of hill roads will admit, and in the evening it forms the nucleus around which groups of ladies and gentlemen are observed to congregate. Sometimes the road is entirely taken up with conveyances, when to avoid accident or inconvenience they are obliged to proceed in slow order, but when no such interruption exists a lady or two escorted by a gay cavalier may be seen on their steeds dashing by thicket and grove. While the evening is so often a scene of animation at this spot, in the morning it is generally one of perfect solitude. At a time when the atmosphere is supposed or proved to be the purest—the more so at this elevation—the people neglect the most favourable opportunity of enjoying the exhilarating effects of an early ramble."

In his 'Travels in India,' 1844 to 1866, Colonel S. Dewé White, of the Bengal Staff Corps, wrote as follows:—

"A little farther to the north there was another hill station, more resorted to than any other, which was quite an accessible sanatorium to Bareilly: this was Simla. To this spot would flock all seekers of appointments. An officer aspiring to get a civil or military appointment, who desired to get to some place where, by currying favour with the great, he might create an influence for himself sufficient to secure that object, would select Simla, which was, and is, pre-eminently the most fashionable sanatorium in India.

Here the place-hunter would stick during the whole period of his leave, taking every opportunity to ingratiate himself with all who could do him a good turn, as it is to Simla that the Governor-General, Commander-in-Chief, and other magnates annually take their flight to escape the scorching heat of the plains. These great personages draw after them a host of minor swells, too numerous to particularize. Simla, then, for six months, becomes the head-quarters of the civil and military government of India, and for that time endless festivities and gaieties and frivolities are the order of the day."

Referring to a *bal masqué* given in 1845 in honour of Prince Waldemar of Prussia, then a visitor to Simla, Dr. Hoffmeister, his physician, wrote:—"It was a bright and merry party, for there are here a great many sprightly old ladies who, loaded with perfect gardens of flowers, rush about in the polkas with incredible zeal. They did not appear, as I had heard they were to do, as Dianas or the Graces, but on the contrary in remarkably pretty antiquated costumes, hooped petticoats and stiff brocades: the elderly gentlemen being equipped to correspond. The fancy dresses were all very successful, and selected with much taste. The oriental masked travesties were also very numerous and natural to a degree which doubtless could never have been attained in any other part of the world; for you may easily imagine, considering the generosity with which all eastern Princes delight in lavishing presents to the right and left, that the British officers, many of them newly arrived from the remotest parts of the East Indies, having been ordered now to the Punjab, now to Scinde or Afghanistan, are richly supplied with costly stuffs which they can turn to account only on occasions such as this. There was however by no means a lack of young ladies, for the kind and thoughtful relatives at Simla never fail to bring up from the plains everything in the shape of young and marriageable nieces or cousins; and here where so many agreeable officers are stationed for pleasure's sake alone, many a youthful pair are thrown together, and many a match is made."

In the life of General Sir Hope Grant we find the following passage written in 1846:—"I returned to Simla (from Kotegarh), and my association with bright ladies and gay gentlemen, all dressed in the height of fashion, for a time caused my love of the quietude and simplicity of a rural life to ooze out of me, and I too thought of nothing but dressing gaily, and wearing polished boots and well turned hat, and attending balls and parties. Music too there had become a great craze."

The 'Delhi Sketch Book,' or Indian Punch, of 1851 contained an amusing skit on a season at Simla showing 'Why they all went up,' and much that was true fifty years ago holds good in the present day. The skit runs:—

"The Governor General wished to make himself acquainted with the

Punjab, so by the advice of Sir Henry * he went up to Simla to take a bird's-eye view of it. On being informed of His Lordship's intention of passing the hot weather in the hills, both His Excellency the Commander-in-Chief of India and His Honour the Lieutenant Governor of Agra felt it their duty to follow him. The Commander-in-Chief went up at a great deal of personal sacrifice, the hot winds always agreed with him, and he had formed a number of very pleasant acquaintances in the barracks. But the head-quarters were at Simla, and so was the Governor General, and where these two were, he felt it his duty to be also. 'It's a —— nuisance,' as he observed to one of his Aides-de-Camp, 'having to go, but still duty is duty, and the Commander-in-Chief, who would avoid going to the hills to shirk it, is a ——,' something we leave the reader to imagine.

"Mr. Thomason † was also very unwilling to leave the plains; he liked his 'tatty'; he liked his bath, and for taking exercise he much preferred his carriage and four to a 'ghoont' (hill pony). Besides there were other reasons that would render a trip to Simla productive of much annoyance. His Honour had always set his face against the hills; and he had left no stone unturned to prevent his subordinates, even the sick, from having access to it, and if there was any truth in common report, he had even gone so far as to remove several persons from their appointments merely to place them out of the way of temptation. His Honour could not help feeling that after preaching so much one way, to practise just the reverse would be giving a great handle to his enemies. How Mr. —— would sneer, and say he knew all along what it would come to, and be more than ever confirmed in his opinion of human nature. How Mr. —— would chuckle and rub his hands. What hollow interest Sir Henry would begin to take in his health? All this was very disagreeable, but when Mr. Thomason feels a thing to be his duty, it is not a few disagreeables that will deter him from doing it. He had a good deal to say to His Lordship in favour of vernacular education that could not be well put in a letter. The Ganges Canal required a friend at court, and last, though not least, in case Sir Henry Lawrence broke down, it was very desirable that there should be some one at hand who could carry out the Punjab settlement.

"The correspondence of the Governor General, the Commander-in-Chief and the Lieutenant Governor, taken collectively, is beyond all question the most important in Upper India. On ascertaining therefore that these illustrious personages intended making Simla their place of residence during the ensuing season, the Post Master General felt it his duty to ascertain by personal inspection and observation that the post office at that station was in a state of efficiency.

* Sir Henry Lawrence. † Lieutenant Governor of N.-W. Provinces.

Reproduced from
"The Delhi Sketch Book."

SIMLA, IN SEASON, 1851

"If, as Pope says, it is only high life that produces high characters, by parity of reason, great official virtue can only be expected to be found in those individuals holding great official situations. Although, as I have shown, the heads of the Government and the head of the Post Office went up to Simla from nothing but the purest regard for the good of the State, I fear the mass of their subordinates were drawn up by much more mixed motives. Some went up for health, some for pleasure, and some few who had an eye to appointments, or a taste for cards, went up on business. Some because they were ill, some because they feared they would be, and some because they were in excellent health and had a mind to enjoy it. Some took sick leave, some took private leave, and some few, I am sorry to say, took no leave at all, but this was only for short periods and from contiguous stations. Old Mr. Slowcoach of the Sudder had only one year more to serve and wished to serve it in the hills, so by great luck his liver broke down and enabled him to do so. Young Mr. Mivins, a very rising man, had rather overworked himself and required change of air. Mr. Pringle was getting middle aged and began to want a wife, so he took four months' leave to inspect the new arrivals. Captain Flint, the great shot, wished to try his luck among the 'gurral' (chamois), and Lieutenant Snorley, that celebrated waltzer, his among the ladies. Captain Lounge of the Dragoons had been up every year since his arrival in India, so he went up this from mere force of habit. Major Drill wished to see the snowy range to tell his friends at home what it was like (he was thinking of selling out), but this being the first leave he had applied for in seven and twenty years, he had some difficulty in obtaining it. Captain Rook and Mr. Sharp went up because they were clever at cards and billiards, and Mr. Spoon and Ensign Jones because they thought they were. In sending in their applications these gentlemen did not think it necessary to state their reasons in too much detail, but hinted in general terms at the existence of urgent private affairs requiring their absence from regimental duties, which indeed was all that was necessary, it being received at that time (I need hardly inform the reader the story is laid under the old *regime*) as an undeniable axiom at head-quarters that every man must be better acquainted with his own private affairs than any third party. If, therefore, an officer thought that they required his absence from his regiment, or his presence in the hills, it was not for those who possessed less information on the subject to contradict.

"Excepting that neither play nor sport were among the inducements, the ladies went up from pretty much the same motives as the gentlemen. Good motherly Mrs. A., because her children's health required it, and little flirting Mrs. B., who had no children, because her own did. Mrs. Clare certainly lived at the dullest of out-stations, and everybody knew the weather half killed her, but I do not believe anything would have induced her to leave her husband, if he, dear old man,—he was a *leettle* her senior—had not absolutely insisted upon it, and then, of course, it was her duty to obey. Miss O. went up because she was Miss O, and did not wish to be so any longer. But what made old match-making Mrs. F. take her (unless, as the gossips said, it was to keep her hand in till Sophia came out) is a mystery. Captain F. wanted staff employ, but had no interest, so he very wisely sent his wife, that very agreeable woman, to make some. Mrs. Lennox was determined her daughters should not be in the plains more than she could help, so she took them up the very first season."

An observant visitor in 1858, whose opinions are tersely recorded, was Dr. W. T. H. Russell, the famous *Times* correspondent, whose graphic description of the United Service Club I have already quoted. Discussing society nearly fifty years ago Dr. Russell said:—"The social distinctions are by no means lost sight of in India;—on the contrary, they are perhaps more rigidly observed here than at home, and the smaller the society the broader are the lines of demarcation. Each man depends on his position in the public service, which is the aristocracy: and those who do not belong to it are out of the pale, no matter how wealthy they may be, or what claims they may advance to the consideration of the world around them. The women depend on the rank of their husbands. Mrs. A., the wife of a barrister making £4,000 or £5,000 a year, is nobody as compared with Mrs. B., who is a deputy commissioner, or with Mrs. C., who is the better half of the station surgeon. Wealth can do nothing for man or woman in securing them honour or precedence in their march to dinner, or on their way to the supper table, or in the dance. A successful speculator, or a 'merchant prince,' may force his way into good society in England; he may be presented at court and flourish at court balls; but in India he must remain for ever outside the sacred barrier which keeps the non-official world from the high society of the services. This is, to some extent, a necessity of position, and at a place like Simla, where there is an annual gathering of all sorts of people, it is desirable to take care whom you know."

Dr. Russell also wrote:—"Soon after our return the reports from the bazaar which reached us—in other words, the stories of the natives respecting the proceedings of the young gentlemen who are up here on leave and sick-certificate—show that Simla must be entitled to a high position as a sanatorium; for its health-restoring properties, to judge from the wildness of these gentlemen's spirits, are well-nigh miraculous.

"There can be no more convincing proof of the very lax no ions of

Reproduced from
"The Delhi Sketch Book."

SIMLA OUT OF, SEASON. 1851.

discipline and decency of these young men than the excesses of their conduct, which would not be endured in any place where a sound public opinion existed, or indeed any public opinion at all. In former days, when Cashmere was visited by the British, their wild exuberance of spirits was so great that the Indian Government was forced to appoint a diplomatic officer of rank to look after these young gentlemen; and I am decidedly of the opinion that a senior officer should be sent to all our hill-stations to exercise a proper, but not a too rigid, control over the fast invalids and riotous sick who recover themselves so boisterously. . . . . I think that every Englishman in India ought to look upon himself as a sort of unrecognized unpaid servant of the State, on whose conduct and demeanour towards the natives may depend some of the political prestige of our rule in the whole empire. He is bound to keep the peace, to obey the law, to maintain order and good government. In the hill-stations he certainly does not exhibit any strong inclination to adopt those views of his position. Our manners are said to be much improved recently, but even now gambling is carried to an excessive and dangerous extent, and there is not a season passes without damage to reputations, loss of fortune, and disgrace to some of the visitors; which are serious social evils affecting the British community directly, but which also bear a very grave aspect in relation to the influence we exercise over the natives."

The same writer continued :—"Somewhat better and able to crawl on my crutches to the verandah" (Dr. Russell was then living in 'The Priory'), "whence I turned from my monkeys and birds to the young ladies and gentlemen who were flirting and philandering, ahorse and afoot, on the road below us, and from the lovers to the monkeys till I was tired. Jacquemont says English society in India is less frivolous than society in general in France; but I do not think he would apply that remark to Simla, if what my gossips tell me be true. Probably Jacquemont's notion of an agreeable evening was realised when he had a party of nice women sitting round him,—in silence if possible,—whilst he held forth in broken English *de omne scribili*. Here we have ball after ball, followed by a little backbiting; the great event of every day being the promenade which is almost of a sacred and devotional character in honour of the god of the mountain who is called Jacko, and who is 'gone round' as if he were a holy well. If he be propitious—'*Veneres cupidinesque*,' he leads to the altar of Hymen."

Mr. John Lang in 'Wanderings in India' published in 1859, said :—"Simla differs from Mussoorie. It is so much more sedate; more than one-half of those who prefer Simla do so in the hope of prepossessing one or other of the great authorities by being brought into contact with them, and thus obtain staff employ or promotion, and very amusing is it to look on at a public entertainment and witness the feelings of jealousy and envy that swell the hearts of the various candidates for notice and favour. . . . . . The season I spent at Simla was a very pleasant one, and notwithstanding that it was enlivened by several exciting incidents, to wit a duel, a police affair, a court-martial, and an elopement, I was very glad when it was over, and we could return to the plains."

In 'A Mingled Yarn,' published in 1898, by Edward Spencer Mott, (formerly Lieutenant of the 19th Regiment and later 'Nathaniel Gubbins' of the *Sporting Times*), the author, in referring to gambling, said:—"Everybody played some game of cards or other at Simla, and here, again, but little actual cash was ever paid out. In 1862 loo, the 'unlimited' brand, flourished like a green bay tree in the highest circles. A select coterie used to assemble in a private house most evenings for the worship of the goddess . . . . On one occasion the play had become so thoroughly exciting that there were 'chits' (pieces of paper) representing over £4,000 on the table. And for this amount was the senior player 'looed.' I think he parted with some cash, but his payments were mostly in kind, and consisted of a furnished house, a mail phæton, and other chattels. When the scandal reached the ears of 'the Chief,' all the gamblers were ordered to return to their regiments with the utmost promptitude. Of that party of 'exiles' Colonel —— is, to the best of my belief, the only survivor. Two, at least, of it were in straitened circumstances—one was driving a hansom in London—the last time I met them."

It was in the early sixties that the feminine chignon attained such a size that it sorely troubled the masculine mind, and a few subalterns in 1863 decided to signify their disapproval of the fashion. They accordingly appeared one evening at the band stand with their ponies' tails tied up in chignon form. Great was the sensation they caused, but history relates that their punishment was greater. Not only were they sent to 'Coventry' by the fair sex, but they received a plain hint from a high military authority that the plains were more suitable for such jokes than the hills. And down they went.

Mr. Carey, a Simla architect, wrote in 1870:—"There are two classes of visitors here—one seeking health, the other amusement, combined no doubt it may be with a renewal of bloom and strength. Many a man pinches himself, or, worse, runs into debt, to enable the drooping wife or the ailing child to take a new lease of life at Simla. Many make a point during their sixty days' leave at least to shake themselves loose from the dreary months vegetated through at some quiet station in the plains. This is their all to

Reproduced from
"The Delhi Sketch Book."

THE KHYBUR PASS, (SIMLA,) 6. P. M. 1851.

look forward to till they can get home. Amusement is to them the *sine quâ non*, and *coûte qui coûte* they will have it. Then you have the head-quarters of the army, their gallant chief at their head. Amalgamate these, and when you have done this, pack them in the small compass they must occupy, comparatively speaking, in Simla, meeting on the mall at least once a day, thronging to Annandale, to balls, picnics, everybody knowing every one,—this alone begets a manner so familiar that it in itself strikes a stranger as something very unusual. It is difficult to understand this world of Simla without seeing it. You go up for a few months, you make acquaintances for the season, many of whom you are not likely to meet again, so matters it you think what they say or do? . . . . The utter absence of occupation on the one hand, and on the other the keen search after amusement, let it be what it may, makes life go at a reckless hand gallop that many come out of in a sore plight."

It was about this time that 'A True Reformer,' by General Francis Rawdon Chesney, R.A., the explorer of the Euphrates, and the founder of the overland route to India, was published by Blackwood & Sons, and the book, which was really written of Simla, contains several vivid descriptions of the life of the day. Writing of a wedding in the hills the author said :— "It has always struck me that the bridegroom looks rather out of place at a wedding, being, so to speak, an awkward, although perhaps a necessary, ingredient in this affair; but nowhere does he appear more so than at a wedding in the Himalaya. The bride must of course return in her sedan, for, to say nothing of the sun, the dust would utterly spoil her dress were she to walk: so the bridegroom must perforce either walk or ride by her side, and most men would prefer the latter alternative, since it is not every one who can keep up gracefully with the pace of four shuffling sedan-bearers in the prime of condition. But even then, ride he never so well, the general effect is a good deal marred by the need which arises every minute either to push on in front or drop behind, at the numerous points where the narrow road affords room for only the sedan to pass, and on such occasions he hardly looks as if he belonged to the bride, or the bride to him."

Mr. Andrew Wilson, the author of the 'Abode of Snow,' appears to have been one of the few of earlier writers who formed a favourable impression of Simla society. His book written in 1873 contains the following passages :— "According to some people, and especially according to the house-proprietors of Calcutta, who view its attractions with natural disfavour, Simla is a very sinful place indeed; and the residence there, during summer, of the Viceroy and his Members of Council ought to be discouraged by a paternal Secretary of State for India. The 'Capua of India' is one of the terms which are applied to it; we hear sometimes of 'The Revels upon Olympus;'

and one of the papers seemed to imagine that to describe any official as 'a malingerer at Simla' was sufficient to blast his future life. Even the roses and the rhododendrons, the strawberries and the peaches, of that 'Circean retreat,' come in for their share of moral condemnation as contributing to the undeserved happiness of a thoughtless and voluptuous community. For this view there is some show of justification. Simla has no open law courts to speak of, or shipping, or mercantile business, or any of the thousand incidents which furnish so much matter to the newspaper of a great city. The large amount of important governmental business which is transacted there is seldom immediately made known, and is usually first communicated to the public in other places. Hence there is little for the newspaper correspondents to write about except the gaieties of the place; and so the balls and picnics, the croquet and badminton parties, the flirtations and rumoured engagements, are given an importance which they do not actually possess, and assume an appearance as if the residents of Simla had nothing to do but to enjoy themselves and 'to chase the glowing hours with flying feet.'

"But, in reality, the dissipation of Simla is not to be compared with the dissipation of a London season; and if the doings of any English provincial town or large watering-place in the season were as elaborately chronicled and looked up to and magnified, maliciously or otherwise, as those of the Indian Capua are, the record would be of a much more scandalous and more imposing kind. Indeed, unless society is to be put down altogether, or conducted on Quaker principles, it is difficult to see how the Anglo-Indians, when they go to the hills, could conduct themselves much otherwise than as they do; and probably more in Simla, than anywhere else, there exists the feeling that life would be intolerable were it not for its amusements.

"But no one who knows European society will accuse Simla, of the present and preceding Viceroyships at least, of being an abode of dissipation or of light morality. Wherever youth and beauty meet, there will, no doubt, be a certain amount of flirtation, even though the youth may be rather shaky from long years of hard work in the hot plains of India, or from that intangible malady which a friend styles as 'too much East,' and though the beauty be often pallid and passé; but anything beyond that hardly exists at Simla at all, and has the scantiest opportunity for developing itself. Overworked secretaries to Government and elderly members of Council, are not given either to indulge in levity of conduct or to wink at it in others; the same may be said of their ladies; and the young officers and civilians who go up to Simla for their leave are usually far-seeing young men who have an eye to good appointments, and, whatever their real character may be, are not likely to spoil their chances of success by attracting attention to themselves as very gay Lotharios. Moreover, at Simla, as almost everywhere in India, people live under glass cases; everything they do is known to their native servants and to the native community, who readily communicate their knowledge of such matters to Europeans."

In July 1877, Mr. Val C. Prinsep, the artist who had travelled out to India in the previous winter to paint a picture of the Delhi assemblage, came up to Simla for a few weeks, and devotes a chapter of 'Imperial India' to life in the station. His impressions of Simla during Lord Lytton's residence are of special interest, as, if Dame Rumour can be believed, life in Simla was never faster than in those days, and even now allusions are frequently made to the society scandals of that time. Mr. Prinsep's remarks, if not altogether complimentary, are brightly recorded.

"The day after my arrival," he writes, "I went to a ball at 'Peterhoff' to see the beauty and fashion. I came to the conclusion that there are a great many captains. I forget what jealous husband it was who said he was glad of the Crimean war. 'For now,' he said, 'there will be fewer captains.' By 'captains' he and I mean people on leave with nothing to do. This place is full of such people, who have a difficulty in passing the day. Of course the devil is busy and provides mischief. Sad tales are told of the place no doubt; but like all such tales there is a great element of exaggeration therein. Of course people gamble, and do what they ought not. They do that everywhere. The play is very high, the whist execrable, and I hope the money lost is paid. I suppose this is the blood-letting necessary after the heat of the plain, and the monotony of regimental duty—excitement provided for by kind nature to restore the equilibrium of the system. . . . . The gaieties of Simla go on wet or dry. Rinking is greatly on the increase, being the only exercise many men and all women can take. . . . . The world of Simla jogs on, or rather pushes along, at its usual pace. All are bent on enjoying themselves, and champagne flows on every side. Every evening at eight the roads are full of 'jampons' conveying the fair sex to their festivities. . . . . . Simla society is a curious study. Simla itself is like an English watering place gone mad. Real sociability does not exist. People pair off directly they arrive at a party, as a matter of course, and the pairs happy in their own conversation do not trouble themselves about the general hilarity.

"Indeed the 'muffin' system, like that in Canada, is the order of the day. If you have not a pair, as in my case, you are likely to die of inanition. When such a state of society exists, there must arise most frequent and terrible squabbles, especially among the fair sex, and it is difficult to find two of the dear creatures who are on friendly terms. . . . . . .

Everything is so English and unpicturesque here that except that the people one meets are those who rule and make our history—a fact one can hardly realise—one would fancy oneself at Margate. . . . Officialism is also rampant. The new order of precedence has just been published, and in this new order everything is settled as to India; but the visitor, however high his rank, has no precedence except by courtesy. I do not find any mention of artists in this document, either with or without Government commissions, and I am in consequence frequently left out in the cold."

On leaving Simla about 15th October Mr. Prinsep wrote, evidently with some relief:—"At length I have left Simla and its civilized gaieties and scandals, and can resume my journal with some chance of recording something more than the flirtation of Captain A. with Mrs. B., or the quarrels and jealousies of C. and his wife, which form the staple conversation of the modern Capua swelled by tittle-tattle of the Viceroy, and his eccentricity, and idle speculation as to the doings of the far-off Turk."

So much for the opinions of those in earlier days of the station. Let us now come down to more recent years. No record of Simla in our own time, however, would be complete which omitted mention of Ruyard Kipling, who in the eighties spent several months in the station, and whose 'Plain Tales from the Hills' first appeared in the columns of the *Civil and Military Gazette.* Wonderfully clever as these short stories were, they have, I fear, led many to regard Simla as a town populated by 'Mrs. Hawksbees,' by frivolous grass-widows, idle hill captains and the genus known as 'bow-wows,' and no writer has perhaps done more than the brilliant genius I have mentioned to give the outside world the idea that Simla is a centre of frivolity, jealousy, and intrigue. Possibly, were he asked, no one would be more ready to admit that several of his characters were exaggerations of an author whom Simla will always be proud to have possessed among her most famous residents.

In an able and interesting article only just published on 'The Hills' by A. H., in the *Pioneer*, the writer has said:—"Nowhere possibly in the world are the passions of human nature laid so open for dissection as they are in remote hill stations on the slopes of the eternal abodes of snow. In the very small communities the round of gossip is incessant, probably inevitable. Resources there are none, save such as are afforded by amusement committees. The men are mostly deprived of sport, the women are overladen with calls and dressing and admiration. . . . . The groove into which Anglo-India is forced by circumstances in the plains becomes narrower still in the hills. There, where every advantage of climate is combined with every imaginable beauty of nature, with few house-keeping cares, with many luxuries, with a constant flow of amusements which few save in the richest society at home can attempt to enjoy incessantly; there, where even the rainy season has its compensations, and the miraculous beauty of a troubled sunset after a storm is a joy to be treasured in the memory always, and where all being more or less equal, none has cause to complain—there discontent breeds and jealousy and scandal dominate. The smallness of society, eddying round in such a tiny backwater, makes for stagnation."

In several of his statements I am obliged to agree with A. H., though I venture to think that, to those men and women who desire them, Simla offers more resources than the casual visitor to the hills imagines. Botany, gardening, the United Service Institute, mission and charitable societies, the Fine Arts Exhibition and other matters—all have a certain following in Simla.

Women, too, are constantly found in Simla who spare neither time, trouble nor personal expense in the interests of local hospitals and orphanages; and the station as a matter of fact has reason to be proud of many English ladies who, I venture to maintain, have set examples not only as wives and mothers, but also as hostesses and leaders in a society which is often over-exacting, critical, and captious.

The fact is that there are two distinct sides to Simla life, *viz.*, the official, and the social. There are two communities—the bees, and the butterflies. The former are the working classes, the men who conduct the work of the Empire, and of whose laborious days I have already written under 'The Government of India;' the latter are those who come up for a holiday, with the express intention of getting as much enjoyment out of that holiday as time and funds will allow. Among these last are the grass widows, the hill captains, already alluded to by other writers, who are encouraged to more or less extent by the wives and daughters of Government officials whose duties are not so heavy as those of their husbands and fathers. Their doings, their picnics, dances, and luncheon parties are continually, as Mr. Andrew Wilson remarked in 1873, given an importance they do not actually possess. In a word, it is in great measure the fault of the Anglo-Indian journals themselves that Simla has attained the reputation for frivolity which she now enjoys, for each week a column or two is invariably devoted by the leading papers to social gatherings which in any other capital would pass unnoticed or unheard of. It is, moreover, an undeniable fact that the work and play of society in Europe are not brought together as they are in India, where the workers themselves are obliged to provide or patronize the amusement which society demands, and which at home is catered for in much larger profusion by professional contractors.

So, as Mr. Andrew Wilson explained, there is often little for newspaper correspondents to write about except the gaieties of the place, and it is largely due to this reason that the tittle-tattle of the hills, the bulletin of the daily doings of the viceregal court assume monstrously exaggerated proportions, and induce jaundiced critics at home to believe that the air of the Himalayas has no other effect but to lighten the heels of the dwellers on the mountain tops.

And now for a few words on the 'calling' question which has come so prominently to the fore, and caused so much discussion during the last two or three years. As all Anglo-Indians are aware, the custom of paying the first call is one which, in Simla, as elsewhere in India, is performed by the newcomer. And one of the things which first strikes the visitor fresh from Europe, is the way in which each residence displays, on a neighbouring tree, its 'not-at-home' box for the reception of cards, when the lady of the house happens to be 'darwaza band' (door closed) to her friends. Gradually, as Simla grew in extent and population, calling, from becoming a pleasurable duty, developed into a serious social nuisance, and at length many ladies found it a practical impossibility to return all the calls made upon them. Especially was the performance of this duty made difficult by the absurd rule which demanded that visits must be made between the hours of twelve and two o'clock, the hottest hours of the day. So a number of leading ladies held a formal meeting, and passed a resolution that those already acquainted, should in future be privileged to call by posting their cards to each other, only strangers being required to make the first call in person. Recently, however, a further concession has been allowed, and all ladies in Simla, whether newcomers or not, are permitted, if they choose, to despatch their cards through the medium of the post. How long the new system will continue in vogue it is difficult to say; it would be ridiculous to say that it is devoid of drawbacks, or that it is universally approved. But that it has come to many as a much-needed relief from an intolerable burden cannot be denied. For calling was fast developing into a farce. Servants were often sent out with 'tickets' which were to be quietly placed in Mrs. So-and-So's box, intimate friends perpetually dropped each other's cards on a third person; 'box-hunting,' instead of visiting, became the rule; every one openly spoke of calling as a bore, yet no one condoned social laxity or remissness in others. Innumerable complications, heart burnings, and squabbles resulted, and the time had clearly arrived for some drastic reform. But the new scheme was not introduced without a certain amount of difficulty. Anonymous skits were circulated; strong protests emanated from the male sex, especially from those tied to their office desks, to whom no relief was suggested, and numberless letters were written to the press decrying the innovation.

Major J. A. Douglas. Mr. H. Housman. Mr. E. Maconochie, C.S. Colonel H. Goad. Captain G. Lubbock, R.E. Captain M. H. P. Barlow.

Mr. C. P. Bennett. Mr. G. R. Irwin, C.S. Sir William Cuningham. Surgeon General R. Harvey. Mr. R. Egerton.

Colonel G. Money. Major Colin Campbell.

THE BLACK HEARTS, SIMLA, 1897.

While the permanent residents welcomed the new custom, the casual visitors and strangers condemned it as unsociable and discourteous. But I think the development is one which arose from a difficulty which had made itself acutely felt, and that time will prove its wisdom. Simla has for some time been growing into too large a town for everyone to know his neighbours as was customary in earlier years. And the sooner this is more generally recognised, the better.

The principal Simla summer festivities may be said to consist of balls at Viceregal Lodge, at the Lieutenant-Governor's and Commander-in-Chief's residences, some eight or nine plays by the Amateur Dramatic Club, weekly gymkhanas on Saturdays at Annandale, and constant tennis, dinner, and evening parties. Dances given by the Club and leading hostesses, and the meetings of the Rifle, Polo, Cricket, and Football Clubs are naturally of frequent occurrence.

Add to these an official garden party or two, a few concerts, picnics for which the surroundings are peculiarly well adapted, rides in and around the station, three days' racing in May and October, an occasional bazaar for charitable purposes, and there is little else to mention. In the autumn a limited amount of partridge and pheasant shooting is obtainable by energetic sportsmen on the neighbouring hills, and last, not least, most delightful excursions of eight or ten days can be enjoyed by those who are able to afford the time, to those woods and forests of Huttoo, on the Tibet high road, which ought to be included in the 'Wonders of the World.'

Prominent among Simla social institutions, and I use the word institutions advisedly, is the 'Most Hospitable Order of the Black Heart.' This order, which was founded in 1891, consists of a grand master and (some twenty) knights associated for the purpose of entertaining their friends at Simla. The motto of the order is 'He is not so——as he is painted,' and the hiatus in the knight's motto originally caused a 'missing word' competition, for which a prize was offered to the lady who supplied the adjective. Luckily perhaps for the knights only one fair dame hit on the solution,—"devil." The motto is really a quaint rendering of a well-known saying given to his pupils by an Italian teacher of English idioms.

Since the knights have been in existence they have known four grand masters, *viz.*, Colonel Newnham Davis, who was largely responsible for their creation, Sir William Cuningham, K.C.S.I., Surgeon-General Sir William Taylor, K.C.B., and the present master, Mr. Albert Williams, C.S. Their social entertainments are invariably run in perfect taste, and contribute in no small degree to the success of a Simla season. They include picnics, dinners, bal-masqués, and dances. When in evening dress, the grand master wears the golden chain of his office, and all the knights don knee breeches, with the black heart of their order suspended by a red ribbon round the neck. The rules of the order are believed to be simple, 'Worthiness and bachelordom' (or at the least grass-widowerdom) are the sole qualifications required of the 'brethren,' or knights, who are elected to this hospitable but select society.

To return, however, to my defence, if such indeed be needed to-day, of Simla society. Were Simla social letters brought within the scope of the Official Secrets Act, and gossiping epistles from Poona or Ootacamund condemned as treasonable documents, the bees would be less often accused of making no honey, while the flitting and flirting butterflies would continue to fulfil the natural object of their existence. More than one critic on Simla life has declared that its society lives in a glass house. This I think undeniable, and it is equally true that Simla in considerable measure takes its tone from the example set to it by the wife of the Viceroy who presides over Viceregal Lodge. For the last twenty years at any rate, no one has found it possible to advert, save in terms of admiration, to the example set by the wives of the Rulers of India. Lady Dufferin's 'Viceregal Life in India' is full of allusions to a delightful and happy home life; and has not Kipling, in 'The Song of the Women,' described with consummate feeling the great work which she inaugurated for the relief of the women of India which still bears her honoured name, and which has since been so greatly developed by her successors?

There are many in Simla to-day who still warmly cherish the memory of Lady Lansdowne, whose winning grace and charm of manner endeared her to all classes of society, and whose visit to a hospital I well remember being likened to 'a ray of sunshine passing through the wards.' It seems but yesterday too that I saw her native bodyservant in Calcutta burst into a flood of tears at the mere mention of her departure from India some days before the event took place.

Has not Lady Elgin left behind her a reputation for many kind acts performed in secret, for the keenest interest in all charitable institutions, for her example as a pattern mother? And though state and Viceregal functions at times proved for her gentle frame a somewhat heavy task, were not her duties performed with a kindliness which all her guests appreciated?

Lady Curzon, the present head of Indian society, has for five years filled a difficult post with not less success than her distinguished predecessors. The youngest wife of a Viceroy who has yet come to India, a charming hostess, the possessor of natural and well cultivated talents, and of beauty and strength of character, she has earned the respect and admiration of all who have come into contact with her. A thorough woman of business, she has doubled the usefulness of Lady Dufferin's great medical scheme by

NEVER GO FAST ROUND THE CORNERS OF JAKHO.

Simla Season 1854.

A LITTLE SCANDAL ON THE MALL.

Simla Season 1854.

Reproduced from
"The Delhi sketch Book."

raising nearly £40,000 for improving the working of one of its branches. Of her qualities as a sympathetic friend to those in distress there are many in India who can testify. To those who would read a further appreciation of Lady Curzon let me recommend Mrs. Craigie's (John Oliver Hobbes) 'The Impressions of an Englishwoman,' written from India during the Delhi Durbar, 1901.

Surely it is women such as these who have done, and who continue to do, more to raise the tone of Simla society, its morals, and its general influence than a dozen carping detractors of ordinary innocent amusements. As Hope Huntly wrote a year or two ago in 'Our Code of Honour,' a novel dedicated to Lord Roberts, and which dealt in some degree with Simla life:—"The Anglo-Indian lives 'en evidence' from morning till night and night till morning, and many a peccadillo is enlarged into a scandal in consequence, in which a Londoner might indulge and go scot-free. Society at home is not, as many suppose, more irreproachable than it is at Calcutta and Simla; and perhaps were the recording angels to compare records, London could not show quite so clean a bill of moral health as would our Eastern City of Palaces."

CHAPTER XII.

Mashobra and Mahasu.

ABOUT six miles from the Simla church, in the Native State of Koti, lies the little suburban village of Mashobra, an ideal retreat from the 'despotism of despatch boxes,' and which, it has been practically settled, is presently to be included with its adjoining slopes within the municipal limits of Simla proper. On the right the ridge stretches away to Mahasu, Kufri, Fagu and the Tibet high road, and on the left to Naldera, Basuntpur, and Suni in the Bujji State, and the Sutlej Valley. During the last few years Mashobra has been steadily growing in favour as a popular week-end resort, and a number of delightful villas are now dotted among its beautiful pine and oak forests. In May and June the heat and dusty roads of Simla are always trying, and both then, and in late September and October, when the climate is superb, Mashobra houses are in great request, and innumerable are the picnics which are held in the maiden-hair clad forest glades. The name Mahasu is derived from Muha Sheo, the Great Sheo, or Shiva, the simple mountaineers holding the belief that the larger and more beautiful trees are each the property and abode of some peculiar divinity. No one in the interior at any rate is suffered to destroy a tree so consecrated unless he has performed the ceremony of offering a goat in sacrifice. The offering is a living one, and is presented to the priest of the nearest temple which is generally on the borders of the forest. Dozens of trees may always be seen decorated with little fluttering pieces of rag which are supposed to be offerings to local deities. The beauty of the Mahasu forests did not fail to strike Miss C. F. Gordon Cumming, who in her book on the Himalayas wrote in 1884:—"The various pine trees here are all more or less gigantic spruce firs, upright as masts, and festooned to the topmost boughs with graceful virginia creeper or clematis which was now starry with beautiful large white blossoms. We felt that at last we had reached something worthy of the name of forest. Not that Mahasoo can show any of the magnificent twisted and gnarled deodars which we find further up the country, but finer specimens of the morinda and rye pine could hardly be found, some of them towering a hundred and fifty or two hundred feet without a bend."

I will now ask the reader to wander out from Simla along the Mashobra road, and notice the principal houses by the way. The first house after leaving the toll bar, about three miles from Simla where the real forest road begins, is 'Maisonette' (once the 'Hermitage'). Built by the late

Mr. Horace B. Goad, it next passed into the possession of Colonel J. Robertson, and is now owned by General A. S. Hunter who has considerably improved the place. Below 'Maisonette' lies 'Fairlawn,' a picturesquely situated house, for many years owned by Mr. R. Dixon, of the Foreign Office, who laid out the fine grass terraces from which the place is named. Sir George White and his family occupied 'Fairlawn' for several months, and the then Commander-in-Chief, who was a wonderful walker, started on several of his pedestrian feats from this residence. Its present proprietor is Mr. Cowell. A mile further is 'Holmdale' with its cleverly terraced gardens, the property of Mr. A. E. Jones, and lying close to the rugged cliff where from time immemorial the 'lamergeyers' (Himalayan eagles) have reared their young in eyries under the overhanging rocks. Popular belief has it indeed that this was the cliff over which 'Tertium Quid,' in Kipling's well-known story, met with his fatal fall.

Close to the quaint little bazaar are the buildings erected in 1866 by Mr. Gilbert Campbell (afterwards Sir Gilbert Campbell, Bart.), in which he resided for several years. Later on the property passed into the hands of Mrs. Martin Towelle and was known as the 'Gables Hotel.' It was regularly rented by Lord Lytton, who with his family made it a constant summer resort, and it has always been a favourite house of call with the Simla public. Close to the hotel is 'Black Rock,' built by Mrs. Towelle, which commands a splendid view of the snows, and numbers among its recent tenants the late Bishop Matthews, Mr. Steedman, C.S., and Mr. Gordon Walker, the Commissioner of the Delhi Division. It was at this house during a summer season in Lord Dufferin's viceroyalty that his Aide-de-Camp, Lord Herbrand Russell (now the Duke of Bedford), kennelled a pack of German hounds he had specially imported from Europe with which to hunt the Indian boar. But the experiment, chiefly owing to the unsuitability of the climate, did not prove a success: many of the hounds died, and the pack was broken up. On the spur above the 'Gables' is 'Mashobra House,' the oldest of all the houses in the neighbourhood. The place, which is extensive and well wooded, belonged in the early fifties to a Colonel Mackenzie, and Mrs. Martin Towelle, who acquired the house in 1864, resided there for over thirty years till her death in 1896. The three last-named houses are now the property of Mr. Lawrie.

'Bendochy,' a delightful little cottage, once occupied by Sir Henry Brackenbury, and recently secured by the United Service Club as an annexe for its members, lies just below Mashobra House, and on the next spur is the villa 'Rahat Mahal' (the abode of bliss), appropriately so called by its owner Mr. T. Bliss. 'The Peak,' which has passed through the hands of several proprietors since 1863, was until lately the property of the late Mr.

J. L. Arathoon. It stands on a commanding hill in some fifteen acres of ground and possesses a striking view of the snowy range. 'Sherwood' and 'Cosy Nook,' the next two houses, are both charming and popular picnic resorts, and their owner, Mr. A. M. Ker (Manager of the Alliance Bank), an enthusiastic amateur gardener, who purchased 'Sherwood' from Mr. Schlich, the Inspector General of Forests in 1888, has since laid out perfect lawns, forest paths and a particularly fine orchard of English fruit trees. The estate comprises over thirty acres of pine forest and is extremely picturesque. Lady Curzon spent several weeks there last autumn while the Viceroy was on tour.

We next come to 'Kenilworth,' one of the largest and most valuable of the Mashobra estates. The place was formerly owned by the late Mr. F. Peterson, of the Simla Bank Corporation, and until 1889 was known as 'The Refuge.' Colonel A. R. D. Mackenzie, however, then purchased the property, built an imposing house and planted out a large orchard and grounds. 'Kenilworth' has been occupied from time to time by several Commanders-in-Chief, and is a perfect country residence. The beautiful weeping willows which adorn both the 'Kenilworth' and 'Sherwood' grounds were propagated from cuttings taken from a tree which once stood at the entrance to Bentinck Castle (now Peliti's hotel). This tree was grown from a slip originally obtained from the willow which grows over Napoleon's now empty tomb in St. Helena, and to which I have already alluded in my account of old Simla houses.

Other noticeable houses on the ridge are 'Honington,' built by General Sir Edwin Collen, now retired, who has owned the ground for over thirty years; 'Belmont,' once held by Mr. A. M. Jacob, to whom allusion has already been made, and now possessed by Mr. Rivett, and 'Villa Carignano,' a striking house in spacious grounds constructed in the Italian style, by Chevalier Peliti the owner of the Grand hotel.

The last house on the Mashobra Spur is 'Hillock Head,' about nine miles from Simla. The land formerly belonged to the late Mr. E. E. Oliver (author of 'Balooch and Pathân'), but about twelve years ago it was purchased by Mr. A. Coutts, and now boasts a market garden which supplies Simla with the choicest English fruits, flowers, and vegetables.

About six miles further on lies the beautiful spur of Naldera, now possibly best known for its golf links, the course being perhaps one of the most sporting in the east. Crowned by a beautiful grove of deodars Naldera is carpeted with a fine springing turf and used to be a favourite camping ground of Lord Lytton's. Lord Lansdowne made more than one visit to the spot, and Lord Curzon with his family has regularly proceeded there for several weeks in June during the last few years.

SHERWOOD, MASHOBRA.

There is however no house either in, or out of, Simla which is better known than 'The Retreat,' Mashobra, and Sir Edward Buck, who for seventeen years owned the estate, has kindly sent me the following account of it.

"My introduction," writes Sir Edward, "to the Retreat was in May 1869, when I passed through its woods on a first day's march to the snows. The oaks were then in their glorious autumn coloured foliage of the spring, and as I sat on the bank opposite the house, half intoxicated with the beauty of the scene, I registered a vow that if ever fate should bring me to Simla those woods should be mine. Fate did lead me there in October 1881, and within a month those woods *were* mine.

"The house was then called 'Larty Sahib Ki Koti,' and it was some time before I discovered that 'Larty' signified Lord William Hay (afterwards Marquis of Tweeddale), who had occupied it for many years when Commissioner of the Simla Hill States. Although the house was not built by him (it was erected by a medical officer Dr. C ——), it was in his name that the permanent lease of the house and surrounding forest was granted by the local Raja of Koti. After Lord William Hay's departure the permanent lease changed hands more than once, while the house itself was occupied by various tenants, among whom were Sir William Mansfield, Commander-in-Chief, and Mr. (now Sir Dietrich) Brandis, Inspector General of Forests. The holder of the lease in 1881 was the widow of a Mr. Lionel Berkeley, a government official, from whom she inherited it, and at the time of my arrival in 1881 she had offered it for sale for Rs. 15,000. The Raja of Koti, who was only receiving a small annual rent of Rs. 100 as ground landlord, was anxious to repurchase the estate, but I had bought it before he intervened. Even then difficulties arose about the boundaries of the estate, but these were settled by the discovery of 'Larty Sahib's' old 'chowkidar,' who on being promised restoration to his old employment showed where the foundations of the boundary pillars were buried. A survey with maps was then made, and the area of the forest proved to be something like 300 acres. The old 'chowkidar' remained a faithful servant of the estate until his death some years later.

"The original lease contained conditions that the two main roads, from Simla and the Mashobra village respectively, towards the hill known as Mahasu, should, in the interests of the native population of the Koti State, be open to the public; that no trees should be cut down without the leave of the Raja; and that no cattle should be slaughtered within the boundaries. After the survey of the estate a fresh lease was drawn up in my name. I agreed to increase the ground-rent to Rs. 200 on condition of being allowed to cut down a limited number of trees, but the other conditions were not abrogated.

A new condition was however added under which the Raja was to have the right of pre-emption.

"On examination of the house it was found to be in a very insecure condition. The foundations were giving way, and the building was, as indicated by rents in the interior walls, parting asunder like a pair of scissors, and would evidently within a short time fall over the cliff on either side. Prompt measures were adopted to save it. The roof was under-pinned by trees cut down in the vicinity, while the rubble foundations were replaced by strong stone masonry, which was further supported by abutment walls. The opportunity was taken to improve the house itself. Hitherto it had been one house with one entrance. Now a second entrance hall was opened; conservatories and a billiard-room added; an unused attic converted into four attic rooms; and an extra room added above the billiard-room. The advantage of this arrangement was proved by the fact that for four years the upper section of the house was occupied by Mr. (now Sir Courtenay) Ilbert and his family, and later on, for four years, by Sir Frederick (now Lord) Roberts, and his family, while I myself retained the lower half."

How fond Lord Roberts was of the 'Retreat' may be judged from the following passage in 'Forty-one Years in India.' Writing of 1862, the author says:—"The new Viceroy Lord Canning remained in Calcutta; but Sir Hugh Rose had had quite enough of it the year before, so he came up to the hills and established himself at 'Barnes Court.' He was very hospitable. We spent a good deal of our time at Mashobra, a lovely place in the heart of the hills, about 6 miles from Simla, where the Chief had a house which he was good enough to frequently place at our disposal when not making use of it himself." Again in 1864 Lord Roberts says:—"Sir Hugh Rose was a most considerate friend to us; he placed his house at Mashobra at my wife's disposal, thus providing her with a quiet resort which she frequently made use of, and which she learned to love so much that when I returned to Simla as Commander-in-Chief her first thought was to secure this lovely 'Retreat' as a refuge from the (sometimes) slightly trying gaiety of Simla."

Sir Edward Buck continues:—"I used the house chiefly as a week-end 'Retreat,' although when any important piece of business had to be done I would stay longer, finding, as others have found, that the seclusion of the house and the healthy air of the oxygen-breathing woods were more conducive to sound work than the 'chit' and 'chuprasi' of the Simla office, and the dust and dirt with which the bazaars filled the Simla atmosphere. Moreover, the Retreat proved an excellent rendezvous for official conferences. In the pleasant surroundings of the Mashobra forests, men were in better

THE RETREAT, MASHOBRA, FEBRUARY 1904.

temper, and of calmer mind than in the midst of Simla interruptions sitting round a long table in a cold office room. Many of the schemes which had to be worked out by the Department of Revenue and Agriculture of which I had charge for fifteen years were finally settled and sealed at the conferences held at the Mashobra Retreat.

"I, with my tenants in the upper chambers, remained in occupation of the Retreat until 1896, when Lord Elgin became my tenant, and as I was then shortly to retire from the service arrangements were in that year made to transfer the estate permanently to the Government as a viceregal residence. The Raja of Koti however was unwilling to surrender the right of pre-emption which I had granted to him, and purchased the estate himself for Rs. 35,000 (which sum barely covered the outlay which had been expended on the house and grounds) and then consigned it to the Government as tenant on a permanent lease. Since the occupation of the estate as a viceregal residence considerable additions and improvements have been made in the outbuildings, but the house itself and the grounds have been little altered.

"During my own residence considerable pains were taken to improve and extend the roads and paths through the grounds (including the main road, part of Lord Dalhousie's cart road to Tibet, at the foot of the northern slope, the measured length of the paths within the estate was in 1896 about 10 miles). At the same time trees and plants were introduced from the Narkanda and Huttoo forests to the northern side of the woods where they were likely to succeed, and at the time that I left many of these were promising well. Most prominent among them were four varieties of maple; the silver fir or *Abies Webbiana*, the hazel nut tree; and 'ringall' bamboos. In years to come these should add much to the beauty of the upper woods, especially on the north side. One of the most successful importations was however from further afield. Early in the seventies I had noticed in the garden of the Deputy Commissioner of Kumaon (Major Garstin) at Almora a green clad bank, which he told me was covered with a creeping raspberry that he had brought from the snows. I was permitted to take some plants to Naini Tal where in a few years it covered the slopes of my garden, and on being ordered to Simla I carried with me some half a dozen roots and put them down in a Jakko compound. In due course the plants were brought over to Mashobra, where the slopes from the house are now covered and protected from erosion by the creeping raspberry of the snows, botanically known as *rubus nutans*. Mashobra in return has supplied some of the slopes of the Viceregal grounds, of Snowdon, and the United Service Club, and of North Bank (my nephew's house) at Simla with the same useful and ornamental plant. Many English shrubs were also imported, but the only one which met with pronounced success was the variegated elder, which was subsequently used for the ornamentation of Simla shrubberies. The Mashobra grounds were also utilized for the experimental cultivation of European fruits and vegetables. The only prominent successes however were apples and rhubarb. The elevation was too high for most fruits, and among others the Spanish chesnut failed. But it may be interesting to note that the chesnuts which I planted at 4,500 feet on the other side of Simla below Taradevi have, especially in dry years, produced excellent fruit, and that the success of that experiment has had much to do with the establishment by the Forest Department of chesnut plantations in other suitable localities with the view of providing food for the hill people in years of drought.

"For many years before my own occupation of the Retreat estate as well as during my tenancy, the woods were freely used by Simla residents for picnic parties. Those who occupied the house in later years including myself invited all Simla to a breakfast in the woods on the day of the Sipi fair, and as the oak trees had then, as a rule, assumed their richest foliage, and the young maiden-hair which clothes the northern slopes was in its dress of brightest green, this picnic gathering was one of the pleasantest memories of the year. How many people do I still meet in various parts of the world, some indeed whom I do not recognize, who come up to me with the remark 'Don't you remember me as one of your guests at the Mashobra picnic of 18—?' Very often I don't! They were so many."

Undoubtedly the most celebrated picnic of the Mashobra woods was that memorable one which gave rise on the 25th June 1862 to the historical 'Pickles Court-Martial,' which created such a sensation in Simla, and indeed throughout India and England. In a word, Sir William Mansfield, the Commander-in-Chief, arraigned Captain E. S. Jervis, A.-D.-C., 106th Bombay Light Infantry, before a court-martial on the charge of feloniously appropriating at the Retreat sundry wines and stores, the property of His Excellency. The details of the trial were published in full, and the incidents which occurred during the two months it lasted were unusually numerous and extraordinary.

Brigadier-General Brind, C.B., was president of the court-martial, which included seven Colonels, four Lieutenant-Colonels, and three Majors. Captain W. K. Elles, who afterwards died as Lieutenant-General of the Bengal Command, was the prosecutor, and Major J. N. Young the Judge Advocate at the trial. The stores which the prisoner was alleged to have misappropriated for his own use included 100 bottles of sherry, 61 of champagne, 88 of claret, and 114 of beer, and amongst other sundries a bottle of pickles; while he was also accused of insubordination. Captain

WILDFLOWER HALL, MAHASU.
JANUARY 1901.

Jervis, who had indignantly protested against a court-martial, and had also written a letter to the Adjutant-General declining to attend, was ably defended by Mr. William Tayler (of Patna fame), and was finally acquitted by the court of dishonest misappropriation. He was, however, sentenced to dismissal from the service for insubordination, but was allowed to rejoin for one day, whereby he obtained £1,800 for his commission.

There were many in Simla, and India generally, who felt that the Commander-in-Chief acted under an erroneous impression of his own private position in bringing Captain Jervis to a court-martial. Constant closures of the court took place during the trial, and Sir William Mansfield, who was in court for several days, went through a very unpleasant examination: his native servants were questioned, his household details and tradesmen's bills produced, his domestic affairs laid bare for public comment, and much soiled linen was washed in the open; and he was certainly placed in a position by no means dignifying to his high command. Party feeling, too, ran high in the station, and the 'Pickles' case was the sole topic of conversation at every dinner table.

I have it on the authority of an official who has just completed thirty-five years in India that the feeling on the subject was so strong, that two members of the opposing factions worked themselves up to such a pitch of excitement over the incident that a duel with pistols actually ensued. With due solemnity the seconds arranged the affair, and the belligerents armed with their weapons faced each other at the opposite ends of a long table. The signal was given and both fired simultaneously. If the result was not deadly, it was certainly ludicrous, for the pistols had been carefully loaded with charges of raspberry jam, and each rival had successfully bespattered his enemy!

Although the court in their sentence of dismissal recommended the accused to mercy in consideration of extenuating circumstances disclosed in the proceedings, the Commander-in-Chief did not assent to the recommendation. During the latter portion of the season while the trial was in progress Mr. William Tayler and his wife who were living at Kennedy House gave a series of dances. Captain Jervis was staying in the house, but "as it was not *en règle* for him while under arrest to appear in public, he had a small room allotted to him with a card table, lamp, and bottle of champagne, and friends at intervals went in to keep him company."

Another well-known old house on the Mahasu range is 'Wildflower Hall,' for many years the property of Mr. G. H. M. Batten, C.S., and a favourite retreat of Lord Ripon's. It commands a magnificent view of the snows, and it was in a sense indirectly responsible for the recent accident to Lord

Kitchener. I take the following account, which I contributed immediately after the Commander-in-Chief's mishap, from the *Englishman* :—" Almost immediately after Lord Kitchener arrived in Simla he secured the lease of 'Wildflower Hall,' a charming old house situated on the Mahasu range about six miles from Simla. The house in former years has often been the temporary residence of a Viceroy or Commander-in-Chief, its elevation is about 8,000 feet, and it now belongs to Mrs. Goldstein, a well known Simla resident. It is an open secret that the Commander-in-Chief is an enthusiastic gardener: indeed, it is said that he is never happier than when improving the grounds at Mahasu, where he impresses into service his staff, syces (grooms), kitmutgars (table servants), and all the coolies he can lay his hands on. The only fault apparently that Lord Kitchener has to find is that shrubs and flowers do not grow quickly enough. The road to 'Wildflower Hall' is really that known as 'the Great Hindustan and Tibet Road' projected by and constructed under the auspices of Lord Dalhousie. About two miles from Simla, just beyond the Sanjouli bazaar, is the tunnel, through which every visitor to Mashobra or Mahasu must of necessity pass.

" This tunnel, which has now for all time gained such an unfortunate notoriety, was commenced by Major Briggs in 1850 and concluded in the winter of 1851-52. It is 560 feet in length, is driven through solid rock, and was almost entirely constructed by prisoners In its excavation, indeed, it is recorded that some 10,000 prisoners and over 8,000 free labourers were employed. The roof is supported by massive beams, and heavy beams also rib the sides. In the early part of the season the tunnel is whitewashed so as to improve the light, but it is always very dim even in midday. In the evening the tunnel is illuminated by some half dozen very miserable lanterns which are attached to side beams, and which ought often to be lighted at a far earlier hour. After the monsoon when the rains have been able to percolate through the hill and trickle down its sides, the whitewash gradually disappears, and the tunnel becomes darker, and damper, and drearier. But the Public Works Department, which is responsible for its control, for its lighting and upkeep, is apparently unable to afford more paint or light, and so it has, in spite of continual complaints, been allowed to remain in its present uncared-for state. Half way between Simla and Mashobra, and about a mile and a half beyond the tunnel, is the toll bar. Here all passengers, each rickshaw, horse, mule, sheep, bullock, or goat, is taxed from three pice to six annas per head, and the toll bar is annually put up to auction and sold. Last year about Rs. 10,000 was paid for it by the present owner, and the proceeds are supposed to be spent on the upkeep of the road, but it is doubtful if

THE SANJOULI TUNNEL.

much was devoted to the improvement of the tunnel, which is only just wide enough to allow a rickshaw to pass through.

"To return, however, to Lord Kitchener. The Chief had informed his staff on Sunday morning that he would not again visit 'Wildflower Hall.' Later on, however, he changed his mind, and rode out. He approached the tunnel as it was growing dark in the evening on the return journey. About the centre was a coolie coming in the opposite direction, and he, as is the custom of all passengers through the tunnel, squeezed himself between two of the side beams to allow the rider to pass. But the light was very dim, the coolie apparently moved, the horse shied slightly, Lord Kitchener caught his foot against a side beam, there was a sudden twist and wrench, and both bones of the leg above the ankle snapped. How the Chief managed to get off his horse can best be imagined. The coolie bolted, and Lord Kitchener lay down in the tunnel suffering as only those who know what a broken leg means can realise. If the tunnel is damp, dark and cold in summer, it is doubly so in November, but for half an hour or so the Jungi Lat Sahib (the Lord of War) lay there, while frightened coolies, it is said, came to the tunnel entrance and fled in fear at the rumour it was the Commander-in-Chief who lay hurt within.

"At length, after what must have been a long period of misery, came relief in the shape of a European, Mr. Jenn (Messrs. Steirt and Co.), a rickshaw and some coolies, and there followed a slow and painful journey to Snowdon, where Colonel Tate in charge of the head-quarters' staff, and Majors Clark and Green, civil surgeons of Simla, were quickly in attendance. The break was declared quite clean, both bones having snapped without any symptoms of a fracture which is sometimes apt to give so much trouble and anxiety. Lord Kitchener bore the operation of having his leg set with much courage and cheeriness, and is doing as well as can be expected, though it is certain that the next few days will be a period of considerable pain and inconvenience. A man with a less strong constitution indeed might well have feared the danger of pneumonia, so damp and chilly was the place where the accident occurred."

Among other prominent houses on the Mahasu heights may be mentioned 'Dukani' (8,200 feet), famous for its picnic ground and terraced flower garden, as well as its visitors' book which contains numerous autographs and quaint remarks. 'Dukani' was originally owned by Colonel T. D. Colyear, and later on by Mr. H. B. Goad and the late Maharaja of Alwar. Among those who have occupied it have been the late Sir John Woodburn, Lieutenant Governor of Bengal, Sir George Robertson, of Chitral fame, and Sir Charles Rivaz, the present Lieutenant Governor of the Punjab. 'The Bower,' originally known as 'Alice Bower,' and for years believed to have been haunted by a ghost of that name, was once a favourite summer house of Sir Charles Elliott, afterwards Lieutenant-Governor of Bengal, and later of Sir Denzil Ibbetson, now a member of the Viceroy's Council. Both 'Dukani' and 'Bower' are now the property of the author. Further on is 'The Nest,' belonging to Mr. J. M. Macpherson, a delightfully secluded house in thick pine forest ; then comes the Government bungalow belonging to the Public Works Department, picturesquely situated on a wooded slope; and last of all 'Kufri House,' formerly the old staging bungalow. This house, which is now owned by Mr. T. S. Bean, possesses a unique and commanding position as well as a flourishing apple orchard.

NATIVE BAZAAR ON THE HILL SIDE

CHAPTER XIII.

The Hill People, some Customs, and Traditions.

NO account of Simla would be complete which omitted mention of its native population, its local traditions, customs, its temples and bazaars. A contributor to a 'Chambers' Journal' of 1872 includes in an article on Simla some interesting remarks on the bazaar and its community, which, although written thirty years ago, remain true to-day. The writer then said :—

"The little town is now one of the capitals of the greatest empire in the world. Subject princes, mighty western nobles, and travellers from every country, are seen in its narrow bazaars. Long lines of camels, and caravans of oxen carts, are unceasingly, for six months of every year, pouring into it the luxuries of Hindustan, and the magnificent comforts of Europe. A thousand beautiful villas look down upon it from the surrounding hills, and on the splendid roads which lead from it in every direction may be seen, of a summer evening, a wonderful show of fashion and beauty—the *crême de la crême* of England in Asia. Amid all her greatness, however, Simla never forgets her origin, but still as of old barters with the simple shepherds of Tibet, supplying all the little luxuries they seek, and absorbing primitive wares brought in exchange. Wild and unkempt-looking fellows are these Tibetans, with their long hair falling over their shoulders and their sheep-skins and woollen jackets hanging down—a mass of rags and dirt. Their sallow faces, small squat noses, and upturned eyes, plainly denote their race, and contrast strangely with the delicate Aryan features of the Punjab hillmen. Always smoking long wooden pipes—like those of the lower classes in Germany—smiling and pleased at everything, ever ready for any amount of conversation or food, they are great favourites with the mountaineers of the lower ranges; and indeed they have many very amiable and lovable qualities. They are eminently truthful, honest, and chaste, easily amused, easily satisfied, very sociable, and of great physical endurance. The women are not characterised by such strongly marked Tartan features as the men, and many of them are exceedingly pretty, though sadly dirty always. A considerable number of these people remain in Simla during the whole summer, finding employment as wood-cutters and coolies. Strings of them are always to be seen carrying in enormous beams from the Fagu forest. They fasten them behind them by ropes suspended over their shoulders, and go staggering along almost bowed to the ground with the weight. You sometimes see a young girl bearing one of these huge logs—the best part of a young pine tree perhaps—and though bent double with the ponderous burden, looking quite happy and contented, and carrying in her hand a wooden pipe to which she occasionally applies for comfort and solace. Or a whole family —papa, mamma, big and little brothers and sisters—all are seen struggling along in single file with loads proportioned to their respective ages and sizes, all smoking, talking, and looking merry enough. These great pieces of timber not only stretch across the whole breadth of the road, but frequently far out over the side, and sometimes indeed are of such length that the unhappy coolie has to sidle along with them the whole way from Phagu to Simla, about eight or ten miles. When riding quickly along this winding road one sometimes comes very awkwardly upon these great timber barriers, stretching one behind and the other across the path, and not unfrequently accidents have happened by this means. But generally the Tibetans arrange by a twist of the body to bring the beams in line with the road with astonishing celerity.

"Now that we have stopped a little in the bazaar, let us take a stroll through it. It is thronged with natives, from the scarlet and golden messenger of the British Government to our old friends the Tibetans. Sauntering through a bazaar is the *summum bonum* of life to a Hindoo. Standing chattering in the middle of the roadway or smoking a pipe with some friends in a shop, or sitting on the edge of the gutter, quietly contemplating the passers-by, he is perfectly happy. Within twenty yards is one of the grandest sights in the world. A splendid panorama of hill and valley with the eternal snows as a background on one side, while on the other the view melts away into the distant plain, across which the great Sutlej is seen like a silver band. But to our brown friends such things possess no attraction. The bustle, closeness, smells, flies, pariah dogs, unowned children of the kennel, and all the attraction of the bazaar are to them more pleasing than the majestic tranquility of mountain and valley and far-off plain. But one ought not to be too severe on the bazaar—it has its spectacle and pretty sights. Do you see that long line of horsemen coming slowly along with the stout little gentleman in front? He is a mountain chieftain, whose home is a lonely castle on the hillside, overlooking a great rich valley which is his own. One cannot help observing how gallantly he is dressed, in gay but well-matched colours, and cloth of the richest coloured material. The horsemen behind are his suite. One is probably his commander-in-chief (for he is sure to have an army, however small), another is the keeper of his privy purse, others lords-in-waiting, and so on. All fine little gentlemen in their way and men in authority. Simla is 'Town' to them, the metropolis of civilisation; the bazaar is Regent Street and Cheapside in

THE LAKKAR BAZAAR

one. As they pass, the shop-keepers come to their thresholds and make low salaams. The short stout little prince who is passing is the representative of a family which for generations has been to their ancestors and themselves the ideal of greatness, the incarnation of power, the pink of nobility. Is it not recorded, in their unwritten traditions, how his grandfather at the head of a great army drove back the Goorkhas who were hovering round the town, and then, out of light-heartedness, looted them himself, and carried away its female population to a woman, and how when the carpenter, goldsmith, and sweetmeat-maker went as a deputation from the burghers to expostulate with him, he relented and wept on their necks, and promised to give back half of their wives and daughters on condition of receiving a sum of tribute yearly for ever, and how they only got their grandmammas after all! With such legends living in their memory, how can they help honouring and fearing those of the rajahs left to them.

"Look at those gaily dressed, fair, and pretty women. They come from the valleys immediately under the snowy range, to buy nose rings and bangles which their souls love. Although some of them have two or three husbands, they are good and happy women, and have pleasant homes among those giant mountains of the Himalaya beyond the Sutlej. Theirs is a cool fruit-growing land, abounding in peaches, strawberries, walnuts, and grapes, and their fair pretty faces and their merry wholesome laughter speak of the happy glens from which they come."

Most localities in India possess their own particular legends and queer stories, and Simla is no exception to the rule. Let me then tell of the native belief concerning the little waterfall which is so prominent a feature on the Mall near the Glenarm hotel in the rainy season. At the foot of this waterfall there once existed a spring known as the 'churail baoli,' which was said to be haunted. Even to-day no hillman will visit the spot at nightfall, and many of those who of necessity pass by sing loudly as they turn the corner. The legend runs that a 'churail,' or the spirit of a woman who had died in childbirth, haunts the place, and lays violent hands on all who would draw water there. It is an Oriental superstition that women who so lose their lives sometimes re-visit the earth, and are recognised by the fact that both their feet are turned inwards. When such a spirit hovers round a household, the immediate relatives lose no time in performing the religious rites, on which the presence of the unwelcome visitor depends. The belief is that the spirit of the 'churail' causes her victims to fall down in a fit, and it is a curious coincidence that a young European was once overtaken with giddiness and fell down unconscious on the spot I have just described.

Among other old 'baolis' (springs) of the station is that of the

Combermere bridge, where in former days natives went only in the day time to draw water on account of the bears who inhabited the ravine, and Kunchum's 'baoli' below the Ripon hospital, constructed by the 'chowdry' (overseer) of the market in Lord William Hay's time. Kunchum's son Dultoo built a temple now occupied by Laljee Pundit.

The oldest 'baoli' in Simla is said to have existed just above the United Service Club, but since the present water supply system has come into use these two sources have naturally been almost completely neglected.

Almost half-way between Mashobra and the golf links at Naldera the traveller passes along a bleak hill-side profusely strewn with curious grey, jagged rocks and boulders, among which snakes and lizards alone seem to thrive. A more desolate God-forsaken piece of hill-side could scarcely be imagined. As the hill men approach the spot they are wont to preserve a strict silence, and the following legend which a local villager told me on the spot will perhaps interest the members of the Naldera Golf Club:—"Once upon a time, Sahib," said my informant, "before Simla was ever thought of, there stood a wealthy and prosperous city on this spot. The people who lived in it were both sinful and profane. Indeed, so great were their sins that the great Mahadeo arose one day in his wrath and hurled the whole city, with all its inhabitants, down the steep hillsides. These grey rocks of to-day are all that remain of it, and only the temple of Naldera, where the gods dwell, is left, but no man is brave enough to live in this place!" The following too is a fair specimen of hill legends from the Simla district, and I give it as related in the Naldera village:— "Far away in one of the valleys near Simla lies a little village, where once lived a good man who had his home beside a field, in which grew a beautiful mulberry tree. A *méla* (festival) was regularly held beneath its shade, and the poor carried away basket-loads of its fruit, so that it came to be an annual meeting place. Now the fame of it reached a certain raja who had rented out the land, and one day he came with all his retinue to see it. 'There is no such tree in the royal gardens,' said the grand vizier. 'It is not meet that a subject should possess what the raja hath not,' added the prime minister. The raja replied not a word, for his heart was filled with envy; and, that night before sleeping, he gave orders that on a certain day at early dawn, before anybody was astir, a party of armed men should take their axes to the village and cut down the mulberry tree. But ill dreams disturbed the raja's rest, and during the night a strange man appeared to him and said, 'O king live for ever! I am the spirit of a 'bunniah' (merchant) who died in yonder village many years ago. During my life time I defrauded the people. I gave them short measure and adulterated their food. When I died, therefore, and passed into the land of spirits, the gods who are

A WRESTLING MATCH AT SIMLA

just, O king! decreed that I should restore all I had stolen. My soul therefore entered a mulberry tree, where, year after year, the people may gather fruit and regain their losses. In one year more they will be repaid to the utmost cowrie; but you mean to destroy the tree and drive my soul I know not whither; therefore have I come to plead with you to spare it this once; for, when the year is past it will die of itself, and my soul return in peace to the land of shadows.' So the raja listened, and the strange man went away. For one year more the people sat under the mulberry tree as of yore; the next it died!"

There are several picturesque temples and shrines in and near Simla which are well worth the attention of the casual visitor. In touching on this subject, however, I must confess I have found it is very difficult to get reliable dates regarding the original buildings; more especially as each fakir in charge unhesitatingly asserts that his own particular temple is more than 4,000 years old! Of the earlier wooden structures now left intact the temple at the Waterfalls is said to be the most ancient, and its present incumbent is believed to have come down in direct succession from the fakir who was in charge of the temple seven generations back. Gokal Bunnia of Boileaugunge, who was in Simla for several years before the Mutiny, and who is now 83 years of age, states that he remembers the time when the first fruit garden was planted in the vicinity of Deo's Mundes near the Waterfalls in about the year 1840. There was no municipality in those days, and the amount he then paid to a sweeper for cleaning away the rubbish before his little shop was 9 pies per month!

Certainly one of the most ancient temples in Simla is that at Annandale, and though old cultivators who live near the Kaithu hill say that religious ceremonies used to be held there, the picturesque old building among the deodars is now falling into silent decay. Better this fate however than that it should be rebuilt, as some of the more modern Simla temples have been, with corrugated iron roofs and inappropriate design.

Kootub's mosque, situated nearly opposite the police station, was constructed in Lord William Bentinck's time by the 'khansamah' of the Commanders-in-Chief Sir Jasper Nicolls and Sir Hugh Gough. This man made a pilgrimage to Mecca, and afterwards died in Calcutta, and later on the only means of support the mosque possessed was the liberality of the Mahomedans who resorted to it.

On the summit of Jakko, about 8,300 feet, is a small temple dedicated to Hunuman, the monkey god, where lives a fakir, chiefly famed as the presiding genius over the troops of brown monkeys which practically own the hill top. Writing of this place in August 1837 Gerard describes his encampment as "situated on Jakko in Simla, a middling sized village where a fakir is stationed to give water to travellers." The shrine as it then existed is no doubt somewhat altered to-day, but it is a spot that all visitors seem to find of special interest. Simla children are occasionally allowed as a special treat to make the steep journey up the hill, where they throw biscuits and grain to the chattering monkey folk.

It is a curious sight, that of the old fakir in his yellow garments standing in front of the temple, and calling "ajao, ajao," to his monkey children. For many he has pet names, such as 'Raja,' 'Ranee,' 'Kotwal,' 'Daroga,' and so on, and numbers of them eat freely from his hand. The 'Raja,' who is monarch of the troop, keeps his subjects under the strictest discipline, scolding and chastising the quarrelsome, and forcibly ejecting any of the younger gallants who approach his wives. Last year as some visitors were watching the old fakir feeding the monkeys, one of the animals in jumping from one tree to the other missed its footing and fell heavily to the ground. The 'jogi' seemed much concerned at this unusual occurrence, but lost no time in making his apologies for the incident. "Forty years ago," he remarked, "when I first knew that monkey, she could climb as well as any here, but even a monkey can grow old in forty years. Alas, poor Budhee!"

In connection with the monkey fakir may be recorded a local incident. Some thirty years ago a Mr. De Russet, a contractor and architect, lived in Simla, and his son became a student at the Bishop Cotton School and a member of the volunteer corps. The boy, however, suddenly declared himself an apostate from Christianity, and joined the fakir as a disciple at the shrine on Jakko. Here he underwent a severe novitiate and for two years he remained under a tree with the sole company of the monkeys, and the attendant who brought him food. Eventually he was admitted into the priesthood, and for some years, from his head-dress of a leopard skin, he was known in Simla as the 'leopard fakir.' He was recently often seen in the station, but has now retired to the seclusion of a temple some distance below Annandale, avoids recognition, shuns Europeans, and appears to have forgotten his mother tongue.

Mr. John C. Oman, formerly professor of natural science at the Government College, Lahore, in his work on the 'Mystics, Ascetics and Saints of India' (1894), reproduced a photograph of the leopard fakir or 'sadhu,' and wrote of him as follows: "Some years ago at Simla I interviewed one Charles de Russeth, a young man of French descent, who although brought up as a Christian, and properly educated in Bishop Cotton's School in that time, had while a mere boy embraced the life of a 'sadhu'. . . . Of his fellow 'sadhus' he spoke in terms of high praise, and assured me that he had seen 'jogi' adepts perform many most wonderful acts. . . . . I have

THE MONKEYS ON THE TOP OF JAKKO.

no doubt he commands the highest respect from the natives, and lives idle, happy, and contented, without any anxiety about the morrow ! !"

If for no other reason, the monkeys of Simla will always have a claim to fame in that they formerly attracted Rudyard Kipling's attention, and have been immortalised in verse. And it must have been on Jakko that he addressed his verses to the 'Gleesome Fleasome Thou,' and has left us the example of the—

> "Artful Bunder, who, never in his life,
> Had flirted at Peliti's with another Bunder's wife."

I am told that in the cold weather many of the monkeys migrate to warmer regions; some authorities indeed declare that they visit the plains considerably below Kalka.

In 1862, however, a subaltern who came up to Simla just before Christmas wrote:—"The monkeys and such leopards and other wild beasts as were gradually being driven in by the all encroaching snows made such a noise that a decent night's rest became out of the question. It was a wonderful sight, the spectacle of the monkeys in their thousands careering about the mall, or seated on the rails or the rocks, in the early morning."

Of recent years, the monkeys have become a decided nuisance in Simla, as they are terribly destructive pests in station gardens and do not improve our houses by frolicking on their roofs. The native population of the station, however, accepts the position with that quiet resignation for which the inhabitant of Hindustan is so famous, and in the Lakkar bazaar the 'bundars' are particularly numerous and mischievous.

There is another fakir named Sewa Chatan who lives on the summit of Prospect Hill near Viceregal Lodge and who, native like, has recently offended the authorities by constant and stealthy enlargement of his dwelling place through encroachment on ground to which he appears to have an uncommonly doubtful claim. When, however, fakirs are informed that they have to submit like ordinary individuals to the law of the land, they are not wanting in plausible excuses, as the following letter addressed by Sewa Chatan to a junior political officer will show. The epistle, evidently drafted by a Secretariat babu, runs:—"With reference to your letter No. 1468 of 19th instant, I have the honour to enquire why you decline to interfere in the above matter. I look upon you 'in loco parentis,' and I expect you to exert yourself in my behalf. I have taken up my abode or domicilium, as the Latins say, for the last many days, and I do not see the reason why I should be ejected, or that if I am, I beg to be compensated in the sum of rupees one hundred; but I prefer the former. Since my stay on this elevated and beautiful country, surrounded by all the beauties of nature, visited by all the *élite* of Simla with special reference to the feminine gender in which I am old enough to gaze upon without perturbation, I have become as it were a part of my surroundings."

There are three principal temples to Kali (the goddess of destruction) in Simla; one on Mount Prospect, a second above the new railway tunnel near the Hazelmere garden, and the third in the centre of the station just below the Grand hotel. The last-named is a hideous modern structure of no architectural beauty, and was erected about 1845 by a Bengali Brahmin called Ram Churn Brumcharee, but it occupies a conspicuous position, and is a popular place of worship within the temple.

The goddess, as described in 1870, was 4 feet in height; but she has since been replaced by a smaller and better made figure from Jeypore, which reposes in a small room with an iron grating before it, while the door is closed at such times as the goddess is supposed to sleep or rest. The temple is adorned by seven metal bells which are rung at irregular intervals "that the sound may bring peace to the hearts of men!" though I fancy the residents of Peliti's hotel may differ in opinion on this point from the Brahmin in charge. For many years a midday gun used to be fired just below this temple, and the two nuisances have always been associated during the past fifty years. Owing, however, to objections being raised by people in the neighbourhood, and also to a distinguished member of the Government making a sudden and involuntary descent from his pony, the guns were removed a couple of years ago to a spot below the cart road. In answer to my query regarding the origin of this shrine the Brahmin in charge told the following story:—"Before Rothney Castle was built there stood in its grounds a small temple surrounded by a verandah, and within it was 'Majee' that old old idol which you see in the corner. One day a sahib came to the place, and seeing no priest in charge he had Majee thrown down the khud; and having pitched his camp he made the temple into his kitchen, and ordered the servants to prepare his dinner in the verandah! Although this greatly shocked the Hindu servants they carried out the orders given to them and presently dinner was finished, and the camp wrapt in slumber. Then old Majee, indignant at her treatment, wreaked her vengeance; and a terrible vision appeared to the sahib. He saw two horsemen approach with spears, and so real appeared their attack upon him that he awoke shouting for help. The servants told him there could be but one reason for this visitation, and, unless the fallen idol were restored to her home, death would surely visit the camp. On this the sahib sent out and had Majee picked up. He is said to have built another temple for her somewhere near Christ Church, and when that land was afterwards required for the Rothney Castle site, the present site was selected about 1835, and the building has from time to time been renovated

HILL WOMEN AT THE SIPI FAIR

and repaired by native public subscriptions largely assisted by the Maharajah Holkar of Indore."

On the Tara Devi hill facing Simla on the south in the Raja of Keonthal's territory, there are two temples, one of which is of great antiquity, and here in the autumn each year is held a special 'mela,' or fair in honour of the goddess Kali. Two buffaloes are invariably offered to the blood-thirsty goddess, their heads being severed at a single blow by a sturdy Gurkha or hillman armed with a keen 'kukri' or sword. Several preliminary ceremonies precede the actual sacrifice: the buffaloe is anointed with sandal wood paste, is sprinkled with rose-water, flowers are thrown over it, it is given sweetmeats, and the tulwar is smeared with oil. The spectators appear to work themselves up into an extraordinary state of nervousness while the preparations are made, and their excitement is intense when the signal is given for the animal's death. The actual deed of killing is over in a second, the buffalo's neck is drawn taut with a rope over his horns, there is a swish, and the animal falls with its head completely severed from its body. Many an animal has been less mercifully despatched in the slaughter houses of the great markets in England. The question of cruelty can scarcely be said to arise. Many years ago a big wooden idol in one of these temples was found to be minus his head and much consternation was caused among the native residents. The Bishop Cotton School was then situated at Jutogh, and the Tara Devi Hill was one of the boys' favourite resorts, so perhaps further comment is unnecessary.

About the 12th May is annually celebrated a hill festival which from time immemorial has been also observed as a public holiday by the official world of Simla. I refer to the Sipi fair, which takes place in a small valley below the Mashobra bazaar in the Rana of Koti's territory. Of recent years the European attendance at the fair has somewhat fallen off, but to the new-comer the festival has an attraction which it would be idle to deny, and I have heard of no Viceroy or Commander-in-Chief who has not visited the fair at some time or other during his stay in Simla. But let me try and describe the fair.

Imagine if you can a small teacup-shaped valley shaded by magnificent deodars. On the one side, if the expression may be permitted, picture dozens of swings and roundabouts crammed with hill people in a blissful state of happiness; on the other a long line of stalls crammed with glass beads, necklaces, and cheap finery of every description, and surrounded by a merry, excited throng of wrangling purchasers. In front you will find row upon row of hill women sitting in terraces on the hill slope decked in costumes of every hue under the sun, many laden with massive silver or turquoise ornaments, and all smiling and gossiping to their hearts' content.

Some are distinctly pretty, all appear wonderfully healthy, and many, it is whispered, are the marriage alliances contracted by purchase or family agreement during the two days' fair. Behind lie the shamianas and tents reserved for European visitors, some provided by the Rana's thoughtfulness, others by the hospitality, perhaps, of the Viceroy's staff. Sitting with considerable dignity under a shamiana the Rana smilingly receives his European and native friends, invites them to ride on his elephant through the excited crowd, or bids his hillmen display their skill in archery, this latter consisting in discharging blunt arrows at each other's legs. Add to the above dozens of sweet shops with their overpowering scent of 'ghi' (butter) and frizzling sweetmeats, the crash of the tom-toms, the chorus of dancing 'jampanies,' the report of countless crackers, with an ever moving crowd of native and European visitors and the merry laugh resounding clear above the din—and you have a faint idea of the fun, bustle, and noise of the Sipi fair. Similar, too, in some respects to an old English rural gathering is the Himalayan fête, for at either can be seen the merry-go-round and performing bear, while farthing toys, cheap sweets, and games of chance are as popular in the East as in the West.

One more allusion to a local custom and I must conclude a chapter which is already too long. There is a curious practice to which a large number of hill children are subjected by their mothers which never fails to interest European visitors to the Himalayas. Having selected a spot where a stream of water is diverted into the fields, the women lull their little ones to sleep, and then having lain them down, they arrange by means of a hollow stick or piece of bark that a tiny stream of water shall be directed to fall on each child's head. Half-a-dozen little ones may often be seen lying in a row, all sound asleep, with a cool stream falling gently on the crowns of their heads. The practice is more or less universal in the Himalayas, and the idea is that it increases hardihood and strength. The 'water babies' never seem to object to the process,—indeed, they hardly ever move, and less seldom wake when once placed under the falling water.

CHAPTER XIV.

The Trees of Simla.

SIMLA itself is essentially 'the hill of deodars,' of which beautiful conifers Kipling and many before him have described the peculiar charm. But there are many other trees in the neighbourhood, specially in the forest-clad slopes of Mashobra, which deserve notice. Of these so picturesque an account has been given in a paper read before the Simla Natural History Society by Sir Edward Buck, in 1885, that I cannot do better than quote *in extenso* from his pamphlet, noting by the way that this little society, which was formed by Sir Courtenay Ilbert, when he ruled the Legislative Department, unfortunately did not survive his departure. Sir Edward Buck confined his note to the twenty-six commoner trees of the neighbourhood. "The twenty to which I draw attention are," he wrote, "seven conifers, three oaks, the rhododendron and its congener the andromeda, four maples, two species of cornus, and two laurels.

"One of the characteristic features of the neighbourhood of Simla is the rapidity with which we pass from one region or belt of vegetation to another. The climate changes rapidly on ascending or descending the precipitous sides of the huge mountain waves of the Himalayan ranges. The most prominent beacons or flags which mark each climatic belt are, perhaps, the conifers; and I think we shall obtain a clearer conception of the distribution of the Simla arboreal flora, if, at the outset, we associate each belt of vegetation with a particular conifer. This arrangement has the undoubted advantage of lifting us at once out of the very low valleys which conifers love not, and through the steam and heat of which I do not propose that we should roam. Let us hasten up from Kalka, then, as quickly as we can, and pass by that noble mango tree which, spreading over the road a few miles from the foot of the hill, always seems to me like a huge boundary mark erected by nature for the purpose of noting the division between the flora of the plains and the flora of the hills. It is not, perhaps, until we come to the end of the third of the seventeen four-mile stages, into which the wearisome ascent of some 60 miles from Kalka to Simla is broken up, that we find ourselves being jolted into the region of *Pinus longifolia*, the cheer pine, which, commencing to appear at an elevation of from 2,000 to 3,000 feet, occupies the landscape for the ten or twelve most tiresome of our seventeen stages. It is hardly necessary, then, to describe to you that poor, thinly-clothed specimen of a conifer, which with the prickly euphorbia (popularly called cactus) is almost the only natural object in view on the scorched and arid slopes of the southern spurs of the Himalayan wall for some 40 or 50 miles of the upward journey. But, miserable tree as it is compared with its allies that live in higher altitudes, we still owe it some gratitude for relieving the barren monotony of the tiresome ascent, since, alone of all trees, it seems able to support existence on those otherwise deserted steeps.

"This circumstance leads me to notice a singular feature of the Himalayan ranges, at any rate of those which face the northern and drier regions of the Indian continent, and I will take the occasion of our protracted drive through the dreary belt of *Pinus longifolia* to ask you to consider it. You observe the northern and north-easterly slopes are covered with a profusion of vegetation of all kinds, while the southern, and specially those which trend westward, are almost bare. So much is this the case that in the extended views which we obtain from the summits of our peaks, such as, for instance, Prospect Hill, Jakko, or Mashobra (8,100 feet), the northern slopes of the distant ranges look as if they had been shaded with a giant paint-brush. If I may attempt an explanation of so striking a phenomenon, it would be this: Young plants and seedlings are, on the southern slopes, thwarted in their first attempts to live by the piercing heat of the unclouded sun, aided by the hot blast of the desert winds from the western Punjab and Rajputana. When, therefore, the tremendous downpour of the monsoon torrents beat upon the hill sides, there is no shelter of vegetation, no protecting tangle of matted roots to hold up the soil, and therefore so much the less chance is there, when the next summer returns with dry hot winds and baking sun, for seeds to germinate or tender plants to live. There is a constant tendency to denudation, which results in bareness. The northern and north-easterly slopes, on the contrary, turning away from the midday sun, are in shade, and are protected also by their aspect from the direct blasts of the desert winds, while they are refreshed occasionally by moist and cool breezes from the snows. Young plants can live. A mass of roots and herbage hold up the soil and jealously guard it against the precipitating rush of the monsoon deluge, while decaying leaves and grasses add, year after year, to the depth of rich humus. There is a constant tendency to the formation of soil, which results in a clothing of vegetation. Just a word more to notice that the phenomenon becomes less apparent on high elevations above, say, 8,000 or 9,000 feet, where the southern heat of the sun and wind is tempered by atmospheric coolness; but even there the character of the vegetation differs much on either side. Look at the Shali cliffs, which rise to a greater height even than 9,000 feet, and you will just see the fringe of forest peering over the edge, a visible sign of the rich forest which we know lies on the further side, while the whole southern face fronting us is bare, save on those shaded slopes of the projecting spurs which veer round towards the north. Stand on the summit of Jakko and face northwards towards the snows, and the whole Himalayan region looks a desert; you can see nothing but southern slopes. Stand again on the summit of Huttoo and face southwards towards Simla and the plains, and the whole Himalayan region looks a forest; you see nothing but northern slopes. The contrast is indeed striking.

"But it is almost time for us to emerge now from our weary miles of *Pinus longifolia*, a tree which has so strange a preference for the southern slopes between 2,000 and 6,000 feet, and while we are passing through the last stage, let me call the attention of our botanists to a singular fact, or at any rate, one that has struck me as singular, which, perhaps, accounts in part for the exceptional vitality of the cheer pine on the southern slopes. 'It makes,' writes Mr. Ribbentrop, our Inspector-General of Forests, 'a long tap-root in its early youth, which must not be injured in transplanting;' and so true is this that my own attempts a few years ago at Naini Tal to transplant even the smallest baby seedlings continually failed, on account of the depth to which the vertical root had descended, and the difficulty of taking it out intact. But that such a habit as this is exceptional and indicative of special adaptability to surrounding circumstances is suggested by a passage which I will quote from John's *Forest Trees of Britain*:—'Firs,' he states, 'both young and old, extend their roots horizontally, or in a direction parallel to the surface of the ground; tap-root they have none, for such an appendage would be useless to trees often growing in soil but a few inches deep.' The necessity of escaping from a furnace sun and burning winds is, of course, not understood in Great Britain.

"Now to our higher levels. Near Simla, at 5,000 or 6,000 feet, *Pinus longifolia* gradually is replaced by a very near ally, *Pinus excelsa*, and so closely connected are the two pines that but for the fact that *excelsa* has an appearance of being better clothed, it is not easy at a little distance to distinguish it from its poorer relation. The barks of the two trees are also quite different—*longifolia* is dark brown in corky slabs, while *excelsa* is compact and in the young trees smooth and greenish blue. Take a tuft of spiny leaves from each tree in the hand, and a ready means of telling the one from the other will be found in the fact that in each tuft of the *Pinus longifolia* there are three spines, and in each of those of *Pinus excelsa* there are five spines. Moreover, the under-surface of each spine of *Pinus excelsa* has a distinct bluish tinge, a circumstance which had led to its being called the blue pine, and on a breezy day, when the spines are upturned by the wind, the blue colouring becomes very apparent. The blue pine is one of the three common trees of Simla, the other two being the deodar and the white oak. It has, in common with *Pinus longifolia*, a virtue which

*

(though many of you are doubtless acquainted with it) ought to be more generally known. The fallen spines of these two trees form excellent stable litter, especially at Simla; on the one hand. their turpentiny nature keeps insects away, at the same time that it prevents animals from attempting to feed on the refuse under their feet; on the other hand, the high price of grass, often the difficulty of getting grass at all, makes it at Simla quite worth while to send our syces and jhampanis down the sides of the valleys to collect pine leaves. You should be warned, however, that the fall of spines varies very greatly in different years. The blue pine of Simla, which afforded plenty of litter in 1884, gave very little in 1885, when *Pinus longifolia* took its place. The leaves of the former have a life of three or four years, and of the latter two or three years, and the annual shedding becomes, therefore, very unequal. Next year the rich orange and russet colouring which marked the slopes of *Pinus longifolia* above the Glen, at the beginning of last rains, will possibly be less conspicuous, although at Mashobra (the Simla head-quarters of *Pinus excelsa*) a large fall of the spines of *excelsa* may be noted. *Pinus excelsa* has a wide range, from 5,000 to 10,000 feet, but seems in this neighbourhood to prefer the warm slopes between 6,000 and 8,000 feet. It has the protection, though not to the same extent as with *Pinus longifolia*, of a long tap-root.

"We come to the next distinguishing conifer, our familiar friend the cedar or deodar. Observe that, like the two species of pines, its spiny leaves are bound into clusters. This character readily separates the pines and deodar from the firs (*Abies*). It has almost the same range as *Pinus excelsa,* though found at both lower and higher elevations, and preferring cooler aspects. *Cedrus Deodara* is, as you know, closely allied to the cedar of Lebanon and would look much more like the tree which we know in Europe under that name, if our predecessors in Simla had given it more room to grow. Crowded as it is on the steep slopes, it has no opportunity of spreading out its branches in its characteristic flat table-like fashion, but when you encounter a solitary specimen in some open space outside the station, the resemblance is very apparent. The trunk of one which we measured the other day at a corner of the road to Kotgurh (where it formed a very conspicuous object) was 20 feet in girth, a size which would, judging from the data given by Brandis and Stewart, make it not less than 500 years old. The deodar is very capricious in its distribution. There are none, for instance, at Naini Tal, at the same height as at Simla; and again on the Tibet road between that Kotgurh giant of which I have spoken, and the seventh mile from Simla, a distance of about 40 miles, hardly a specimen is to be observed, while it is conspicuous again by its absence from the rich forests on the nearest ranges of Narkanda and Huttoo, even when these dip down to the Simla level. The deodars of Simla are just now displaying a phenomenon common to all conifers, which is not very conducive to household cleanliness, and is productive, some people say, of hay-fever. Late in autumn, the pollen-bearing cones, standing erect in great profusion on the lower branches, scatter to the winds a sulphur-coloured powder, of which a small percentage only reaches its destination in the larger pollen-receiving cones, which sit vertically, with gaping mouths, anxious to receive the fructifying powder as it is borne on the breeze. The greater part of the yellow pollen stains our verandahs, or mixes with the dust on the roads, and continues to be dispersed throughout the winter, the fallen pollen-bearing cones staining the snow.

"But I must not dwell longer among our Simla conifers. We must pass to Mashobra, where we first meet the next conifer on our list, the spruce fir, or *Abies Smithiana* (*Picea Smithiana*, as the botanists say we ought now to call it), allied as it is to *Picea Peculiata*, or the spruce fir of northern Europe. The peculiarity of the tree which most strikes the ordinary observer is the singular manner in which the lateral branchlets droop down as if hung out to dry from the larger horizontal branches. The latter, on the contrary, have a way of tilting their tips heavenwards, which forms a marked contrast to the gracefully drooped ends of the deodar. The gentle droop on the spreading deodar branches and the vertical fall of the spruce branchlets, are both doubtless due to the necessity of shifting off the burden of falling snow. The spruce fir ranges in these hills from about 7,500 to 9,500 feet, and thus marks a belt distinctly above the Himalayan cedar, and from Mashobra to Huttoo it is one of the commonest—the commonest I may say—of the conifer tribe. A curious phenomenon is exhibited occasionally in the young spruce firs before they have assumed their hoary character, both of the Himalayas and of Europe, which in the case of some seedlings in the Bhagi forest, which may be seen growing in an exposed position some 50 miles from Simla, lately led a distinguished botanist to suspect the occurrence of altogether another species of *Abies* or rather *Picea*. This is the formation of a false cone on certain trees, generally young ones, by the agency of an insignificant little insect of the Aphis family. In the case of our new Himalayan species, the dissection of the cones soon led to the discovery by our botanical friend of the deception, and Colonel Collett's microscope subsequently led to the identification of the deceiver as a small Aphis! The following account of the formation of these cones is taken from a descriptive account of the European tree :—'In the autumn, this insect lays its eggs on the under-side of the buds on the side branches. When these begin to burst in spring, the young leaves grow together into a solid mass, composed of a number of cells. Each of these contains an embryo insect, and towards the end of summer, opens and suffers the perfect insect to escape. These galls resemble imperfect cones.' The resemblance was perfect enough on the Huttoo trees to deceive a botanist, but, either due to the nature of the locality or the soil, the foliage and general characters of these stunted firs aided the deception. 'The Laplanders,' says the English account from which I have quoted, 'eat the gall;' so, perhaps, we may add another food product to our Himalayan list, though we did not eat the Huttoo specimens. The mimicry is probably another instance of protective habit, the cone-forming Aphis thus escaping most effectually the attacks of hungry birds, which know by experience or instinct how unpleasant is the taste of a turpentiny pine cone.

"Having taken you to Huttoo, I may introduce you to the last of our belt-distinguishing conifers in the *Abies Webbiana*, or silver fir. When I first saw the *Smithiana* and the *Webbiana* together, I had no friend to tell me which I ought to call the spruce and which the silver fir, and as I thought the *Webbiana* looked much sprucer and far less silvery than its companion, I attached the English epithets to the wrong trees. I did not know then, what I afterwards learned, that the rich dark-green silver firs, *Nigra*, as a Roman author calls the *Abies*, owe their name to the bright whitish streak on either side of the mid-rib on the underside of the leaf. Virgil writes of it as the fairest ornament of the mountains of Italy—*pulcherrima abies in montibus altis*—and you who have visited Huttoo will agree that the poet who is to describe the glories of the Himalayas must award his most rapturous verses to the forests of Bhagi, in which the king that stands pre-eminent is—paradoxical as the name may sound—the dark-green silver fir. Looking down even on the lofty spruce, which rises by its side almost to the same height, the silver fir towers to a height of often 150 feet, and in one instance (my authority is an eminent forester) even to 200 feet. But now I have to halt to ask the pardon of our botanical members. The tree is not *Abies Webbiana* at all. It is *Picea* not *Abies; Pindrow*, not *Webbiana*. I won't give, because I do not understand, the reasons which lead our botanical authorities to forbid the Virgilian name of *Abies*; but I am told that our Indian botanists are inclined to believe that the tree first marked down as *Webbiana* is confined to the inner ranges of Sikkim, Nepal, and Bhootan, is smaller and more like the silver fir of Europe, than the *Pindro* variety which occupies the Western Himalayas. It is a pity, for there was a symmetrical simplicity about the names of *Smithiana* and *Webbiana* which made them easy to remember for those of us who are not scientific botanists.

"I have now carried you up five conifer steps. The cheer pine from 2,000 to 6,000, the blue pine 5,000 to 7,000, the deodar up to 8,000, the spruce fir from 7,000 to 9,000, and the silver fir, 8,000 to 10,000. I shall now ask you to leave for the present the two pines and the two lower belts, and concentrate your attention on the three arboreal strata of the higher ranges, marked by the cedar and the two firs. To each of the distinguishing conifers of these ranges, I propose to give a mate from among the oaks. For this arrangement I have the authority of Dr. Brandis, late Inspector-General of Forests, who, in his description of the arboreal vegetation between Simla and the snows, divides the hills into three strata, of which the main trees are,—in the lowest stratum, the deodar and white oak; in the middle stratum, the spruce fir and the green oak; and in the highest, the silver fir and the brown oak. For the simple epithets which I have attached to the oaks, I am indebted to Dr. Brandis's successor, Dr. Schlich, who pointed out to me that the underleaf of the three oaks are respectively white, green, and brown. The white oak is *Quercus incana*, which in company with the deodar covers Jakko, and you may have often noticed, when a western breeze turns up the leaves to the afternoon sun, the glistening silver of the underleaves. In early spring the young leaves of this tree are pinkish, shining through a dusty grey which gives the Simla neighbourhood a sombre tint, relieved only by the bright sparkling flowers of the peaches and plums. The green oak is *Quercus dilatata*, and is with the spruce fir the chief component of the Mashobra woods. Its green, shiny leaves, of the same colour on both sides, and twisted and covered with spines, make it, when young, very like the English holly; and I would here draw your attention to yet another instance of protective habit, in the fact that the younger the tree, and the nearer the ground, the more prickly and the more like those of an English holly are the leaves. 'The leaves,' says Dr. Brandis, 'are prized as fodder for sheep and goats; the trees are often (as alas! we know) severely lopped for that purpose.' Nature has therefore done her best to arm the tree against her enemies by furnishing the leaves within reach of animals with 'sharp spinescent teeth,' as Brandis and Stewart have described them. The brown oak is *Quercus semiscarpifolia*, and what I have called the brown of the underleaf is, perhaps, better described by Brandis and Stewart's adjective 'ferruginous,' or russet-brown. It covers the summits of Matyana, Narkanda, and Huttoo in some places to the exclusion of every other tree, but always in the neighbourhood of silver firs. All three oaks, but especially the green and brown oak, often present a very miserable appearance from the severe lopping of which I have spoken, for the leaves of all three are utilised as fodder, and the higher the elevation the more recourse is had to them during the season that the snow is on the ground. Talking one day to a native cultivator of the neighbourhood, I pointed to a hillside, and asked if there was not good grazing there. 'No,' said my agricultural friend, 'there is no grazing there; there are no oaks.' Before I part company with our three oaks, I must tell those of you who have not seen it what a gorgeous dress is assumed by my favourite of the three—the green or Mashobra oak—in the early summer. In April and May last, the woods which surround us—now, in October, an almost unbroken green, save where lighted up by the reddening leaves of the Virginian creeper—presented every shade of colour that can be imagined, from light yellow and pink, through all the tints of orange and crimson, down to a deep copper brown. I do not remember ever to have seen a richer display of colouring in nature. My only regret was that so few Simla residents came out to see it; for, short as the distance is between us, there is not a specimen of this tree that I know of in the whole of Simla. I hope that the brief description I have given now of the spring glories of these woods will attract more visitors in future years. It is a sight that I could go a hundred miles to see.

"I must now complete my conifers. The two of the promised seven of which I have not yet spoken are the yew, *Taxus baccata*, and a cypress, *Cupressus torulosa*. The yew is found in the silver fir belt, and is the same tree as the one we know in England, though I have never myself seen any such large specimens in the Himalayas as in England. Here it is more like a giant bush, densely branched, and, what is curious, it seems to suffer from some fatal disease, as every now and then in these forests we come across a leafless bush of tangled branches, not thrown over like the stately pine or fir to rot on the ground, but remaining erect until, branch by branch, it disappears. The yew is very common on the Narkanda and Huttoo ridges, but as it is so familiar a tree to us all, I will not detain you by stopping to describe it further. *Cupressus torulosa*, of which I can show you a specimen planted on this hill, will not be so familiar to you. It is found, however, on the back of Shali and below the Water Works road, about one mile beyond the toll-bar, on the south-east slope which faces the municipal orchards, and again in Simla itself. It may be recognised in the tall trees which form a short avenue just above the tonga station. The cypress belongs to the spruce fir level, but is said by Brandis to prefer a limestone soil, which would account for its selection of the north side of the Shali as its dwelling-place. Those of you who have been to Naini Tal will recognise it as the tree that grows on the slopes of the Cheena mountain overhanging the station. It is not such a tidy-looking tree as the rest of our conifers, but at Naini Tal, where the only other of the fir tribe is the *Pinus longifolia*, it is much prized, and there is a very severe law against cutting it down. An energetic member of the Naini Tal Club, however, finding a well-grown specimen very much in the way of a projected tennis court, dug it up and removed it by sliding it down the hill to a newly-dug hole. Of course the tree died, and of course the energetic member knew that it would die; and then ensued one of the most protracted and virulent 'station-rows' that I ever witnessed—and I have witnessed many. The energetic member protested that he had not broken the law, having only transplanted, or attempted to transplant the tree, but the municipal committee, of course, took an opposite view.

"I have now done with the conifers. I have given you five conifer strata or belts, and associated with the three upper strata, the three oaks, white, green and brown. I next come to a tree which in outward similarity is not unlike the green oak, though it is far removed from it botanically. The one, for instance, has an acorn, the other a berry. I refer to the Himalayan holly, or *Ilex dipyrena*, and I am sure that on looking at the two branches you see here, one of a young 'green oak,' the other of a Himalayan holly, you will pronounce the former far more like the English holly than the latter. I was for some time very much puzzled how to distinguish the holly until it was pointed out to me by a botanist, Dr. Watt, that the underside of the holly leaf is smoother and less transparent than that of the oak, in which latter the reticulations of the nerves and veins are seen almost as plainly on the back of the leaf as on the face, whereas on the back of the holly leaf, they can be scarcely distinguished. Further, that the lateral nerves in the oak leaf are regular and parallel, whereas in the holly they are irregular and often crooked. The *Ilex dipyrena* runs through all three of our oak belts, and is much commoner in Simla than most people seem to be aware. There are several trees along the Mall on the north side of Jakko, and one of the finest I have seen is just above the Commander-in-Chief's house. Last year it was full of berries.

"Still remaining in Simla, we have a tree to notice, which is the glory of our Himalayan spring—the familiar rhododendron, *Rhododendron arboreum*, whose flowers greet our annual arrival with a blaze of rich crimson and scarlet. Which colour is it? I have turned to Brandis's 'Forest Flora' for a judgment, and find apparent confusion. 'Flowers,' he says, 'are commonly crimson-scarlet, occasionally white, pink, or rose colour or marked with purple or yellowish spots.' It is certainly the fact that the colouring depends somewhat on aspect and elevation, and as far as I have observed, the deep crimsons are most prevalent in the cold high ravines with north aspect, and the light pinks in sunny dry aspects. Occasionally, as all who were here last year know, it flowers twice, and it may be possible that the check to growth caused by a prolonged drought from spring to midsummer, such as we had last season, has the effect not unknown in the case of other trees of bringing out a second crop. The second flowering occurred at Naini Tal and Mussoorie, and was therefore common to an extended area along the Himalayan range. The tree rhododendron belongs distinctly to the white oak or deodar belt, ranging generally between 5,000 and 8,000 feet, with a preference for the lower elevations on the north side, and it avoids arid dry positions. Dr. Watt has told me that this tree has a wider and more varied range than any other tree of his acquaintance in the Himalayan regions. To go back to its flowers. You may have often observed a richly-coloured carpet of strewn blossoms, apparently fresh and undecayed, lying under the trees. These have been probably thrown down by monkeys which are fond of plucking out each separate flower, from what botanists call the 'terminal cluster or corymb,' and sucking the honeyed base. Our president, Mr. Ilbert, first drew my attention to this circumstance, having observed our Mashobra *lungoors* hard at work at a repast of rhododendron flowers, and scattering the blossoms on the ground as fast as they sucked them dry; but men eat them, too, and make of them what is said to be a 'pleasant sub-acid jelly,' and perhaps like them none the less because at times they are intoxicating. It may interest you to know that in these north-westerly Himalayas there are three other rhododendron shrubs,—one the tobacco rhododendron (*R. campanulatum*), with a blush pink flower, which ranges from Kashmir to Nepal above 10,000 feet, and of which the leaves are brought to the plains to be used as snuff; the second, a small Alpine shrub (*R. anthopogon*), distributed from Kashmir to Sikkim, also above forest level and up to 16,000 feet, of the flowers of which, passing from bluish through snowy white to a faint sulphur, Hooker writes in rapturous language; a third, also a small Alpine shrub (*R. lepidotum*), has the same range and elevation. The last is found on Huttoo, and comes therefore within the range of our beat, and although very far from being a 'tree,' you will perhaps permit me to introduce it to your closer attention on account of its relationship with our familiar Simla friend. I captured a few specimens on my last visit to the Huttoo forest, and as you will observe from these specimens, the leaves are very like those of the Azalea. It has flowers growing singly or in twos and threes, in shape like the bowl of a small salt-spoon and, says Brandis, of various colours, from red to dingy yellow, but generally in my experience of a magenta-tinged red. It does not grow above a foot high, and is fond of spreading itself over a mossy stone with very little soil for its nourishment. But I must come back again to our Simla trees. Our rhododendron often takes unto itself a partner, or keeps company with a pretty little tree, which may almost be called a first cousin. Botanists know it by the name of *Andromeda* (*Pieris*) *ovalifolia*, and natives, in the North-West Provinces at least, by the name of ayár.

The hill on which I once lived at Naini Tal was known by the name of Ayárpata, or the hill of the ayár, and my attention was first called to the tree by the dread which the servants had of letting their cows and goats get near it, for it has the virtue of being poisonous to goats, and if I thought that goats would take generally to eating it, I would ask the Forest Department to plant it 'with the least possible delay' wherever it would grow, with the object of ridding the country of that common enemy to foresters and naturalists. Goats should at any rate beware of the back of Jakko, for on the slopes of our Simla mountain, facing the Chor, the ayár is found in great abundance. Most of those who have not seen it may recognise it by its twisted gnarled branches, and the untidy appearance of its bark, resembling somewhat in these respects its cousin the rhododendron, both, as those who are not botanists will be as surprised as I was to learn, being members of the heath family, or *Ericaceæ*. The flower of the *Andromeda* has indeed some actual likeness on a large scale to that of a heath, and it is quite worth while to pay a visit to the back of Jakko just before the rains to collect the pretty white or flesh-coloured *racemes* which may then be found in profusion on its branches, with their little white heatherbell-shaped flower drooping gracefully, as our president once happily remarked, like grains of rice along the flower-stalk.

"I will now deal with two trees of whose existence I am ashamed to say I was, until a very short time ago, very ignorant. My attention was first called to one of them by a blaze of yellow in a ravine opposite the Matyana dâk bungalow, and half a mile or so from it. Anxious to know what so conspicuous a flower could be, we sent for a branch, and the flowers proved to be a puzzle even to the most botanical members of our party. At last it turned out that the four large yellow petals, as we thought them, which formed the conspicuous part of the apparent flower, were not petals at all, but bracts, the real flowers being packed together in a bunch in the centre of the four bracts, and being quite indistinguishable as separate flowers until placed under the microscope. Simla residents who wander to the Glen and Chadwick Falls, know it as the 'strawberry-tree,' and botanists have called it *Cornus capitata*, a member of the Cornel or Dogwood family. I should be inclined to place it in the *Pinus excelsa* belt, and though it ascends to 8,500 feet, it only does so in sheltered situations. Dr. Watt writes that in the valley commencing at the Elysium Hill, and extending towards Mashobra, the *Cornus capitata*, along with the barberry, the white rose, and the pomegranate, will be found in June to be one blaze of yellow, white, and red flowering bushes. Its strawberry-like fruit is made into preserves by natives. It is, however, worthy to be called a small tree rather than a bush. Closely allied is the *Cornus macrophylla*, but this is a much finer tree than the preceding, with large leaves, pale green underneath. The tree grows to a height of 40 or 50 feet. In this case the flowers are free from each other, forming an open panicle of small white flower without the embracing bracts of the last species. It is therefore less showy in blossom, but as a tree is more handsome than *Cornus capitata*. It is not uncommon near Simla. There is a very fine specimen near the Commander-in-Chief's house, and a good many in and below the Glen and underneath Annandale. The fruit of this tree is also eaten. The *Cornus macrophylla* belongs distinctly to the belt of which the distinguishing conifer is *Pinus excelsa*.

"I must next tell you what you will, perhaps, be interested to hear, that there are two wild laurels not at all uncommon in the neighbourhood of Simla. One, called *Machilus* (or *Laurus*) *odoratissima*, has a pleasantly orange-scented leaf. It grows (writes Dr. Watt) in abundance at the bottom of the Glen around the ruined hut, where its large sweetly-scented leaves, spreading from a somewhat clumsily branched tree, cannot be mistaken. It is the favourite tree of the '*Muga*' silk-worm, domesticated in Assam.

"The other laurel is the common Indian laurel *Litsæa zeylanica*, found not only on the Himalayas, but on the hills of Ceylon and Southern India. It grows from 3,000 to 8,000 feet, and I would therefore associate this tree also with the *Pinus excelsa* belt. It likes, however, more shady places to live in. It is described by Dr. Watt as an erect, elegant tree, with shining pale-green pendulous leaves. It is common from Mashobra to Narkanda, and you will see a specimen on the valley side of the road not a hundred yards from the place where the Fagu and Mashobra roads meet.

"We have now done for to-day with the trees close to Simla, and I must take you for a few minutes up to Huttoo and the silver fir belt, to tell you of the maples. On my first visit to the Baghi forest on the Huttoo slopes, the maples puzzled me. I called them sycamores. I was so far right that the sycamore is a maple, but these maples were, I afterwards found, not sycamores. As far as we have at present made out, there are four of them—*Acer cæsium*, with five-lobed leaves; *Acer caudatum*, the same, but with lobes having long tail-like ends, whence the name; *Acer pictum*, with seven-lobed leaves; *Acer villosum*, with five-lobed leaves but much thicker and coarser than the others. It is difficult for me, however, to present any precise idea of the difference between these four trees without specimens, and I must ask you to study them for yourselves on Huttoo with Brandis and Stewart's 'Forest Flora.' Suffice it to say that the maples form one of the chief beauties of the Baghi forest, brightening it up, as they do through the summer with their fresh bright green—a pleasing contrast to the dark firs amid which they grow, and again in autumn painting the woods with rich orange and scarlet. *Acer oblongum* is much more tropical in its likings and belongs to the *Pinus longifolia* region. It may be seen in the Ushan valley, below Chota Simla, and ought to be freely planted on the warmer slopes of Simla itself.

"The beauty which the Baghi forests owe to the spruce and silver firs and to these four maples, leads me now to deplore the apathy of past Simla generations who have made no attempt to beautify the slopes of Jakko with any of these trees. Still more am I led to deplore the irreparable destruction which has removed the rich forests through which even in 1869 I walked without break for some 30 miles from Mashobra to Matyana. The trees of ages were cut down, that for a brief decade potatoes might be grown. But the soil, protected no longer by vegetation, is now in great part washed away, gaping ravines are forming on every side, and soon neither potatoes nor forest will be able to grow. Even as near as the seventh mile from Simla, was a fine sample of the silver fir and maple forest, of which only a few miserable relics remain. Let me earnestly beg each member of our club to raise his voice, and use what influence he has for the restoration of these protecting forests, as well as for the embellishment of Simla with the Huttoo beauties. The latter lies at any rate in our power. At least one of our members is also a member of the municipal committee, and we are fortunate enough to have a well-wisher and co-operating supporter in Mr. (now Sir) James Walker, the president of the municipality. Already he has, I understand, sanctioned a nursery for the growth of forest seedlings, which in due time will be planted out and call forth the gratitude of posterity. Do not think that because nature has not placed the Mashobra or Huttoo trees on Jakko that they will not therefore grow there. Possibly the Simla climate is more favourable to the deodar and white oak, than to the silver fir and maple, and that in the struggle for existence the former have driven the latter to hills where they themselves find it less easy to flourish. But if you protect the spruce or silver fir and maples from the surrounding trees, the climate on all the northern slopes of Jakko is sufficiently like that of the lower part of Huttoo to admit of the successful growth of the Huttoo trees; in proof whereof I may remind you that there are a few maples growing happily in Simla gardens, while the excellent condition of three silver firs (planted, possibly, twenty years ago) close to this house, where silver firs never grew before, shows, by practical example, the favourable results attending transplantation."

Thus far Sir Edward Buck. It is due to him to state that during his occupation of the Mashobra 'Retreat' he did much to carry his precepts into practice by introducing into the Retreat grounds many of the trees of the Huttoo forest, notably the silver fir and the maples, which go far to enhance the beauty of the Mashobra woods.

A privately printed volume on Simla flowers, described as 'an annotated list of flowers collected in the neighbourhood of Simla and Mashobra,' was compiled by Lady Elizabeth Bruce and Mr. H. Babington Smith in 1897. A preface by the latter explains that the list had no claim to any original or scientific value, nor did it make any pretension to supply the place of a complete Simla Flora, but nevertheless it is a delightfully interesting volume for those interested in the botany of the neighbourhood. The compilers acknowledge the unfailing kindness they received from Mr. T. F. Duthie, of the Botanical Survey of Upper India.

Another volume which deals with Simla Flora is Thomson's 'Western Himalaya and Tibet.'

CHAPTER XV.

The Cemeteries.

IT may not be generally known that although only two are now in use, there are no less than four European cemeteries in Simla. The oldest, situated just behind a shelter shed in Chota Simla, where the road to 'Barnes Court' takes off from the Mall, is a relic of a period prior to the annexation of the Punjab. It occupies a small space of about 30 yards by 15, and contains in all about forty graves dating between the years 1829 and 1840. All the monuments are of ancient design, and are mostly constructed of roughly chiselled stones of the size of ordinary bricks with heavy slabs on the top. Some of them are so dilapidated that they might well be razed to the ground, while from others the slabs have evidently been carried off for use elsewhere. The tablets in many cases have disappeared altogether, and in others are so weather worn, or densely covered with ivy, as to be undecipherable. In one corner is a family vault with a very old and time-worn shingle roof, whose tablets record the deaths in the year 1840 of the wife and four children of a Captain Codrington, three of the children dying within the short space of two weeks. In another corner there is a cenotaph to the memory of Captain Matthew Ford, who died at Peshawar on the 17th March, 1841. The oldest decipherable monument is to the memory of Charles Corbet, infant son of Captain Henry Garston, 10th Regiment, Light Cavalry, who died on the 18th July, 1829, aged eight months and eight days; another contains a tablet to the memory of Margaret, daughter of Dr. R. M. M. Thompson, who died on the 28th May, 1829, and a third records the decease of Lieutenant-Colonel J. L. Gale, who was also buried there on 3rd May, 1832.

Three monuments that bear the following inscriptions may bring recollections of the past to descendants now in India: "Sacred to the memory of John Edward De Brett, Captain in the Bengal Artillery, who departed this life on 10th May, 1835, aged 46 years." (This monument, erected by his son in 1863, is the last monument included in the cemetery.) "Sacred to the memory of Captain Zouch Henry Turton, 15th Regiment of Native Infantry, who died on 29th September, 1835, aged 36 years." "Sacred to the memory of Lieutenant-Colonel Robert Chalmers, Honorable East India Company's Service, who departed this life at Simla, 7th November, 1840, aged 48 years." A fourth is—"To the memory of John Shaw, Junior, late of Wolverhampton, England, who died 25th October, 1839, aged 21 years;"

and another to that of "Major John Elliott, Captain in H. M.'s 4th Light Dragoons, and Assistant-Adjutant General, King's Troops in India, who departed this life on the 5th July, 1837." Here, too, lie the mortal remains of Colonel Parker, who died of fever contracted while out on a shooting expedition in the neighbourhood of Simla. A monument subscribed for by his brother officers was not erected at the site of the grave (now untraceable), but is to be seen as a cenotaph near a small cemetery, to be referred to presently, belonging to the Convent of Jesus and Mary at Chota Chelsea, at the back of Jakko; an arrangement due to the action of Colonel Tapp, then Superintendent of the Hill States, who considered the spot near the Convent to be more picturesque than that of the old graveyard. The tablet bears the following epitaph: "To the memory of Colonel Charles Parker, Bengal Artillery, who died at Simla, 27th April, 1837. Ætat 54. This monument has been erected by his brother officers in token of their regard for a warm friend and an ornament to their profession." The cemetery was little used after this day. In the guide books to Simla it is said:—"In process of time this resting place of the dead was found to be too near to the abodes of the living, so was closed;" but it was probably abandoned as too small for the needs of a growing settlement. There could have been no houses so near to it in 1840 as to make the little cemetery in any way objectionable. There are no houses very close to it even now, and the small deserted graveyard, although adjacent to the busy Mall, is a peaceful spot. At present the little cemetery surrounded by a wall with spiked stones on the top has a somewhat neglected look, and the entrance door is but poorly closed with a rusty chain and lock. The staple can be easily removed by hand, and no responsible person seems to have been placed in charge of the ground.

The second cemetery, also a small one, about 80 yards by 40, is situated under the cart road immediately below the Bullock Train Office, and at the apex of what may be described as the heart of one of the most thickly populated and busy parts of Simla. Dwelling places surround it on all sides, the brisk traffic of the cart road goes on day by day just above it, while immediately beneath is the house called 'Glen Hogan,' for many years the residence of Mr. William Hogan, a prominent member of the early Simla community, and, at the time of his death, head clerk of the office of the Commander-in-Chief's Military Secretary. This Mr. Hogan is reported to have married seven times, and it is a local tradition that his wives lie in the cemetery in sight of his old residence, but at the present day the monument of one only is traceable. The cemetery was consecrated by Bishop Wilson, Metropolitan of India, on the 24th October, 1840, and was brought into use in 1841. It contains monuments dating from that year up to 1876.

The monuments are typical of the gradually improved change in style that has taken place in memorials to the dead within the past few years. None of the monuments are so cumbrous and heavy as those in the old cemetery at Chota Simla. The earlier ones, however, though lighter in construction than those in the first cemetery, are of the ugly stone slab type. Then comes the very tall pillar type of monument with an iron or other ornamental top and black marble, gold-lettered tablet, and following this there is the simple white marble head-stone or cross of the present day. Many of the older monuments are in a very dilapidated state, and in many instances the tablets have fallen out and disappeared. The oldest monuments in this cemetery are to the memory of Letitia Margaret, wife of Captain D. M. Cameron, H. M.'s 3rd Foot, who died 2nd April, 1841, aged 23, and to the memory of Sophia Matilda, wife of Mr. James Christie, of the Subathoo Agency Office, died 6th November, 1841, aged 19. Other records interesting from the names which link the present with the past, or from the character of the epitaphs are the following:—Felicite Anne, second wife of T. T. Metcalfe, Esq., C.S., died 26th November, 1842, aged 34. Lieutenant James Montgomery, died 18th April, 1843. Erected by his brother officers as a token of their sincere esteem and respect. Captain Parker, 1st European Infantry Regiment, died 4th November, 1843. Erected by brother officers as a mark of their esteem. Maria, wife of Mr. James Christie, Deputy Collector, Cis-Sutlej States, died 27th May, 1847, aged 26.

An interesting tablet runs:—"This monument was erected by a few friends as a token of regard and affection to the memory of Captain Partrick Gerard, Honorable East India Company's service. His was a family noted for talent and enterprise, he and his brothers, Alexander and James, being among the first who explored the Trans-Himalayan regions. His equable disposition endeared him to all. He died at Simla on 3rd October, 1848, aged 54, and his remains are here interred." Patrick Gerard was a skilled meteorologist, and kept registers of the weather at Simla, Subathu, and Kotegarh. His brother, Alexander, was a man of scientific attainments, who was associated with the explorers Lambton and Everest, and James Gerard was the medical officer of the Nusseeree battalion, and is reported to have been the first European to penetrate the hill tracts beyond Kotegarh.

Other tablets mark the resting places of Philip Valentine, Mines Superintendent of the Sutlej Timber Agency, who died 24th July, 1848, aged 51; Michael Wilkinson, Clerk of Ipswich, Suffolk, "after upwards of 20 years spent in this country as a missionary to the heathen departed this life on the 6th November, 1848, aged 51 years;" Margaret, wife of Lieut.-Col. J. B. Gough, C.B., 3rd Light Dragoons, Quartermaster-General, H. M.'s Forces in India, died 3rd July, 1849; Rev. L. Pitcaithly, died 19th December

P 2

1849, aged 44, "having left a family of six young children with unfaltering confidence to the care of his God;" Lieut.-Colonel John Byrne, C.B., died 21st July, 1851, aged 51, the monument being a particularly handsome one; and Lieut. J. Mallock, Bengal Artillery, died 1st June, 1852, the memorial being erected, as in so many other cases, by his brother officers.

Mrs. Mary Ann Hogan, who died 21st June, 1852, aged 36, wife of Mr. William Hogan already mentioned, has the following verse on her tombstone:—

"Tread gently, stranger, on this sacred spot
Where sleeps divinely one who's not forgot,
A wife, a mother, Christian and a friend
Such as Heaven to Earth may in blessing send.
Then for your own salvation's sake forbear
To disturb the ashes in deposit here."

Among other memorials may be mentioned those to John Kyffin Williams, Headmaster of Agra College, died at Simla 5th November, 1852, 36 years and 4 months; Mary Emma, wife of James Craddock, died January 26th, 1870; and John Pengree, who was at one time a large householder in Chota Simla, Invalid Establishment, died 9th October 1875, aged 68 years. In close proximity are the graves of his wife, two sons and a grandson. A handsome polished Aberdeen granite monument is to the memory of W. Byrne-Johnson, late Lieut., H. M.'s 55th Foot, died 6th August, 1876, aged 40 years.

A simple stone marks the grave of one of old Simla's most influential citizens—Major Samuel Boileau Goad—1st Bengal Light Cavalry, who died on the 13th December, 1876. Major Goad's burial appears to have been the last interment in the cemetery. Between the years 1852 and 1870 there are no tablets, with the exception of those mentioned, and the few funerals subsequent to 1852 were therefore probably by special permission in accordance with the expressed wish of relatives. The number of the monuments indeed shows that by this time the graveyard was becoming overcrowded, and probably for this reason it was finally closed.

The third cemetery, or that now in general use, is situated on a well-wooded spur above the old Brewery, about a mile and a quarter from the Church, is well removed from inhabited dwellings, and is approached by a picturesque forest road which leaves the Mall at the old bandstand, just beyond the Metropole Hotel. The cemetery, originally a small one, has had three extensions made to it, and is now quite a large ground. Burials commenced in the year 1850, but the first portion of the cemetery was not consecrated until the 10th of January, 1857, and this site was extended in the year 1871. Although there is no record of the actual date of the early consecrations, or of the clergy who officiated thereat, the ceremonies were probably performed by Bishops Wilson and Milman, respectively, of the Calcutta Diocese, who in bye-gone days held ecclesiastical jurisdiction in the Punjab. A third extension at the lower end of the cemetery was consecrated by the Right Rev. Valpy T. French, D.D., first Bishop of Lahore, on the 8th July, 1882. A fourth by the Right Rev. G. Lefroy, D.D., third and present Bishop of Lahore, on 14th August, 1902. This extension, which is at the top of the ground, now constitutes the main entrance to the cemetery. The new entrance gate, with robing and retiring rooms, all painted in black and white, in the utilitarian Public Works Department style of the present day, with a flight of ninety steps between the terraces of the last extension, has a somewhat formal appearance; but when the older part of the ground is reached, the eye is relieved by splendid deodars, handsome shrubs, and a quiet and restful beauty which shows the ground was well selected for its special purpose by the early residents of Simla. Nothing indeed could be in greater contrast than the old and new portions of the cemetery. Many years ago, when land was easily obtainable and of but little value, the dead were laid under the spreading boughs of the forest trees. Now, these latter are cut down and uprooted so as to make the most of the ground, and are replaced by small shrubs and flowering plants, which present a rather formal appearance and modern aspect to the newer ground. The whole cemetery is in charge of a chaukidar (or keeper), who, with an adequate staff of gardeners, keeps it in admirable order. This is more than can be said of the two older cemeteries, as their state can only be described as disgraceful and a reproach to Simla.

The earliest memorial in the latest cemetery is to the memory of Mr. Joseph Anderson, of Alnwick, Northumberland, who died at Gauzar, on the 26th June, 1850. From among the hundreds of graves, a number which indicates the rapidity with which the population of Simla has increased during the past half century, and more especially of late years, I have selected inscriptions at random from tablets which are sacred to the memory of old and respected residents of bye-gone days, which are names carrying with them memories of the past, or which commemorate those who met their deaths under circumstances of an unusual character.

Rev. Henry Beddy, Pastor of the first Baptist Church at Simla. Died 3rd June, 1852, aged 64. "Tandem Felix."

Major-General Sir Henry T. Godwin, K.C.B., Colonel, H. M.'s 20th Regiment. Born 26th October, 1853. Aged 69 years. This officer served in the first Burmese war in 1825, and afterwards, as Major-General, commanded the troops that formed the second expedition in 1852 and gained Lower Burma.

Harriette, widow of the Ven'ble Archdeacon Ed. Vaughan, of Madras. Died 11th October, 1858. Aged 66.

Colonel C. D. Blair, C.B., Invalid Establishment, formerly of the 10th Bengal Light Cavalry. Died 27th September, 1860.

In the centre of the oldest part of the cemetery is a cumbrous dome-like and very unsightly family vault. A tablet on this vault is to the memory of one who in his day displayed considerable public spirit for the progress and improvement of Simla, for many of the more superior among the old houses and places of business are due to his initiative. The tablet runs:—"Underneath, rest the remains of Charles Harris Barrett Born at Cambridge, 29th July, 1793. Died at Simla, 29th December, 1860."

A handsome marble cross, also in the oldest part of the cemetery, bears the following inscription:—"Sacred to the memory of Nora Frederica, only child of Major (recently Commander-in-Chief of H. M.'s Forces) Fred. Roberts. Born at Mean Mir, 10th March, 1860. Died at Simla, 31st March, 1861." A stone slab subsequently placed on the grave records the deaths of two more infant children of Lord and Lady Roberts, as it runs: —"Also to the memory of Evelyn Santille. Born at Clifton, 18th July, 1868. Died at Sea, 8th February, 1869; and of Frederick Henry. Born at Simla, 27th July, 1869. Died 20th August, 1869."

Another inscription runs:—"The grave of Sir Alexander H. Lawrence, Baronet, son of Sir H. W. W. Lawrence, K.C.B. Born, 6th September, 1838. Died, 27th August, 1864." (Sir Alexander fell with his horse through a bridge which gave way, on the Hindustan-Tibet road, and was killed instantaneously.)

Gustave F. W. Belle. Died 20th August, 1867. Aged 37 years. Also, adds an additional stone, Eliza, his widow, who entered into rest, October 7th, 1891. Aged 66 years.

Sergeant-Major Fred. Bender, A-22, R.A. Mountain Battery, who died at Jutogh on the 12th of July, 1869, from an accident met with on duty.

Catherine Sophia, daughter of R. Cloette, Esquire, of the Cape of Good Hope, and wife of G. H. W. Batten, Esquire, Her Majesty's Bengal Civil Service. Born 23rd January, 1831; married 4th October, 1854; died 5th August 1870.

John Cumming Anderson, Colonel, R.E., C.S.I. Died 12th October, 1870. Erected by the brother officers associated with him in the Public Works Secretariat of the Government of India.

Peter Innes, of the 14th Regiment, B. N. I. and the Bengal Staff Corps, Lieutenant-General in the Army. Born 20th May, 1804. Died 10th May, 1871.

In a quiet corner of the cemetery are interred, side by side, the remains of four youthful members of an itinerant band of Italian musicians, who, on their way up to Simla, were crushed to death on the 28th June 1871, by a piece of rock falling from the hill side on the bullock cart in which they were travelling. An interesting fact in connection with this accident was that Lord Mayo was one of the first to hear of it, and proceeded at once with the men of the Viceroy's band to the spot which was some little distance below the last posting stage into Simla. No head-stones mark their last resting places, but the register of burials gives the following names and ages: Nicola Navallo, aged 13; Francis Pizzo, aged 14; Joseph Di Girardi, aged 14; Ferdinand Depasqua, aged 17. The sad fate of these poor little fellows caused quite a sensation in Simla, and the expenses of their funeral—very largely attended—were defrayed by the public.

Among other graves may be mentioned those of Janette Barbarie, wife of the Revd. H. W. Crofton, Chaplain of Simla. Died 18th July, 1872. Colonel Robert Christopher Tytler, Bengal Army, died 10th September, 1872. Aged 54. William Cotton (of the firm of Cotton and Morris), died June 17th, 1873, aged 35 years, from injuries received by a fall from his horse. Surgeon-General George Stewart Beatson, C.B., M.D., died at Simla, 7th June, 1874, aged 61 years. Alice Maude, infant daughter of Lord and Lady Napier of Magdala. Born 28th December, 1874. Died 17th July, 1875.

One noticeable monument in the Italian style, a stone surmounted by a cherub, is conspicuous among the sober and unpretentious English monuments with which it is surrounded, and bears this inscription:—"Cara Memoria di Giovenna Peliti, defuncto 30 Giugno 1878, il Fratello Federico Rosa."

Other tablets record the death of Mary, wife of Whitley Stokes, who was for many years Secretary in the Legislative Department. Died 30th January, 1879, aged 37. William Hogan. Died at Glen Hogan, Simla, on 15th October, 1879, aged 87. Susan Nind Hogan. Widow of the late William Hogan. Died 11th January, 1891, aged 73; and Edward Newberry, Major, Bengal Staff Corps, Personal Assistant to the Inspector-General of Police, Punjab. Died at Simla, 2nd June, 1884, aged 42 years. This latter monument was erected by his brother officers of the police force and many friends, all of whom admired his worth and deplored his loss.

Thomas David Colyear, Lieutenant-Colonel, 7th Bengal Light Cavalry, "Died at Dukani, near Simla, on the 8th August, 1875, aged 70 years, and here awaits the sound of the last trumpet."

Colonel Colyear had married a native Mahomedan lady who predeceased him in the year 1865, and he buried her in the compound of Juba House, on the road to the Bishop Cotton School. Here he erected a mausoleum of native type with carved marble screen panels to her memory, which bore the following inscription on a tablet:—"Beneath this stone rest the remains of the dearly beloved and devoted wife of Lieutenant-Colonel T. D. Colyear Retired List, a good mother and firm friend, who lived in the service of her God and died at Simla on Monday, 30th January, 1865, deservedly and sincerely lamented by her relatives and friends." After Colonel Colyear's death Juba House was sold, but the purchasers objecting to a grave on the estate declined to conclude the sale unless the body was removed. It being reported that a quantity of jewellery had been buried with Mrs. Colyear, the grave was opened in the presence of the Deputy Commissioner, a representative of the family, a solicitor, the district police officer, the civil surgeon, and a few friends. No jewellery was found, and the remains were re-coffined, and removed to the cemetery where they rest with those of Colonel Colyear, and the tablet to his wife's memory can now be seen at the foot of his grave. The mausoleum was afterwards levelled to the ground and a garden covers its site.

A tombstone with a particularly sad story attached to it is that in memory of Ralph Broughton, Lieutenant, 9th Lancers, of Barlaston and Cotton, Staffordshire; son of John Lambert and Selina Broughton of Tumstall, Market Drayton. Born 17th July, 1863. Died 17th July, 1885. Erected by his brother officers. The young Lancer, who was on the eve of his marriage with Miss Bridge, daughter of the Principal Medical Officer at Amballa, lost his life through his pony bolting between Alloa Cottage and the Public Works Department offices, the animal having been frightened by the rattle of some empty kerosine tins carried by a cooly. Another fatal accident I may mention occurred on the occasion of the first Queen's Birthday ball, given by Lord Mayo at Peterhoff. After the dance was over two young officers mounted the same pony, and one was thrown over the khud near Armsdell and killed on the spot.

A simple head-stone in the shape of a cross has on it the letters I. H. S. Underneath is the crest of the Royal Artillery—a field piece with its motto "*Ubique quo fas et gloria ducunt,*" and the inscription, Thomas Elliott Hughes, Major-General, Royal Artillery. Died May 24th, 1886, aged 56.

Among others laid to rest in the cemetery I find:—Richard William Rumsby, Superintendent, Civil Secretariat, Punjab. Died 15th August, 1889. Aged 27 years. Elizabeth, wife of Charles Arthur Roe, B.C.S. Died 11th July, 1891. Aged 43 years. Felix Von Goldstein, Band Master to His Excellency the Viceroy and so well known for years as the conductor of the 'Monday Pops' at Benmore, the fashionable resort of Simla society on Monday afternoons. Died 1st July, 1892, aged 58; and James Craddock. Born January 1st, 1833. Died January 31st, 1894, aged 61.

Two graves which lie side by side possess tablets in loving memory of John William Rebsche, for 57 years a Missionary in India. Died May 17th, 1895. Aged 79 years; and of Albertine Adelaide, the wife of the Revd. W. Rebsche. At rest June 27th, 1899, aged 73 years.

Not far off two other graves, also side by side, bear tablets to the memory of Captain Archibald Litster of the 79th Highlanders. Born at Wemyss, Fifeshire, on the 10th January, 1831. Died at Simla on 30th October, 1897. (Captain Litster, also a Volunteer officer, was the first Adjutant of the Simla Volunteers.) Mary, relict of Captain Litster, 79th Highlanders. Born at Nenach, Tipperary, Ireland, on the 17th March, 1832. Died at Simla, on the 12th May, 1899.

Demetrius Panioty, Assistant Private Secretary to His Excellency the Viceroy, son of Emanuel Panioty, a Greek gentleman of Calcutta. Born at Calcutta, 1st October, 1830. Died at Simla, 17th July, 1895. "A devoted husband, a good father, a true friend and faithful servant of Government. He tried to do his duty."

Katherine Mary, the dearly loved wife of Lieutenant-Colonel Robert A. Wahab, Royal Engineers, who died at Simla on the 7th May, 1896. Aged 34 years. (Mrs. Wahab succumbed to injuries occasioned by falling with her horse over the cliff on the beautiful forest road between Narkanda and Bagi, about 46 miles from Simla.)

Alexander Herbert Mason, Brevet-Lieut.-Colonel, R.E. Born June 10th, 1856. Died May 8th, 1896. "Erected by his widow and brother officers of the Corps at Simla." The funerals of both the last named took place on the same day, and cast a sad gloom over Simla.

Two well remembered and highly respected residents of Simla who also rest in the cemetery are Alexander Chisholm. Died 8th July, 1896, aged 68 years: and John Alexander Stowell, of Merlin Park, Simla. Died 28th May, 1902, aged 70 years. The latter was for many years the Registrar of the Home Department, Government of India.

The following inscriptions taken from the tombstones of well known Freemasons are of special interest in the Punjab. "Sacred to the memory of Worshipful Brother John Burt, who was summoned from the Eastern Chair of Lodge Himalayan Brotherhood to the Grand Lodge above, on 3rd March, 1888. Born 2nd June, 1844. Erected in fraternal remembrance by the members of the Lodge." 'Shall not the Judge of all the world do right.'—Gen. xviii. 23.

"Sacred to the memory of worshipful Brother W. Bull, Past Grand Sword Bearer of England and for many years District Grand Secretary of the District Grand Lodge of the Punjab. Born 2nd November, 1838. Died 9th September, 1901. Erected by the Freemasons of the Punjab, in memory of a good and worthy Mason." "Faith, Hope and Charity, but the greatest of these is Charity" is also inscribed on this stone.

The fourth cemetery is the private property of the Convent of Jesus and Mary at Chota Simla. It is called the 'Nuns' Graveyard,' and was laid out in the year 1872, and the ground was blessed in 1873 by Father Ildefonsus of Pestora, at that time Vicar-General of the Agra Archdiocese, assisted by the Convent and Chaplain of Simla. In 1892 and the following year the ground was enlarged and beautified by Mr. Philip Sheridan, for many years Postmaster-General of the Punjab. The cemetery is situated on a picturesque spur below the Convent premises, and the approach to it by a forest path leaving the Mall just beyond 'Bohemia,' is one of the pleasantest walks in Simla. Always beautiful, it is exquisite in the rainy season when the forest trees are covered with moss and numerous little rills run across the path, and the little cemetery is moreover carefully tended. Its entrance is decorated by an ornate iron gate supported by stone pillars with ornamental iron railings on each side, the cemetery itself being charmingly laid out with trees, shrubs, rose bushes and flowering plants and with its perfect sense of calm and quiet it is an ideal last resting place for the dead. Most of the graves are without monuments, and are those of orphan children who have died in the Convent, but one or two are to the memory of sisters and priests. One noticeable tablet is to the memory of the wife of Philip Sheridan, who died on the 22nd August, 1891, aged 46 years. The cemetery is some distance from Simla and is only intended for those who have resided in the Convent; but as both Mr. Sheridan and his wife took a great interest in everything connected with the Convent, Mrs. Sheridan was buried there instead of in the large cemetery generally used by the Simla community.

Just outside the gate of the cemetery is, as already stated, the cenotaph to Colonel Parker, whose mortal remains lie in the old cemetery in Chota Simla.

APPENDIX I.

Personal Staffs of the Governors-General and Viceroys who have visited Simla.

WILLIAM PITT, BARON AMHERST, P.C. (afterwards EARL AMHERST) Governor-General of Fort William in Bengal, 1st August 1823 to 12th March 1828.

Arrived in Simla . April 1827. Left Simla . June 1827.

Military Secretary.	Aides-de-Camp.	Surgeons.
Major W. Fendall, 4th Light Dragoons.	Capt. G. S. Crole, 41st Foot. Lieut. the Hon'ble F. G. Howard, 13th Foot. Lieut. R. R. Gillespie, 4th Light Dragoons. Cornet T. H. Pearson, 11th Light Dragoons. Lieut. Hon'ble H. Gordon, 23rd N. I. Lieut. W. Brownlow, 46th N. I. Major J. Maling, 64th N. I. (Supy.)	Asst. Surgeon H. Cavell, Bengal Medical Service. Asst. Surgeon E. W. W. Raleigh, Bengal Medical Service.

W. B. Bailey, Esq., officiated as Senior Member, 13th March 1828 to 3rd July 1828.

LORD WILLIAM CAVENDISH BENTINCK, G.C.B., G.C.H., P.C., 4th July 1828 to 19th March 1835. (Governor-General of Fort William in Bengal, 4th July 1828 to 15th June 1834. Governor-General of India, 16th June 1834 to 19th March 1835.)

Arrived in Simla . {April 1831. April 1832. Left Simla . {October 1831. October 1832.

Private Secretary.	Military Secretary and Aide-de-Camp.	Aides-de-Camp.	Surgeon.
Thos. Pakenham, Esq.	Capt. R. Benson, 11th N. I.	Major H. Caldwell, 49th N. I. Lieut. J. Higginson, 58th N. I.	Surgeon J. Turner.

Charles Lord Metcalfe officiated from 20th March 1835, but his nomination by the Directors was disallowed by His Majesty's Government.

The Most Noble JAMES ANDREW, EARL (afterwards MARQUESS) OF DALHOUSIE, K.T., P.C., 12th January 1848 to 28th February 1856.

Arrived in Simla . { About 20th April 1849. About last week of April 1850. Left Simla . { About 30th November 1849. About 29th October 1850.

Private Secretary.	Military Secretaries.	Aides-de-Camp.	Surgeon.
F. F. Courtenay, Esq.	Lieut.-Col. R. Benson, C.B., 41st N. I. (Offg.) Capt. J. Ramsay, 22nd Foot.	Major the Hon'ble F. W. H. Fane, 25th Foot. Capt. J. DeCourcy Sinclair, Madras Arty. Capt. J. Metcalfe, 3rd N. I. Capt. H. O. Mayne, 6th Madras Lt. Cavy. Capt. C. B. Bowie, Arty.	Asst. Surgeon A. Grant.

The Right Hon'ble CHARLES JOHN, VISCOUNT (afterwards EARL) CANNING, G.C.B., 29th February 1856 to 11th March 1862(*a*).

Arrived in Simla . April 1860. Left Simla . June 1860.

Private Secretary.	Military Secretary.	Aides-de-Camp.	Surgeon.
Lewin Bentham Bowring, Esq., C.S.	Major Sir E. FitzG. Campbell, *Bart.*, 60th Foot (and Aide-de-Camp).	Capt. R. Baring, 1st Euro. Lt. Cavy. Capt. the Hon'ble J. C. Stanley, Grendr. Guards. Major H. M. Jones, 73rd Foot. Lieut. J. Hills, Arty.	Surgeon A. Beale.

(*a*) Viceroy, 1st November 1858.

His Excellency JAMES, EARL OF ELGIN and KINCARDINE, K.T., G.C.B., K.C.S.I., 12th March 1862 to 20th November 1863(*b*).

Arrived in Simla . About first week of April 1863. Left Simla . About second week of October 1863.

Private Secretary.	Military Secretary.	Aides-de-Camp.	Surgeon.
The Hon'ble Thomas John Havell Thurlow.	Lieut.-Col. S. J. Blane, 52nd Lt. Infy.	Major A. Scott, 5th Fusiliers. Capt. R. Baring, 19th Hussars. Lieut. the Hon'ble A. Stewart, R.A.	Asst.-Surgeon W. B. Beatson, M.D.

(*b*) Died at Dharmsala, 20th November 1863.

Major General Sir Robert Napier, K.C.B., (afterwards Lord Napier of Magdala), officiated as Senior Member of Council, pending the arrival of the Governor of Madras, 21st November 1863 to 1st December 1863.

Colonel Sir William Thomas Denison, K.C.B., acted as Viceroy and Governor-General of India from 2nd December 1863 to 11th January 1864.

His Excellency the Right Hon'ble SIR JOHN LAIRD MAIR LAWRENCE (afterwards BARON LAWRENCE), BART., G.C.B., G.C.S.I., 12th January 1864 to 11th January 1869.

Arrived at Simla .	July 1864. July 1865. April 1866. July 1867. July 1868.	Left Simla .	November 1864. November 1865. November 1866. November 1867. October 1868.

Private Secretaries.	Military Secretaries.	Aides-de-Camp.	Surgeon.
Surgeon-Major C. Hathaway, M.D. J. D. Gordon, Esq., C.S.I.	Capt. E. C. Impey, S.C. Lieut.-Col. S. J. Blane, Rifle Brigade (and A.-D.-C.).	Major H. G. A. Vicars, 18th Foot Capt. W. L. Randall, 59th N. I. Capt. R. Baring, 19th Hussars. Capt. R. G. Kennedy, 18th Hussars. Capt. H. B. Lockwood, late 4th European Lt. Cavy. Capt. E. F. B. Brooke, 41st Foot.	Surgeon T. Farquhar, M.D.

His Excellency the Right Hon'ble RICHARD SOUTHWELL, EARL OF MAYO, 12th January 1869 to 8th February 1872. (*a*)

Arrived in Simla .	April 1869. 1st May 1870. April 1871.	Left Simla .	19th October 1869. 4th October 1870. 1st November 1871.

Private Secretary.	Military Secretary.	Aides-de-Camp.	Surgeon.
Major O. T. Burne, 20th Foot.	Major the Hon'ble R. Bourke, 3rd Hussars.	Cornet the Hon'ble H. J. L. Wood, 10th Hussars. Capt. E. F. B. Brooke, 41st Foot. Capt. H. B. Lockwood, late 4th Euro. Lt. Cav. Major C. C. Taylor, S.C. Lieut. C. L. C. deRobeck, 60th Foot. Lieut. R. H. Grant, R.A. Capt. H. N., Visct. Lascelles, Grenadier Guards (Extra). Capt. F. H. Gregory, 15th Hussars (Extra).	Staff Surgeon O. Barnett.

(*a*) Assassinated at Port Blair by convict Shere Ali, 8th February 1872.

Sir John Strachey, G.C.S.I., C.I.E., officiated as Senior Member of Council, pending the arrival of the Governor of Madras, from 9th February 1872 to 22nd February 1872.

Baron Napier of Merchistoun, K.T. (afterwards Baron Napier and Ettrick), acted as Viceroy and Governor General of India from 23rd February 1872 to 2nd May 1872.

His Excellency the Right Hon'ble THOMAS GEORGE BARING, Baron NORTHBROOK of STRATTON, G.M.S.I. (afterwards Earl NORTHBROOK), 3rd May 1872 to 11th April 1876.

Arrived in Simla { On 25th May 1872. On 18th April 1873. About 2nd April 1875. Left Simla . { 14th October 1872. 29th October 1873. 15th October 1875.

Private Secretary.	Military Secretary.	Aides-de-Camp.	Surgeon.
Capt. E. Baring, R.A.	Col. W. Earle, Grendr. Guards.	Capt. J. Biddulph, 19th Hussars. Capt. G. C. Jackson, late 2nd E. L. C. Capt. C. B. Reynardson, 1st Foot Guards. Lieut. C. L. C. deRobeck, 60th Foot. Capt. G. L. M'L. Farmer, 60th Foot. Lieut. E. Hartopp, 10th Hussars. Major C. C. Taylor, s.c. (Extra.) Lieut the Hon'ble F. G. Baring, Rif. Brigade (Extra).	Staff Surgeon O. Barnett.

His Excellency the Right Hon'ble EDWARD ROBERT, Baron LYTTON of KNEBWORTH (afterwards Earl LYTTON), 12th April 1876 to 7th June 1880.

Arrived in Simla . { 25th April 1876. End of April 1877. Beginning of April 1878. April 1879. 5th April 1880. Left Simla . . { 10th October 1876. 5th November 1877. 18th November 1878. 20th November 1879.

Private Secretaries.	Military Secretaries.	Aides-de-Camp.	Surgeon.
Lieut.-Col. O. T. Burne, C.S.I., 20th Foot (Offg.) Col. Sir G. Pomeroy Pomeroy-Colley, C.B., K.C.S.I. C.M.G., 2nd Foot. G. H. M. Batten, Esq., C.S. (Offg.) Lieut.-Col. H. Brackenbury, R.A.	Col. Sir G. P. Pomeroy-Colley, C.B., 2nd Foot. Lieut.-Col. the Hon'ble G. P. H. Villiers, Grendr. Guards. Col. T. D. Baker, C.B., 18th Foot (A.-D.-C. to the Sovereign). Major A. C. W. Crookshank, 32nd N.I. (Offg.) Lieut.-Col. W. L. Dalrymple, 88th Foot.	Major G. C. Jackson, late 2nd Euro. Lt. Cavalry. Capt. Lord W. L. DeLa P. Beresford, 9th Lancers. Lieut.-Col. the Hon'ble G. P. H. Villiers, Grendr. Guards. Capt. W. Loch, 19th B.C. Lieut. A. F. Liddell, R.A. Capt. J. Biddulph, 19th Hussars (Extra). Lieut. H. R. Rose, 34th Foot. Lieut. H. S. H. Riddell, 60th Foot. Lieut. C. W. Muir, s.c. Lieut. J. P. Brabazon, 10th Hussars (Extra). Lieut. C. Herbert, s.c. (Extra). Capt. R. Pole-Carew, Colds. Guards (Extra). Lieut. G. C. Kitson, 60th Foot, (Offg.). Lieut. B. M. Hamilton, 15th Foot (Extra).	Surgeon Maj. O. Barnett.

His Excellency the Most Hon'ble GEORGE FREDERICK SAMUEL, MARQUESS OF RIPON, K.C., P.C., G.M.S.I., 8th June 1880 to 12th December 1884.

Arrived in Simla		Left Simla .	
	8th June 1880.		28th October 1880.
	On or about 21st March 1881.		1st November 1881.
	On or about 21st March 1882.		6th November 1882.
	On or about the 17th March 1883.		16th October 1883.
	On or about the 22nd March 1884.		10th November 1884.

Private Secretary.	Military Secretaries.	Aides-de-Camp.	Surgeon.
H. W. Primrose, Esq.	Lieut.-Col. G. S. White, C.B., Gord. Highrs. Capt. Lord W. DeLa P. Beresford, V.C., 9th Lancers.	Capt. C. W. Muir, Staff Corps. Lieut. E. L. S. Brett, 5th Bn., Scots Guards. Capt. F. O. B. Foote, R.A. Capt. the Hon'ble W. C. Wentworth FitzWilliam, Roy. Horse Guards. Capt. E. H. Clough-Taylor, R. Welsh Fus. Lieut. the Hon'ble C. Harbord, Scots Guards. Lieut. Lord A. F. Compton, 10th Hussars. Capt. A. N. Rochford, R.A. Lieut. F. S. St. Quentin, 30th N. I. Lieut C. R. Burn, 8th Hussars. Lieut. A. W. Perry, Rif. Brig. (Extra). Lieut. A. G. A. Durand, 1st C.I.H. Lieut. C. Herbert, Deoli Irreg. Force (Extra). Lieut. H. W. Pollen, R.E. (Extra). Capt. E. R. Owen, Lanc. Fus. (Extra). Lieut. L. Gordon, K. O. Sco. Borderers (Extra).	Surgn. Maj. J. Anderson, C.I.E.

His Excellency the Right Hon'ble FREDERICK-TEMPLE, EARL OF DUFFERIN, (afterwards MARQUESS OF DUFFERIN AND AVA), K.P., G.C.B., G.M.S.I., G.C.M.G., P.C., G.M.I.E., 13th December 1884 to 9th December 1888.

Arrived in Simla .		Left Simla .	
	April 1885.		20th October 1885.
	12th April 1886.		28th October 1886.
	18th April 1887.		3rd November 1887.
	9th May 1888.		13th November 1888.

Private Secretary.	Military Secretaries.	Aides-de-Camp.	Surgeon.
Sir Donald Mackenzie Wallace, K.C.I.E.	Bt. Lieut.- Col. Lord W. L. De La P. Beresford, V. C., C.I.E., 9th Lancers.	Major H. Cooper, N. Lanc. R. Lieut. Hon'ble C. Harbord, Scots Guards. Lieut. Lord H. A. Russell, Grendr. Guards. Lieut. A. G. Balfour, High. L. I.	Maj. J. Findlay, M.B., I.M.S.

Private Secretary.	Military Secretary.	Aides-de-Camp.	Surgeon.
		Capt. C. R. Burn, 1st Dragoons. Lieut. K. O. Gordon, K.O.S. Borderers (Extra). Major F. J. R. Hamilton, Norfolk Regt. Capt. George, Lord Binning, Royal Horse Guards. Lieut. A. J. L., Viscount Clandeboye, 17th Lancers (Extra). Lieut. L. G. F. Gordon, R. A. (Extra). Capt. J. W. Currie, 20th M. I. (Extra). Lieut. G. C. Birdwood, 1st Bo. L. (Extra). Lieut. J. A. Henderson, 8th Hussars (Extra). Lieut. H. L. Pennell, 1st Dragoon Guards.	

His Excellency the Most Hon'ble HENRY CHARLES KEITH, MARQUESS OF LANSDOWNE, G.M.S.I., G.C.M.G., G.M.I.E., 10th December 1888 to 26th January 1894.

Arrived in Simla { 15th April 1889. About the end of April 1890. About the end of April 1891. On 21st April 1892. 22nd April 1893.

Left Simla { 22nd October 1889. 21st October 1890. 14th October 1891. 27th October 1892. 7th November 1893.

Private Secretary.	Military Secretary.	Aides-de-Camp.	Surgeon.
Col. J. C. Ardagh, C.B., C.I.E., R.E.	Col. Lord W.L. de la P. Beresford, V.C. K.C.I.E., 9th Lancers.	Major F. T. Rowan Hamilton, Norfolk Regt. Capt. H. Streatfeild, Grendr. Guards. Capt. Hon'ble C. Harbord, Scots Guards. Lieut. H. A. Pakenham, Grendr. Guards. Lieut. G. P. Brazier-Creagh, 9th B.L. Lieut. S. H. Pollen, Wilts. R. Capt. L. Herbert, C. I. Horse. Capt. R. E. Grimston, 6th B.C. Lieut. G. C. Lister, K. R. Rif. C. (Extra). Lieut. H. E. Wise, Sco. Rifles (Extra). Capt. P.A.H., Viscount Valletort, Duke of Cornwall's L. I. (Extra). 2nd Lieut. W. L. DeM., Visct. Milton, Oxf. L. I. (Extra).	Surgn. Lieut.-Col. E. H. Fenn, Medl. Staff.

His Excellency the Right Hon'ble VICTOR ALEXANDER, EARL OF ELGIN and KINCARDINE, P.C., G.M.S.I., G.M.I.E., 27th January 1894 to 5th January 1899.

Arrived in Simla		Left Simla	
	9th April 1894.		24th October 1894.
	6th April 1895.		24th October 1895.
	9th April 1896.		2nd November 1896.
	6th April 1897.		25th November 1897.
	25th April 1898.		7th November 1898.

Private Secretary.	Military Secretary.	Aides-de-Camp.	Surgeon.
Henry Babington Smith, Esq., C.S.I.	Bt. Lieut.-Col. A. G. A. Durand, C.B., 2nd C. I. H.	Capt. R. E. Grimston, 6th B. C. Lieut. S. H. Pollen, Wilts. R. Lieut. F. L. Adam, Scots Guards. Lieut. F. E. G. Ponsonby, Grendr. Guards. Lieut. A. E., Viscount Fincastle, 16th Lancers. Bt. Major C. P. Campbell, 2nd C. I. Horse. Lieut. R. G. T. Baker-Carr, Rifle Brigade. Lieut. R. J. Bentinck, 4th Lancers, H. C. (Extra). Lieut. J. M. J. Fuller, Wilts. Yeo. Cavy. (Extra). Lieut. C. P. A. Hull, R. Scots Fus. (Extra). Lieut. L. L. Maxwell, 2nd B. L. (Extra). Lieut. F. C. Marsh, R. W. Kent R. (Extra). Lieut. C. Wigram, 18th B. L. (Extra). Lieut. E. FitzClarence, Dorset. R. (Extra). Capt. R. W. Morley, 4th D. G. (Extra). Lieut. H. McN. Patterson, 5th B. C. (Extra). Second Lieut. Lord G. Stewart-Murray, R. Highrs. (Extra). Lieut. the Hon'ble R. H. J. L. deMontmorency, 21st Hussars (Extra). Lieut. A. D. G. Ramsay, 12th B. C. (Extra). Lieut. L. S. Bayley, R. A. (Extra). Capt. M. H. K. Pechell, King's Royal Rifle Corps (Extra). Lieut. the Hon'ble H. Baring, 4th Hussars (Extra). Lieut. R. N. Greathed, R. A. (Extra).	Brigade Surgn. Lieut.-Col. B. Franklin, C.I.E., I.M.S.

His Excellency the Right Hon'ble GEORGE NATHANIEL, BARON CURZON of KEDLESTON, P.C., G.M.S.I., G.M.I.E., 6th January 1899 to date.

Arrived in Simla .	6th April 1899. End of April 1900. April 1901. End of first week, May 1902. 24th April 1903.	Left Simla . .	27th October 1899. 25th October 1900. 4th November 1901. 25th October 1902. 6th November 1903.

Private Secretaries.	Military Secretaries.	Aides-de-Camp.	Surgeons.
W. R. Lawrence, Esq., C.I.E. (Now Sir Walter Lawrence, K.C.I.E.) H. W. C. Carnduff, Esq., C.I.E. (offg.) J. O. Miller, Esq., C.S.I.	Bt. Lieut.-Col. A. E. Sandbach, R. E. Lieut.-Col. the Hon'ble E. Baring, 10th Hussars, C.V.O.	Capt. R. G. T. Baker-Carr, Rif. Brig. Capt. R. J. Marker, Colds. Gds. Capt. F. L. S. Adam, Scots Guards. Lieut. C. Wigram, 18th B. L. Capt. W. McL. Campbell, C. Highrs. Capt. H. B. desV. Wilkinson, Durham L. I. Lieut. R. A. Steel, 17th B. C. Capt. C. Champion-de-Crespigny, 2nd Life Guards. Lieut. the Hon'ble G. B. Portman, 10th Hussars. Lieut. F. M. B. Robertson, Royal Highrs. Lieut. the Hon'ble J. R. L. Yarde-Buller, Scots Guards. Capt. the Hon'ble R. H. Lindsay, late 2nd Dragoons. Lieut. G. A. Akers-Douglas, Arg. and Suthd. Highrs. Lieut. A. V. S. Keighley, 18th B. L. Major F. L. Adams, Scots Guards. Capt. E. A. Fagan, 6th Bo. C. (Extra). Capt. Henry M. P., Earl of Suffolk and Berkshire, 4th Glouc. R. (Extra). Lieut. H. N. Holden, 5th B. C. (Extra). Capt. A. W. S. Knox, 5th P. C. (Extra). Capt. L. J. L., Earl of Ronaldshay, York Vol. Arty. (Extra). Capt. G. E. Tyrrell, R. G. A. (Extra). Lieut. C. L. W. Wallace, R. Irish Rifles (Extra). Major A. V. Poynter, D. S. O., late Scots Guards (Extra). Lieut. C. M. the Hon'ble Hore-Ruthven, D. S. O., Royal Highrs. (Extra). Lieut. L. A. Jones-Mortimer, Somerset L. I. (Extra).	Lieut.-Col. E. H. Fenn, C.I.E., R.A.M.C. Capt. W. E. A. Armstrong, I.M.S. Lieut.-Col. C. P. Lukis, I.M.S. Major R. Bird, M.D., I.M.S.

Major J. Strachey, 11th Rajputs, holds the appointment of Comptroller of the Viceregal Household.

APPENDIX II.

Personal Staffs of the Commanders-in-Chief in India who have visited Simla.

General STAPLETON, VISCOUNT COMBERMERE, G.C.B., G.C.H.
Arrived in Simla . 8th April 1828. Left Simla . 17th October 1828.

Military Secretary.	Persian Interpreter.	Aides-de-Camp.	Medical Officer.
Lieut.-Col. Hon'ble J. Finch, C. B., His Majesty's Service.	Capt. T. Macan, 16th Lancers. Lieut. W. Parker, 10th Bengal Light Cavalry (Offg.).	Lieut.-Col. F. H. Dawkins, His Majesty's Service. Capt. E. C. Archer, 41st Foot. Capt. G. C. Mundy, 2nd Foot. Lieut. C. Cotton, 16th Lancers. Lieut. W. Parker, 10th Bengal Light Cavalry. Capt. W. H. Agnew, 2nd Madras N. I. Lieut.-Col. E. Kelly, His Majesty's Service. Capt. Baron W. Osten, 16th Lancers.	Asst. Surgn. D. Murray, M.D., His Majesty's Service.

General GEORGE, EARL OF DALHOUSIE, G.C.B.
Arrived in Simla . 24th March 1831. Left Simla . 5th October 1831.

Military Secretary.	Persian Interpreter.	Aides-de-Camp.	Medical Officer.
Major-General the Hon'ble John Ramsay, His Majesty's Service.	Lieut. W. M. Ramsay, 62nd Bengal N. I.	Major A. Maclachlan, Royal Arty. Capt. George, Lord Ramsay, 49th Foot. Capt. John Byrne, 31st Foot.	Asst.-Surgeon D. Murray, M.D., 38th Foot.

General SIR EDWARD BARNES, G.C.B.
Arrived in Simla . { 24th April 1832. May 1833. } Left Simla . 3rd November 1832.

Military Secretary.	Persian Interpreter.	Aides-de-Camp.	Medical Officer.
Colonel C. H. Churchill, His Majesty's Service.	Lieut. W. M. Ramsay, 62nd Bengal N. I.	Lieut. R. Fawkes, 4th Light Dragoons. Lieut. W. E. F. Barnes, 26th Foot. Lieut. G. S. Deverill, 16th Lancers. Capt. F. C. Barlow, 20th Foot.	Asst. Surgeon A. Wood, M.D., 49th Foot.

General Sir HENRY FANE, G.C.B.

Arrived in Simla . { 22nd April 1837. 3rd January 1838. Left Simla . { 26th October 1837. 4th November 1838.

Military Secretary.	Persian Interpreter.	Aides-de-Camp.	Medical Officer.
Colonel M. Beresford, 3rd Foot.	Capt. J. Hay, 35th Bengal N. I.	Major H. Fane, 9th Foot. Capt. J. Michel, 3rd Foot. „ R. Campbell, 43rd Bengal N. I. Lieut. H. Fane, 57th Foot. Ensign R. H. Yea, 13th Foot.	Asst.-Surgeon A. Wood, M.D., 11th Light Dragoons.

General Sir JASPER NICOLLS, K.C.B.

Arrived in Simla . { 24th March 1842. 22nd March 1843. Left Simla . { 29th October 1842. August 1843.

Military Secretary.	Persian Interpreter.	Aides-de-Camp.	Medical Officers.
Lieut.-Col. J. Luard, 21st Foot.	Capt. C. Graham, 55th Bengal N. I.	Lieut. G. N. Harrison, 63rd Foot. Capt. W. Lydiard, 11th Bengal N. I. Lieut. T. R. Crawley, 15th Hussars. Capt. C. J. Oldfield, 4th Bengal N. I. Capt. W. Lamb, 57th Bengal N. I. Capt. E. T. Erskine, 63rd Bengal N. I.	Asst.-Surgeon G. Turner, Bengal Medical Department. Asst.-Surgeon J. Steel, M.D., Bengal Medical Department.

General Sir HUGH GOUGH, G.C.B. (afterwards Viscount GOUGH).

Arrived in Simla . { 12th April 1844. 9th April 1845. 11th April 1846. 5th March 1847. 23rd April 1849. Left Simla . . { 11th November 1844. 13th November 1845. 8th December 1846. 19th October 1848. May 1849.

Military Secretaries.	Persian Interpreters.	Aides-de-Camp.	Medical Officer.
Lieut.-Col. J. B. Gough, C.B., 3rd Light Dragoons. Capt. F. P. Haines, 10th Foot.	Lieut.-Col. H. Havelock, 13th Foot. Lieut. W. G. Prendergast, 8th Bengal Light Cavalry. Capt. C. J. Otter, 61st Foot (Acting).	Capt. R. Smith, 28th Bengal N. I. Lieut. A. Bagot, 15th Bengal N. I. Major F. R. Evans, 26th Bengal N. I. Lieut. A. S. Galloway, 3rd Bengal Light Cavalry. Lieut. F. P. Haines, 4th Foot.	Asst.-Surgeon J. E. Stephens, M.D., 63rd Foot (afterwards of the 10th Light Dragoons).

Military Secretary.	Persian Interpreter.	Aides-de-Camp.	Medical Officer.
		Capt. the Hon'ble C. R. West, 21st Foot. Cornet Lord J. DeB. Browne, 16th Lancers. Capt. H. Bates, 82nd Foot. Cornet W. F. Stephens, 5th Bengal Light Cavalry. Cornet H. B. Loch, 3rd Bengal Light Cavalry. Capt. H. Boyd, 15th Bengal N. I. Lieut. S. J. Hire, 22nd Bengal N. I. Lieut. W. Fraser-Tytler, 9th Bengal Light Cavalry. Capt. W. M. Gabbett, Madras Arty. Capt. C. J. Otter, 61st Foot.	

General Sir CHARLES JAMES NAPIER, G.C.B.

Arrived in Simla . {18th June 1849. 22nd April 1850. Left Simla . {23rd October 1849. 17th November 1850.

Military Secretary.	Persian Interpreter.	Aides-de-Camp.	Medical Officers.
Major J. P. Kennedy, 25th Foot.	Capt. F. P. Harding, 22nd Foot.	Major W. C. E. Napier, 25th Foot. Major W. M. S. McMurdo, 78th Foot. Lieut. E. D. Byng, 1st Bengal European Regt. (Fusiliers). Lieut. Sir E. FitzG. Campbell, Bart., 60th Foot. Capt. H. W. Bunbury, 33rd Foot.	Asst.-Surgn. J. Anderson, M.D., 22nd Foot. Asst.-Surgn. A. Gibson, M.D., 22nd Foot.

General Sir W. M. GOMM, G.C.B.

Arrived in Simla . {14th April 1851. 1st May 1852. 4th April 1853. 5th April 1854. 1855. Left Simla . {7th November 1851. 13th December 1852. 30th October 1853. 26th October 1854. 1855.

Military Secretary.	Persian Interpreter.	Aides-de-Camp.	Medical Officers.
Capt. E. R. W. Wingfield Yates, 82 Foot.	Major C. J. Otter, 61st Foot.	Capt. J. Halkett, Coldstream Guards.	Asst.-Surgn. H. Franklin, 3rd Lt. Dragoons.

Military Secretary.	Persian Interpeter.	Aides-de-Camp.	Medical Officers.
		Ensign the Hon'ble E. W. Douglas, 17th Bombay N. I. Capt. G. G. C. Stapylton, 98th Foot. Capt. Lord F. J. Fitz Roy, Grenadier Guards. Lieut.-Col. H. Bates, 98th Foot. Cornet E. Howard Vyse, 3rd Lt. Dragoons. Capt. O. Hamilton, 7th Beng. Lt. Cav. Lieut. C. L. Peel, 52nd Foot. Lieut. Lord W. C. M. Douglas-Scott, 52nd Foot. Capt. the Hon'ble E. G. Curzon, 52nd Foot. Lieut. E. B. Johnson, Beng. Arty.	Surgeon W. Carson, H. M.'s Service. Asst.-Surgn. W. Peskett, Beng. Medl. Dept.

General the Hon'ble G. ANSON.

Arrived in Simla . 1st April 1857. Left Simla . 15th May 1857.

Military Secretary.	Persian Interpreter.	Aides-de-Camp.	Medical Officer.
Lieut.-Col. the Hon'ble R. W. P. Curzon, Grenadier Guards.	(None appointed.)	Capt. the Hon'ble E. F. W. Forester, 83rd Foot. Lieut. R. H. D. Lowe, 74th Foot. Lieut. G. H. W. Clive, 52nd Foot. Capt. the Hon'ble A. H. A. Anson, 18th Foot.	Asst. Surgn. W. F. Mactier, M.D., Beng. Medl. Dept.

General SIR COLIN CAMPBELL, G.C.B. (afterwards LORD CLYDE).

Arrived in Simla . {Last week of April 1859. / Second week of April 1860.} Left Simla . {First week of October 1859. / May 1860.}

Military Secretary.	Persian Interpreter.	Aides-de-Camp.	Medical Officers.
Col. A. C. Sterling, C.B., Unattached.	Lieut.-Col. J. Metcalfe, 4th European Regt.	Maj. F. M. Alison, 19th Foot. Maj. the Hon'ble J. C. Dormer, 13th Foot. Capt. G. Allgood, 49th N. I. Lieut.-Col. J. Metcalfe, 4th European Regt.	Asst.-Surgn. W. A. Mackinnon, 29th Foot. Asst.-Surgn. W. Sinclair, 93rd Foot.

General Sir HUGH HENRY ROSE, G.C.B.

Arrived in Simla . 1st April 1862. 31st March 1863. 6th April 1864. — Left Simla . 25th October 1862. 14th November 1863. 1st November 1864.

Military Secretaries.	Persian Interpreter.	Aides-de-Camp.	Medical Officers.
Lieut. O. T. Burne, 20th Foot. Lieut.-Col. H. A. Sarel, 17th Lancers.	Capt. H. Moore, Bombay Staff Corps.	Capt. H. H. Lyster, V.C, late 72nd N. I. Lieut. H. Moore, Bombay Staff Corps. Lieut. J. F. Elton, late 7th N. I. (afterwards of 98th Foot). Maj. H. J. Wilkin, 7th Hussars. Capt. O. T. Burne, 20th Foot. Maj. The Hon'ble R. Baillie-Hamilton, 44th Foot. Maj. G. E. Rose, Rifle Brigade. Capt. A. H. Lindsay, R. A.	Asst.-Surgn. A. E. T. Longhurst, 13th Foot. Asst.-Surgn. G., A. Cheke, Bengal Medical Service.

General Sir WILLIAM ROSE MANSFIELD, K.C.B., G.C.S.I.—1865-70.

Military Secretary.	Persian Interpreter.	Aides-de-Camp.	Medical Officers.
Maj. F. R. S. Flood, 82nd Foot.	Maj. T. E. Gordon, Bombay Staff Corps.	Capt. E. Scott Jervis, 106th Foot. Lieut. H. T. Christie, Bombay Infantry. Capt. The Hon'ble W. Harbord, 7th Hussars. Lieut. J. E. Buller, 91st Foot. Lieut. G. S. Byng, Rifle Brigade. Lieut. The Hon'ble C. Dutton, 85th Foot.	Surgn. J. T. C. Ross, Bengal Medical Service. Asst.-Surgn. A. F. Bradshaw, R. A.

General ROBERT C., Lord NAPIER of MAGDALA, G.C.B., G.C.S.I.—1870-76.

Military Secretary.	Persian Interpreter.	Aides-de-Camp.	Medical Officer.
Col. M. Dillon, C.B., C.I.E., Rifle Brigade.	Lieut.-Col. H. Moore, Bombay Staff Corps.	Capt. W. W. H. Scott, Bengal Infantry. Capt. The Hon'ble R. W. Napier, Bengal Infantry.	Surgn.-Maj. A. F. Bradshaw, British Medical Department.

Military Secretary.	Persian Interpreter.	Aides-de-Camp.	Medical Officer.
	Capt. M. H. Court, Bengal Cavalry (Offg.).	Lieut. A. C. F. FitzGeorge, Rifle Brigade. Lieut. F. E. Walter, R. A. Lieut. Hon'ble J. S. Napier, 92nd Foot. Capt. R. G. Kennedy, 18th Hussars (afterwards of the 1st Dragoons). Capt. J. H. Vivian, 85th Foot. Capt. F. H. Gregory, 15th Hussars. Lieut. W. L. Davidson, R. A.	

General Sir FREDERICK PAUL HAINES, G.C.B.—1876-81.

Military Secretaries.	Persian Interpreter.	Aides-de-Camp.	Medical Officer.
Lieut.-Col. G. T. Gough, Her Majesty's Service. Col. R. Preston, 44th Foot. Maj. J. Goldie, 6th Dragoon Guards (Offg.). Col. H. C. Wilkinson, Her Majesty's Service.	Col. H. Moore, C.B., C.I.E. Bombay Staff Corps.	Maj. H. G. Grant, 78th Foot. Lieut. W. L. Davidson, R. A. Capt. H. B. MacCall, 60th Foot. Capt. H. S. Gough, 10th Hussars. Lieut. G. Haines, 6th Foot. Second-Lieut. G. S. Haines, 54th Foot.	Surgn.-Maj. A. F. Bradshaw, British Service.

General Sir DONALD MARTIN STEWART, Bart., G.C.B.—1881-85.

Military Secretaries.	Interpreter.	Aides-de-Camp.	Medical Officer.
Col. E. F. Chapman, C.B., R. A. Lieut.-Col. M. W. E. Gosset, Dorsetshire Regt. Col. B. A. Combe, 10th Hussars.	Col. H. Moore, C.B., C.I.E., Bombay Staff Corps.	Capt. F. J. W. Eustace, R. A. Capt. G. Haines, Roy. Warwickshire Regt. Lieut. E. L. Maisey, Liverpool Regt. Capt. R. Owen, 14th Hussars (afterwards of the 21st Hussars). Capt. C. H. H. Mayne, R. A. Lieut. D. W. Stewart, Gordon Highlanders. Lieut. J. G. Turner, Bengal Staff Corps.	Surgn.-Maj. R. W. Davies, Army Medical Department.

General Sir FREDERICK SLEIGH (afterwards Lord) ROBERTS, v. c., g.c.b., g.c.i.e.—1885-93.

Military Secretaries.	Interpreters.	Aides-de-Camp.	Medical Officers.
Col. R. Pole-Carew, c.b., Coldstream Guards. Col. W. G. Nicholson, c.b., r. e.	Lieut.-Col. N. F. Fitz G. Chamberlain, Central India Horse. Lieut.-Col. I. S. M. Hamilton, Gordon Highlanders. Maj. E. A. Travers, 2nd Gurkha Regt.	Capt. R. Owen, 21st Hussars. Lieut. J. G. Turner, 19th Bengal Lancers. Capt. C. V. Hume, r. a. Lieut. H. S. Rawlinson, King's Royal Rifle Corps. Capt. W. M. Sherston, Rifle Brigade. Lieut.-Col. I. S. M. Hamilton, Gordon Highlanders. Capt. The Hon'ble F. E. Allsopp, r. a. Maj. E. A. Travers, 2nd Gurkha Regt. Capt. E. A. P. Hobday, r. a. Lieut. P. Holland, 5th P. I. Lieut. R. S. Oxley, King's Royal Rifle Corps. Capt. C. J. Mackenzie, Seaforth Highlanders. Lieut. H. C. Ricketts, 15th Bengal Cavalry. Lieut. W. T. Furse, r. a. Lieut. A. C. M. Waterfield, 11th Bengal Lancers. Lieut. A. G. Maxwell, 6th Bengal Cavalry. Lieut. A. W. Cotton, Grenadier Guards. Lieut. C. H. H. Gough, 12th Bengal Cavalry. Second-Lieut. The Hon'ble F. H. S. Roberts, King's Royal Rifle Corps.	Surgn.-Maj. W. Taylor, Medical Staff. Surgn.-Maj. C. W. Owen, c.m.g., c.i.e., Indian Medical Service. Surgeon W. A. Edwards, m.d., Indian Medical Service.

General Sir GEORGE S. WHITE, v.c., k.c.b., g c.i.e.—1893-98.

Military Secretaries.	Interpreters.	Aides-de-Camp.	Medical Officers.
Col. I. S. M. Hamilton, d.s.o., British Service. Lieut.-Col. B. Duff, 39th B.I.	Maj. L. Herbert, 1st Central India Horse. Capt. C. H. H. Gough, 12th Bengal Cavalry.	Capt. S. C. F. Jackson, d.s.o., Hampshire Regt. Capt. C. H. H. Gough, 12th Bl. Cavy. Capt. Q. G. K. Agnew, Roy. Scots Fusiliers.	Surgn.-Maj. F. H. Treherne, Medl. Staff. Surgn.-Lieut. J. N. Macleod, Indian Medical Service (Offg.).

Military Secretary.	Interpreter.	Aides-de-Camp.	Medical Officer.
	Capt. Q. G. K. Agnew, Roy. Scots Fusiliers.	Capt. C. H. Stuart, Roy. Inniskilling Fusiliers. Capt. W. A. Watson, 1st Central India Horse (Tempy.). Lieut. F. Lyon, R. A. Capt. C. O. Swanston, 18th Bengal Lancers. Capt. N. C. Taylor, 14th Bengal Lancers. Capt. R. G Brooke, 7th Hussars. Lieut. A. H. Marindin, Roy. Highlanders. Capt. W. A. Boulnois, R. A.	

General Sir CHARLES E. NAIRNE, K.C.B.—1898 (provisional).

Military Secretary.	Interpreter.	Aides-de-Camp.	Medical Officer,
Lieut.-Col. B. Duff, C.I.E., 39th B. I.	Maj. H. F. Mercer, R. A.	Lieut. W. P. Dimsdale, Roy. Irish Rifles. Lieut. E. S. Nairne, R.A. Lieut. A. H. Marindin, Roy. Highlanders. Lieut. H. B. DesV. Wilkinson, Durham Light Infy. (Offg.).	Surgn.-Maj. A. E. J. Croly, Army Medl. Staff.

General Sir WILLIAM S. A. LOCKHART, G.C.B., K.C.S.I.—1898-1900.

Military Secretaries.	Interpreter.	Aides-de-Camp.	Medical Officer.
Lieut.-Col. B. Duff, C.I.E., 39th B. I. Capt. F. S. Gwatkin, Staff Corps.	Maj. A. W. Money, R. A.	Capt. J. A. L. Haldane, Gordon Highlanders. Capt. Q. G. K. Agnew, Roy. Scots Fusiliers. Capt. L. N. Beatty, 1st Bombay Lancers. Capt. G. deS. Barrow, 4th Bengal Cavy. (Offg.). Lieut. G. E. Tyrrell, R. A.	Capt. W. G. Beyts, Roy. Army Medl. Corps.

General SIR ARTHUR POWER PALMER, K.C.B., G.C.I.E.—1900-02.

Military Secretaries.	Interpreters.	Aides-de-Camp.	Medical Officer.
Maj. J. M. Burt, R. A. Lieut.-Col. C. deC. Hamilton, R.A.	Capt. G. de S. Barrow, 4th Bengal Lancers. Capt. A. W. Chaldecott, 1st Punjab Cavalry (Offg.). Capt. L. N. Beatty, 1st Bombay Lancers. Maj. G. W. Rawlins, 12th Bengal Cavy. (Offg.).	Capt. L. N. Beatty, 1st Bombay Lancers. Lieut. J. H. Watson, 13th Bengal Lancers. Lieut. L A. Jones-Mortimer, Somerset Light Infy. Lieut. T. B. Olive, Lancashire Fusiliers. Capt. G. deS. Barrow, 4th Bengal Lancers. Lieut. J. T. Weatherby, Oxford Light Infy. Lieut. C. L. Storr, 4th Sikh Infy.	Maj. A. G. Kay, M.B., Roy. Army Medl. Corps.

General the Right Hon'ble H. H., VISCOUNT KITCHENER of KHARTOUM, G.C.B., O.M., G.C.M.G.—1902—

Military Secretary.	Assistant Military Secretary and Interpreter.	Aides-de-Camp.	Medical Officer.
Col. H. I. W. Hamilton, D.S.O., A.-D.-C. to His Majesty, British Service.	Lieut.-Col. W. R. Birdwood, 11th Bengal Lancers.	Maj. R. J. Marker, D.S.O., Coldstream Guards. Maj. F. A. Maxwell, V.C., D.S.O., 18th Bengal Lancers. Capt. V. R. Brooke, D.S.O., 9th Lancers. Capt. R. W. R. Barnes, D.S.O. 4th Hussars.	

APPENDIX III.

Hints to Travellers in the Himalayas and Simla Hills.

The following is an extract from Major Gordon Forbes' well-known Guide Book [1893]:—

Things to be taken on a march into the interior and hints for travellers.—Biscuits, ginger bread-nuts, tins of butter (Irish), jams, cocoa (Van Houten), cocoa and milk, tea, sugar, potted meats, bacon (in canvas), extract of meat (Brand), cornflour, a few tins of milk (very rarely wanted), rice, flour, oatmeal, pepper, salt, spices, raisins, and currants, curry-powder, carbonate of soda or baking powder, candles (the best), matches; of course, stores *ad lib.* may be taken, but the above are almost necessaries. A few 1-lb. tins of corned beef should be taken in case of supplies failing. Kerosine oil can be bought at Rampur.

Light hatchet. small spade for trenching tent, trowel, light strong rope, whipcord, hammer, nails, brad-awl, sail-maker's needle and twine for repairing tent, spare boot nails, spring candlestick with globe and top, candle lantern, bucket, cobbler's wax, a few coils of thin copper wire, needles and thread, buttons, tape, etc.

The tent known as the Light Field Service Cabul tent is about the best pattern, it is light and roomy, the poles should, however, be jointed in the middle. For servants—*tent d'abris.* The bed known as the 'Cashmir,' it is very light and strong; a light folding table and chair, wash-hand basin stand, folding canvas or Indian-rubber bath.

All loads should be of such a shape that they can be carried on the back; the Simla coolies will carry them on their heads in preference, but once in the interior they are carried the other way.

The 'Bigarri' brings with him his own rope which he fastens round the load in such a manner as to leave two projecting loops through which he puts his arms up to the shoulder; in some districts they only hitch the loop over the shoulders.

Skin-covered wicker trunks for carrying stores, clothes, etc., and open basket ones for the numerous odds and ends required in camp life; these last are cylindrical in shape and are called 'Khiltas.'

All bundles of bedding should be tightly strapped up in waterproof sheeting, not only to keep it dry, but also to protect it from the numerous pests which infest the persons and clothes of these unwashed folk.

Tent-pegs of strong tough wood and about 2 feet long should be provided for the corner and storm ropes; the small iron pegs sold with the tents are only useful for minor ropes and side-walls.

Supplies for the interior should be taken from Simla.

Potatoes, onions, flour, and *atta* for the servants can be bought at Kotgarh and Rampur, but it is not always wise to trust to doing so.

Fowls and eggs can be obtained in small quantities up to Pangi; small hill sheep can be obtained all along the road, but notice, sometimes as much as three days, is required as they have to be brought from elevated grazing grounds.

Milk is obtained throughout the whole route up to Tibet, in fact much better than can be got at Simla; the half-bred 'Yak,' the 'Zo Po' gives excellent sweet milk, rich in cream. Some of the bungalows have small gardens from which beans and pumpkins of sorts can be got.

Strong boots or shoes, well furnished with nails, should be taken, as after the Hindustan and Tibet Road ceases, the path is dreadfully rough on shoe leather.

Money should be taken principally in small change, and the traveller will, if he is wise, invariably pay his coolies himself, and for everything he buys; if left to servants, they take a percentage and the people get dissatisfied.

The coolies should never be paid until all the loads are in, and then they should be paid at once.

Always, when marching early in the morning, let them halt for half an hour for their morning meal; if marching late, see that they have it before they start. Take quinine, Eno, Lorbeer's cholera and snake antidotes, chlorodyne, ipecacuanha, arsenical soap (for skins), zinc eye ointment, carbolic ointment, lint and plaster, Cockle's pills and Seidlitz powders. People suffering from various ailments, as well as injuries, are sure to be brought to you for treatment; and if supplied with a few ordinary medicines one can often alleviate a good deal of suffering. Take blue or neutral tinted goggles for the snow.

The water is, as a rule, good, but do not drink much on the march, particularly when climbing.

Take a 'Warren' cooking-pot; it will be found invaluable; keep a stew going in it, and follow the instructions sold with it carefully. Do not let your servants have the management of it; do it yourself; take also sauce-pan and frying-pan—enamelled iron or aluminium is the best, and a kettle, tea pot and sulky; copper cooking-pots are always a source of danger—the tin wears off and leaves the copper exposed; all cooking vessels should be either of block tin, enamelled iron or aluminium.

Have the flour, rice, etc., sewn up in strong bags made of linen or drill.

Have tops made for jam and butter tins, so that when the tins are opened, the top can be put on; one top will do for each kind of tin; it should fit pretty tight.

It is just as well to make up one's mind to make tea one's principal beverage; beer is of course out of the question on an extended trip. One cooly can carry a box of two dozen bottles; whisky or brandy are more portable, but one very quickly gets into the habit of only taking an occasional drink, and the water met with is generally excellent.

* * * * * * *

Routes.

(The following routes are taken from Major Gordon Forbes' Guide Book [1893]:—)

Simla to Shipki.

Name of Stage.	Distance.	Elevation.	Remarks.
	miles.	ft.	
Simla . . .	...	7,220	Leave the 'Mashobra' road after passing the toll bar, long ascent to 'Mahasu,' then level.
Fagu . . .	12	8,178	The road to 'Mussoorie' and that to the 'Chor' Peak branch off here.
Theog . . .	4¾	7,421	A short cut, about 3 miles out, for pedestrians only.
Matiana . .	11¼	7,691	Level road.
Narkunda . .	11	8,799	Through the forest on the slopes of 'Huttoo,' at about 5 miles; 'Kotgarh' road turns off to the left, rather a steep descent.
Kotgarh . .	10¾	5,600	Road through 'Komarsen' to Kulu *viâ* Dularsh.
Nirit . . .	10	3,660	Descent by short cut, for pedestrians only, for 2 hours, then strike road, reach the 'Sutlej' in 3, and 'Nirit' in 4 hours.

Name of Stage.	Distance.	Elevation.	Remarks.
	miles.	ft.	
Bridge over 'Nogri.'	7	...	Road fairly level along bank of river. Ascend gradually from the 68th mile.
Rampur City .	5	3,870	Suspension Bridge across Sutlej. There is a Post Office here.
Rampur Bungalow	2	...	
Gaura . . .	6½	6,512	Ascend for about 5 miles. The last mile very steep, then fairly level.
Manglad Stream .	...	...	At 83rd mile steep descent to bridge over 'Manglad' stream, then steep ascent to 87th mile, join the Upper or Forest road, from 'Bagi,' then level.
Sarahan . .	10½	6,713	The scenery is very fine on this march, road level to about the 94th mile, between 95th and 97½th ascent and descent over the 'Maneoti' Pass; from 100th mile descend to bridge over mountain torrent, then ascent, first gradual then steep, passing village with two fine deodars to crest of ridge, then level for ¼ mile.
Bridge . .	...	...	
Manaspur . .	...	...	
Taranda . .	14	7,015	At 105th mile steep descent to bridge over torrent, then gradual ascent.
Bridge . .	...	...	
Paunda . .	4½	6,124	Gradual ascent; fine deodar and elm forest with quaint temple at 110th mile in deodar forest. The scenery is particularly fine.
Nachar . .	4½	7,125	Steady descent to Bungalow, which is about 100 feet above the river.
Wangtu Bridge .	3	5,361	Cross 'Wangtu' bridge and a little further on a bridge over the 'Wangar' torrent (from here there is a path over the 'Bhabeh' Pass to 'Dankar'); road fairly level along river bank, at 122nd mile road turns to left up hill; the road to 'Kilba,' the Forest Head-Quarters, continues along the bank for a mile, then crosses to left bank by a wooden bridge.
Chagaon . .	...	...	Change coolies, ascend for 1½ miles, then level.
Urni . . .	9¾	7,900	Road level for one hour, then gradual ascent for another hour. The scenery now begins to be very fine; the view of the 'Morang' snows across the Sutlej being magnificent. the principal peaks being the 'Kailas,' 19,866; 'Raldang,' 21,250; and 'Castle Rock,' 18,110; the 'Baspa' river here flows into the Sutlej from the S. E. This valley is noted for its fine scenery, and is more open than most Himalayan valleys. A road follows the course of the river up to near its source, then crosses the high range to the S. and descends into the valley of the 'Bhagirathi' by the 'Nela' Pass.
Rogi . . .	10¼	9,361	The road to 'Roghi' rises gradually with a slight ascent at the very end to the Bungalow which is finely situated, Raldang being immediately opposite. 'Burrel' are to be got on 'Rakchora,' a fine rugged hill, which rises behind the Bungalow.
Chini . . .	3	9,196	Good camping ground; fine view.
Pangi . . .	7	8,950	Road fairly level; cross two fine torrents at head of ravine at 145th mile, then gradual ascent.
Bridge over Koz-hang . .	...	...	Level to 149th mile; then gradual, followed by steep ascent, then descent, and last two miles level.

Name of Stage.	Distance.	Elevation.	REMARKS.
	miles.	ft.	
Rarang . .	8	9,068	Camping ground. A forest bridge here connects with the road on left bank; a strong prevailing wind blows over the ridge on which the camping ground is. (There is a road through 'Riba' along the 'Todang Gar' river to the 'Gamrang' or Winter Pass; closed between May and September, as all the snow bridges are swept away. Also a way down to 'Gangotri,' but which is said to be very difficult; it goes by way of the 'Charang' Pass to 'Chitkul' on the 'Baspa;' also another road to 'Rispa' and the 'Morang' Fort up the 'Talgagar' river to the 'Zeoozang' Pass in to Tibet.)
Akpa . . .	3	...	The road is fairly level (change coolies at 'Akpa').
Jangi . . .	4	9,000	Through fine deodar forest. There is a large prayer-wheel here in a temple; the Hindus call it a 'Tarkudwara.' From this point the length of the marches is given in hours, as it is almost impossible to estimate miles on the sort of road that has to be traversed; also if miles were correctly given it would convey nothing to the intending traveller. The times given are those taken by laden coolies well kept up to their work.
Jangi . . .	...	9,000	Gradual descent for four miles, when the road comes to an abrupt termination; from henceforward it is only a rough hill track.
End of road .	...	...	Descend by rough path to the 'Taite' river, cross by a crazy bridge, then very steep ascent up a bad path for one hour, after which $\frac{3}{4}$ mile along a fairly level path. A rather rough descent and ascent round the
Kola. . .	$5\frac{1}{2}$	...	end of a spur, then level to 'Kola' and passing above 'Pilo' to 'Labrang.'
Labrang . .	$\frac{3}{4}$	9,000	Instead of the long and fairly level road round the spur, there is a short cut by a rather steep ascent over the 'Kilmerung' Pass, from which although the elevation is trifling, the view is superb. The road passes through a deodar forest down to the upper part of 'Labrang' and thence to 'Tabang;' this is, perhaps, a better way, certainly more picturesque.
Labrang . .	...	...	Camping ground very bad, rough, stony, and on a slant. 'Khanum,' a large village, is opposite across the valley, a mile distant.
Tabang . .	1	10,000	Steep ascent for one hour to the hamlet of 'Tabang.' The camping ground is good here, but all supplies as well as coolies, except milk, must be got from 'Labrang' or 'Khanum.' From here a gradual ascent; at 2 hours is a stream. This is a good place for the coolies to have their morning meal; then steady ascent for $2\frac{1}{2}$ hours to the top of the Pass.
Runang Rang Pass	$4\frac{1}{2}$	14,360	A bitter cold wind generally blows over the crest; then descent for about $3\frac{1}{2}$ hours down stony desolate
Thanum . .	$3\frac{1}{2}$	...	valley (passing 'Thaling' village towards the end) to the 'Thanum' river, the last bit of descent very steep and rough. Cross the river, a clear rushing stream, by a very ricketty bridge, then a gradual ascent to village about 15 miles.
Sugnam . .	10	8,000	'Sugnam' is a large flourishing village, chiefly Buddhist. There is a road up the river through 'Rupa,' 'Pama-

Name of Stage.	Distance.	Elevation.	REMARKS.
	miles.	feet.	
			chang' and the 'Namgang' Pass to 'Dankar,' in 'Spiti' and another by the 'Hangerang' Pass 14,354 over the northern spur of 'Thugirigga' by 'Hango' to 'Chango' on the 'Li' or 'Spiti' river on the road to 'Lahoul.' There are two ways of getting to 'Pooi,'—one by the way of the 'Charling' Pass over the southern spur of 'Thugirigga' 16,684, and the other by the cliff road down the gorge of the Sutlej. These roads diverge near 'Shaso;' the latter is very bad and rough, and in places very dangerous, and is impassable by animals; either way is a long tiring 12 hours' journey. The cliff road should not be attempted by anyone who has not a good head. In August and again in September the only available space for a tent was the flat roof of a house. The road to 'Pooi' or 'Spuch,' as it is spelt on the map, drops sharply down into the bed of the stream from the 'Hangerang' Pass and ascends to a corresponding level on the opposite side.
Shaso . . .	3	...	From here there is a fairly good path to 'Shaso,' a small village (before reaching it the road up to the 'Charling La' branches off to the left with a gradual ascent of about 3 miles to 'Lafang' Dogri; good milk can be obtained here, not anything else. From the 'Dogri' there is a very stiff climb up a steep slope of loose stones and shale to the top of the Pass 14,600. About an hour further is another 'Dogri;' no supplies of any sort or firewood, but a good place to camp and break the journey. From here is a long and rough but not difficult descent to 'Pooi'). There is a path from here to 'Labrang' crossing the 'Thanum' and ascending the almost precipitous spur of 'Cheladt' by the 'Benang' Pass, but it is very dangerous and very often impassable.
Cliff . . .	$1\frac{1}{2}$	...	The cliff road continues along the hill-side, a good bit of it over slate avalanches now at rest, for an hour and a half, when it reaches the cliffs of the Sutlej just above the point where the two streams join. From here for the next five hours the path works across the face of the cliffs, is bad throughout, and in many places exceedingly dangerous. It then leaves the cliffs; and after an hour and three-quarters (coolies $2\frac{1}{2}$) of good going, with a drop into and a steep climb out of a deep ravine, 'Pooi' is reached. About 18 miles. Coolies take a good 12 hours with two short halts for food; one at 'Shaso,'—one in the cliffs.
Pooi . . .	12	10,000	'Pooi' is a large flourishing village with many well-built houses; it is purely Buddhist. The only camping ground, before the crops are cut, is the open space in front of the 'Mani' house or Lama Serai, which answers to the village green, and is used for public meetings, festivals, etc. There is a Moravian Mission here. The Mission House stands above the village; it is very small; only two rooms with office, and a school-room used as a church. There is a fine prayer-wheel in the Lama Serai. Before leaving 'Pooi' or 'Namgea' it is advisable to send on word to 'Shipki' to prepare the way as some travellers have been very rudely treated and not allowed to pitch their tents. Take on also from 'Pooi' a man who can talk both Hindustani and Tibetan to act as interpreter. He can also perhaps smooth over any difficulties that may arise. Wilson, when he went there in 1876, was very rudely treated. The 'Mookyar' or head man of 'Pooi,' by name 'Stopki,' is very civil, and will give every assistance in his power to help travellers on.

Name of Stage.	Distance.	Elevation.	Remarks.
	miles.	feet.	
Bridge over Sutlej .	½	...	From 'Pooi' there is a steep descent of about a thousand feet to the Sutlej, which is crossed by a very unpleasant kind of bridge, 100 feet long and about 70 feet above the water, here very deep and rapid. From here to 'Dubling,' where coolies are changed, the road is bad and rocky. 'Dubling' is some little way above the road, and notice should be sent on ahead to prevent delay.
Dubling . .	2	...	
Khalb . . .	3	...	Road very rough and bad, up and down over rocks and through streams along the river bank. Coolies are again changed here. A bit of rough ascent and descent, and the last bit level to camping ground on a field above the village, under a huge rock. A rope bridge here crosses the river and ascends to the Monastery of 'Tashigang,' high upon the side of 'Lio Porgyulle.' There is also a way too, round the shoulder of the spur to 'Nako' and 'Chango.' From 'Namgea' there are two ways of reaching 'Shipki,'—one by the gorge through which the Sutlej enters India, and the other over the Kung Ma La. The first is bad and quite impracticable for animals, but is preferred by the coolies to the long, tiring ascent and great height of the Pass.
Namgea . .	1	10,000	
Namgea Dogri .	1	...	One hour's climb up a steep rocky path to a few terraced fields and tumble-down stone huts fenced with hedges of wild gooseberry and a stream of clear cold water, then a steady ascent up a rocky pathway, rough and arduous certainly, but not in the least dangerous or difficult; the last half-hour being up a very steep slope of loose stones and gravel, and the 1st crest of Pass is reached. An hour's scrambling over a boulder-strewn slope brings you to the 2nd or Tibetan crest, the frontier line being somewhere between the two; the view is magnificent.
1st Crest . .	3½	...	
Kung Ma La .	...	15,500	
2nd Crest . .	1	...	
			The first part of the descent is like the last part of the ascent,—loose stones and shale with no firm foothold; it then gets easier as the slope becomes less, and before reaching 'Shipki' is very fairly good; two-thirds of the way down is the 'Dogri' of 'Shipki.'
Shipki . . .	3¼	10,000	A large Tartar village; good milk, flower, pumpkins, and sometimes sheep can be obtained; wood and water plentiful; coolies by the lower road take 10 hours.

'Pooi' to 'Sugnam' over 'Charling' or 'Lafang' Pass.

Name of Stage.	Distance.	Elevation.	Remarks.
			Began the ascent behind 'Pooi' at 6-30 A.M., road rough; halted at a spring for about 9 minutes to allow the coolies to eat; then steady ascent, bad in places to 'Charling Dogri,' which I reached at 1 P.M., halted ½ hour, reached top of Pass after a stiff climb; at 2-30 halt 10 minutes. (Coolies took a lower but longer path after leaving the 'Dogri,' as they would not face the steep ascent.) Descended half running, half walking, ankle-deep in loose stones and gravel, down a very steep slope, and reached 'Lafang Dogri' at 3-15; waited for the coolies until 3-45; struck into the Shaso road at 5; went on with the two strongest coolies with my tent, and reached 'Sugnam' at 6-15; the remainder of the coolies arrived at 7-30 P.M.; 13 hours out from 'Pooi.' A long, tiring day.
Charling Dogri .	6½	...	
Charling Pass .	1	14,700	
Lafang Dogri .	35	...	
Sugnam . .	11¾	...	
(Coolies) . .	13	...	

'Sarahan' to 'Narkunda' by the Upper or Forest Road.

Name of Stage.	Distance.	Elevation.	REMARKS.
	miles.	feet.	
Sarahan . .	...	...	At 87th mile the road turns off to the left and follows the course of the 'Manglad' stream, which it crosses by a bridge at about 3 miles; then gradual ascent through lovely forest scenery passing 'Moshnu' village in about an hour; $\frac{3}{8}$ later cross bridge in ravine and ascend for another $\frac{3}{4}$ hour to village of 'Darun.' The Bungalow is one hour further on,—about 14 miles altogether.
Moshnu . .	4	...	
Darun . . .	$1\frac{1}{2}$	...	
Forest Bungalow .	1	...	
Darun . . .	...	...	Descent through forest, then over open hill-side passing 'Tola' village; at $1\frac{1}{2}$ hours cross stream; $1\frac{1}{2}$ hours later by bridge over end of spur to bridge across the 'Nogri,' a clear green stream; then ascent for one hour,—about 10 miles.
Forest Bungalow Tachlech . .	...	...	Steady ascent at times through fine forest for $2\frac{1}{2}$ hours to crest of ridge. Here is a small grassy plateau and a pond with a bubbling spring; then level road through forest and across fine rocks; one place where a pony could not cross, as the beams of the road had given way,—about 10 miles.
Bhali . . .	...	...	Road fairly level through fine forest scenery; cross large stream at head of valley at $2\frac{3}{4}$ hours; then gradual ascent for one hour to a place where the road had given way and a detour is necessary; a steep bit of up and down for 20 minutes.
Soongiri . .	4	...	About 10 miles level road, fine scenery,—occasionally bits of forest.
Kudrelli . .	3	...	About 9 miles; Forest Rest House.
Bagi . . .	$3\frac{1}{2}$	...	About 9 miles.
Narkunda . .	...	...	A level road through the forest on the slopes of 'Huttoo' 12 miles; it is quite worth while, if time allows, to do this march *viâ* the top of 'Huttoo' (about 11,000 feet).

Name of Stage.	Bungalow Rooms.	Miles.	Cooly hire.		REMARKS.
			a.	*p.*	
Simla to Fagu .	D B* 5	12	5	6	
Theog . .	D B* 3	5	2	6	
Matiana . .	D B* 4	$11\frac{1}{4}$	4	0	
Narkunda . .	D B* 5	11	4	0	
Kotgarh . .	D B* 2	$10\frac{3}{4}$	4	0	

* At these Bungalows there is a khansamah and staff of servants.

Name of Stage.	Bungalow Rooms.	Miles.	Cooly hire.	Remarks.
			a. p.	
Nirit . . .	R B 2	10	4 0	
Rampur . .	R B 1	13	4 0	
Gaura . . .	R B 1	6½	4 0	
Sarahan . .	R B 2	10½	4 0	
Taranda . .	R B 2	14	5 0	
Paunda . .	R B 2	4½	2 0	
Nachar . .	F B 2	4½	2 0	
Wangtu . .	R B 2	3	1 0	
Urni . . .	R B 2	9¾	4 0	Change at Chagaon 3 *as.* Urni 1.
Rogi . . .	R B 2	10	4 0	
Pangi . . .	R B 4	10	4 0	Two sets of rooms.
Rarang . .	Camp	8	4 0	
Jangi . . .	R B 2	7	4 0	Akpa 2 *as.* Jangi 2 *as.*
Labrang . .	Camp	11	5 0	
Sugnam . .	Do.	14	6 0	
Pooi . . .	Do.	20	6 0	
Namgea . .	Do.	11	5 0	Dubling 2 *as.* Khalb 2 *as.* Namgea 1
Shipki . .	Do.	11	4 0	
Total distance—				
Viâ Rampur .	...	228	...	
Viâ Bagi . .	...	250	...	

Upper or Forest Road.

Name of Stage.	Bungalow Rooms.	Miles.	Cooly hire.	Remarks.
Narkunda to Bagi	D B* 5	12	4 0	
Kudrelli . .	F B 2	9	4 0	
Soongri . .	D B 2	9	4 0	
Bhali . . .	D B 2	10	4 0	
Tachlech . .	F B 1	10	5 0	
Daran . .	F B 2	10	5 0	
Sarahan . .	R B 2	14	5 0	

* At these Bungalows there is a khansamah and staff of servants.

'Simla' to the 'Chor Mountain.'

Name of Stage.	Distance.	Elevation.	Remarks.
	miles.		
Fagu . . .	12	8,178	Road well-known.
	2½	...	
Kot . . .	8¾	...	'Cheog' forest, fine deodars and temple; road lies on a level straight through forest, then descends to 'Kot' (4,300).
Digtall . .	...	4,330	Descend to bed of river; during the rains may be difficult to cross. After crossing there is a steep ascent for ¾ mile; then the road goes on very easy gradient, with slight rise to 'Bhujjil.' ¾ mile level; 2½ miles of easy ascent of 10 in 100,—good road; the remainder —8 in 100—easy ascent by good road through a fine forest of fir to 'Madhain' Ghat, which is the watershed on the north shoulder of the 'Chor.' Steep ascent all the way; pony no good; room at 'Kalabagh' for a small camp.
Giri River . .	½	...	
Bhujjil . .	...	5,475	
Bahla . . .	7	7,600	
Madhain Ghat .	3	8,600	
Kalabagh . .	4⅓	10,800	
Chor Peak . .	1	11,892	A rough but quite easy ascent.

'Pooi' in 'Upper Kunowar' to 'Dankar' in 'Spiti.'

Name of Stage.	Distance.	Elevation.	Remarks.
Pooi . . .	...	...	
Pass . . .	...	10,094	Ascend from behind the village for about 5 hours to the top of the 'Chuling' Pass, then a descent of about 3 hours.
Chuling . .	8	11,000	About 10 miles of descent; road fairly easy.
Lio . . .	...	...	Cross 'Spiti' river soon after starting by a wooden bridge; and during the march, which is about 15 miles, several small streams by bridges for pedestrians only.
Chango . .	...	...	
Lepcha Pass .	...	13,700	Cross 'Spiti' river by bridge near 'Shalkar' Fort, then cross the 'Lepcha' Pass and descend to 'Somra' on the 'Spiti' river. From 'Chango' there is a road by way of the 'Para' river through Chinese territory into 'Ladak.'
Somra . .	...	...	
Lari . . .	...	...	Cross 'Spiti' river by a 'jhula' and up left bank of river to 'Lari.' Up left bank crossing several small streams. Same as last march.
Pol or Pok . .	6	...	
Dankar . .	...	12,700	Capital of 'Spiti.'

'Chini' to 'Landour.'

Name of Stage.	Distance.	Elevation.	Remarks.
Chini . . .	...	...	Descend to Sutlej, cross by a 'jhula' at Poari, then ascend to 'Barang.'
Poari . . .	3	...	
Barang . .	10	...	Steep ascent followed by level to 'Meibar' change coolies, then ascend Pass about 12,000, then rough descent into 'Baspa' valley.
Pass . . .	9	...	
Janga . . .	16	...	Up right bank of 'Baspa,' change coolies at 'Rukchum;' road is rough; take supplies for coolies from here.

Name of Stage.	Distance.	Elevation.	REMARKS.
	miles.	feet.	
Chitkul	16	...	Up right bank of 'Baspa,' no trees, road rough.
Sancha	10	...	Road rough, at four miles descend into river bed; follow it for about six miles, ford stream several times, camp near Neela Glacier.
Camp	12	...	Ascend glacier and ascend to Neela Pass about 18,000 feet, steep snow ascent near top, descend two miles to stream along which for two miles and camp.
Neela Pass	8	...	
Karkuti	12	...	Descend into Ganges valley.
Derali	16	...	Good but narrow road.
Jangla	4½	...	Then ascent followed by descent, at four miles, confluence of Ganges and 'Neela' rivers; from here visit 'Gangotri' and 'Gowmukhi.'
Bungalow Camp	9	...	
Jangla	...	...	Cross river at 'Hirsai,' then down right bank of Ganges; cross several streams.
Jhala	9	...	
Dangal	9	...	
Bathari	11	...	Gradual descent by right bank of Ganges, change coolies at 'Minarie.'
Barahat	15	...	
Darasu	15	...	Ascent, then descent, followed by steep ascent.
Lalluri	9	...	Long ascent to top of Pass, then long descent.
Bhowanee	16	...	First three miles level, then ascent to 'Magar,' after which very steep ascent to 'Teree' road, seven miles from Landour.
Landour	18	...	
Total, about	200	...	

NOTE.—A better way is to ascend the 'Baspa' from its junction with the Sutlej, near Kilba.

Simla to Dharmsala, *viâ* Kotgurh, Dularsh, Bajaora, and Beijnath.

Name of Stage.	Distance.	Elevation.	REMARKS.
Fagoo	12	...	Supplies—Dák Bungalow.
Theog	4½	...	Do. do. Joined the road from Fagoo at 7½ miles.
			Theog *viâ* Fagoo, is distant from Simla 16½ miles.
Muttiana	11	...	Travellers' Bungalow. Water and supplies.
Narkunda	12	...	Travellers' Bungalow. Bazaar most picturesquely situated. Scenery magnificent. On Mount Huttoo, 10,469, just above Narkunda, there is splendid shooting. Narkunda is charmingly adapted for a short trip from Simla. Elevation 9,000 feet.
Kôtgurh	9½	...	Travellers' Bungalow, latter part of road leads into Kôtgurh. Very steep descent. This is a British possession. There is mission house and small church, and there are two tea plantations.

Name of Stage.	Distance.	Elevation.	REMARKS.
	miles.	feet.	
Kumarsen . .	3¾	...	Small village, supplies scarce, water plentiful.
Dularsh . .	9½	...	Village, supplies and water, camping ground good. On leaving Kumarsen 4 miles descent to Sutlej, which is crossed at Kêpoo, by a bridge 180 feet span. Then ascent by steep and broad road to Dularsh.
Chuhaie . .	7	...	Village, few supplies, but water plentiful, encamping ground.
Kot . . .	9	...	Small village, supplies and water, limited encamping ground, tiring ascents and descents on this march.
Jeebhee . .	11¼	...	Village, supplies and water plentiful. A temple. Road tolerably good, steep ascent for four miles to Jalori Pass (elevation 11,500 feet), then descent to Jeebhee, cross a bridge at 9 miles.
Munglour . .	8¾	...	Small village situated below Platch, supplies and water. Road tedious, several nullas. There is another route from Kôtgurh to Munglour—as follows :— Nirth . . . . 11¼ miles. Rampore . . . . 12 ,, Cross Sutlej. Ursua . . . . 7 ,, Suronee . . . . 12 ,, Thar . . . . 9 ,, Munglour . . . 12 ,,
Largi . . .	8½	...	Village—on bank of Synj at its junction with the Chôta, and about 200 yards from confluence with Beas.
Bajaora . .	12	...	Steep ascents and descents, nulla bridged. Bazaar, old Fort, few supplies, water plentiful, very limited encamping ground. Road runs for some distance along valley of the Beas about 1,000 feet above the river. Cross the Beas at 9 miles, where it is wide and the current strong. There is a tea plantation at Bajaora, and Sultanpoor lies ten miles north, on the road to Lahol.
Dolchie . .	10	...	Villages, few supplies, water, small encamping ground. Road bad, ascends for eight miles to summit of Pass (elevation 9,150 feet), then descends to Dolchie, where the road from Amballa *viâ* Roopur joins on.
Jugroo Kooproo .	8	...	Water scarce, supplies ditto. Encamping ground. Road ascends, and crosses Ool at 4½ miles.
Fatakul . .	11	...	Small bungalow, almost in ruins, no supplies, water scarce—good encamping ground. Road along bare hill, no water to be met with. Pheasants and black partridge plentiful. (Elevation 7,100 feet.)
Haurbaug . .	8½	...	Village, supplies, water limited, encamping ground. Road descending all the way.
Piproleh . .	14	...	Village, supplies, water, shady encamping ground. Road level for 10 miles, then tedious descents to Beijnath, and the Binnoo; at Beijnath there is a tea plantation. An ancient temple, a great resort of pilgrims. (Elevation, 3,337 feet.) From Piproleh to Kangra 3 marches, *via* :— Burwaneh . . . . 9 miles. Nugrotch . . . . 11 ,, Kangra . . . . . 8 ,,

Name of Stage.	Distance.	Elevation.	REMARKS.
	miles.	feet.	
Holta . . .	6	...	Village, tea plantation, supplies, water and encamping ground good.
Puthyar . .	12	...	Village, supplies, water, encamping ground good. Road crosses several streams.
Dharmsala . .	8	...	

Simla to Leh, *viâ* Kotgurh, Rampoor, Sultanpoor, the right bank of the Beas, and the Rotang and Bara Lacha passes.

Name of Stage.	Distance.	Elevation.	REMARKS.
Fagoo . .	12	...	Travellers' Bungalow and supplies.
Theog . .	4½	...	Do. do.
Muttiana . .	11	...	Do. do.
Narkunda . .	12	...	Do. do.
Kôtgurh (British) .	9½	...	Do. do.
Nirth (on bank of Sutlej.)	11½	...	Small Travellers' Bungalow and supplies.
Rampur (Capital of Bussahir).	12	3,300 A. S. L.	Do. do. (½ mile beyond the town.)
Ursur. . .	7	...	Good encamping ground, supplies, cross Sutlej by bridge at Rampoor.
Surone . .	12	6,000 A. S. L.	Half-way up the Dhol Pass, encamping ground, supplies, and water.
Thar or Bather .	9	...	Supplies scarce, camping ground and water.
Munglour . .	12	...	Village, supplies scarce, water plentiful. The road from Kôtgurh *viâ* Dularsh joins in at the Chôta, which is crossed by a bridge. The marches from Kotgurh are— Komarsen . . . . 3¾ miles. Dularsh . . . . 9½ " Chuahie . . . . 7 " Kot . . . . 9 " Jeebhee . . . . 11¼ " Munglour . . . . 9 "
Larji . . .	8½	...	
Bajaora . .	12	...	
Sultanpoor (Capital of Kooloo).	10	4,092	Supplies and water, accommodation in Baradurree, and camping ground. Country richly cultivated. The Beas flows close by Sultanpoor.
Nuggur . .	13	5,780 A. S. L.	Supplies, water and accommodation, a small civil station. On leaving Sultanpoor descend by an easy flight of steps to the Beas, which is then crossed by a bridge.

Name of Stage.	Distance.	Elevation.	Remarks.
	miles.	feet.	
Jagatsuk . .	$8\frac{3}{4}$	5,985 A. S. L.	Village, supplies and water, camping ground, country very beautiful. There is a magnificent cascade here. From Jagatsuk there is a road to Chataloo, in Lahoul, *viâ* Cheka.
Burwa . . .	$8\frac{1}{2}$	...	Village, supplies and water. It is necessary to take supplies and coolies from here, before crossing the Rotang Pass.
Rahla . . .	5	9,000 A. S. L.	Encamping ground small, no supplies, water plentiful. Rahla is the head of the Kooloo valley and at the foot of the Rotang Pass. From Sultanpoor there is another road to Rahla on the right bank of the Beas. Dewara . . . . . 12 miles. Munauli . . . . . 13 „ Rahla . . . . . 30 „
Kokser (in Lahoul)	14	...	Supplies and fuel scarce, water procurable. On leaving Rahla the ascent of the Rotang Pass is commenced, either by a flight of steps 4 miles in length or by a very bad zig-zag; in August the pass is clear of snow, elevation of the crest is 15,200 feet, after descending a steep road and crossing numerous torrents at the foot the Chundra is crossed by a bridge, which is made of birch twigs. Lahoul is chiefly inhabited by Tibetans.
Sisu . . .	9	9,938	Small village on right bank of Chundra—supplies and fuel scarce—road very bad, five torrents are crossed.
Gondla . .	8	10,300	Village, supplies and water plentiful.
Kailing . .	10	...	Large village, supplies plentiful. On the opposite bank of the river is Korbung, a large village with a travellers' Bungalow. The confluence of the Chundra and Bhaga is just above Tandi, where the road turns off to Dhurmsála, *viâ* Chumba and to Srinuggur, *viâ* Kishtwar; these places are distant from India 120 and 277 miles respectively.
Kolang . .	12	...	Village, supplies and water.
Darcha . .	11	10,844	Do. do. The country becomes less inhabited as the Bhaga is ascended. From Darcha the road turns off to Leh by the Shinkul Pass. By this route Leh is distant 23 marches or about 200 miles.
Patsco . . .	11	12,464	Village, supplies and water, country desolate, supplies and coolies must be taken on from this, as nothing is procurable beyond, for 8 or 9 marches.
Zingzingbar .	$7\frac{1}{2}$	...	Small encamping ground half-way up the Bara Lacha Pass, no supplies, water procurable, road bad, crossing the Bhaga at Patsco.
Talaoki . .	12	...	Small encamping ground, no supplies, water procurable. Road difficult, leading for 2 miles over the Bara Lacha Pass, which is 16,200 feet at crest.

Name of Stage.	Distance.	Elevation.	REMARKS.
	miles.	feet.	
Chasung . .	12	..	Few huts, no supplies, water procurable, road over a black tableland.
Sundu . . .	9	...	No coolies or supplies, road bad, leading over a difficult pass.
Pung . .	9	...	Small village, few supplies occasionally procurable.
Roksing . .	15	...	Do. supplies procurable.
Tahlung . .	12	...	Do. do.
Ghair . .	12	...	Do. do.
Machilung . .	15	...	Do. do.
Leh (Capital of Ladak) Lat., 34° 10′, Long., 77° 40′.	11	10,500	Supplies and water abundant; there are between 500 and 550 houses and a population of about 2,500 souls.

From Simla to Srinagar.

Name of Stage.	Distance.	Elevation.	REMARKS.
Fagoo . .	12	...	
Theog . .	4½	...	
Mutteana . .	11	...	
Narkunda . .	12	...	Or *viâ* Bagee.
Kotgurh . .	9½	...	
Nirth . .	11½	...	
Rampur . .	12	...	
Ursur . .	7	...	
Surone . .	9	...	
Thar or Bather .	9	...	
Munglour . .	12	...	
Largi . .	8½	...	
Bajora . .	12	...	
Sultanpoor . .	10	...	
Dwara . .	12	...	Village. supplies and water.
Munauli . .	13	...	Do. do.
Rahla . .	10	...	Encamping ground at foot of Rotang Pass, no supplies, water plentiful.

Name of Stage.	Distance.	Elevation.	Remarks.
	miles.	feet.	
Kokser . .	14	...	
Sisu . .	9	...	
Gundla . .	8	...	The other route by the left bank of Beas from Sultanpoor is as follows :— Nuggur . . . . 13 miles. Jugatsuk . . . . . . $8\frac{3}{4}$,, Burwa . . . . $8\frac{1}{2}$,, Rahla . . . . 5 ,,
Tandi . .	7	...	Village, supplies and water.
Jurma . .	14	...	Do. do.
Triloknath . .	12	9,566	Do. do.
Odapoor . .	6	...	Do. do.
Miyar . .	10	10,215	Few huts, no supplies.
Chirpat . .	3	...	Do. do.
Leias . .	15	...	Do. do.
			Road difficult, a long steep ascent to the top of the Gurdaar Pass, 17,500 feet, then a very difficult descent, almost impracticable for laden coolies, footsteps have to be cut in the snow; the last 2 or 3 miles the descent is somewhat easier, but very stony.
Bataor . .	6	11,633	Few huts, no supplies.
Lechoo . .	8	...	Small village, no supplies.
Sauch . .	10	7,886	Village, supplies and water.
Kilar . .	8	8,411	Do. do.
Darwas . .	6	8,411	Do. do.
Usdari . .	10	...	No supplies.
Sohul . .	11	...	Village, supplies and water.
Goolabgurh .	6	...	Do. do.
Jhar . .	4	...	Do. do.
Sireree . .	10	...	No supplies.
Lidrari . .	7	...	Do.
Pyas . .	7	...	Do.
Bhagna . .	9	...	No supplies and water.

Name of Stage.	Distance.	Elevation.	REMARKS.
	miles.	feet.	
Kishtw r . .	12	...	Large town, supplies and water.
Mogul Maidan .	16	...	
Singpur . .	16	...	
Wankringi . .	16	...	
Wangam . .	9	...	
Islamabad . .	17	...	
Avantipur . .	17	...	
Srinagar . .	18	...	

From Simla to Chakrata, *viâ* Fagu and Mundol.

Name of Stage.	Distance.	Elevation.	REMARKS.
Fagu . .	12	...	A good Dak Bungalow, supplies, elevation 8,300 feet.
Synj . .	8	...	A village, from which camping ground half a mile, steep descent to the Giri, fordable, after which road level.
Dhar . .	7	...	Large village, prettily situated, supplies abundant, shady camping ground; the latter part of the stage the road runs through dense forest.
Paternalla . .	6	...	No supplies. Water, road ascends to village near summit of hill, elevation 9,370 feet. Descent to a torrent, then another steep ascent through forest of oak and holly.
Chepal . .	10	...	A village, water, a few supplies, road through forest, steep descent about half way just before coming to the road to the Chor. From this the summit of the Chor is distant about 24 miles. Elevation 7,695 feet.
Peontree . .	11	...	A village, supplies scarce, water available, road running near the bank of the Shallu, for about 3 miles through cultivations.
Tikri . .	8	...	A village, supplies scarce, water, the road descends to the Shallu, which is crossed at 2 miles, then an ascent, another descent to a valley. Again an ascent of about 3 miles.
Mundol . .	5	...	A village, supplies scarce, water, road through forests, crossing a small stream, the end of the march road steep.
Maindrot . .	...	...	Water plentiful, good camping ground. Steep descent to the Tonse, which is crossed at 5 miles by a wire suspension bridge; as far as the river the road is the old one from Simla to Landour, from there a new forest road.
Jakin Lani . .	...	...	Gradual ascent through forest, water at a distance from road, no camping ground.

Name of Stage.	Distance.	Elevation.	REMARKS.
	miles.	feet.	
Kinanipani . .	11	...	Water abundant, camping ground extensive, road at first precipitous, then easy to Lokur at 6 miles. This is usually made the march from Maindrot, as there is a Forest Bungalow there.
Chakrata . .	15	...	A Cantonment, supplies and water plentiful, road an easy gradient along the top of the main ridge between the Tonse and Jumna rivers. Pass Deobun at 11 miles, from thence a decent of 2,000 feet to Chakrata.
Total 12 marches .	112	...	Elevation 7,364 feet.

Simla to Dalhousie, *viâ* Buddee, Hajeepoor and Pathankot.

Syrie . .	10	...	A small bazaar, supplies and water, camping ground extremely limited, constant ascents and descents, cross the Gumbur at 1⅓ miles, pass Hurripoor at 2½ miles, the road to Belaspoor at 6¾ miles, Belaspoor distant 38 miles.
Kukkur Huttee .	10	...	Small village, supplies, water, an hotel, camping ground limited. Bridge over Gumbur.
Khudlee . .	7	...	A small village, supplies scarce, water, camping ground limited, steep ascents and descents, pass Jharmajra at 1⅝, Runahal at 4, Dhajar at 6, and Pata at 9¼ miles.
Buddeo . .	11	...	Small village, at the foot of the Himalayas, supplies, water, small camping ground, road good, except in a few places where it runs along banks of the Sirsa, which is forded at 10 miles.
Jugatkhana . .	8	...	Small village, supplies and water, good camping ground, country cultivated, road fair, pass Kotlah at 1, Meanpoor at 4½ and Mundwara at 7½ miles.
Abseanah . .	8	...	Cross Sutlej by ferry. Village right bank Sutlej, water good, camping ground, country well cultivated, road stony, but fair; pass Fort Plassi, belonging to Rajah of Nalaghur at 2 miles on bank of Sirsa.
Noorpoor . .	7	...	Large village and thana, snpplies and water abundant, camping ground very good, country well cultivated. Road heavy, cross several nullas, a matter of some difficulty after much rain.
Phulan . . .	9	...	A village, supplies have to bo collected, water, good camping ground, river Sohan to be forded half way, road as in last stage, pass Mawa at 2 miles.
Suntokhgurh .	7	...	A small village, camping ground good, country and road as in the last stage.
Conah . . .	9	...	A small town, with a tehsil and thana, supplies and water to be had, camping ground good, country fertile; road good, cross and recross tho Sohan half-way fordable.
Churooroo . .	10	...	A small village, supplies and water, camping ground good, country hilly, road fair.

Name of Stage.	Distance.	Elevation.	REMARKS.
	miles.	feet.	
Mubarikpoor . .	10	...	A village at the foot of the Sola Singhee range. Supplies procurable on notice given, water, country very hilly, road tolerable, pass Huttee at 3 and Umb at 7 miles. Road from Hoshyarpoor to Dhurmsála, *viâ* Nadaon passes through Umb, and *viâ* Gopeepúr Derah through Mubarikpoor. Five nullas to cross.
Dowlatpoor . .	7	...	A small village, country and road as in last stage, supplies and water. Eleven nullas to cross.
Tulwara . .	14	...	Several nullas to cross Village on right bank of Beas, camping ground good, supplies and water available. Pass Huttee on the banks of the Sohan at 6 miles. No water between Huttee and Tulwara.
Hajipoor . .	9¼	...	A large village, supplies and water, camping ground good; pass Buhera at 1 and Hindwall at 6¾ miles.
Meerthul . .	12	...	A village on right bank of Beas, supplies and water; river Beas crossed by ferry.
Pathankot . .	11¼	...	A small town with an old fort. at the foot of the hills, a serai for Europeans, supplies and water abundant, camping ground good; pass Nipwall at 2¼, Hounterpura at 3½, and cross the Chukee by a ford at 10 miles. Noorpoor is 17½ miles from Pathankot.
Dhar . . .	17	...	Small village, supplies and water, camping ground on the top of the Dhar range of hills, close to the bungalow. Country mountainous, road fit for carts except in the rains.
Dooneira . .	11	...	Small village at the foot of the high range of hills; supplies and water, camping ground good, four nullas to cross. Road joins the one from Noorpoor at 9 miles; the road from Dhurmsala to Dalhousie passes through Dooniera, the former distant 48½, the latter 22¼ miles.
Mamool . .	9	...	A village, supplies and water, country hilly, road descends steeply for 2 miles, when it crosses the Naini Khud, where it becomes difficult, and in the rainy season even dangerous on ascent to Mamool; from here Bakloh is distant 2½ miles.
Buleyra . .	5½	...	A village, supplies and water, country hilly, ascents and descents practicable for camels in dry weather, and laden mules at all times.
Dalhousie .	7¼	...	Station, Cantonment and Sanitarium.
Total 22 marches .	219		

The following are taken from "Routes in the Western Himalayas, Kashmir, etc., by the late Lieut.-Colonel T. G. Montgomerie, R.E., F.R.S., F.R.G.S."

Mussoorie to Simla; by Chakrata (New Road.)

Name of Stage.	Distance.	Elevation.	REMARKS.
	miles.	feet.	
Mussoorie to .	...	6,599	Top of library.
Lakwar D.B. .	15	...	Cross Jumna by suspension bridge. Supplies plentiful.

Name of Stage.	Distance.	Elevation.	REMARKS.
	miles.	feet.	
Nagtat R.B. .	7	...	Road good. Supplies procurable.
Pokri „ .	8	...	Do. Supplies scarce.
Chakrata D.B.	9	7,300	Do.
Kinanipani .	15	...	Do. Some precipices passed through.
Kutiyan F.B.	12	...	Do.
Maindrot „ .	9	...	Gradual descent. On the Tons.
Mandholi „ .	9	...	Cross Tons R. at 4 miles, after which road rather steep and bad. Supplies scarce.
Tikri or Pekri	5	...	Road pretty good. Supplies scarce.
Piantra or Kedi	8	...	Cross the Shallu R. at 6 miles. Supplies scarce.
Chipal .	11	7,695	Road good. Supplies scarce.
Patarnala .	10	9,368	Change coolies. No supplies.
Dhar or Godhna	6	...	Large village. Supplies plentiful.
Sainj .	7	8,300	Cross the R. Giri (fordable). Supplies procurable Road fair.
Fagu .	8	...	Bungalow. Supplies procurable. Road fair.
Simla .	12	7,084	Road good.
Total	151		

Mussoorie to Simla; by Old Road.

Name of Stage.	Distance.	Elevation.	REMARKS.
Mussoorie to	...	6,599	Top of library.
Mudarsu .	13	...	......
Thoina or Thyna	8	...	Cross R. Jumna by suspension bridge.
Pokri D.B. .	14	...	......
Deoband .	13	9,347	Bungalow.
Bandraoli .	13	...	......
Kanda .	11	...	......
Tikri or Pekri	11	...	Cross the Tons R. at 3 miles.
Simla .	62	7,084	As in No. 41.
Total	145		

Simla to Belaspur and Mandi; by Jutogh.

Name of Stage.	Distance.	Elevation.	REMARKS.
	miles.	feet.	
Simla to . .	...	7,084	Church.
Jutogh . . .	5	...	Supplies and water procurable.
Erki . . .	16	...	Road fair. Supplies and water procurable.
Namuli . .	14	...	Do. Supplies and water scarce.
Belaspur . .	12	...	On left bank of the Sutlej; supplies and water plentiful.
Suket . . .	22	2,965	Cross the Sutlej by bridge.
Mandi . . .	11	3,006	On left bank of the Beas R.; cross Sukaty river a little below Chugwan village and follow the left bank of it.
Total .	80		

Simla to Srinagar (Kashmir); by Kangra and Chamba.

Name of Stage.	Distance.	Elevation.	REMARKS.
Simla to . .	...	7,084	Church.
Sairi . . .	10	...	Dâk Bungalow.
Sahiki Hati . .	20	...	Bungalow. Supplies procurable after due notice.
Belaspur . .	21½	...	Supplies and water plentiful, road fair.
Kunar Hati . .	9	...	Cross Sutlej R. bridge. Supplies procurable after due notice.
Dangah . .	8	...	......
Hamirpur . .	16	...	Bungalow and Thana.
Nadaon . .	14¼	...	......
Juala Mukhi .	6½	1,883	Serai. Cross the Beas by ferry.
Ranital . .	11⅓	...	Dâk Bungalow. Supplies and water procurable.
Kangra . .	9	2,419	Dâk Bungalow and encamping ground.
Rilloo (Hutli) .	13	...	......
Sihanta . .	12	...	Road bad for ponies.
Rapir . . .	9	...	Do. do.
Chuari . . .	7	...	Do. do.
Rareri . . .	14	...	Cross pass; steep ascent for 5 miles.
Chamba . .	6	3,033	Road bad. Cross Ravee by bridge. Báradari.
Manjeri . .	16	...	Steep ascent; cross low pass. Cross R. School on massaks.

Names of stages.	Distance.	Elevation.	Remarks.
	miles.	feet.	
Digi or Kirah .	11	...	Bad road. Cross Kandi Marl to left bank.
Bungul . .	11	...	Bad road.
Camp (Mur) .	10	...	......
Badrawar . .	12	5,427	Cross Padri Pass; short ascent and very steep descent. (Digi to Badrawar: or Manjeri — Thunun . . . 12; Langera . . . 9; Thannala . . . 15; Badrawar . . . 8)
Kalen . . .	11	...	......
Doda . . .	10	...	Cross R. Chandra Bhaga or Chenab by rope bridge.
Bhagwan . .	7	...	......
Gayi . . .	9	...	Bad road. Follow up the source of Lider Khol stream.
Camp . . .	7	...	......
Chaon . . .	13	...	Cross Braribal; steep ascent and descent.
Vernag . .	10	6,500	Báradari. Supplies and coolies abundant.
Srinagar . .	52	5,235	
Total .	355¾		

Simla to Srinagar (Kashmir); by Kulu, Chamba and Badrawar.

Names of stages.	Distance.	Elevation.	Remarks.
Simla to . .	...	7,084	Church.
Bajaora . .	120	...	Dâk Bungalow.
Komand . .	13	...	Cross pass (6,000 ft.); steep ascent.
Sauri . . .	8	...	Cross Ul river by bridge; ascent. (Sauri to Haurbaug: Old route.)
Fatakal . .	11	...	
Haurbaug . .	10	...	
Baijnath . .	17	3,337	Dâk Bungalow and encamping ground.
Bundleh . .	11	...	Putiyar is about half-way between Bundleh and Bhagsu.
Bhagsu Cant. .	19	4,058	Cross several torrents; Dhurmsála is just above Bhagsu. Encamping ground.
Rilloo (Hutli) .	17	...	
Srinagar . .	227	5,235	
Total .	453		

Simla to the top of the Shali Peak.

From Major Gordon Forbes' "Simla to Shipki."

Leave Simla after early breakfast; first to Mashobra, then descent, easy to Sipi, after which it is steeper and in places rather rough, down to the Nowle Gad river, which must be forded, as there is no bridge. After crossing there is a steep ascent to the village of Kūtnōl, which should be reached during the afternoon; there is a very good place to camp in a grove of pine trees above the village. Start early next morning, taking food and *water also* for the day as there is none to be found further up the mountain; the last part of the ascent is very steep; a pony can be taken up part of the way. The actual summit is very small, most of it being taken up with a temple. The height of the peak is about 9,400. Kūtnōl is about the same level as Mashobra.

A *purwana* should be procured from the Deputy Commissioner, Simla, for the supplies required.

INDEX.

A

B

M

N

S